THE WORKS OF
WILKIE COLLINS

My Miscellanies

VOLUME TWENTY

NEW YORK
P. F. COLLIER & SON

𝕬𝖋𝖋𝖊𝖈𝖙𝖎𝖔𝖓𝖆𝖙𝖊𝖑𝖞 𝖅𝖓𝖘𝖈𝖗𝖎𝖇𝖊𝖉

:O

HENRY BULLAR,

(OF THE WESTERN CIRCUIT).

PREFACE.

THE various papers of which the following collection is composed were most of them written some years since, and were all originally published —with many more, which I have not thought it desirable to reprint—in *Household Words* and in the earlier volumes of *All the Year Round.* They were fortunate enough to be received with favor by the reader, at the period of their first appearance, and were thought worthy in many instances of being largely quoted from in other journals. After careful selection and revision, they are now collected in book-form; having been so arranged, in contrast with each other, as to present specimens of all the shorter compositions which I have contributed in past years to periodical literature.

My object in writing most of these papers— especially those collected under the general heads of "Sketches of Character" and "Social Grievances"—was to present what I had observed and what I had thought, in the lightest and the least pretentious form; to address the public (if I could) with something of the ease of letter-writing, and something of the familiarity of friendly talk. The literary Pulpit appeared to me at that time—as it appears to me still—to be rather overcrowded with the Preachers of Lay Sermons. Views of life and society to set us thinking penitently in some cases, or doubting contemptuously in others, were, I thought, quite plentiful enough already. More freshness and novelty of appeal to the much-lectured and much-enduring reader seemed to lie in views which might put us on easier terms with ourselves and with others; and which might encourage us to laugh good-humoredly over some of the lighter eccentricities of character, and some of the more palpable absurdities of custom —without any unfair perversion of truth, or any needless descent to the lower regions of vulgarity and caricature. With that idea, all the lighter contributions to these Miscellanies were originally written; and with that idea they are now again dismissed from my desk, to win what approval they may from new readers.

HARLEY STREET, LONDON.

MY MISCELLANIES.

TALK–STOPPERS.

WE hear a great deal of lamentation nowadays, proceeding mostly from elderly people, on
the decline of the Art of Conversation among us.
Old ladies and gentlemen with vivid recollections
of the charms of society fifty years ago, are constantly asking each other why the great talkers
of their youthful days have found no successors
in this inferior present time. Where—they inquire mournfully—where are the illustrious men
and women gifted with a capacity for perpetual
outpouring from the tongue, who used to keep
enraptured audiences deluged in a flow of eloquent monologue for hours together? Where are
the solo-talkers, in this degenerate age of nothing
but choral conversation?

The solo-talkers have vanished. Nothing but
the tradition of them remains, imperfectly preserved in books for the benefit of an ungrateful
posterity, which reviles their surviving contempo-

raries, and would perhaps even have reviled the illustrious creatures themselves as Bores. If they could rise from the dead, and wag their unresting tongues among us now, would they win their reputations anew, just as easily as ever? Would they even get listeners? Would they be actually allowed to talk? I venture to say, decidedly not. They would surely be interrupted and contradicted; they would have their nearest neighbors at the dinner-table talking across them; they would find impatient people opposite, dropping things noisily, and ostentatiously picking them up; they would hear confidential whispering, and perpetual fidgeting in distant corners, before they had got through their first half dozen of eloquent opening sentences. Nothing appears to me so wonderful as that none of these interruptions (if we are to believe report) should ever have occurred in the good old times of the great talkers. I read long biographies of that large class of illustrious individuals whose fame is confined to the select circle of their own acquaintance, and I find that they were to a man, whatever other differences may have existed between them, all delightful talkers. I am informed that they held forth entrancingly for hours together, at all times and seasons, and that I, the gentle, constant, and patient reader, am one of the most unfortunate and pitiable of human beings in never having enjoyed the luxury of hearing them; but, strangely enough, I am never told whether they were occasionally interrupted or not in the course of their outpourings. I am left to infer that their friends sat under them just as a congregation sits under a pulpit; and I ask myself amazedly (remembering what society is at the present day), whether human nature can have changed altogether since that time. Either the reports in the biographies are one-sided and imperfect, or the race of people whom I frequently meet with now—and whom I venture to call talk-stoppers, because their business in life seems to be the obstructing, confusing, and interrupting of all conversation—must be the peculiar and portentous growth of our own degenerate era.

Perplexed by this dilemma, when I am reading in long biographies about great talkers, I do not find myself lamenting, like my seniors, that they have left no successors in our day, or doubting irreverently, like my juniors, whether the famous performers of conversational solos were really as well worth hearing as eulogistic report would fain have us believe. The one invariable question that I put to myself under these cricumstances runs thus: Could the great talkers, if they had lived in my time, have talked at all? And the answer I receive is: In the vast majority of cases, certainly not.

Let me not unnecessarily mention names, but let me ask, for example, if some such famous talker as, say—the Great Glib—could have discoursed uninterruptedly for five minutes together in the presence of my friend Colonel Hopkirk?

The colonel goes a great deal into society; he is the kindest and gentlest of men; but he unconsciously stops, or confuses conversation everywhere, solely in consequence of his own sociable horror of ever differing in opinion with anybody. If A should begin by declaring black to be black, Colonel Hopkirk would be sure to agree with him before he had half done. If B followed, and declared black to be white, the colonel would be on his side of the question before he had argued it out; and, if C peaceably endeavored to calm the dispute with a truism, and trusted that every one would at least admit that black and white in combination made gray, my ever-compliant friend would pat him on the shoulder approvingly all the while he was talking; would declare that C's conclusion was, after all, the common sense of the question; and would set A and B furiously disputing which of them he agreed or disagreed with now, and whether on the great Black, White and Gray question, Colonel Hopkirk could really be said to have any opinion at all.

How could the Great Glib hold forth in the company of such a man as this? Let us suppose that delightful talker, with a few of his admirers (including, of course, the writer of his biography), and Colonel Hopkirk, to be all seated at the same table; and let us say that one of the admirers is anxious to get the mellifluous Glib to discourse on capital punishment for the benefit of the company. The admirer begins, of course, on the approved method of stating the objections to capital punishment, and starts the subject in this manner: "I was dining out, the other day, Mr. Glib, where capital punishment turned up as a topic of conversation—"

"Ah!" says Colonel Hopkirk, "a dreadful necessity—yes, yes, yes, I see—a dreadful necessity—eh?"

"And the arguments for its abolition," continues the admirer, without noticing the interruption, "were really handled with great dexterity by one of the gentlemen present, who started, of course, with the assertion that it is unlawful, under any circumstances, to take away life—"

"Unlawful, of course!" cries the colonel. "Very well put. Yes, yes—unlawful—to be sure—so it is—unlawful, as you say."

"Unlawful, sir?" begins the Great Glib, severely. "Have I lived to this time of day, to hear that it is unlawful to protect the lives of the community by the only certain means—?"

"No, no—oh dear me, no!" says the compliant Hopkirk, with the most unblushing readiness. "Protect their lives, of course—as you say, protect their lives by the only certain means—yes, yes, I quite agree with you."

"Allow me, colonel," says another admirer, anxious to assist in starting the great talker, "allow me to remind our friend, before he takes this question in hand, that it is an argument of the abolitionists that perpetual imprisonment would answer the purpose of protecting society—"

The colonel is so delighted with this last argument that he bounds on his chair, and rubs his hands in triumph. "My dear sir!" he cries, before the last speaker can say another word, "you have hit it—you have, indeed! Perpetual imprisonment—that's the thing—ah, yes, yes, yes, to be sure—perpetual imprisonment—the very thing, my dear sir—the very thing!"

"Excuse me," says a third admirer, "but I think Mr. Glib was about to speak. You were saying, sir—?"

"The whole question of capital punishment," begins the delightful talker, leaning back luxuriously in his chair, "lies in a nutshell." ("Very true," from the colonel.) "I murder one of you —say Hopkirk here." ("Ha! ha! ha!" loudly from the colonel, who thinks himself bound to laugh at a joke when he is only wanted to listen to an illustration.) "I murder Hopkirk. What is the first object of all the rest of you, who represent the community at large?" ("To have you hanged," from the colonel. "Ah, yes, to be sure! to have you hanged. Quite right! quite right!") "Is it to make me a reformed character, to teach me a trade, to wash my bloodstains off me delicately, and set me up again in society, looking as clean as the best of you? No!" ("No!" from the compliant colonel.) "Your object is clearly to prevent me from murdering any more of you. And how are you to do that most completely and certainly? Can you accomplish your object by perpetual imprisonment?" ("Ah! I thought we should all agree about it at last," cries the colonel, cheerfully. "Yes, yes— nothing else for it but perpetual imprisonment, as you say.") "By perpetual imprisonment? But men have broken out of prison." ("So they have," from the colonel.) "Men have killed

their jailers; and there you have the commission
of that very second murder that you wanted to
prevent." ("Quite right," from the compliant
Talk-Stopper. "A second murder — dreadful!
dreadful!") "Imprisonment is not your certain
protective remedy, then, evidently. What is?"

"Hanging!!!" cries the colonel, with another
bound in his chair, and a voice that can no
longer be talked down. "Hanging, to be sure!
I quite agree with you. Just what I said from
the first. You have hit it, my dear sir. Hanging, as you say—hanging, by all manner of
means!"

Has anybody ever met Colonel Hopkirk in society? And does anybody think that the Great
Glib could possibly have held forth in the company of that persistently-compliant gentleman,
as he is alleged, by his admiring biographer, to
have held forth in the peculiar society of his own
time? The thing is clearly impossible. Let us
leave Glib, congratulating him on having died
when the Hopkirks of these latter days were as
yet hardly weaned; let us leave him, and ascertain how some other great talker might have got
on in the society of some other modern obstructer
of the flow of eloquent conversation.

I have just been reading the Life, Letters, Labors, Opinions, and Table-Talk of the matchless
Mr. Oily; edited—as to the Life, by his mother-
in-law; as to the Letters, by his granddaughter's
husband; and as to the Labors, Opinions, and
Table-Talk, by three of his intimate friends, who
dined with him every other Sunday throughout

the whole of his long and distinguished life. It
is a very pretty book in a great many volumes,
with pleasing anecdotes—not only of the eminent man himself, but of all his family connec-
tions as well. His shortest notes are preserved,
and the shortest notes of others to him. "My
dear O., how is your poor head? Yours, P."
"My dear P., hotter than ever. Yours, O."
And so on. Portraits of Oily, in infancy, childhood, youth, manhood, old age active, and old
age infirm, concluding with a post-mortem mask,
abound in the book—so do fac-similes of his
handwriting, showing the curious modifications
which it underwent when he occasionally ex-
changed a quill for a steel pen. But it will be
more to my present purpose to announce for the
benefit of unfortunate people who have not yet
read the Memoirs, that Oily was, as a matter of
course, a delightful and incessant talker. He
poured out words, and his audience imbibed the
same perpetually three times a week from tea-
time to past midnight. Women especially rev-
eled in his conversation. They hung, so to
speak, palpitating on his lips. All this is told
me in the Memoirs at great length, and in several places; but not a word occurs anywhere
tending to show that Oily ever met with the
slightest interruption on any one of the thousand
occasions when he held forth. In relation to
him, as in relation to the Great Glib, I seem
bound to infer that he was never staggered by
an unexpected question, never affronted by a
black sheep among the flock, in the shape of an

inattentive listener, never silenced by some careless man capable of unconsciously cutting him
short and starting another topic before he had
half done with his own particular subject. I
am bound to believe all this—and yet, when I
look about me at society as it is constituted now,
I could fill a room, at a day's notice, with people
who would shut up the mouth of Oily before it
had been open five minutes, quite as a matter of
course, and without the remotest suspicion that
they were misbehaving themselves in the slightest degree. What (I ask myself), to take only
one example, and that from the fair sex—what
would have become of Oily's delightful and incessant talk, if he had known my friend Mrs.
Marblemug, and had taken her down to dinner
in his enviable capacity of distinguished man?

Mrs. Marblemug has one subject of conversation—her own vices. On all other topics she is
sarcastically indifferent and scornfully mute.
General conversation she consequently never
indulges in; but the person who sits next to
her is sure to be interrupted as soon as he attracts her attention by talking to her, by receiving a confession of her vices—not made repent-
antly, or confusedly, or jocularly—but slowly
declaimed with an ostentatious cynicism, with a
hard eye, a hard voice, a hard—no, an adaman-
tine—manner. In early youth, Mrs. Marblemug
discovered that her business in life was to be eccentric and disagreeable, and she is one of the
women of England who fulfills her mission.

I fancy I see the ever-flowing Oily sitting next

to this lady at dinner, and innocently trying to make her hang on his lips like the rest of his tea-table harem. His conversation is reported by his affectionate biographers as having been for the most part of the sweetly pastoral sort. I find that he drove that much-enduring subject, Nature, in his conversational car of triumph, longer and harder than most men. I see him, in my mind's eye, starting in his insinuating way from some parsley garnish round a dish of lobsters—confessing, in his rich, full, and yet low voice (*vide* Memoirs) that garnish delights him, because his favorite color is green—and so getting easily on to the fields, the great subject from which he always got his largest conversational crop. I imagine his tongue to be, as it were, cutting its first preliminary capers on the grass for the benefit of Mrs. Marblemug; and I hear that calmly-brazen lady throw him flat on his back by the utterance of some such words as these:

"Mr. Oily, I ought to have told you, perhaps, that I hate the fields. I think Nature in general something eminently disagreeable—the country, in short, quite odious. If you ask me why, I can't tell you. I know I'm wrong; but hating Nature is one of my vices."

Mr. Oily eloquently remonstrates. Mrs. Marblemug only says, "Yes, very likely—but, you see, it's one of my vices." Mr. Oily tries a dexterous compliment. Mrs. Marblemug only answers, "Don't! I see through that. It's wrong in me to see through compliments, being a woman, I know. But I can't help seeing through them, and saying I do. That's another of my vices." Mr. Oily shifts the subject to Literature, and thence, gently but surely, to his own books—his second great topic after the fields. Mrs. Marblemug lets him go on, because she has something to finish on her plate—then lays down her knife and fork—looks at him with a kind of wondering indifference, and breaks into his next sentence thus:

"I'm afraid I don't seem quite so much interested as I know I ought to be," she says; "but I should have told you, perhaps, when we first sat down, that I have given up reading."

"Given up reading?" exclaims Mr. Oily, thunderstruck by the monstrous confession. "You mean only the trash that has come into vogue lately; the morbid, unhealthy—"

"No, not at all," rejoins Mrs. Marblemug. "If I read anything, it would be morbid literature. My taste is unhealthy. That's another of my vices."

"My dear madam, you amaze—you alarm me —you do, indeed!" cries Mr. Oily, waving his hand in graceful deprecation and polite horror.

"Don't!" says Mrs. Marblemug; "you'll knock down some of the wine-glasses, and hurt yourself. You had better keep your hand quiet—you had, indeed. No; I have given up reading, because all books do me harm—the best—the healthiest. Your books even, I suppose, I ought to say; but I can't, because I see through compliments, and despise my own, of course, as much as other people's! Suppose, we say, I don't read, because books do me harm — and leave it there. The thing is not worth pursuing. You think it is? Well, then, books do me harm, because they increase my tendency to be envious (one of my worst vices). The better the book is, the more I hate the man for being clever enough to write it —so much cleverer than me, you know, who couldn't write it at all. I believe you call that Envy. Whatever it is, it has been one of my vices from a child. No, no wine—a little water. I think wine nasty, that's another of my vices— or, no, perhaps, that is only one of my misfortunes. Thank you. I wish I could talk to you about books; but I really can't read them—they make me so envious."

Perhaps Oily (who, as I infer from certain passages in his Memoirs, could be a sufficiently dogged and resolute man on occasions when his dignity was in danger) still valiantly declines to submit and be silent, and, shifting his ground, endeavors to draw Mrs. Marblemug out by asking her questions. The new effort, however, avails him nothing. Do what he will, he is always met and worsted by the lady in the same quiet, easy, indifferent way; and, sooner or later, even his distinguished mouth is muzzled by Mrs. Marblemug, like the mouths of all the degenerate talkers of my own time whom I have ever seen in contact with her. Are Mr. Oily's biographers not to be depended on, or can it really be the fact that, in the course of all his long conversational career, that illustrious man never once met with

a check in the shape of a Mrs. Marblemug? I
have no tender prepossession in favor of the lady;
but when I reflect on the character of Mr. Oily,
as exhibited in his Memoirs, I am almost inclined
to regret that he and Mrs. Marblemug never met.
In relation to some people, I involuntarily regard
her as a dose of strong moral physic; and I really
think she might have done my distinguished coun-
tryman some permanent good.

To take another instance, there is the case of
the once brilliant social luminary, Mr. Endless—
extinguished, unfortunately for the new generation, about the time when we were most of us
only little boys and girls.

What a talker this sparkling creature must have
been, if one may judge by that racy anonymous
publication (racy was, I think, the word chiefly
used in reviewing the book by the critics of the
period), "Evenings with Endless, by A Constant
Listener!" "I could hardly believe," I remember the Listener writes, "that the world was the
same after Endless had flashed out of this mortal
scene. It was morning while he lived—it was
twilight, or worse, when he died. I was very intimate with him. Often has the hand that writes
these trembling lines smacked that familiar back
—often have those thrilling and matchless ac-
cents syllabled the fond diminutive of my Christian name. It was not so much that his talk was
ceaseless (though that is something), as that it
moved incessantly over all topics from heaven to
earth. His variety of subject was the most amazing part of this amazing man. His fertility of

allusion to topics of the past and present alike, was truly inexhaustible. He hopped, he skipped, he fluttered, he swooped from theme to theme. The butterfly in the garden, the bee in the flower-bed, the changes of the kaleidoscope, the sun and shower of an April morning, are but faint emblems of him.'' With much more to the same eloquent purpose; but not a word from the first page to the last to hint even that Endless was ever brought to a full stop, on any single occasion, by any one of the hundreds of enchanted listeners before whom he figured in his wonderful performances with the tongue from morning to night.

And yet there must surely have been Talk-Stoppers in the world, in the time of the brilliant Endless—talk-stoppers, in all probability, possessing characteristics similar to those now displayed in society by my exasperating connection by marriage, Mr. Spoke Wheeler.

It is impossible to say what the consequences might have been if my relative and Mr. Endless had ever come together. Mr. Spoke Wheeler is one of those men—a large class, as it appears to me—who *will* talk, and who have nothing whatever in the way of a subject of their own to talk about. His constant practice is to lie silently in ambush for subjects started by other people; to take them forthwith from their rightful owners; turn them coolly to his own uses, and then cunningly wait again for the next topic, belonging to somebody else, that passes within his reach. It is useless to give up, and leave him to take the

lead—he invariably gives up, too, and declines
the honor.   It is useless to start once more, seeing him apparently silenced—he becomes talkative again the moment you offer him the chance
of seizing on your new subject—disposes of it
without the slightest fancy, taste, or novelty of
handling, in a moment—then relapses into utter
speechlessness as soon as he has silenced the rest
of the company by taking their topic away from
them.   Wherever he goes, he commits this social
atrocity with the most perfect innocence and the
most provoking good-humor, for he firmly believes in himself as one of the most entertaining
men who ever crossed a drawing-room or caroused
at a dinner-table.

Imagine Mr. Spoke Wheeler getting an invitation to one of those brilliant suppers which assisted in making the evenings of the sparkling
Endless so attractive to his friends and admirers.
See him sitting modestly at the table with every
appearance in his face and manner of being the
most persistent and reliable of listeners.   Endless
takes the measure of his man, as he too confidently believes, in one bright glance—thinks to
himself, Here is a new worshiper to astonish;
here is the conveniently dense and taciturn human pedestal on which I can stand to let off my
fireworks — plunges his knife and fork, gayly
hospitable, into the dish before him (let us say
a turkey and truffles, for Endless is a gastronome
as well as a wit), and starts off with one of those
"fertile allusions" for which he was so famous.

"I never carve turkey without thinking of

what Madame de Pompadour said to Louis the Fifteenth," Endless begins, in his most off-hand manner. "I refer to the time when the superb Frenchwoman first came to court, and the star of the fair Chateauroux waned before her. Who remembers what the Pompadour said when the king insisted on carving the turkey?"

Before the company can beg Endless, as usual, to remember for them, Mr. Spoke Wheeler starts into life and seizes the subject.

"What a vicious state of society it was in the time of Madame De Pompadour!" he says, with moral severity. "Who can wonder that it led to the French Revolution?"

Endless feels that his first effort for the evening is nipped in the bud, and that the new guest is not to be depended on as a listener. He, however, waits politely, and every one else waits politely to hear something more about the French Revolution. Mr. Spoke Wheeler has not another word to say. He has snatched his subject—has exhausted it—and is now waiting, with an expectant smile on his face, to lay hands on another. Disastrous silence reigns, until Mr. Endless, as host and wit, launches a new topic in despair.

"Don't forget the salad, gentlemen," he exclaims. "The emblem, as I always fancy, of human life. The sharp vinegar corrected by the soft oil, just as the misfortune of one day is compensated by the luck of another. Heigh-ho! let moralists lecture as they will, what a true gambler's existence ours is, by the very nature of it! Love, fame, wealth, are the stakes we all play for; the world is the table; Death keeps the house, and Destiny shuffles the cards. According to my definition, gentlemen, man is a gambling animal, and woman—" Endless pauses for a moment, and lifts the glass to his lips to give himself a bacchanalian air before he amazes the company with a torrent of eloquence on the subject of woman. Unhappy man! in that one moment Mr. Spoke Wheeler seizes on his host's brilliant gambling metaphor, and runs away with it as his own property immediately.

"The worst of gambling," he says, with a look of ominous wisdom, "is, that when once a man takes to it, he can never be got to give it up again. It always ends in ruin. I know a man whose son is in the Fleet, and whose daughter is a maid of all work at a lodging-house. The poor devil himself once had twenty thousand pounds, and he now picks up a living by writing begging-letters. All through gambling. Degrading vice, certainly; ruins a man's temper and health, too, as well as his property. Ah! a very degrading vice—very much so, indeed!"

"I am afraid, my dear sir, you have no vices," says Endless, getting angry and sarcastic as a fresh pause follows this undeniable commonplace. "The bottle stands with you. Do you abjure even that most amiable of human failings—the cheerful glass? Ha!" exclaims Endless, seeing that his guest is going to speak again, and vainly imagining that he can cut him short this time. "Ha! what a debt we owe to the first man who

discovered the true use of the grape! How drunk
he must have got in making his immortal preliminary experiments! How often his wife must have
begged him to consider his health and his respectability, and give up all further investigations!
How he must have shocked his family with perpetual hiccoughs, and puzzled the medical men of
the period with incurable morning headaches!
To the health of that marvelous, that magnificent, that inestimable human being, the first
toper in the world! The patriarchal Bacchus
quaffing in his antediluvian vineyard! What a
picture, gentlemen; what a subject for our artists! Scumble, my dear friend," continues Endless, breathlessly, feeling that Mr. Spoke Wheeler
has got his topic again, and anxious to secure assistance in preventing that persistent gentleman
from making any use of the stolen property—
"Scumble, your pencil alone is worthy of the
subject. Tell us, my prince of painters, how
would you treat it?"

The prince of painters has his mouth full of
turkey, and looks more puzzled than flattered
by this complimentary appeal. He hesitates, and
Mr. Spoke Wheeler darts into the conversation
on the subject of drunkenness forthwith.

"I'll tell you what," says the Talk-Stopper,
"we may all joke about drunkenness as much as
we please—I'm no saint, and I like a joke as well
as anybody—but it s a deuced serious thing for
all that. Seven-tenths of the crime in this country is owing to drunkenness; and of all the incurable diseases that baffle the doctors, delirium-

tremens is (next to hydrophobia) one of the worst.
I like a cheerful glass myself—and this is un-
commonly good wine we are drinking now—but
there's more than you think for to be said on the
temperance side of the question; there is, indeed!"

Will even the most indiscriminate of the surviving admirers of Endless, and of the great
talkers generally, venture to assert that he, or
they, could have shown off with the slightest
approach to success in the company of Mr. Spoke
Wheeler, or of Mrs. Marblemug, or of Colonel
Hopkirk, or of any of the other dozens on dozens
of notorious talk-stoppers whose characters I refrain from troubling the reader with? Surely not!
Surely I have quoted examples enough to prove
the correctness of my theory, that the days when
the eminent professors of the Art of Conversation
could be sure of perpetually attentive audiences,
have gone by. Instead of mourning over the loss
of the great talkers, we ought to feel relieved (if
we have any real regard for them, which I sometimes doubt) by their timely departure from the
scene. Between the members of the modern generation who would not have listened to them, the
members who could not have listened to them,
and the members who would have confused, interrupted, and cut them short, what extremities of
compulsory silence they must have undergone if
they had lasted until our time! Our case may
be lamentable enough in not having heard them;
but how much worse would theirs be if they
came back to the world now, and tried to show
us how they won their reputations!

SOCIAL GRIEVANCES.—I.

A JOURNEY IN SEARCH OF NOTHING.

[Communicated by an Anonymous Traveler.]

NOTE THE FIRST.   TRYING FOR QUIET.

"YES," said the doctor, pressing the tips of his fingers with a tremulous firmness on my pulse, and looking straight forward into the pupils of my eyes, "yes, I see: the symptoms all point unmistakably toward one conclusion—Brain. My dear sir, you have been working too hard; you have been following the dangerous example of the rest of the world in this age of business and bustle. Your brain is overtaxed—that is your complaint. You must let it rest—there is your remedy."

"You mean," I said, "that I must keep quiet, and do nothing?"

"Precisely so," replied the doctor. "You must not read or write; you must abstain from allowing yourself to be excited by society; you must have no annoyances; you must feel no anxieties; you must not think; you must be neither elated nor depressed; you must keep early hours and take an occasional tonic, with moderate exercise, and a nourishing but not too full a diet—above all, as perfect repose is essential to your restoration, you must go away into the country, taking any direction you please, and living just as you like, so long as you are quiet and so long as you do nothing."

"I presume he is not to go away into the country without ME?" said my wife, who was present at the interview.

"Certainly not," rejoined the doctor with an acquiescent bow. "I look to your influence, my dear madam, to encourage our patient to follow my directions. It is unnecessary to repeat them, they are so extremely simple and easy to carry out. I will answer for your husband's recovery, if he will but remember that he has now only two objects in life—to keep quiet, and to do nothing."

My wife is a woman of business habits. As soon as the doctor had taken his leave, she produced her pocket-book, and made a brief abstract of his directions for our future guidance. I looked over her shoulder and observed that the entry ran thus:

"Rules for dear William's restoration to health. No reading; no writing; no excitement; no annoyance; no anxiety; no thinking. Tonic. No elation of spirits. Nice dinners. No depression of spirits. Dear William to take little walks (with me). To go to bed early. To get up early. N.B.—Keep him quiet. Mem.: Mind he does nothing."

Mind I do nothing? No need to mind about that. I have not had a holiday since I was a boy. Oh, blessed Idleness, after the years of

merciless industry that have separated us, are
you and I to be brought together again at last?
Oh, my weary right hand, are you really to ache
no longer with driving the ceaseless pen? May
I, indeed, put you in my pocket, and let you rest
there, indolently, for hours together? Yes! for
I am now at last to begin—doing nothing. Delightful task that performs itself! Welcome responsibility that carries its weight away smoothly
on its own shoulders!

These thoughts shine in pleasantly on my mind
after the doctor has taken his departure, and dif-
fuse an easy gayety over my spirits when my
wife and I set forth, the next day, for the country. We are not going the round of the noisy
watering-places, nor is it our intention to accept
any invitations to join the circles assembled by
festive country friends. My wife, guided solely
by the abstract of the doctor's directions in her
pocket-book, has decided that the only way to
keep me absolutely quiet, and to make sure of
my doing nothing, is to take me to some pretty,
retired village, and to put me up at a little primitive, unsophisticated country inn. I offer no
objection to this project—not because I have no
will of my own and am not master of all my
movements—but only because I happen to agree
with my wife. Considering what a very independent man I am naturally, it has sometimes
struck me, as a rather remarkable circumstance,
that I always do agree with her.

We find the pretty, retired village. A charming place, full of thatched cottages with creepers

at the doors, like the first easy lessons in drawing-masters' copy-books. We find the unsophisticated inn—just the sort of house that the novelists are so fond of writing about, with the snowy curtains and the sheets perfumed by lavender, and the matronly landlady and the amusing sign-post. This Elysium is called the Nag's Head. Can the Nag's Head accommodate us? Yes, with a delightful bedroom and a sweet parlor. My wife takes off her bonnet and makes herself at home, directly. She nods her head at me with a look of triumph. Yes, dear, on this occasion also I quite agree with you. Here we have found perfect quiet; here we may make sure of obeying the doctor's orders; here we have, at least, discovered—nothing.

Nothing! Did I say nothing? We arrive at the Nag's Head late in the evening, have our tea, go to bed tired with our journey, sleep delightfully till about three o'clock in the morning, and at that hour begin to discover that there are actually noises even in this remote country seclusion. They keep fowls at the Nag's Head, and at three o'clock the cock begins to crow and the hens to cluck under our window. Pastoral, my dear, and suggestive of eggs for breakfast whose reputation is above suspicion; but I wish these cheerful fowls did not wake quite so early. Are there likewise dogs, love, at the Nag's Head, and are they trying to bark down the crowing and clucking of the cheerful fowls? I should wish to guard myself against the possibility of making a mistake, but I think I hear three dogs. A shrill dog who barks rapidly; a melancholy dog who howls monotonously; and a hoarse dog who emits barks at intervals like minute-guns. Is this going on long? Apparently it is. My dear, if you will refer to your pocket-book, I think you will find that the doctor recommended early hours. We will not be fretful and complain of having our morning sleep disturbed; we will be contented, and will only say that it is time to get up.

Breakfast. Delicious meal, let us linger over it as long as we can—let us linger, if possible, till the drowsy midday tranquillity begins to sink over this secluded village.

Strange! but now I think of it again, do I, or do I not, hear an incessant hammering over the way? No manufacture is carried on in this peaceful place, no new houses are being built; and yet there is such a hammering that, if I shut my eyes, I can almost fancy myself in the neighborhood of a dock-yard. Wagons, too. Why does a wagon, which makes so little noise in London, make so much noise here? Is the dust on the road detonating powder, that goes off with a report at every turn of the heavy wheels? Does the wagoner crack his whip or fire a pistol to encourage his horses? Children, next. Only five of them, and they have not been able to settle for the last half-hour what game they shall play at. On two points alone do they appear to be unanimous—they are all agreed on making a noise, and on stopping to make it under our window. I think I am in some danger of forgetting

one of the doctor's directions; I rather fancy I
am actually allowing myself to be annoyed.

Let us take a turn in the garden, at the back
of the house. Dogs again. The yard is on one
side of the garden. Every time our walk takes
us near it, the shrill dog barks and the hoarse
dog growls. The doctor tells me to have no
anxieties. I am suffering devouring anxieties.
These dogs may break loose and fly at us, for
anything I know to the contrary, at a moment's
notice. What shall I do? Give myself a drop
of tonic, or escape for a few hours from the perpetual noises of this retired spot by taking a
drive? My wife says, take a drive. I think 1
have already mentioned that I invariably agree
with my wife.

The drive is successful in procuring us a little
quiet. My directions to the coachman are to
take us where he pleases, so long as he keeps
away from secluded villages. We suffer much
jolting in by-lanes, and encounter a great variety
of bad smells. But a bad smell is a noiseless
nuisance, and I am ready to put up with it patiently. Toward dinner-time we return to our
inn. Meat, vegetables, pudding, all excellent,
clean, and perfectly cooked. As good a dinner
as I wish ever to eat; shall I get a little nap after
it? The fowls, the dogs, the hammer, the children, the wagons, are quiet at last. Is there
anything else left to make a noise? Yes: there
is the working population of the place.

It is getting on toward evening, and the sons
of labor are assembling on the benches placed

outside the inn to drink. What a delightful scene they would make of this homely every-day event on the stage! How the simple creatures would clink their tin mugs, and drink each other's healths and laugh joyously in chorus! How the peasant maidens would come tripping on the scene and lure the men tenderly to the dance! Where are the pipe and tabor that I have seen in so many pictures; where the simple songs that I have read about in so many poems? What do I hear as I listen, prone on the sofa, to the evening gathering of the rustic throng? Oaths—nothing, on my word of honor, but oaths! I look out, and see gangs of cadaverous savages, drinking gloomily from brown mugs, and swearing at each other every time they open their lips. Never in any large town, at home or abroad, have I been exposed to such an incessant fire of unprintable words as now assail my ears in this primitive village. No man can drink to another without swearing at him first. No man can ask a question without adding a mark of interrogation at the end in the shape of an oath. Whether they quarrel (which they do for the most part), or whether they agree; whether they talk of their troubles in this place or their good luck in that; whether they are telling a story, or proposing a toast, or giving an order, or finding fault with the beer, these men seem to be positively incapable of speaking without an allowance of at least five foul words for every one fair word that issues from their lips. English is reduced in their mouths to a brief vocabulary of all the vilest expressions in the language. This is an age of civilization; this is a Christian country; opposite me 1 see a building with a spire, which is called, 1 believe, a church; past my window, not an hour since, there rattled a neat pony-chaise with a gentleman inside, clad in glossy black broadcloth, and popularly known by the style and title of clergyman. And yet, under all these good influences, here sit twenty or thirty men whose ordinary table-talk is so outrageously beastly and blasphemous that not one single sentence of it, though it lasted the whole evening, could be printed, as a specimen, for public inspection in these pages. When the intelligent foreigner comes to England, and when I tell him (as I am sure to do) that we are the most moral people in the universe, I will take good care that he does not set his foot in a secluded British village when the rural population is reposing over its mug of small beer after the labors of the day.

I am not a squeamish person, neither is my wife; but the social intercourse of the villagers drives us out of our room, and sends us to take refuge at the back of the house. Do we gain aanything by the change? Nothing whatever.

The back parlor, to which we have now retreated, looks out on a bowling-green; and there are more benches, more mugs of beer, more foul-mouthed villagers on the bowling-green. Immediately under our window is a bench and table for two, and on it are seated a drunken old man and a drunken old woman. The aged sot in trousers is offering marriage to the aged sot in petticoats, with frightful oaths of endearment. Never before did I imagine that swearing could be twisted to the purposes of courtship. Never before did I suppose that a man could make an offer of his hand by bellowing imprecations on his eyes, or that all the powers of the infernal regions could be appropriately summoned to bear witness to the beating of a lover's heart under the influence of the tender passion. I know it now, and I derive so little satisfaction from gaining the knowledge of it, that I determine on having the two intolerable old drunkards removed from the window, and sent to continue their cursing courtship elsewhere. The hostler is lounging about the bowling-green, scratching his bare, brawny arms, and yawning grimly in the mellow evening sunlight. I beckon to him, and ask him if he does not think those two old people have had beer enough? Yes, the hostler thinks they have. I inquire next if they can be removed from the premises, before their language gets worse, without the risk of making any great disturbance. The hostler says, Yes, they can, and calls to the pot-boy. When the pot-boy comes, he says, "Now then, Jack!" and snatches the table away from the two ribald old people without another word. The old man's pipe is on the table; he rises and staggers forward to possess himself of it; the old woman rises, too, to hold him by the arm for fear he should fall flat on his face. The moment they are off the bench, the pot-boy snatches their seat away from behind them, and quietly joins the hostler, who is carrying their table into the inn. None of the other drinkers laugh at this proceeding, or pay any attention to it; and the two intoxicated old people, left helpless on their legs, stagger away feebly without attracting the slightest notice. The neat stratagem which the hostler and the pot-boy have just performed, is evidently the customary and only possible mode of letting drinkers know when they have had enough at the Nag's Head. Where did those savage islanders live whose manners a certain sea-captain once upon a time described as no manners at all, and some of whose customs he reprobated as being very nasty? If I did not know that we are many miles distant from the coast, I should be almost disposed to suspect that the seafaring traveler whose opinion I have just quoted had been touching at the Nag's Head.

As it is impossible to snatch away all the tables and all the benches of all the company drinking and swearing in front of the house and behind it, I inquire of the hostler, the next time he comes near the window, at what time the tap closes? He tells me at eleven o'clock. It is hardly necessary to say that we put off going to bed until that time, when we retire for the night, drenched from head to foot, if I may so speak, in floods of bad language.

I cautiously put my head out of window, and see that the lights of the tap-room are really extinguished at the appointed time. I hear the drinkers oozing out grossly into the pure fresh-

ness of the summer night. They all growl together; they all go together. All? Sinner and
sufferer that I am, I have been premature in
arriving at that happy conclusion! Six choice
spirits, with a social horror in their souls of going home to bed, prop themselves against the
wall of the inn, and continue the evening's con-
versazione in the darkness. I hear them cursing
at each other by name. We have Tom, Dick,
and Sam, Jem, Bill, and Bob to enliven us under
our window after we are in bed. They begin improving each other's minds, as a matter of course,
by quarreling. Music follows and soothes the
strife, in the shape of a local duet, sung by voices
of vast compass, which soar in one note from
howling bass to cracked treble. Yawning follows the duet; long, loud, weary yawning of all
the company in chorus. This amusement over,
Tom asks Dick for "baccer," and Dick denies
that he has got any, and Tom tells him he lies,
and Sam strikes in and says, "No, he doan't,"
and Jem tells Sam he lies, and Bill tells him that
if he was Sam he would punch Jem's head; and
Bob, apparently snuffing the battle from afar off,
and not liking the scent of it, shouts suddenly a
pacific good-night in the distance. The farewell
salutation seems to quiet the gathering storm.
They all roar responsive to the good-night roar
of Bob. A moment of silence, actually a moment, follows; then a repetition of the long, loud,
weary yawning in chorus; then another moment
of silence; then Jem suddenly shouts to the retiring Bob to come back; Bob refuses, softened by

distance; Jem insists, and his four friends join him; Bob relents, and returns. A shriek of indignation, far down the village; Bob's wife has her window open, and has heard him consent to go back to his friends. Hearty laughter from Bob's five friends; screams from Bob's wife— articulate screams, informing Bob that she will "cut his liver out," if he does not come home directly. Answering curses from Bob; he will "mash" his wife, if she does not hold her tongue. A song in chorus from Bob's five friends. Outraged by this time past all endurance, I spring out of bed and seize the water-jug. My wife, having the doctor's directions ever present to her mind, implores me in heart-rending tones to remember that I am under strict medical orders not to excite myself. I pay no heed to her remonstrances, and advance to the window with the jug. I pause before I empty the water on the heads of the assembly beneath; I pause, and hear — oh! most melodious, most welcome of sounds —· the sudden fall of rain! The merciful sky has anticipated me; the "clerk of the weather" has been struck by my idea of dispersing the Nag's Head Night Club by water. By the time I have put down the jug and got back to bed, silence—the primeval silence, the first, the foremost of all earthly influences—falls sweetly over our tavern at last.

That night, before sinking wearily to rest, I have once more the satisfaction of agreeing with my wife. Dear and admirable woman! she proposes to leave this secluded village the first thing

to-morrow morning.   Never did I share her opinion more cordially than I share it now.   Instead
of keeping myself composed, I have been living
in a region of perpetual disturbance; and, as for
doing nothing, my mind has been so agitated and
perturbed that I have not even had time to think
about it.   We will go, love—as you so sensibly
suggest—we will go the first thing in the morning to any place you like, so long as it is large
enough to swallow up small sounds.   Where,
over all the surface of this noisy earth, the blessing of tranquillity may be found, I know not;
but this I do know: a secluded English village
is the very last place toward which any man
should think of turning his steps, if the main
object of his walk through life is to discover
quiet.

NOTE THE SECOND.   DISCOVERY OF—NOTHING.

The next morning we continue our journey in
the direction of the coast, and arrive at a large
watering-place.

Observing that it is, in every respect, as unlike
the secluded village as possible, we resolve to
take up our abode in this populous and perfectly
tranquil town.   We get a lodging fronting the
sea.   There are noises about us — various and
loud noises, as I should have thought, if I had
not just come from a village; but everything is
comparative, and, after the past experience I
have gone through, I find our new place of abode
quiet enough to suit the moderate expectations
which I have now learned to form on the subject

of getting peace in this world. Here I can at least think almost uninterruptedly of the doctor's orders. Here I may surely begin my new life, and enjoy the luxury of doing nothing.

I suppose it *is* a luxury; and yet so perverse is man, I hardly know whether I am not beginning to find it something more like a hardship at the very outset. Perhaps my busy and active life has unfitted me for a due appreciation of the happiness of being idle. Perhaps I am naturally of a restless, feverish constitution. However that may be, it is certain that on the first day when I seriously determine to do nothing, I fail to find in the execution of my resolution such supreme comfort as I had anticipated. I try hard to fight against the conviction (which will steal on me, nevertheless) that I have only changed one kind of hard work for another that is harder. I try to persuade myself that time does not hang at all heavily on my hands, and that I am happier with nothing to do than ever I was with a long day's work before me. Do I succeed or do I fail in this meritorious attempt? Let me write down the results of my first day's experience of the art of doing nothing, and let the reader settle the question for me.

Breakfast at nine o'clock, so as not to make too long a day of it. Among the other things on the table are shrimps. I find myself liking shrimps for an entirely new reason—they take such a long time to eat. Well, breakfast is over at last: I have had quite enough, and yet I am gluttonously sorry when the table is cleared. If I were in health I should now go to my desk, or take up a book. But I am out of health, and I must do nothing. Suppose I look out of window? I hope that is idle enough to begin with.

The sea—yes, yes, the sea! Very large, very gray, very calm; very calm, very gray, very large. Anything else about the sea? Nothing else about the sea.

Yes—ships. One big ship in front, two little ships behind. (What time shall we have dinner, my dear? At five? Certainly at five!) One big ship in front, two little ships behind. Nothing more to see. Nothing.

Let me look back into the room, and study the subjects of these prints on the walls. First print: Death of the Earl of Chatham in the House of Lords, after Copley, R. A. Just so. Curious idea this picture suggests of the uniformity of personal appearance which must have distinguished the Peers in the last century. Here is a house full of noble lords, and each one of them is exactly like the other. Every noble lord is tall, every noble lord is portly, every noble lord has a long, receding forehead, and a majestic Roman nose. Odd; and leading to reflections on the physical changes that must have passed over the peerage of the present day, in which I might respectfully indulge, if the doctor had not ordered me to abstain from thinking.

Circumstanced as I am, I must mournfully dismiss the death of the Earl of Chatham, and pass from the work of Copley, R. A., to the other prints on the walls. Dear, dear me! Now I look again, there is nothing to pass to. There are only two other prints, and they are both classical landscapes. Deteriorated as the present condition of my faculties may be, my mind has not sunk yet to the level of Classical Landscape. I have still sense enough left to disbelieve in Claude and Poussin as painters of Italian scenery. Let me turn from the classical counterfeit to the modern reality. Let me look again at the sea.

Just as large, just as gray, just as calm as ever. Any more ships? No; still the one big ship in front; still the two little ships behind. They have not altered their relative positions the least in the world. How long is it to dinner-time? Six hours and a quarter. What on earth am I to do? Nothing.

Suppose I go and take a little walk? (No, dear, I will not tire myself; I will come back quite fresh to take you out in the afternoon.) Well, which way shall I go, now I am on the doorstep? There are two walks in this place. First walk, along the cliff westward; second walk, along the cliff eastward. Which direction shall I take? I am naturally one of the most decided men in the world; but doing nothing seems to have deprived me already of my usual resolute strength of will. I will toss up for it. Heads, westward; tails, eastward. Heads! Ought this to be considered conclusive? or shall I begin again, and try the best of three? I will try the best of three, because it takes up more time.

Heads, tails, heads! Westward still. Surely this is destiny. Or can it be that doing nothing has made me superstitious as well as irresolute? Never mind; I will go westward, and see what happens.

I saunter along the path by the iron railings; then down a little dip, at the bottom of which there is a seat overlooking a ship-builder's yard. Close under me is a small coasting vessel on the slips for repair. Nobody on board, but one old man at work. At work, did I say? Oh, happy chance! This aged repairer of ships is the very man, of all others, whom I had most need of meeting, the very man to help me in my present emergency. Before I have looked at him two minutes, I feel that I am in the presence of a great professor of the art of doing nothing. Toward this sage, to listen to his precepts and profit by his example, did destiny gently urge me, when I tossed up to decide between eastward and westward. Let me watch his proceedings; let me learn how to idle systematically by observing the actions of this venerable man.

He is sitting on the left side of the vessel when I first look at him. In one hand he holds a crooked nail; in the other, a hammer. He coughs slowly, and looks out to sea; he sighs slowly, and looks back toward the land; he rises slowly, and surveys the deck of the vessel; he stoops slowly, and picks up a flat bit of iron, and puts it on the bulwark, and places the crooked nail upon it, and then sits down and looks at the effect of the arrangement so far. When he has had enough of the arrangement, he gives the sea a turn again, then the land. After that, he steps back a little and looks at the hammer, weighs it gently in his hand, moistens his hand, advances to the crooked nail on the bit of iron, groans softly to himself and shakes his head as he looks at it, administers three delicate taps with the hammer, to straighten it, finds that he does not succeed to his mind; again groans softly, again shakes his head, again sits down and rests himself on the left side of the vessel. Since I first looked at him I have timed him by my watch; he has killed a quarter of an hour over that one crooked nail, and he has not straightened it yet! Wonderful man, can I ever hope to rival him? Will he condescend to talk to me? Stay! I am not free to try him; the doctor has told me not to excite myself with society; all communion of mind between me and this finished and perfect idler is, I fear, prohibited. Better to walk on, and come back, and look at him again.

I walk on and sit down; walk on a little further and sit down again; walk on for the third time, sit down for the third time, and still there is always the cliff on one side of me, and the one big ship and the two little ships on the other. I retrace my steps, occupying as much time as I possibly can in getting back to the seat above the coasting vessel. Where is my old friend, my esteemed professor, my bright and shining example in the difficult art of doing nothing? Sitting on the right side of the vessel this time, with the bit of flat iron on the right side also, with the

hammer still in his hand, and, as I live, with
the crooked nail not straightened yet! I observe
this, and turn away quickly with despair in my
heart. How can I, a tyro Do-Nothing, expect to
imitate that consummate old man? It is vain to
hope for success here—vain to hope for anything
but dinner-time. How many hours more?
Four. If I return home now, how shall I
go on doing nothing? Lunch, perhaps, will
help me a little. Quite so! Let us say a glass
of old ale and a biscuit. I should like to add
shrimps—if I were not afraid of my wife's disap-
probation—merely for the purpose of trying if I
could not treat them, as my old friend of the
coasting vessel treated the crooked nail.

Three hours and a half to dinner-time. I have
had my biscuit and my glass of old ale. Not
being accustomed to malt liquor in the middle of
the day, my lunch has fuddled me. There is a
faint singing in my ears, an intense sleepiness in
my eyelids, a genial warmth about my stomach,
and a sensation in my head as if the brains had
oozed out of me, and the cavity of my skull was
stuffed with cotton-wool steeped in laudanum.
Not an unpleasant feeling altogether. I am not
anxious; I think of nothing. I have a stolid
power of staring immovably out of window at
the one big ship and the two little ships, which I
had not hitherto given myself credit for possessing. If my wife would only push an easy-chair
up close behind me, I could sink back in it and
go to sleep; but she will do nothing of the sort.
She is putting on her bonnet; it is the hour of

the afternoon at which we are to take each other out fondly for our little walk.

The company at the watering-place is taking its little walk also at this time. But for the genial influence of the strong ale, I should now be making my observations and flying in the face of the doctor's orders by allowing my mind to be occupied. As it is, I march along slowly, lost in a solemn trance of beer.

One circumstance only, during our walk, is prominent enough to attract my sleepy attention. I just contrive to observe, with as much surprise and regret as I am capable of feeling at the present moment, that my wife apparently hates all the women we meet, and that all the women we meet seem, judging by their looks, to return the compliment by hating my wife. We pass an infinite number of girls, all more or less plump, all more or less healthy, all more or less overshadowed by eccentric seaside hats; and my wife will not allow that any one of these young creatures is even tolerably pretty. The young creatures on their side look so disparagingly at my wife's bonnet and gown, that I should feel uneasy about the propriety of her costume, if I were not under the comforting influence of the strong ale. What is the meaning of this unpleasant want of harmony among the members of the fair sex? Does one woman hate another woman for being a woman —is that it? How shocking if it is! I have no inclination to disparage other men whom I meet on my walk. Other men cast no disdainful looks on me. We lords of the creation are quite content to be handsome and attractive in our various ways, without snappishly contesting the palm of beauty with one another. Why can not the women follow our meritorious example? Will any one solve this curious problem in social morals? Doctor's orders forbid me from attempting the intellectual feat. The dire necessity of doing nothing narrows me to one subject of mental contemplation—the dinner-hour. How long is it —now we have returned from our walk—to that time? Two hours and a quarter. I can't look out of window again, for I know by instinct that the three ships and the calm gray sea are still lying in wait for me. I can't heave a patriot's sigh once more over the "Death of the Earl of Chatham." I am too tired to go out and see how the old man of the coasting vessel is getting on with the crooked nail. In short, I am driven to my last refuge. I must take a nap.

The nap lasts more than an hour. Its results may be all summed up in one significant and dreadful word—Fidgets. I start from the sofa convulsively, and sit down bolt upright in a chair. My wife is opposite to me, calmly engaged over her work. It is an hour and five minutes to dinner-time. What am I to do? Shall I soothe the fidgets and soften my rugged nature by looking at my wife, to see how she gets on with her work?

She has got a strip of calico, or something of that sort, punched all over with little holes, and she is sewing round each little hole with her needle and thread. Monotonous, to a masculine mind. Surely the punching of the holes must be the pleasantest part of this sort of work? And that is done at the shop, is it, dear? How curious!

Does my wife lace too tight? I have never had leisure before to look at her so long and so attentively as I am looking now; I have been uncritically contented hitherto to take her waist for granted. Now I have my doubts about it. I think the wife of my bosom is a little too much like an hour-glass. Does she digest? Good heavens! In the existing state of her stays, how do I know whether she digests?

Then, as to her hair: I do not object to the dressing of it, but I think—strangely enough, for the first time since our marriage—that she uses too much bear's grease and bandoline. I see a thin rim of bandoline shining just outside the line of hair against her temples, like varnish on a picture. This won't do—oh dear no—this won't do at all. Will her hands do? Certainly not! I discover, for the first time, that her hands won't do either. I am mercifully ready to put up with their not being quite white enough, but what does the woman mean by having such round tips to her fingers? Why don't they taper? I always thought they did taper until this moment. I begin to be dissatisfied with her; I begin to think my wife is not the charming woman I took her for. What is the matter with me? Am I looking at her with perceptions made morbid already by excessive idleness? Is this dreadful necessity of doing nothing to end by sapping the foundations of my matrimonial tranquillity, and letting down my whole connubial edifice into the bottomless abyss of Doctors' Commons?   Horrible!

The door of the room opens, and wakes me, as it were, from the hideous dream in which my wife's individuality has been entirely altered to my eyes.   It is only half an hour to dinner; and the servant has come in to lay the cloth.   In the presence of the great event of the day I feel myself again.   Once more I believe in the natural slimness of my wife's waist; once more I am contented with the tops of her fingers.   Now at last I see my way to bed-time.   Assuming that we can make the dinner last two hours; assuming that I can get another nap after it; assuming—

No!   I can assume nothing more, for I am really ashamed to complete the degrading picture of myself which my pen has been painting up to this time.   Enough has been written—more than enough, I fear—to show how completely I have failed in my first day's attempt at doing nothing.   The hardest labor I ever had to get through was not so difficult to contend with as this enforced idleness.   Never again will I murmur under the wholesome necessities of work. Never again—if I can only succeed in getting well—will a day of doing nothing be counted as pleasant holiday-time by me.   I have stolen away at the dead of the night, in flat defiance of the doctor's directions, to relieve my unspeakable weariness by writing these lines. I cast them on the world as the brief personal narrative of a most unfortunate man. If I systematically disregard medical advice, I shall make myself ill. If I conscientiously obey it, how am I to get through to-morrow? I mustn't work, and I can't idle. Will anybody kindly tell me what I am to do?

NOOKS AND CORNERS OF HISTORY.—1.

A QUEEN'S REVENGE.

THE name of Gustavus Adolphus, the faithful Protestant, the great general, and the good King of Sweden, has been long since rendered familiar to English readers of history. We all know how this renowned warrior and monarch was beloved by his soldiers and subjects, how successfully he fought through a long and terrible war, and how nobly he died on the field of battle. With his death, however, the interest of the English reader in Swedish affairs seems to terminate. Those who have followed the narrative of his life carefully to the end may remember that he left behind him an only child—a daughter named Christina. But of the character of this child, and of her extraordinary adventures after she grew to womanhood, the public in England is, for the most part, entirely ignorant. In the popular historical and romantic literature of France, Queen Christina is a notorious character. In the literature of this country, she has hitherto been allowed but little chance of making her way to the notice of the world at large.

And yet the life of Christina is in itself a romance. At six years old she was Queen of

Sweden, with the famous Oxenstiern for guardian. This great and good man governed the kingdom in her name until she had lived through her minority. Four years after her coronation she, of her own accord, abdicated her rights in favor of her cousin, Charles Gustavus. Young and beautiful, the most learned and most accomplished woman of her time, she resolutely turned her back on the throne of her inheritance, and set forth to wander through civilized Europe in the character of an independent traveler, who was resolved to see all varieties of men and manners, to collect all the knowledge which the widest experience could give her, and to measure her mind boldly against the greatest minds of the age.

So far, the interest excited by her character and her adventures is of the most picturesquely attractive kind. There is something strikingly new in the spectacle of a young queen who prefers the pursuit of knowledge to the possession of a throne, and who barters a royal birthright for the privilege of being free. Unhappily, the portrait of Christina cannot be painted throughout in bright colors only. It must be recorded to her disgrace that, when her travels brought her to Rome, she abandoned the religion for which her father fought and died. And it must be admitted in the interests of truth that she freed herself from other restraints besides the restraint of royalty. Mentally distinguished by her capacities, she was morally degraded by her vices and her crimes.

The events in the strange life of Christina—
especially those connected with her actions in the
character of a Queen - Errant — present ample
materials for a biography, which might be regarded in England as a new contribution to our
historical literature.   One among the many extraordinary adventures which marked the Queen's
wandering career may be related in these pages
as an episode in the history of her life which is
complete in itself.   The events of which the narrative is composed throw light, in many ways,
on the manners, habits, and opinions of a past
age; and they can, moreover, be presented in the
remarkable words of an eye-witness who beheld
them two centuries ago.

The scene is the Palace of Fontainebleau, the
time is the close of the year sixteen hundred and
fifty-seven, the persons are the wandering Queen
Christina; her grand equerry, the Marquis Monaldeschi; and Father Le Bel, of the Convent of
Fontainebleau, the witness whose testimony we
are shortly about to cite.

Monaldeschi, as his name implies, was an Italian by birth.   He was a handsome, accomplished
man, refined in his manners, supple in his disposition, and possessed of the art of making himself
eminently agreeable in the society of women.
With these personal recommendations, he soon
won his way to the favor of Queen Christina.
Out of the long list of her lovers, not one of the
many whom she encouraged caught so long and
firm a hold of her capricious fancy as Monaldes-

chi. The intimacy between them probably took its rise, on her side at least, in as deep a sincerity of affection as it was in Christina's nature to feel. On the side of the Italian, the connection was prompted solely by ambition. As soon as he had reaped all the advantages of the position of chief favorite in the Queen's court, he wearied of his royal mistress, and addressed his attentions secretly to a young Roman lady, whose youth and beauty powerfully attracted him, and whose fatal influence over his actions ultimately led to his ruin and his death.

After endeavoring to ingratiate himself with the Roman lady in various ways, Monaldeschi found that the surest means of winning her favor lay in satisfying her malicious curiosity on the subject of the secret frailties of Queen Christina. He was not a man to be troubled by any scrupulous feelings of honor when the interests of his own intrigues happened to be concerned, and he shamelessly took advantage of the position that he held toward Christina, to commit breaches of confidence of the most meanly infamous kind. Not contented with placing in the possession of the Roman lady the series of the Queen's letters to himself, containing secrets that she had revealed to him in the fullest confidence of his worthiness to be trusted, he wrote letters of his own to the new object of his addresses, in which he ridiculed Christina's fondness for him, and sarcastically described her smallest personal defects with a heartless effrontery which the most patient of women would have found it impossible

to forgive.   While he was thus privately betraying the confidence that had been reposed in him,
he was publicly affecting the most unalterable
attachment and the most sincere respect for the
Queen.

For some time this disgraceful deception proceeded successfully.   But the hour of discovery
was at hand, and the instrument of effecting it
was a certain cardinal who was desirous of sup-
planting Monaldeschi in the Queen's favor.   The
priest contrived to get possession of the whole
correspondence, which had been privately confided to the Roman lady, including, besides Christina's letters, the letters which Monaldeschi had
written in ridicule of his royal mistress.   The
whole collection of documents was inclosed by
the cardinal in one packet, and was presented
by him, at a private audience, to the Queen.

It is at this critical point of the story that the
testimony of the eye-witness whom we propose
to quote begins.   Father Le Bel was present at
the terrible execution of the Queen's vengeance
on Monaldeschi, and was furnished with copies
of the whole correspondence, which had been ab-
stracted from the possession of the Roman lady.
Having been trusted with the secret, he is wisely
and honorably silent throughout his narrative on
the subject of Monaldeschi's offense.   Such particulars of the Italian's baseness and ingratitude
as have been presented here have been gathered
from the contradictory reports which were current at the time, and which have been preserved
by the old French collectors of historical anec-

dotes. The details of the extraordinary punishment of Monaldeschi's offense, which are now to follow, may be given in the words of Father Le Bel himself. The reader will understand that his narrative begins immediately after Christina's discovery of the perfidy of her favorite.

The sixth of November, sixteen hundred and fifty-seven (writes Father Le Bel), at a quarter past nine in the morning, Queen Christina of Sweden, being at that time lodged in the Royal Palace of Fontainebleau, sent one of her menservants to my convent, to obtain an interview with me. The messenger, on being admitted to my presence, inquired if I was the superior of the convent, and, when I replied in the affirmative, informed me that I was expected to present myself immediately before the Queen of Sweden.

Fearful of keeping her Majesty waiting, I followed the man at once to the palace, without waiting to take any of my brethren from the convent with me.

After a little delay in the antechamber, I was shown into the Queen's room. She was alone; and I saw, by the expression of her face, as I respectfully begged to be favored with her commands, that something was wrong. She hesitated for a moment; then told me, rather sharply, to follow her to a place where she might speak with the certainty of not being overheard. She led me into the Galerie des Cerfs, and, turning round on me suddenly, asked if we had ever met before. I informed her Majesty that I had once had the honor of presenting my respects to her; that she had received me graciously, and that there the interview had ended. She nodded her head and looked about her a little; then said, very abruptly, that I wore a dress (referring to my convent costume) which encouraged her to put perfect faith in my honor; and she desired me to promise beforehand that I would keep the secret with which she was about to intrust me as strictly as if I had heard it in the confessional. I answered respectfully that it was part of my sacred profession to be trusted with secrets; that I had never betrayed the private affairs of any one; and that I could answer for myself as worthy to be honored by the confidence of a queen.

Upon this, her Majesty handed me a packet of papers sealed in three places, but having no superscription of any sort. She ordered me to keep it under lock and key, and to be prepared to give it her back again before any person in whose presence she might see fit to ask me for it. She further charged me to remember the day, the hour, and the place in which she had given me the packet; and with that last piece of advice she dismissed me. I left her alone in the gallery, walking slowly away from me, with her head drooping on her bosom, and her mind, as well as I could presume to judge, perturbed by anxious thoughts.*

---

* Although Father Le Bel discreetly abstains from mentioning the fact, it seems clear, from the context, that he was permitted to read, and that he did read, the papers contained in the packet.

On Saturday, the tenth of November, at one o'clock in the afternoon, I was sent for to the palace again. I took the packet out of my private cabinet, feeling that I might be asked for it, and then followed the messenger as before. This time he led me at once to the Galerie des Cerfs. The moment I entered it, he shut the door behind me with such extraordinary haste and violence that I felt a little startled. As soon as I recovered myself, I saw her Majesty standing in the middle of the gallery, talking to one of the gentlemen of her court, who was generally known by the name of The Marquis, and whom I soon ascertained to be the Marquis Monaldeschi, Grand Equerry of the Queen of Sweden. I approached her Majesty and made my bow, then stood before her, waiting until she should think proper to address me.

With a stern look on her face, and with a loud, clear, steady voice, she asked me, before the Marquis, and before three other men who were also in the gallery, for the packet which she had confided to my care.

As she made that demand, two of the three men moved back a few paces, while the third, the captain of her guard, advanced rather nearer to her. I handed her back the packet. She looked at it thoughtfully for a little while, then opened it and took out the letters and written papers which it contained, handed them to the Marquis Monaldeschi, and insisted on his reading them. When he had obeyed, she asked him, with the same stern look and the same steady voice, whether he had any knowledge of the documents which he had just been reading. The Marquis turned deadly pale, and answered that he had now read the papers referred to for the first time.

"Do you deny all knowledge of them?" said the Queen. "Answer me plainly, sir. Yes or No?"

The Marquis turned paler still. "I deny all knowledge of them," he said, in faint tones, with his eyes on the ground.

"Do you deny all knowledge of these, too?" said the Queen, suddenly producing a second packet of manuscript from under her dress, and thrusting it in the Marquis's face.

He started, drew back a little, and answered not a word. The packet which the Queen had given to me contained copies only. The original papers were those which she had just thrust in the Marquis's face.

"Do you deny your own seal and your own handwriting?" she asked.

He murmured a few words, acknowledging both the seal and the handwriting to be his own, and added some phrases of excuse, in which he endeavored to cast the blame that attached to the writing of the letters on the shoulders of other persons. While he was speaking, the three men in attendance on the Queen silently closed round him.

Her Majesty heard him to the end. "You are a traitor," she said, and turned her back on him.

The three men, as she spoke those words, drew their swords.

The Marquis heard the clash of the blades against the scabbards, and, looking quickly round, saw the drawn swords behind him. He caught the Queen by the arm immediately, and drew her away with him, first into one corner of the gallery, then into another, entreating her in the most moving terms to listen to him, and to believe in the sincerity of his repentance. The Queen let him go on talking without showing the least sign of anger or impatience. Her color never changed; the stern look never left her countenance. There was something awful in the clear, cold, deadly resolution which her eyes expressed while they rested on the Marquis's face.

At last she shook herself free from his grasp, still without betraying the slightest irritation. The three men with the drawn swords, who had followed the Marquis silently as he led the Queen from corner to corner of the gallery, now closed round him again, as soon as he was left standing alone. There was perfect silence for a minute or more. Then the Queen addressed herself to me.

"Father Le Bel," she said, "I charge you to bear witness that I treat this man with the strictest impartiality." She pointed, while she spoke, to the Marquis Monaldeschi with a little ebony riding-whip that she carried in her hand. "I offer that worthless traitor all the time he requires—more time than he has any right to ask for—to justify himself if he can."

The Marquis, hearing these words, took some

letters from a place of concealment in his dress, and gave them to the Queen, along with a small bunch of keys. He snatched these last from his pocket so quickly, that he drew out with them a few small silver coins which fell to the floor. As he addressed himself to the Queen again, she made a sign with her ebony riding-whip to the men with the drawn swords, and they retired toward one of the windows of the gallery. I, on my side, withdrew out of hearing. The conference which ensued between the Queen and the Marquis lasted nearly an hour. When it was over, her Majesty beckoned the men back again with the whip, and then approached the place where I was standing.

"Father Le Bel," she said, in her clear, ringing, resolute tones, "there is no need for me to remain here any longer. I leave that man," she pointed to the Marquis again, "to your care. Do all that you can for the good of his soul. He has failed to justify himself, and I doom him to die."

If I had heard sentence pronounced against myself, I could hardly have been more terrified than I was when the Queen uttered those last words. The Marquis heard them where he was standing, and flung himself at her feet. I dropped on my knees by his side, and entreated her to pardon him, or at least to visit his offense with some milder punishment than the punishment of death.

"I have said the words," she answered, addressing herself only to me; "and no power under heaven shall make me unsay them. Many a man has been broken alive on the wheel for offenses which were innocence itself, compared with the offense which this perjured traitor has committed against me. I have trusted him as I might have trusted a brother; he has infamously betrayed that trust, and I exercise my royal rights over the life of a traitor. Say no more to me. I tell you again, he is doomed to die."

With those words the Queen quitted the gallery, and left me alone with Monaldeschi and the three executioners who were waiting to kill him.

The unhappy man dropped on his knees at my feet, imploring me to follow the Queen and make one more effort to obtain his pardon. Before I could answer a word, the three men surrounded him, held the points of their swords to his sides—without, however, actually touching him—and angrily recommended him to make his confession to me without wasting any more time. I entreated them, with the tears in my eyes, to wait as long as they could, so as to give the Queen time to reflect, and perhaps to falter in her deadly intentions toward the Marquis. I succeeded in producing such an impression on the chief of the three men that he left us to obtain an interview with the Queen, and to ascertain if there was any change in her purpose. After a very short absence he came back, shaking his head.

"There is no hope for you," he said, addressing Monaldeschi. "Make your peace with Heaven. Prepare yourself to die!"

"Go to the Queen!" cried the Marquis, kneeling before me with clasped hands. "Go to the Queen yourself; make one more effort to save

me! Oh, Father Le Bel, run one more risk—
venture one last entreaty—before you leave me
to die!"

"Will you wait till I come back?" I said to
the three men.

"We will wait," they answered, and lowered
their swordpoints to the ground.

I found the Queen alone in her room, without
the slightest appearance of agitation in her face
or her manner. Nothing that I could say had
the slightest effect on her. I adjured her by all
that religion holds most sacred to remember that
the noblest privilege of any sovereign is the privilege of granting mercy; that the first of Christian duties is the duty of forgiving. She heard
me unmoved. Seeing that entreaties were thrown
away, I ventured, at my own proper hazard, on
reminding her that she was not living now in her
own kingdom of Sweden, but that she was the
guest of the King of France, and lodged in one
of his own palaces; and I boldly asked her if she
had calculated the possible consequences of authorizing the killing of one of her attendants inside the walls of Fontainebleau, without any
preliminary form of trial, or any official notifica-
tion of the offense that he had committed. She
answered me coldly, that it was enough that she
knew the unpardonable nature of the offense of
which Monaldeschi had been guilty; that she
stood in a perfectly independent position toward
the King of France; that she was absolute mistress of her own actions, at all times and in all
places; and that she was accountable to nobody

under Heaven for her conduct toward her subjects and servants, over whose lives and liberties
she possessed sovereign rights, which no consideration whatever should induce her to resign.

Fearful as I was of irritating her, I still ventured on reiterating my remonstrances. She cut
them short by hastily signing to me to leave her.

As she dismissed me, I thought I saw a slight
change pass over her face; and it occurred to me
that she might not have been indisposed at that
moment to grant some respite, if she could have
done so without appearing to falter in her resolution, and without running the risk of letting
Monaldeschi escape her. Before I passed the
door, I attempted to take advantage of the disposition to relent which I fancied I had perceived
in her; but she angrily reiterated the gesture of
dismissal before I had spoken half a dozen words.
With a heavy heart, I yielded to necessity, and
left her.

On returning to the gallery, I found the three
men standing round the Marquis, with their
swordpoints on the floor, exactly as I had left
them.

"Is he to live or to die?" they asked when I
came in.

There was no need for me to reply in words;
my face answered the question. The Marquis
groaned heavily, but said nothing. I sat myself
down on a stool, and beckoned to him to come to
me, and begged him, as well as my terror and
wretchedness would let me, to think of repentance, and to prepare for another world. He be-

gan his confession kneeling at my feet, with his
head on my knees.   After continuing it for some
time, he suddenly started to his feet with a scream
of terror.   I contrived to quiet him, and to fix
his thoughts again on heavenly things.   He
completed his confession, speaking sometimes
in Latin, sometimes in French, sometimes in
Italian, according as he could best explain himself in the agitation which now possessed him.

Just as he had concluded, the Queen's chaplain entered the gallery.   Without waiting to
receive absolution, the unhappy Marquis rushed
away from me to the chaplain, and, still clinging
desperately to the hope of life, besought him to
intercede with the Queen.   The two talked together in low tones, holding each other by the
hand.   When their conference was over, the
chaplain left the gallery again, taking with him
the chief of the three executioners who were appointed to carry out the Queen's deadly purpose.
After a short absence, this man returned without
the chaplain.   "Get your absolution," he said
briefly to the Marquis, "and make up your mind
to die."

Saying these words, he seized Monaldeschi,
pressed him back against the wall at the end of
the gallery, just under the picture of Saint Ger-
main, and, before I could interfere, or even turn
aside from the sight, struck at the Marquis's
right side with his sword.   Monaldeschi caught
the blade with his hand, cutting three of his fingers in the act.   At the same moment the point
touched his side and glanced off.   Upon this, the

man who had struck at him exclaimed, "He has armor under his clothes!" and at the same moment stabbed Monaldeschi in the face. As he received the wound, he turned round toward me, and cried out loudly, "Father Le Bel! Father Le Bel!"

I advanced toward him immediately. As I did so, the man who had wounded him retired a little, and signed to his two companions to withdraw also. The Marquis, with one knee on the ground, asked pardon of God, and said certain last words in my ear. I immediately gave him absolution, telling him that he must atone for his sins by suffering death, and that he must pardon those who were about to kill him. Having heard my words, he flung himself forward on the floor. While he was falling, one of the three executioners, who had not assailed him as yet, struck at his head, and wounded him on the surface of the skull.

The Marquis sank on his face; then raised himself a little, and signed to the men to kill him outright by striking him on the neck. The same man who had last wounded him obeyed by cutting two or three times at his neck, without, however, doing him any great injury. For it was indeed true that he wore armor under his clothes, which armor consisted of a shirt of mail weighing nine or ten pounds, and rising so high round his neck, inside his collar, as to defend it successfully from any chance blow with a sword.

Seeing this, I came forward to exhort the Marquis to bear his sufferings with patience, for the remission of his sins. While I was speaking, the chief of the three executioners advanced, and asked me if I did not think it was time to give Monaldeschi the finishing stroke. I pushed the man violently away from me, saying that I had no advice to offer on the matter, and telling him that, if I had any orders to give, they would be for the sparing of the Marquis's life, and not for the hastening of his death. Hearing me speak in those terms, the man asked my pardon, and confessed that he had done wrong in addressing me on the subject at all.

He had hardly finished making his excuse to me, when the door of the gallery opened. The unhappy Marquis hearing the sound, raised himself from the floor, and, seeing that the person who entered was the Queen's chaplain, dragged himself along the gallery, holding on by the tapestry that hung from the walls, until he reached the feet of the holy man. There he whispered a few words (as if he was confessing) to the chaplain, who, after first asking my permission, gave him absolution, and then returned to the Queen.

As the chaplain closed the door, the man who had struck the Marquis on the neck stabbed him adroitly with a long, narrow sword in the throat just above the edge of the shirt of mail. Monaldeschi sank on his right side, and spoke no more. For a quarter of an hour longer he still breathed, during which time I prayed by him, and exhorted him as I best could. When the bleeding from this last wound ceased, his life ceased with it. It was then a quarter to four o'clock. The death-agony of the miserable man had lasted, from the time of the Queen's first pronouncing sentence on him, for nearly three hours.

I said the De Profundis over his body. While I was praying, the three executioners sheathed their swords, and the chief of them rifled the Marquis's pockets. Finding nothing on him but a prayer-book and a small knife, the chief beckoned to his companions, and they all three marched to the door in silence, went out, and left me alone with the corpse.

A few minutes afterward I followed them, to go and report what had happened to the Queen.

I thought her color changed a little when I told her that Monaldeschi was dead; but those cold, clear eyes of hers never softened, and her voice was still as steady and firm as when I first heard its tones on entering the gallery that day. She spoke very little, only saying to herself, "He is dead, and he deserved to die!" Then, turning to me, she added, "Father, I leave the care of burying him to you; and, for my own part, I will charge myself with the expense of having masses enough said for the repose of his soul." I ordered the body to be placed in a coffin, which I instructed the bearers to remove to the churchyard on a tumbril, in consequence of the great weight of the corpse, of the misty rain that was falling, and of the bad state of the roads. On Monday, the twelfth of November, at a quarter to six in the evening, the Marquis was buried in the parish

church of Avon, near the font of holy water.   The
next day the Queen sent one hundred livres, by
two of her servants, for masses for the repose of
his soul.

Thus ends the extraordinary narrative of Father
Le Bel.   It is satisfactory to record, as some evidence of the progress of humanity, that this barbarous murder, which would have passed unnoticed in the feudal times, as an ordinary and
legitimate exercise of a sovereign's authority over
a vassal, excited, in the middle of the seventeenth
century, the utmost disgust and horror throughout Paris.   The prime minister at that period,
Cardinal Mazarin (by no means an overscrupu-
lous man, as all readers of French history know),
wrote officially to Christina, informing her that
"a crime so atrocious as that which had just been
committed under her sanction, in the Palace of
Fontainebleau, must be considered as a sufficient
cause for banishing the Queen of Sweden from
the court and dominions of his sovereign, who,
in common with every honest man in the kingdom, felt horrified at the lawless outrage which
had just been committed on the soil of France."
To this letter Queen Christina sent the following answer, which, as a specimen of spiteful
effrontery, has probably never been matched:

"MONSIEUR MAZARIN—Those who have communicated to you the details of the death of my
equerry, Monaldeschi, knew nothing at all about
it.   I think it highly absurd that you should have

compromised so many people for the sake of informing yourself about one simple fact. Such a
proceeding on your part, ridiculous as it is, does
not, however, much astonish me. What I am
amazed at is, that you and the king your master
should have dared to express disapproval of what
I have done.

"Understand, all of you—servants and masters, little people and great—that it was my
sovereign pleasure to act as I did. I neither
owe nor render an account of my actions to any
one—least of all, to a bully like you.

.   .   .   .

"It may be well for you to know, and to report to any one whom you can get to listen to
you, that Christina cares little for your court,
and less still for you. When I want to revenge
myself, I have no need of your formidable power
to help me. My honor obliged me to act as I
did; my will is my law, and you ought to know
how to respect it. . . . Understand, if you please,
that wherever I choose to live, there I am Queen;
and that the men about me, rascals as they may
be, are better than you and the ragamuffins whom
you keep in your service.

.   .   .   .

"Take my advice, Mazarin, and behave yourself for the future so as to merit my favor; you
cannot, for your own sake, be too anxious to deserve it. Heaven preserve you from venturing
on any more disparaging remarks about my conduct! I shall hear of them, if I am at the other
end of the world; for I have friends and follow-

ers in my service who are as unscrupulous and as vigilant as any in yours, though it is probable enough that they are not quite so heavily bribed.''

After replying to the prime minister of France in those terms, Christina was wise enough to leave the kingdom immediately.

For three years more she pursued her travels. At the expiration of that time, her cousin, the King of Sweden, in whose favor she had abdicated, died. She returned at once to her own country, with the object of possessing herself once more of the royal power. Here the punishment of the merciless crime that she had sanctioned overtook her at last. The brave and honest people of Sweden refused to be governed by the woman who had ordered the murder of Monaldeschi, and who had forsaken the national religion for which her father died. Threatened with the loss of her revenues as well as the loss of her sovereignty, if she remained in Sweden, the proud and merciless Christina yielded for the first time in her life. She resigned once more all right and title to the royal dignity, and left her native country for the last time. The final place of her retirement was Rome. She died there in the year sixteen hundred and eighty-nine. Even in the epitaph which she ordered to be placed on her tomb, the strange and daring character of the woman breaks out. The whole record of that wild and wicked existence was summed up with stern brevity in this one line:

CHRISTINA LIVED SEVENTY-TWO YEARS.

SOCIAL GRIEVANCES.—II.

A PETITION TO THE NOVEL-WRITERS.

[Communicated by a Romantic Old Gentleman.]

I HOPE nobody will be alarmed if I confess
that I am about to disclose the existence of a
Disreputable Society, in one of the most respectable counties in England. I dare not be more
particular as to the locality, and I cannot possibly mention the members by name.   But I have
no objection to admit that I am perpetual Secre-
tary, that my wife is President, that my daughters are Council, and that my nieces form the
Society. Our object is to waste our time, mis-
employ our intellects, and ruin our morals—or,
in other words, to enjoy the prohibited luxury of
novel-reading.

It is a settled opinion of mine that the dull
people in this country are the people who, privately as well as publicly, govern the nation.
By dull people, I mean people of all degrees of
rank and education who never want to be amused.
I don't know how long it is since these dreary
members of the population first hit on the cunning idea of calling themselves respectable; but
I do know that, ever since that time, this great

nation has been afraid of them—afraid in religious, in political and in social matters.   If my present business were with the general question, I think I could prove this assertion by simple reference to those records of our national proceedings which appear in the daily newspapers.   But my object in writing is of the particular kind.   I have a special petition to address to the writers of novels, on the part of the Disreputable Society to which I belong; and if I am to give any example here of the supremacy of the dull people, it must be drawn from one or two plain evidences of their success in opposing the claims of our fictitious literature to popular recognition.

The dull people decided years and years ago, as every one knows, that novel-writing was the lowest species of literary exertion, and that novel-reading was a dangerous luxury and an utter waste of time; they gave, and still give, reasons for this opinion, which are very satisfactory to persons born without fancy or imagination, and which are utterly inconclusive to every one else. But, with reason or without it, the dull people have succeeded in affixing to our novels the stigma of being a species of contraband goods.   Look, for example, at the prospectus of any librarian. The principal part of his trade of book-lending consists in the distributing of novels; and he is uniformly ashamed to own that simple fact. Sometimes, he is afraid to print the word novel at all in his lists, and smuggles in his contraband fiction under the head of Miscellaneous Literature.   Sometimes, after freely offering all his-

tories, all biographies, all voyages, all travels,
he owns self-reproachfully to the fact of having
novels, too, but deprecatingly adds—Only the
best! As if no other branch of the great tree
of literature ever produced tasteless and worthless fruit! In all cases, he puts novels last on
his public list of the books he distributes, though
they stand first on his private list of the books
he gains by. Why is he guilty of all these sins
against candor? Because he is afraid of the dull
people.

Look again—and this brings me to the subject
of these lines—at our Book Clubs. How para-
mount are the dull people there! How they hug
to their rigid bosoms Voyages and Travels! How
they turn their intolerant backs on novels! How
resolutely they get together, in a packed body,
on the committee, and impose their joyless laws
on the yielding victims of the club, who secretly
want to be amused! Our book club was an example of the unresisted despotism of their rule.
We began with a law that novels should be occasionally admitted, and the dull people abrogated
it before we had been in existence a twelvemonth.
I smuggled in the last morsel of fiction that our
starving stomachs were allowed to consume, and
produced a hurricane of virtuous indignation at
the next meeting of the committee.

All the dull people of both sexes attended that
meeting. One dull gentleman said the author
was a pantheist, and quoted some florid ecstasies
on the subject of scenery and flowers in support
of the opinion. Nobody seemed to know exactly

what a pantheist was, but everybody cried "Hear, hear"—which did just as well for the purpose. Another dull gentleman said the book was painful because there was a death-bed scene in it. A third reviled it for morbid reveling in the subject of crime because a shot from the pistol of a handsome highwayman dispatched the villain of the story. But the great effect of the day was produced by a lady, the mother of a large family, which began with a daughter of eighteen years and ended with a boy of eight months. This lady's objection affected the heroine of the novel—a respectable married woman, perpetually plunged in virtuous suffering, but an improper character for young persons to read about, because the poor thing had two accouchements— only two!—in the course of three volumes. "How can I suffer my daughters to read such a book as that?" cried our prolific subscriber indignantly. A tumult of applause followed. A chorus of speeches succeeded, full of fierce references to "our national morality," and "the purity of our hearths and homes." A resolution was passed excluding all novels for the future; and then, at last, the dull people held their tongues, and sat down with a thump in their chairs, and glared contentedly on each other in stolid controversial triumph.

From that time forth (histories and biographies being comparatively scarce articles) we were fed by the dull people on nothing but Voyages and Travels. Every man (or woman) who had voyaged and traveled to no purpose, who

had made no striking observations of any kind,
who had nothing whatever to say, and who said
it at great length in large type on thick paper,
with accompaniment of frowzy lithographic illus-
trations, was introduced weekly to our hearths
and homes as the most valuable guide, philoso-
pher, and friend whom our rulers could possibly
send us. All the subscribers submitted; all partook the national dread of the dull people, with
the exception of myself and the members of my
family enumerated at the beginning of these
pages. We resolutely abandoned the club; got
a boxful of novels for ourselves, once a month,
from London; lost caste with our respectable
friends in consequence; and became for the future, throughout the length and breadth of our
neighborhood, the Disreputable Society to which
I have already alluded. If the dull people of our
district were told to-morrow that my wife,
daughters, and nieces had all eloped in different directions, leaving just one point of the compass open as a runaway outlet for me and the
cook, I feel firmly persuaded that not one of
them would be inclined to discredit the report.
"This is what comes of novel-reading!" they
would say—and would return, with renewed
zest, to their Voyages and Travels, their accouchements in real life, their canting "national
morality," and their blustering "purity of our
hearths and homes."

And now, to come to the main object of this
paper—the humble petition of myself and family
to certain of our novel-writers. We may say of

ourselves that we deserve to be heard, for we have braved public opinion for the sake of reading novels; and we have read, for some years past, all (I hold to the assertion, incredible as it may appear)—all the stories in one, two, and three volumes that have issued from the press. What, then, have we got to petition about? A very slight matter. Marking, first of all, as exceptions, certain singular instances of originality, I may mention, as a rule, that our novel-reading enjoyments have hitherto been always derived from the same sort of characters and the same sort of stories—varied, indeed, as to names and minor events, but fundamentally always the same, through hundreds on hundreds of successive volumes, by hundreds on hundreds of different authors. We none of us complain of this, so far, for we like to have as much as possible of any good thing; but we beg deferentially to inquire whether it might not be practicable to give us a little variety for the future. We have no unwholesome craving after absolute novelty—all that we venture to ask for is, the ringing of a slight change on some of the favorite old tunes which we have long since learned by heart.

To begin with our favorite Hero. He is such an old friend that we have by this time got to love him dearly. We would not lose sight of him altogether on any consideration whatever. Far be it from us to hint at the withdrawal of this noble, loving, injured, fascinating man! We adore his aquiline nose, his tall form, his wavy hair, his rich voice. Long may we continue to weep on his deep chest, and press respectfully to our lips the folds of his ample cloak! Personally speaking, it is by no means of him that we are getting tired, but of certain actions which we think he has now performed often enough.

For instance, may we put it respectfully to the ladies and gentlemen who are so good as to exhibit him, that he had better not "stride" any more? He has stridden so much, on so many different occasions, across so many halls, along so many avenues, in and out at so many drawing-room doors, that he must be knocked up by this time, and his dear legs ought really to have a little rest. Again, when his dignity is injured by irreverent looks or words, can he not be made to assert it for the future without "drawing himself up to his full height"? He has really been stretched too much by perpetual indulgence in this exercise for scores and scores of years. Let him sit down—do, please, let him sit down next time! It would be quite new, and so impressive. Then, again, we have so often discovered him standing with folded arms, so often beheld him pacing with folded arms, so often heard him soliloquize with folded arms, so often broken in upon him meditating with folded arms, that we think he had better do something else with his arms for the future. Could he swing them for a change, or put them akimbo, or drop them suddenly on either side of him? Or could he give them a holiday altogether, and fold his legs by way of variety? Perhaps not. The word legs

—why, I cannot imagine—seems always suggestive of jocularity. "Fitzherbert stood up and folded his arms," is serious. "Fitzherbert sat down and folded his legs," is comic. Why, I should like to know?

A word—one respectful word of remonstrance to the lady novelists especially. We think they have put our Hero on horseback often enough. For the first five hundred novels or so, it was grand, it was thrilling, when he threw himself into the saddle after the inevitable quarrel with his lady-love, and galloped off madly to his bachelor home. It was inexpressibly soothing to behold him, in the milder passages of his career, moody in the saddle, with the reins thrown loosely over the arched neck of his steed, as the gallant animal paced softly with his noble burden, along a winding road, under a blue sky, on a balmy afternoon in early spring. All this was delightful reading for a certain number of years; but everything wears out at last; and trust me, ladies, your hero's favorite steed, your dear, intelligent, affectionate, glossy, long-tailed horse, has really done his work, and may now be turned loose, for some time to come, with great advantage to yourselves and your readers.

Having spoken a word to the ladies, I am necessarily and tenderly reminded of their charming representatives—the Heroines. Let me say something, first, about our favorite two sisters— the tall dark one, who is serious and unfortunate; the short light one, who is coquettish and happy.

Being an Englishman, I have, of course, an ardent attachment to anything like an established rule, simply because it is established. I know that it is a rule that, when two sisters are presented in a novel, one must be tall and dark, and the other short and light. I know that five feet eight of female flesh and blood, when accompanied by an olive complexion, black eyes, and raven hair, is synonymous with strong passions and an unfortunate destiny. I know that five feet nothing, golden ringlets, soft blue eyes, and a lily brow, cannot possibly be associated by any well-constituted novelist with anything but ringing laughter, arch innocence, and final matrimonial happiness. I have studied these great first principles of the art of fiction too long not to reverence them as established laws; but I venture respectfully to suggest that the time has arrived when it is no longer necessary to insist on them in novel after novel. I am afraid there is something naturally revolutionary in the heart of man. Although I know it to be against all precedent, I want to revolutionize our favorite two sisters. Would any bold innovator run all risks, and make them both alike in complexion and in stature? Or would any desperate man (I dare not suggest such a course to the ladies) effect an entire alteration, by making the two sisters change characters? I tremble when I see to what lengths the spirit of innovation is leading me. Would the public accept the tall dark-haired sister, if she exhibited a jolly disposition and a tendency to be flippant in her talk?

Would readers be fatally startled out of their sense of propriety if the short charmer with the golden hair appeared before them as a serious, strong-minded, fierce-spoken, miserable, guilty woman? It might be a dangerous experiment to make this change; but it would be worth trying—the rather (if I may be allowed to mention anything so utterly irrelevant to the subject under discussion as real life) because I think there is some warrant in nature for attempting the proposed innovation. Judging by my own small experience, I should say that strong minds and passionate natures reside principally in the breasts of little, light women, especially if they have angelic blue eyes and a quantity of fair ringlets. The most facetiously skittish woman for her age with whom I am acquainted is my own wife, who is three inches taller than I am. The heartiest laugher I ever heard is my second daughter, who is bigger even than my wife, and has the blackest eyebrows and the swarthiest cheeks in the whole neighborhood. With such instances as these, producible from the bosom of my own family, who can wonder if I want, for once in a way, to overthrow the established order of things, and have a jovial dark sister and a dismal light one introduced as startling novelties in some few of the hundred new volumes which we are likely to receive next season from the Circulating Library?

But, after all, our long-established two sisters seem to be exceptional beings, and to possess comparatively small importance, the moment our minds revert to that vastly superior single person, THE HEROINE.

Let me mention, to begin with, that we wish no change to be made in our respectable, recognized, old-fashioned Heroine, who has lived and loved and wept for centuries. I have taken her to my bosom thousands of times already, and ask nothing better than to indulge in that tender luxury thousands of times again. I love her blushing cheek, her gracefully-rounded form, her chiseled nose, her slender waist, her luxuriant tresses which always escape from the fillet that binds them. Any man or woman who attempts, from a diseased craving after novelty, to cheat me out of one of her moonlight walks, one of her floods of tears, one of her kneeling entreaties to obdurate relatives, one of her rapturous sinkings on her lover's bosom, is a novelist whom I distrust and dislike. He or she may be a very remarkable writer; but their books will not do for my family and myself. The Heroine, the whole Heroine, and nothing but the Heroine—that is our cry, if you drive us into a corner and insist on our stating precisely what we want in the plainest terms possible.

Being thus faithfully attached to the established Heroine, it will not, I trust, appear a very unaccountable proceeding, if we now protest positively, and even indignantly, against her modern successor—a bouncing, ill-conditioned, impudent young woman, who has been introduced among us of late years. I venture to call this wretched and futile substitute for our dear, tender, gentle, loving old Heroine, the Man-Hater; because, in every book in which she appears, it is her mission from first to last to behave as badly as possible to every man with whom she comes in contact. She enters on the scene with a preconceived prejudice against my sex, for which I, as a man, abominate her; for which my wife, my daughters, my nieces, and all other available women whom I have consulted on the subject, despise her. When her lover makes her an offer of marriage, she receives it in the light of a personal insult, goes up to her room immediately afterward, and flies into a passion with herself, because she is really in love with the man all the time—comes down again, and snubs him before company instead of making a decent apology—pouts and flouts at him, on all after occasions, until the end of the book is at hand—then suddenly turns round and marries him! If we feel inclined to ask why she could not, under the circumstances, receive his advances with decent civility at first, we are informed that her "maidenly consciousness" prevented it. This maidenly consciousness seems to me very like new English for our old-fashioned phrase, bad manners. And I am the more confirmed in this idea, because on all minor occasions the Man-Hater is persistently rude and disobliging to the last. Every individual in the novel who wears trousers and gets within range of her maidenly consciousness becomes her natural enemy from that moment. If he makes a remark on the weather, her lip curls; if he asks leave to give her a potato at dinner-time (meaning, poor soul, to pick out for her the mealiest in the dish), her neck curves in scorn; if he offers a compliment, finding she won't have a potato, her nostril dilates. Whatever she does, even in her least aggressive moments, she always gets the better of all the men. They are set up like nine-pins for the Man-Hater to knock down. They are described, on their introduction, as clever, resolute fellows; but they lose their wits and their self-possession the instant they come within hail of the Man-Hater's terrible tongue. No man kisses her, no man dries her tears, no man sees her blush (except with rage), all through the three volumes. And this is the opposition Hero-ine who is set up as successor to our soft, femi-nine, lovable, sensitive darling of former days!

Set up, too, by lady-novelists, who ought sure-ly to be authorities when female characters are concerned. Is the Man-Hater a true representa-tive of young women nowadays? If so, what is to become of my son—my unlucky son, aged twelve years?

In a short time this boy will be marriageable, and he will go into the world to bill and coo, and offer his hand and heart, as his father did before him. My unhappy offspring, what a prospect awaits you! One forbidding phalanx of Man-Haters, bristling with woman's dignity, and armed to the teeth with maidenly conscious-ness, occupies the wide matrimonial field, look where you will! Ill-fated youth, yet a few years, and the female neck will curve, the fe-male nostril dilate, at the sight of you. You see that stately form, those rustling skirts, that ample brow, and fall on your knees before it, and make your proposal with the impassioned imbecility which your father exhibited before you. My deluded boy, that is not a woman—it is a Man-Hater—a whited sepulcher, full of violent expostulations and injurious epithets. She will lead you the life of a costermonger's ass, until she has exhausted her whole stock of maidenly consciousness; and she will then say (in effect, if not in words), "Inferior animal, I loved you from the first—I have asserted my dignity by making a fool of you in public and private—now you may marry me!" Marry her not, my son! Go rather to the slave-market at Constantinople, buy a Circassian wife who has heard nothing and read nothing about Man-Haters, bring her home (with no better dowry than pots of the famous Cream from her native land to propitiate your mother and sisters), and trust to your father to welcome an Asiatic daughter-in-law, who will not despise him for the unavoidable misfortune of being a Man!

But I am losing my temper over a hypothetical case. I am forgetting the special purpose of my petition, which is to beg that the Man-Hater may be removed altogether from her usurped position of heroine. The new-fashioned heroine is a libel on her sex. As a husband and a father, I solemnly deny that she is in any single respect a natural woman. Am I no judge? I have a wife, and I made her an offer. Did she receive it as the Man-Haters receive offers? Can I ever forget the mixture of modest confusion and perfect politeness with which that admirable woman heard me utter the most absolute nonsense that ever issued from my lips? Perhaps she is not fit for a heroine. Well, I can give her up in that capacity without a pang. But my daughters and nieces have claims, I suppose, to be considered as examples of what young ladies are in the present day. Ever since I read the first novel with a Man-Hater in it, 1 have had my eye on their nostrils, and 1 can make affidavit that I have never yet seen them dilate under any circumstances or in any society. As for curling their lips and curving their necks, they have attempted both operations at my express request, and have found them to be physical impossibilities. In men's society, their manners (like those of all other girls whom I meet with) are natural and modest; and—in the cases of certain privileged men— winning into the bargain. They open their eyes with astonishment when they read of the proceedings of our new-fashioned heroines, and throw the book indignantly across the room, when they find a nice man submitting to be bullied by a nasty woman, because he has paid her the compliment of falling in love with her. No, no; we positively decline to receive any more Man-Haters, and there is an end of it!

With this uncompromising expression of opinion, I think it desirable to bring the present petition to a close. There are one or two other good things in fiction, of which we have had enough; but I refrain from mentioning them, from modest apprehension of asking for too much at a time. If the slight changes in general, and the sweeping reform in particular, which I have ventured to suggest, can be accomplished, we are sure, in the future as in the past, to be grateful, appreciating, and incessant novel-readers. If we cannot claim any critical weight in the eyes of our esteemed authors, we can at least arrogate to ourselves the minor merit, not only of reading novels perpetually, but (and this is a rarer virtue) of publicly and proudly avowing the fact. We only pretend to be human beings with a natural desire for as much amusement as our workaday destinies will let us have. We are just respectable enough to be convinced of the usefulness of occasionally reading for information; but we are also certain (and we say it boldly, in the teeth of the dull people) that there are few higher, better, or more profitable enjoyments in this world than reading a good novel.

FRAGMENTS OF PERSONAL EXPERIENCE.—I.

LAID UP IN LODGINGS.

MY PARIS LODGING.

IT has happened rather whimsically, and not very fortunately for me, that my first experience of living in furnished lodgings abroad, as well as in England, has occurred at the very time when illness has rendered me particularly susceptible to the temporary loss of the comforts of home. I have been ill, alone, in furnished lodgings in Paris—ill, alone, on the journey back to England—ill, alone, again, in furnished lodgings in London. I am a single man; but as I have already intimated, I never knew what it was to enjoy the desolate liberty of the bachelor until I became an invalid. Some of my impressions of things and persons about me formed under these anomalous circumstances, may, perhaps, prove not altogether unworthy of being written down, while they are still fresh in my mind.

How I happen, for a temporary period, to be away from the home in which I have hitherto lived with my nearest relatives, and to which I hope soon to return, it is of no importance to the

reader to know.   Neither is it at all worth while
to occupy time and space with any particular description of the illness from which I have been
and am still suffering.   It will be enough for
preliminary purposes, if I present myself at once
in the character of a convalescent visiting Paris,
with the double intention of passing agreeably
an interval of necessary absence from home, and
of promoting, by change of air and scene, my recovery from a distressing and a tedious illness.
When I add to this, that although I lived alone
in my French bachelor apartment, I had the
good fortune at Paris, as afterward in London,
to be in the near neighborhood of the most kind,
attentive, and affectionate friends, I have said as
much as is needful by way of preface, and may
get on at once to my main purpose.

What my impressions of my apartment in
Paris might have been, if I had recovered there
according to my anticipations, I cannot venture
to say; for, before I had got fairly settled in my
new rooms, I suffered a sudden relapse.   My
life again became the life of an invalid, and my
ways of thought and observation turned back
disastrously to the old invalid channel.   Change
of air and scene—which had done nothing for
my body—did nothing either for my mind.   At
Paris, as before in London, I looked at the world
about me purely from the sick man's point of
view—or, in other words, the events that passed,
the sights that appeared, and the persons who
moved around me, interested or repelled me only
as they referred more or less directly to myself

and my own invalid situation. This curious narrowness of view, of which I am not yet well enough entirely to rid myself, though as conscious as another of the mental weakness that it implies, has no connection that I can discover with excessive selfishness or vanity; it is simply the result of the inevitable increase of a man's importance to himself which the very fact of sickness is only too apt to produce.

My own sensations as a sick man now fill up the weary blank of my daily existence when I am alone, and form the main topic of inquiry and conversation when my doctor and my friends enliven my solitude. The concerns of my own poor body, which do not, I thank Heaven, occupy my attention for much more than one hour out of the twenty-four when I am well, become the main business and responsibility of all my waking moments now that 1 am ill. Pain to suffer, and the swallowing of drugs and taking of nourishment at regulated periods, daily restraints that I must undergo, and hourly precautions that I am forced to practice, all contribute to keep my mind bound down to the level of my body. A flight of thought beyond myself and the weary present time—even supposing I were capable of the exertion—would lead me astray from the small personal rules and regulations on which I now depend absolutely for the recovery of my health.

Have my temper and disposition changed for the worse under these unfavorable circumstances? Not much, I hope. I can honestly say for myself that I envy no other man's health and happiness. I feel no jealous pang when I hear laughter about me. I can look at people out of my window running easily across the road, while I can hardly crawl from one end of my chamber to the other, without feeling insulted by their activity. Still, it is true, at the same time, that I warm to people now exactly in proportion as I see them sensibly and sincerely touched by my suffering condition; and that I like or dislike my habitation for the time being, just as it happens to suit or not to suit all the little requirements of my temporary infirmity. If I were introduced to one of the most eminent men in the country at this moment, and if he did not look sorry to see me ill, I should never care to set eyes on the eminent man again. If I had a superb room with the finest view in the world, but no bedside conveniences for my pill-boxes and medicine-bottles, I would leave that superb room and fine view, and go cheerfully to a garret in an alley, provided it adapted itself comfortably to the arrangement of my indispensable invalid's lumber. This is, doubtless, a humiliating confession; but it is well that I should make it once for all—for the various opinions and impressions which I am about frankly to write down will be found to be more or less colored by what I venture to describe as the involuntary egotism of a sick man.

Let us see how my new lodging in Paris suits me, and why it is that I immediately become fond of it.

I live in a little building of my own, called a

Pavilion. Outside it resembles, as to size, brightness, and apparent insubstantiality, a private
dwelling-house in a Pantomime. I expect as
I drive up to it, for the first time, to see Clown
grinning at the door, and Harlequin jumping
through the window. A key is produced, and
an odd little white door, through which no fat
man could penetrate even sidewise, is opened; I
ascend a steep flight of a dozen steps, and enter
my toy castle; my own independent, solitary,
miniature mansion.

The first room is the drawing-room. It is
about the size of a large packing-case, with a
gay looking-glass and clock, with bright red
chairs and sofa, with a cozy round table, with
a big window looking out on another Pavilion
opposite and on a great house set back in a
courtyard. To my indescribable astonishment,
it actually possesses three doors! One I have
just entered by. Another leads into a bed-chamber of the same size as the drawing-room, just
as brightly and neatly furnished, with a window
that looks out on the everlasting gayety and
bustle of the Champs Elysées. The third door
leads into a dressing-room half the size of the
drawing-room, and having a fourth door which
opens into a kitchen half the size of the dressing-room, but of course possessing a fifth door,
which leads out again to the head of the staircase. As no two people meeting in the kitchen
could possibly pass each other, or remain in the
apartment together without serious inconven-
ience, the two doors leading in and out of it may

be pronounced useful as well as ornamental. Into
this quaint little culinary crevice the coal-mer-
chant, the wood-merchant, and the water-carrier
squeeze their way, and find a doll's cellar and
cistern all ready for them. They might be followed, if I were only well enough to give dinners, by a cook and his scullions; for I possess,
besides the kitchen and cistern, an elaborate char-
coal stove in the kitchen, at which any number
of courses might be prepared by any culinary
artist who could cook composedly with a row of
small fires under his nose, a coal-cellar between
his legs, a cistern scrubbing his shoulder, and a
lukewarm wall against his back.

But what is the main secret of my fondness for
the Pavilion? It does not, I am afraid, lie in the
brightness and elegance of the little rooms, or
even in the delightful independence of inhabiting
a lodging, which is also a house of my own,
where I can neither be disturbed nor overlooked
by any other lodgers. The one irresistible appeal
which my Parisian apartment makes to my sympathies consists in the perfect manner in which
it fits my wants and flatters my weaknesses as
an invalid.

I have quite a little druggist's stock in trade
of physic-bottles, glasses, spoons, card-boxes, and
prescriptions; I have all sorts of queer vestments
and coverings, intended to guarantee me against
all variations of temperature and all degrees of
exposure, by night as well as by day; I have
ready remedies that must be kept in my bed-
chamber, and elaborate applications that I must

find handy in my dressing-room. In short, I
myself am nothing but the center of a vast medical litter, and the closer the said litter revolves
round me the more comfortable I am. In a
house of the usual size, and in rooms arranged on
the ordinary plan, I should be driven distracted
(being an untidy man even in my healthiest moments) by mislaying things every hour in the
day, by having to get up to look for them, and
by being compelled to walk up and downstairs,
or to make others do so for me, when I want to
establish communications between dressing-room,
bedroom, drawing-room, coal-cellar, and kitchen.
In my tiny Parisian house of one small story, I
can wait on myself with the most perfect ease;
in my wee sitting-room, nine-tenths of the things
I want are within arms-length of me, as I repose
in my elbow-chair; if I must move, I can get
from my bed-chamber to my kitchen in less time
than it would take me to walk across an English
drawing-room; if I lose my morning draught,
mislay my noontide drops, or leave my evening
pill-box under my afternoon dressing-gown, I
can take my walking-stick or my fire-tongs and
poke or fish for missing articles in every corner
of the room, without doing more than turning
round in my chair. If I had been well and had
given dinner-parties, I might have found my
habitation rather too small for me. As it is, if
my Pavilion had been built on purpose for a solitary lodger to fall ill in with the least possible
amount of personal discomfort, it could not have
suited my sad case better. Sick, I love and honor

the skillful architect who contrived it. Well, I am very much afraid I should never have bestowed so much as a single thought on him.

Why do I become, in one cordial quarter of an hour, friendly, familiar, and even affectionate with my portress? Because it is part of my unhealthy condition of body and mind that I like nothing so well as being pitied; and my portress sweetens my daily existence with so much compassion that she does me more good, I think, than my doctor or my drugs.

Let me try to describe her. She is a thin, rapid, cheerful little woman, with a tiny face and bright brown eyes. She has a husband (Hippolyte senior) and a son (Hippolyte junior), and a lodge of one room to live in with her family. She has not been in bed, for years past, before two or three in the morning; for my Pavilion and the second Pavilion opposite and the large house behind are all shut in from the roadway by handsome iron gates, which it is the business of somebody in the porter's lodge to open (by pulling a string communicating with the latch) at all hours of the night to homeward-bound lodgers. The large house has so many tenants that some one is always out at a party or a theater—so the keeping of late hours becomes a necessary part of the service in the lodge, and the poor little portress is the victim who suffers as perpetual night-watch. Hippolyte senior absorbs his fair share of work in the day, and takes the early-rising department cheerfully, but he does not possess the gift of keeping awake at

night.   By eleven o'clock (such is sometimes the
weakness even of the most amiable human nature) it is necessary that Hippolyte senior should
be stretched on his back on the nuptial bedstead,
snoring impervious to all sounds and all in-comers.
Hippolyte junior, or the son, is too young to be
trusted with the supervision of the gate-string.
He sleeps, sound as his father, with a half-de-
veloped snore and a coiled-up body, in a crib at
the foot of the parental bed.   On the other side
of the room, hard by the lodgers' keys and can-
dlesticks, with a big stove behind her and a gas-
light before her eyes, sits the faithful little portress, watching out the weary hours as wakefully
as she can.   She trusts entirely to strong coffee
and the near flare of the gas-light to combat the
natural sleepiness which follows a hard day's
work begun at eight o'clock every morning.
The coffee and the gas deserve, to a certain extent, the confidence she places in them.   They
keep her bright brown eyes wide open, staring
with unwinking pertinacity at the light before
them.   They keep her back very straight against
her chair, and her arms crossed tightly over her
bosom, and her feet set firmly on her footstool.
But though they stop sleep from shutting her
eyes or relaxing her limbs, they cannot prevent
some few latent Morphian influences from stealthily reaching her.   Open as her eyes may be, the
little woman nevertheless does start guiltily when
the ring at the bell comes at last; does stare
fixedly for a moment before she can get up; has
to fight resolutely with something drowsy and

clinging in the shape of a trance, before she can
fly to the latch-string, and hang on to it wearily,
instead of pulling at it with the proper wakeful
jerk. Night after night she has now drunk the
strong coffee, and propped herself up stiffly in
her straight chair, and stared hard at the flaring
gas-light, for nearly seven years past. Some
people would have lost their tempers and their
spirits under these hard circumstances, but the
cheerful little portress has only lost flesh. In a
dark corner of the room hangs a daguerreotype
likeness. It represents a buxom woman, with
round cheeks and a sturdy waist, and dates from
the period when she was the bride of Hippolyte
senior, and was thinking of following him into
the porter's lodge. "Ah, my dear sir," she says,
when I condole with her, "if we do get a little
money sometimes in our way of life, we don't
earn it too easily. Aïe, Aïe, Aïe! I should like
a good sleep; I should like to be as fat as my
portrait again!"

The same friendly relations—arising entirely,
let it always be remembered, out of my illness
and the portress's compassion for me — which
have let me into the secrets of the strong coffee,
the daguerreotype portrait, and the sleepy constitution of Hippolyte senior, also enable me to ascertain, by special invitation, how the inhabitants
of the lodge dispose of some of the hardly-earned
profits of their situation.

I find myself suffering rather painfully one
morning, under some aggravated symptoms of
my illness, and my friend, the portress, comes

into the Pavilion to talk to me and keep up my
spirits. She has had an hour's extra sleep, for
a wonder, and is in a chirping state of cheerfulness in consequence. She shudders and makes
faces at my physic-bottles; entreats me to throw
them away, to let her put me to bed and administer a light tea to begin with, and a broth to follow (un Thé léger et un Bouillon). If I will only
stick to these remedies, she will have them ready,
if necessary, every hour in the day, and will
guarantee my immediate restoration to health
and strength. While we are arguing the question of the uselessness of drugs and the remedial
excellence of tea and broth, Hippolyte senior,
with a look of mysterious triumph, which immediately communicates itself to the face of his
wife, enters the room to tell her that she is
wanted below in the lodge. She goes to his
side and takes his arm, as if he was a strange
gentleman waiting to lead her down to dinner,
nods to him confidentially, then glances at me.
Her husband follows her example, and the two
stand quite unconfusedly, arm in arm, smiling
upon me and my physic-bottles, as if they were
a pair of lovers, and I was the venerable parent
whose permission and blessing they were waiting
to receive.

"Have you been getting a new doctor for me?"
I ask, excessively puzzled by their evident desire
to connect me with some secret in the lodge.

"No," says the portress, "I believe in no doctors. I believe in nothing but a light tea and a
broth."

("My sentiments also!" adds her husband, parenthetically.)

"But we have something to show you in the lodge," continues the portress.

(Hippolyte senior arches his eyebrows, and says "Aha!")

"And when you feel better," proceeds my cheerful little friend, "only have the politeness to come down to us, and you will see a marvelous sight!"

Hippolyte senior depresses his eyebrows, and says "Hush!"

"Enough," replies the portress, understanding him; "let us retire."

And they leave the room immediately, still arm in arm—the fondest and most mysterious married couple that 1 have ever set eyes on.

That day I do not feel quite strong enough to encounter great surprises; so my visit to the lodge is deferred until the next morning. Rather to my amazement, the portress does not pay me her usual visit at my waking on the eventful day. 1 descend to the lodge, wondering what this change means, and see three or four strangers assembled in the room, which is bed-chamber, parlor, and porter's office all in one. The strangers, I find, are admiring friends; they surround Hippolyte senior, and all look one way with an expression of intense pleasure and surprise. My eyes follow the direction of theirs, and I see, above the shabby little lodge table, a resplendent new looking-glass in the brightest of frames. On either side of it rise two blush-colored wax-tapers.

Below it are three ornamental pots, with blooming rose-trees in them, backed by a fan-like screen
of fair white paper. This is the surprise that
was in store for me; and this is also the security
in which the inhabitants of the lodge have invested their last hard-earned savings. The whole
thing has the effect upon my mind of an amateur
high altar; and I admire the new purchase accordingly with such serious energy of expression
that Hippolyte senior, in the first sweetness of
triumph, forgets the modesty proper to his position as proprietor of the new treasure, and apostrophizes his own property as Magnifique, with
a power of voice and an energy of gesticulation
which I have never noticed in him before. When
his enthusiasm has abated, and just as I am on
the point of asking where my friend the portress
is, I hear a faint little voice speaking behind the
group of admiring friends:

"Perhaps, messieurs et mesdames, you think
this an extravagance for people in our situation,"
says the voice, in feebly polite tones of apology;
"but, alas! how could we resist it? It is so
beautiful; it brightens the room so; it gives us
such a noble appearance. And, then, it is also
a property—something to leave to our children
—in short, a pardonable extravagance. ˙ Aïe!
I am shaking all over again; I can say no
more!"

While these words are in course of utterance,
the group of friends separate, and I see sitting
behind them, close to the big stove, the little portress, looking sadly changed for the worse. Her

tiny face has become very yellow; her bright
brown eyes look disproportionately large; she
has an old shawl twisted round her shoulders,
and shivers in it perpetually. I ask what is the
matter, imagining that the poor little woman has
got a fit of the ague. The portress contrives to
smile as usual before she answers, though her
teeth are chattering audibly.

"You will not give me drugs, if I tell you?"
she says.

"I will do nothing that is not perfectly agreeable to you," I reply, evasively.

"My complaint is a violent indigestion (une forte
indigestion)," continues the portress, indicatively
laying one trembling forefinger on the region of
her malady. "And I am curing myself with a
light tea."

Here the forefinger changes its direction and
points to a large white earthenware tea-pot, with
an empty mug by the side of it. To save the
portress the trouble of replenishing her drinking-
vessel, I pour out a dose of the light tea. It is a
liquid of a faint straw color, totally unlike any
English tea that ever was made; and it tastes as
a quart of hot water might taste after a wisp of
hay had been dipped into it. The portress swal-
lows three mugfuls of her medicine in my presence, smiling and shivering, looking rapturously
at the magnificent new mirror with its attendant
flower-pots and tapers, and rejecting, with grimaces of comic disgust, all overtures of medical
help on my part, even to the modest offering of
one small pill. An hour or two later I descend to

the lodge again to see how she is. She has been persuaded to go to bed; is receiving, in bed, a levée of friends; in answering, in the same interesting situation, the questions of all the visitors of the day relating to all the lodgers in the house; has begun a fresh potful of the light tea; is still smiling; still shivering; still contemptuously skeptical on the subject of drugs.

In the evening I go down again. The teapot is not done with yet, and the hay-flavored hot water is still pouring inexhaustibly into the system of the little portress. She happens now to be issuing directions relative to the keeping awake of Hippolyte senior, who, for this night at least, must watch by the gate-string. He is to have a pint of strong coffee and a pipe; he is to have the gas turned on very strong; and he is to be excited by the presence of a brisk and wakeful friend. The next morning, just as I am thinking of making inquiries at the lodge, who should enter my room but the dyspeptic patient herself, cured, and ready to digest anything but a doctor's advice or a small pill? Hippolyte senior, I hear, has not fallen asleep over the gate-string for more than half an hour every now and then, and the portress has had a long night's rest. She does not consider this unusual occurrence as reckoning in any degree among the agencies which have accomplished her rapid recovery. It is the light tea alone that has done it; and, if I still doubt the inestimable virtues of the hot hay water-cure, then, of all the prejudiced gentlemen the portress has ever heard of, I am the most

deplorably obstinate in opening my arms to error
and shutting my eyes to truth.

Such is the little domestic world about me, in
some of the more vivid lights in which it presents itself to my own peculiar view.

As for the great Parisian world outside, my
experience of it is bounded by the prospect I obtain of the Champs Elysées from my bedroom
window.   Fashionable Paris spins and prances
by me every afternoon in all its glory; but what
interest have healthy princes and counts and
blood-horses, and blooming ladies, plunged in
abysses of circumambient crinoline, for me, in
my sick situation?   They all fly by me in one
confused phantasmagoria of gay colors and rush-
ing forms, which l look at with lazy eyes.   The
sights I watch with interest are those only which
seem to refer in some degree to my own invalid
position.   My sick man's involuntary egotism
clings as close to me when I look outward at
the great highway, as when I look inward at my
own little room.   Thus the only objects which l
now notice attentively from my window are, oddly
enough, chiefly those which I should have missed
altogether, or looked at with indifference if I
had occupied my bachelor apartment in the enviable character of a healthy man.

For example, out of the various vehicles which
pass me by dozens in the morning, and by hundreds in the afternoon, only two succeed in making anything like a lasting impression on my
mind.   I have only vague ideas of dust, dash-
ing, and magnificence in connection with the

rapid carriages late in the day, and of bells and hollow yelping of carters' voices in connection with the deliberate wagons early in the morning. But I have, on the other hand, a very distinct remembrance of one sober brown omnibus, belonging to a sanitary asylum, and of a queer little truck which carries baths and hot water to private houses, from a bathing establishment near me. The omnibus, as it passes my window at a solemn jog-trot, is full of patients getting their airing. I can see them dimly, and I fall into curious fancies about their various cases, and wonder what proportion of the afflicted passengers are near the time of emancipation from their sanitary prison on wheels. As for the little truck, with its empty zinc bath and barrel of warm water, I am probably wrong in sympathetically associating it as frequently as I do with cases of illness. It is doubtless often sent for by healthy people, too luxurious in their habits to walk abroad for a bath. But there must be a proportion of cases of illness to which the truck ministers; and when I see it going faster than usual, I assume that it must be wanted by some person in a fit, grow suddenly agitated by the idea, and watch the empty bath and the hot-water barrel with breathless interest until they rumble away together out of sight.

So, again, with regard to the men and women who pass my window by thousands every day; my view of them is just as curiously circumscribed as my view of the vehicles. Out of all the crowd, I now find, on taxing my memory, that I have noticed particularly just three people (a woman and two men) who have chanced to appeal to my invalid curiosity.

The woman is a nursemaid, neither young nor pretty, very clean and neat in her dress, with an awful bloodless paleness in her face, and a hopeless consumptive languor in her movements. She has only one child to take care of—a robust little girl of cruelly active habits. There is a stone bench opposite my window; and on this the wan and weakly nursemaid often sits, not bumping down on it with the heavy thump of honest exhaustion, but sinking on it listlessly, as if in changing from walking to sitting she were only passing from one form of weariness to another. The robust child remains mercifully near the feeble guardian for a few minutes — then becomes, on a sudden, pitilessly active again, laughs and dances from a distance, when the nurse makes weary signs to her, and runs away altogether when she is faintly entreated to be quiet for a few minutes longer. The nurse looks after her in despair for a moment, draws her neat black shawl, with a shiver, over her sharp shoulders, rises resignedly, and disappears from my eyes in pursuit of the pitiless child. I see this mournful little drama acted many times over, always in the same way, and wonder sadly how long the wan nursemaid will hold out. Not being a family man, and having nervously acute sympathies for sickness and suffering just now, it would afford me genuine satisfaction to see the oppressed nurse beat the tyrannical child; but she seems fond of the little despot; and besides, she is so weak that, if it came to blows, I am afraid, grown woman as she is, she might get the worst of it.

The men whom I observe are not such interesting cases, but they exhibit, in a minor degree, the peculiarities that are sure to attract my attention. The first of the two is a gentleman—lonely and rich, as I imagine. He is fat, yellow, and gloomy, and has evidently been ordered horse exercise for the benefit of his health. He rides a quiet English cob; never has any friend with him; never—so far as I can see—exchanges greetings with any other horseman; is never smiled at from a carriage, nor bowed to by a foot-passenger. He rides with his flaccid chin sunk on his fat breast; sits his horse as if his legs were stuffed, and his back boneless; always attracts me because he is the picture of dyspeptic wretchedness, and always passes me at the same mournful jog-trot pace. The second man is a police agent. I cannot sympathize with him, in consequence of his profession; but I can observe, with a certain lukewarm interest, that he is all but worked to death. He yawns and stretches himself in corners; sometimes drops furtively on to the stone bench before my window; then starts up from it suddenly, as if he felt himself falling asleep the moment he sat down. He has hollow places where other people have cheeks; and, judging by his walk, must be quite incapable of running after a prisoner who might take to flight. On the whole, he presents to my mind the curious spectacle of a languid man trying to adapt himself to a brisk business, and failing palpably in the effort. As the sick child of a thriving system, he attracts my attention. I devoutly hope that he will not return the compliment by honoring me with his notice.

Such are the few short steps that I take in advance to get a moderately close glance at French humanity. If my view is absurdly limited to my own dim horizon, this defect has at least one advantage for the reader: it prevents all danger of my troubling him with my ideas and observations at any great length. If other people value this virtue of brevity in writers, orators, and preachers as sincerely as I do, perhaps I may hope, on account of my short range of observation and my few words, to get another hearing, if I write the second chapter of my invalid experiences. I began the first half of them (as herein related) in France; and I am now completing the second (yet to be recorded) in England. When the curtain rises on my sick-bed again, the scene will be London.

CHAPTER THE SECOND.—MY LONDON LODGING.

I last had the honor of presenting myself to the reader's notice in the character of an invalid laid up in lodgings at Paris. Let me now be permitted to reappear as an invalid laid up, for the time being, in a London cab. Let it be imagined that I have got through the journey from Paris, greatly to my own surprise and satisfaction, without breaking down by the way; that I have slept one night at a London hotel for the first time in my life; and that I am now helplessly adrift, looking out for furnished apartments as near as may be to my doctor's place of abode.

The cab is fusty, the driver is sulky, the morning is foggy. A dry dog-kennel would be a pleasant refuge by comparison with the miserable vehicle in which I am now jolting my way over the cruel London stones. On our road to my doctor's neighborhood, we pass through Smeary Street—a locality well known to the inhabitants of Northern London. I feel that I can go no further. I remember that some friends of mine live not far off, and I recklessly emancipate myself from the torment of the cab by stopping the driver at the very first house in the windows of which I see a bill with the announcement that apartments are to let.

The door is opened by a tall, muscular woman, with a knobbed face and knotty arms besprinkled with a layer of grate-dust in a state of impalpable powder. She shows me up into a second-floor front bedroom. My first look of scrutiny is naturally directed at the bed. It is of the negative sort, neither dirty nor clean; but by its side I see a positive advantage in connection with it, in the shape of a long mahogany shelf, fixed into the wall a few inches above the bed, and extending down its whole length from head to foot. My sick man's involuntary egotism is as predominant an impulse within me at London as at

Paris. I think directly of my invalid's knick-
knacks; I see that the mahogany shelf will serve
to keep them all within my reach when I am in
bed; I know that it will be wanted for no other
purpose than that to which I design to put it;
that it need not be cleared for dinner every day,
like a table, or disturbed when the servant cleans
the room, like a movable stand. I satisfy myself
that it holds out all these rare advantages to me,
in my peculiar situation, and I snap at them on
the instant—or, in other words, I take the room
immediately.

If I had been in health, I think I should have
had two cogent reasons for acting otherwise, and
seeking apartments elsewhere. In the first place,
I should have observed that the room was not
very clean, or very comfortably furnished. I
should have noticed that the stained and torn
drugget on the floor displayed a margin of dirty
boards all round the bed-chamber; and I should
no sooner have set eyes on the venerable armchair by the bedside than I should have heard it
saying privately in my ear, in an ominous language of its own, "Stranger, I am let to the
Fleas; take me at your peril." Even if these
signs and portents had not been enough to send
me out into the street again, I should certainly
have found the requisite warning to quit the
house written legibly in the face, figure, and
manner of the landlady. I should probably have
seen something to distrust and dislike in everything connected with her, down even to her
name, which was Mrs. Glutch; I should have

made my escape into the street again, and should not have ventured near it any more for the rest of the day. But as it was, my fatal invalid prepossessions blinded me to everything but the unexpected blessing of that mahogany shelf by the bedside. I overlooked the torn drugget, the flea-peopled armchair, and the knotty-faced landlady with the ominous name. The shelf was bait enough for me, and the moment the trap was open I collected my train of medicine-bottles and confidently walked in.

It is a general subject of remark among observant travelers, that the two nations of the civilized world which appear to be most widely separated as to the external aspects of life respectively presented by them are also the two which are most closely brought together by the neighborly ties of local situation. Before I had been many days established in Smeary Street, I found that I myself, in my own circumscribed sphere, offered a remarkable example of the truth of the observation just recorded. The strong contrast between my present and my past life was a small individual proof of the great social contrasts between England and France.

I have truly presented myself at Paris as living independently in a little toy house of my own; as looking out upon a scene of almost perpetual brightness and gayety; and as having people to attend on me whose blessed levity of disposition kept them always cheerful, always quaintly characteristic, always unexpectedly amusing, even to the languid eye of a sick man.

With equal candor I must now record of my in-
door life in London that it was passed, with
many other lodgers, in a large house, without a
vestige of toy-shop prettiness in any part of it. I
must acknowledge that I looked out upon drab-
colored walls and serious faces through a smoke-
laden atmosphere; and I must admit that I was
waited on (so far as the actual house service was
concerned) by people whose cloudy countenances
seemed unconscious of a gleam of inner sunshine
for days and days together. Nor did the contrast end here. In my lodgings at Paris, I have
represented myself as having about me a variety
of animate and inanimate objects, which I might
notice or not, just as I pleased, and as using my
freedom of choice in a curiously partial and re-
stricted manner, in consequence of the narrowing
effect of my illness on my sympathies and powers
of observation. In my London lodging, I enjoyed no such liberty. I could not get even a
temporary freedom of selection, except by fighting for it resolutely at odds and ends of time.
1 had but one object which offered itself to my
observation, which perpetually presented itself,
which insisted on being noticed, no matter how
mentally unfit and morally unwilling my illness
rendered me to observe it; and that object was—
my landlady, Mrs. Glutch.

Behold me, then, now no longer a free agent;
no longer a fanciful invalid with caprices to
confide to the ear of the patient reader. My
health is no better in Smeary Street than it was
in the Champs Elysees; I take as much medicine

in London as I took in Paris; but my character is altered in spite of myself, and the form and color of my present fragment of writing will, I fear, but too truly reflect the change.

I *was* a sick man, with several things to discourse of—I *am* a sick man, with only one topic to talk about. I may escape from it for a few sentences at a time in these pages, as I escaped from it for a few minutes at a time in Smeary Street; but the burden of my song will be now what the burden of my life has been lately—my landlady. I am going to begin with her—I shall go on with her—I shall try to wander away from her—I shall get back to her—I shall end with her. She will mix herself up with everything I have to say; will intrude on my observations out of window; will get into my victuals and drink, and drops, and draughts, and pills; will come between me and my studies of character among maids of all work, in this too faithful narrative, just as she did in the real scenes which it endeavors to represent. While I make this acknowledgment as a proper warning to the reader that I have changed into a monotonous sick man since we met last, let me add, in justice to myself, that my one subject has at least the advantage of being a terrible one. Think of a sick fly waited on by a healthy blue-bottle, and you will have a fair idea of the relative proportions and positions of myself and Mrs. Glutch.

I have hardly been settled an hour in my second-floor front room before the conviction is forced on my mind that Mrs. Glutch is resolved

to make a conquest of me—of the maternal or
platonic kind, let me hasten to add, so as to stop
the mouth of scandal before it is well opened. I
find that she presents herself before me in the
character of a woman suffused in a gentle melancholy, proceeding from perpetual sympathy for
my suffering condition. It is part of my character as a sick man that I know by instinct when
people really pity me, just as children and dogs
know when people really like them; and I have,
consequently, not been five minutes in Mrs.
Glutch's society before I know that her sympathy for me is entirely of that sort of which (in
the commercial phrase) a large assortment is always on hand. I take no pains to conceal from
Mrs. Glutch that I have found her out; but she
is too innocent to understand me, and goes on
sympathizing in the very face of detection. She
becomes, in spite of her knobbed face, knotty
arms, and great stature and strength, languidly
sentimental in manner the moment she enters
my room. Language runs out of her in a perpetual flow, and politeness encircles her as with
a halo that can never be dimmed. "I have been
so anxious about you!" is her first morning's
salutation to me. The words are preceded by a
faint cough, and followed by an expressively
weary sigh, as if she had passed a sleepless night
on my account. The next morning she appears
with a bunch of wall-flowers in her mighty fist,
and with another faint prefatory cough, "I beg
pardon, sir; but I have brought you a few flowers. I think they relieve the mind." The ex-

pressively weary sigh follows again, as if it would suggest this time that she has toiled into the country to gather me the flowers at early dawn. I do not find, strange as it may seem, that they relieve my mind at all; but of course I say, "Thank you."—"Thank *you*, sir," rejoins Mrs. Glutch; for it is a part of this woman's system of oppressive politeness always to thank me for thanking her. She invariably contrives to have the last word, no matter in what circumstances the courteous contention which is the main characteristic of our daily intercourse may take its rise.

Let us say, for instance, that she comes into my room and gets into my way (which she always does) at the very time when she ought to be out of it—her first words are necessarily, "I beg pardon." I growl (not so brutally as I could wish, being weak), "Never mind."— "Thank you, sir," says Mrs. Glutch, and coughs faintly, and sighs, and delays going out as long as possible. Or, take another example: "Mrs. Glutch, this plate's dirty."—"I am much obliged to you, sir, for telling me of it." "It isn't the first dirty plate I have had." —"Really now, sir?" "You may take away the fork; for that is dirty, too."—"Thank you, sir." Oh, for one hour of my little Parisian portress! Oh, for one day's respite from the politeness of Mrs. Glutch!

Let me try if I cannot get away from the subject for a little while. What have I to say about the other lodgers in the house? Not much; for how can I take any interest in people who never make inquiries after my health, though they must all know, by the frequent visits of the doctor and the chemist's boy, that I am ill?

The first floor is inhabited by a mysterious old gentleman and his valet. He brought three cart-loads of gorgeous furniture with him, to fit up two rooms; he possesses an organ, on which, greatly to his credit, he never plays; he receives perfumed notes, goes out beautifully dressed, is brought back in private carriages, with tall footmen in attendance to make as much noise as possible with the door-knocker. Nobody knows where he comes from, or believes that he passes in the house under his real name. If any aged aristocrat be missing from the world of fashion, we rather think we have got him in Smeary Street, and should feel willing to give him up to his rightful owners on payment of a liberal reward. Next door to me, in the second floor back, I hear a hollow cough and sometimes a whispering; but I know nothing for certain—not even whether the hollow cougher is also the whisperer, or whether they are two, or whether there is or is not a third silent and Samaritan person who relieves the cough and listens to the whisper. Above me, in the attics, there is a matutinal stamping and creaking of boots, which go downstairs at an early hour in a hurry, which never return all day, but which come upstairs again in a hurry late at night. The boots evidently belong to shop-men or clerks. Below, in the parlors, there seems to be a migratory population, which comes in one week and goes out the next, and is, in some cases, not at all to be depended upon in the matter of paying rent. I happen to discover this latter fact, late one night, in rather an alarming and unexpected manner. Just before bed-time I descend, candle in hand, to a small back room at the end of the passage, on the ground-floor (used all day for the reception of general visitors, and empty, as I rashly infer, all night), for the purpose of getting a sofa-cushion to eke out my scanty allowance of pillows. I no sooner open the door and approach the sofa, than I behold, to my horror and amazement, Mrs. Glutch coiled up on it, with all her clothes on, and with a wavy, coffee-colored wrapper flung over her shoulders. Before I can turn round to run away, she is on her legs, wide awake in an instant, and politer than ever. She makes me a long speech of explanation, which begins with "I beg pardon," and ends with "Thank you, sir;" and from the substance of which I gather that the parlor lodgers for the past week are going away the next morning; that they are the likeliest people in the world to forget to pay their lawful debts; and that Mrs. Glutch is going to lie in ambush for them all night in the coffee-colored wrapper, ready the instant the parlor door opens to spring out into the passage and call for her rent.

What am I about? I am relapsing insensibly into the inevitable and abhorrent subject of Mrs. Glutch, exactly in accordance with my foreboding of a few pages back. Let me make one more attempt to get away from my landlady. If I try to describe my room, I am sure to get back to her, because she is always in it. Suppose I get out of the house altogether, and escape into the street?

All men, I imagine, have an interest of some kind in the locality in which they live. My interest in Smeary Street is entirely associated with my daily meals, which are publicly paraded all day long on the pavement. In explanation of this rather original course of proceeding, I must mention that I am ordered to eat "little and often," and must add that I cannot obey the direction if the food is cooked on the premises in which I live, because I have had the misfortune to look down certain underground stairs and to discover that in the lowest depth of dirt, which I take to be the stairs themselves, there is a lower deep still, which is the kitchen at the bottom of them. Under these peculiar circumstances, I am reduced to appeal for nourishment and cleanliness in combination to the tender mercies (and kitchen) of the friends in my neighborhood, to whom I have alluded at the outset of this narrative. They commiserate and help me with the readiest kindness. Devoted messengers, laden with light food, pass and repass all day long between their house and my bedroom. The dullness of Smeary Street is enlivened by perpetual snacks carried in public procession. The eyes of my opposite neighbors, staring out of window, and not looking as if they cared about my being ill, are regaled from morning to night by passing dishes and basins, which go westward full and steaming, and return eastward eloquently empty. My neighborhood knows when I dine, and can smell out, if it pleases, what I have for dinner. The early housemaid kneeling on the doorstep can stay her scrubbing hand, and turn her pensive head and scan my simple breakfast, before I know what it will be myself. The midday idler, lounging along Smeary Street, is often sweetly reminded of his own luncheon by meeting mine. Friends who knock at my door may smell my dinner behind them, and know how I am keeping up my stamina, before they have had time to inquire after my health. My supper makes the outer darkness savory as the evening closes in; and my empty dishes startle the gathering silence with convivial clatter as they wend on their homeward way the last thing at night.

Is there no dark side to this bright picture? Is there never any hitch in these friendly arrangements for feeding me in the cleanest way, on the most appetizing diet? Yes, there is a hitch. Will you give it a name? I will. Its name is Mrs. Glutch.

It is, I am well aware, only to be expected that my landlady should resent the tacit condemnation of her cleanliness and cookery implied in the dietary arrangements which I have made with my friends. If she would only express her sense of offense by sulking or flying into a passion, I should not complain; for, in the first case supposed, I might get the better of her by noticing nothing, and, in the second, I might hope in

course of time to smooth her down by soft answers and polite prevarications.   But the means
she actually takes of punishing me for my too
acute sense of the dirtiness of her kitchen are of
such a diabolically ingenious nature, and involve
such a continuous series of small persecutions,
that I am rendered, from first to last, quite powerless to oppose her.   Shall I describe her plan of
annoyance?   I *must* describe it—I must return
to my one prohibited topic (as I foreboded I
should) in spite of myself.

Mrs. Glutch, then, instead of visiting her
wrath on me, or my food, or my friends, or my
friends' messengers, avenges herself entirely on
their tray-cloths and dishes.   She does not tear
the first nor break the second—for that would be
only a simple and primitive system of persecution
—but she smuggles them, one by one, out of my
room, and merges them inextricably with her
own property, in the grimy regions of the kitchen.
She has a power of invisibly secreting the largest
pie-dishes and the most voluminous cloths under
my very eyes, which I can compare to nothing
but slight of hand.   Every morning I see table
utensils which my friends lent me, ranged ready
to go back, in my own room.   Every evening,
when they are wanted, I find that some of them
are missing, and that my landlady is even more
surprised by that circumstance than I am myself.
If my friends' servant ventures to say, in her
presence, that the cook wants her yesterday's
tray-cloth, and if I refer him to Mrs. Glutch, the
immovable woman only sniffs, tosses her head,

and "wonders how the young man can have demeaned himself by bringing her such a peremptory message." If I try on my own sole responsibility to recover the missing property, she lets me see, by her manner at the outset, that she thinks I suspect her of stealing it. If I take no notice of this maneuver, and innocently persist in asking additional questions about the missing object, the following is a sample of the kind of dialogue that is sure to pass between us:

"I think, Mrs. Glutch—"

"Yes, sir!"

"I think one of my friends' large pudding-basins has gone downstairs."

"Really, now, sir? A large pudding-basin? No, I think not."

"But I can't find it up here, and it is wanted back."

"Naturally, sir."

"I put it on the drawers, Mrs. Glutch, ready to go back, last night."

"Did you, indeed, sir?"

"Perhaps the servant took it downstairs to clean it?"

"Not at all likely, sir. If you will please to remember, you told her last Monday evening— or, no, I beg pardon—last Tuesday morning, that your friends cleaned up their own dishes, and that their things was not to be touched."

"Perhaps you took it downstairs, then, yourself, Mrs. Glutch, by mistake?"

"I, sir! I didn't. I couldn't. Why should I? I think you said a large pudding-basin, sir?"

"Yes, I did say so."

"I have ten large pudding-basins of my own, sir."

"I am very glad to hear it. Will you be so good as to look among them, and see if my friends' basin has not got mixed up with your crockery?"

Mrs. Glutch turns very red in the face, slowly scratches her muscular arms, as if she felt a sense of pugilistic irritation in them, looks at me steadily with a pair of glaring eyes, and leaves the room at the slowest possible pace. I wait and ring—wait and ring—wait and ring. After the third waiting and the third ringing, she re-appears, redder of face and slower of march than before, with the missing article of property held out before her at arms-length.

"I beg pardon, sir," she says, "but is this anything like your friends' large pudding-basin?"

"That is the basin itself, Mrs. Glutch."

"Really, now, sir? Well, as you seem so positive, it isn't for me to contradict you. But I hope I shall give no offense if I mention that I had ten large pudding-basins of my own, and that I miss one of them."

With that last dexterous turn of speech, she gives up the basin with the air of a high-minded woman, who will resign her own property rather than expose herself to the injurious doubts of a morbidly suspicious man. When I add that the little scene just described takes place between us nearly every day, the reader will admit that, although Mrs. Glutch cannot prevent me from en-

joying on her dirty premises the contraband
luxury of a clean dinner, she can at least go
great lengths toward accomplishing the secondary annoyance of preventing me from digesting
it.

I have hinted at a third personage in the shape
of a servant, in my report of the foregoing dialogue, and I have previously alluded to myself
(in paving the way for the introduction of my
landlady) as extending my studies of human
character, in my London lodging, to those forlorn members of the population called maids of
all work. The maids—I use the plural number
advisedly—present themselves to me to be studied,
as apprentices to the hard business of service, under the matronly superintendence of Mrs. Glutch.
The succession of them is brisk enough to keep
all the attention I can withdraw from my landlady constantly employed in investigating their
peculiarities. By the time I have been three
weeks in Smeary Street, I have had three maids
of all work to study—a new servant for each
week! In reviewing the three individually before the reader, I must be allowed to distinguish
them by numbers insetad of names. Mrs. Glutch
screams at them all indiscriminately by the name
of Mary, just as she would scream at a succession of cats by the name of Puss. Now, although
I am always writing about Mrs. Glutch, I have
still spirit enough left to vindicate my own individuality by abstaining from following her example. In obedience, therefore, to these last
relics of independent sentiment, permit me the

freedom of numbering my maids of all work as
I introduce them to public notice in these pages.
Number One is amazed by the spectacle of my
illness, and always stares at me.   If I fell ill one
evening, went to a dispensary, asked for a bottle
of physic, and got well on it the next morning;
or if I presented myself before her at the last
gasp, and died forthwith in Smeary Street, she
would, in either case, be able to understand me.
But an illness on which medicine produces no
immediate, effect and which does not keep the
patient always groaning in bed, is beyond her
comprehension.   Personally, she is very short
and sturdy, and is always covered from head to
foot with powdered black, which seems to lie
especially thick on her in the morning.   How
does she accumulate it?   Does she wash herself
with the ordinary liquid used for ablutions, or
does she take a plunge-bath every morning under
the kitchen-grate?   I am afraid to ask this question of her, but I contrive to make her talk to
me about other things.   She looks very much
surprised, poor creature, when I first let her see
that I have other words to utter, in addressing
her, besides the word of command, and seems to
think me the most eccentric of mankind when she
finds that I have a decent anxiety to spare her
all useless trouble in waiting on me.   Young as
she is, she has drudged so long over the wicked-
est ways of this world, without one leisure moment to look up from the everlasting dirt on the
road at the green landscape around and the pure
sky above, that she has become hardened to the

saddest, surely, of human lots before she is yet a woman grown. Life means dirty work, small wages, hard words, no holidays, no social station, no future, according to her experience of it. No human being ever was created for this. No state of society which composedly accepts this, in the cases of thousands, as one of the necessary conditions of its selfish comforts, can pass itself off as civilized, except under the most audacious of all false pretenses. These thoughts rise in me often when I ring the bell, and the maid of all work answers it wearily. I cannot communicate them to her; I can only encourage her to talk to me now and then on something like equal terms. Just as I am succeeding in the attainment of this object, Number One scatters all my plans and purposes to the winds by telling me that she is going away.

I ask why; and am told that she cannot bear being a-railed at and a-hunted about by Mrs. Glutch any longer. The oppressively polite woman who cannot address me without begging my pardon can find no hard words in the vocabulary hard enough for the maid of all work. "I am frightened of my life," says Number One, apologizing to me for leaving the place. "I am so little, and she's so big. She heaves things at my head, she does. Work as hard as you may, you can't work hard enough for her. I must go, if you please, sir. Whatever do you think she done this morning? She up and druv the creases at me." With these words (which I find mean in genteel English that Mrs. Glutch has enforced

her last orders to the servant by throwing a
bunch of water-cresses at her head), Number One
courtesies and says "Good-by!" and goes out resignedly once again into the hard world. I follow her a little while, in imagination, with no
very cheering effect on my spirits—for what do
I see awaiting her at each stage of her career?
Alas for Number One, it is always a figure in
the likeness of Mrs. Glutch!

Number Two fairly baffles me. I see her grin
perpetually at me, and imagine at first that I
am regarded by her in the light of a new kind of
impostor, who shams illness as a way of amusing
himself. But I soon discover that she grins at
everything—at the fire that she lights, at the
cloth she lays for dinner, at the medicine-bottles
she brings upstairs, at the furibund visage of Mrs.
Glutch, ready to drive whole basketfuls of creases
at her head every morning. Looking at her with
the eye of an artist, I am obliged to admit that
Number Two is, as the painters say, out of drawing. The longest things about her are her arms;
the thickest thing about her is her waist. It is
impossible to believe that she has any legs, and
it is not easy to find out the substitute which, in
the absence of a neck, is used to keep her big
head from rolling off her round shoulders. I try
to make her talk, but only succeed in encourag-
ing her to grin at me. Have ceaseless foul words
and ceaseless dirty work clouded over all the little light that has ever been let in on her mind?
I suspect that it is so, but I have no time to ac-
quire any positive information on the subject.

At the end of Number Two's first week of service, Mrs. Glutch discovers, to her horror and indignation, that the new maid of all work possesses nothing in the shape of wearing-apparel except the worn-out garments actually on her back; and, to make matters worse, a lady-lodger in the parlor misses one of a pair of lace cuffs, and feels sure that the servant has taken it. There is not a particle of evidence to support this view of the case; but Number Two being destitute, is consequently condemned without a trial, and dismissed without a character. She, too, wanders off forlorn into a world that has no haven of rest or voice of welcome for her—wanders off, without so much as a dirty bundle in her hand—wanders off, voiceless, with the unchanging grin on the smut-covered face. How shocked we should all be if we opened a book about a savage country and saw a portrait of Number Two in the frontispeice as a specimen of the female population!

Number Three comes to us all the way from Wales; arrives late one evening, and is found at seven the next morning, crying as if she would break her heart, on the doorstep. It is the first time she has been away from home. She has not got used yet to being a forlorn castaway among strangers. She misses the cows of a morning, the blessed fields with the blush of sunrise on them, the familiar faces, the familiar sounds, the familiar cleanliness of her country home. There is not the faintest echo of mother's voice, or of father's sturdy footfall here. Sweetheart John Jones

is hundreds of miles away; and little brother Joe
toddles up doorsteps far from these to clamor for
the breakfast which he shall get this morning
from other than his sister's hands. Is there nothing to cry for in this? Absolutely nothing, as
Mrs. Glutch thinks.   What does this Welsh bar-
barian mean by clinging to my area railings when
she ought to be lighting the fire; by sobbing in
full view of the public of Smeary Street when the
lodgers' bells are ringing angrily for breakfast?
Will nothing get the girl indoors? Yes, a few
kind words from the woman who passes by her
with my breakfast will.   She knows that the
Welsh girl is hungry as well as homesick, questions her, finds out that she has had no supper
after her long journey, and that she has been
used to breakfast with the sunrise at the farm
in Wales. A few merciful words lure her away
from the railings, and a little food inaugurates
the process of breaking her in to London service.
She has but a few days allowed her, however, to
practice the virtue of dogged resignation in her
first place.   Before she has given me many opportunities of studying her character, before she
has done knitting her brows with the desperate
mental effort of trying to comprehend the mystery of my illness, before the smut has fairly settled on her rosy cheeks, before the London dirt
has dimmed the pattern on her neat print gown,
she, too, is cast adrift into the world. She has
not suited Mrs. Glutch (being, as I imagine, too
offensively clean to form an appropriate part of
the kitchen furniture); a friendly maid of all

work in service near us has heard of a place for her, and she is forthwith sent away, to be dirtied and deadened down to her proper social level in another lodging-house.

With her, my studies of character among maids of all work come to an end. I hear vague rumors of the arrival of Number Four. But before she appears, 1 have got the doctor's leave to move into the country, and have terminated my experience of London lodgings by making my escape with all convenient speed from the perpetual presence and persecutions of Mrs. Glutch. I have witnessed some sad sights during my stay in Smeary Street, which have taught me to feel for my poor and forlorn fellow-creatures as I do not think I ever felt for them before, and which have inclined me to doubt for the first time whether worse calamities might not have overtaken me than the hardship of falling ill.

SKETCHES OF CHARACTER.—II.

A SHOCKINGLY RUDE ARTICLE.

[Communicated by a Charming Woman.]

BEFORE I begin to write, I know that this will be an unpopular composition in certain select quarters. I mean to proceed with it, however, in spite of that conviction, because when I have got something on my mind I must positively speak. Is it necessary after that to confess that I am a woman? If it is, I make the confession —to my sorrow. I would much rather be a man.

I hope nobody will be misled, by my beginning in this way, into thinking that I am an advocate of the rights of women. Ridiculous creatures! they have too many rights already; and if they don't hold their chattering tongues, one of these days the poor dear, deluded men will find them out.

The poor dear men! Mentioning them reminds me of what I have got to say. I have been staying at the seaside, and reading an immense quantity of novels and periodicals, and all that sort of thing, lately; and my idea is, that the men writers (the only writers worth reading) are in the habit of using each other very unfairly in books and articles, and so on. Look where I may, I find, for instance, that the large proportion of the bad characters in their otherwise very charming stories are always men. As if women were not a great deal worse! Then, again, most of the amusing fools in their books are, strangely and unaccountably, of their own sex, in spite of its being perfectly apparent that the vast majority of that sort of character is to be found in ours. On the other hand, while they make out their own half of humanity (as I have distinctly proved) a great deal too bad, they go to the contrary extreme the other way, and make out our half a great deal too good. What in the world do they mean by representing us as so much better, and so much prettier, than we really are? Upon my word, when I see what angels the dear, nice, good men make of their heroines, and when I think of myself, and of the whole circle of my female friends besides, I feel quite disgusted—I do, indeed.

I should very much like to go into the whole of this subject at once, and speak my sentiments on it at the fullest length. But I will spare the reader, and try to be satisfied with going into a part of the subject instead; for, considering that I am a woman, and making immense allowances for me on that account, I am really not altogether unreasonable. Give me a page or two, and I will show in one particular, and, what is more, from real life, how absurdly partial the men writers are to our sex, and how scandalously unjust they are to their own.

Bores.—What I propose is, that we take for

our present example characters of Bores alone.
If we were only to read men's novels, articles,
and so forth, I don't hesitate to say we should assume that all the Bores in the human creation
were of the male sex. It is generally, if not always, a man, in men's books, who tells the long-
winded story, and turns up at the wrong time,
and makes himself altogether odious and intolerable to everybody he comes in contact with, without being in the least aware of it himself. How
very unjust, and, I must be allowed to add, how
extremely untrue! Women are quite as bad, or
worse. Do, good gentlemen, look about you impartially, for once in a way, and own the truth.
Good gracious! is not society full of Lady-Bores?
Why not give them a turn when you write next?

Two instances: I will quote only two instances
out of hundreds I could produce from my own
acquaintance. Only two; because, as I said before, I am reasonable about not taking up room.
I can put things into a very small space when I
write, as well as when I travel. I should like
the literary gentleman who kindly prints this (I
would not allow a woman to print it for any sum
of money that could be offered me) to see how
very little luggage I travel with. At any rate,
he shall see how little room I can cheerfully put
up with in these pages.

My first Lady-Bore—see how quickly I get to
the matter in hand, without wasting so much as
a single line in prefatory phrases!—my first Lady-
Bore is Miss Sticker. I don't in the least mind
mentioning her name, because I know, if she got

the chance, she would do just the same by me. It is of no use disguising the fact, so I may as well confess at once that Miss Sticker is a fright. Far be it from me to give pain where the thing can by any means be avoided; but if I were to say that Miss Sticker would ever see forty again, I should be guilty of an unwarrantable deception on the public. I have the strongest imaginable objection to mentioning the word petticoats; but if that is the only possible description of Miss Sticker's figure which conveys a true notion of its nature and composition, what am I to do? Perhaps I had better give up describing the poor thing's personal appearance. I shall get into deeper and deeper difficulties if I attempt to go on. The very last time I was in her company, we were strolling about Regent Street, with my sister's husband for escort. As we passed a hairdresser's shop, the dear, simple man looked in, and asked me what those long tails of hair were for that he saw hanging up in the windows. Miss Sticker, poor soul, was on his arm, and heard him put the question. I thought I should have dropped.

This is, I believe, what you call a digression. I shall let it stop in, however, because it will probably explain to the judicious reader why I carefully avoid the subject—the meager subject, an ill-natured person might say—of Miss Sticker's hair. Suppose I pass on to what is more importantly connected with the object of these pages—suppose I describe Miss Sticker's character next.

Some extremely sensible man has observed somewhere that a Bore is a person with one idea. Exactly so. Miss Sticker is a person with one idea. Unhappily for society, her notion is that she is bound by the laws of politeness to join in every conversation which happens to be proceeding within the range of her ears. She has no ideas, no information, no flow of language, no tact, no power of saying the right word at the right time, even by chance. And yet she *will* converse, as she calls it. "A gentlewoman, my dear, becomes a mere cipher in society unless she can converse." That is her way of putting it; and I deeply regret to add, she is one of the few people who preach what they practice. Her course of proceeding is, first, to check the conversation by making a remark which has no kind of relation to the topic under discussion. She next stops it altogether by being suddenly at a loss for some particular word which nobody can suggest. At last the word is given up, another subject is started in despair, and the company become warmly interested in it. Just at that moment Miss Sticker finds the lost word, screams it out triumphantly in the middle of the talk, and so scatters the second subject to the winds, exactly as she has already scattered the first.

The last time I called at my aunt's—I merely mention this by way of example—I found Miss Sticker there, and three delightful men. One was a clergyman of the dear old purple-faced Port-wine school; the other two would have looked military, if one of them had not been an engineer, and the other an editor of a newspaper. We should have had some delightful conversation if the Lady-Bore had not been present. In some way, I really forget how, we got to talking about giving credit and paying debts; and the dear old clergyman, with his twinkling eyes and his jolly voice, treated us to a professional anecdote on the subject.

"Talking about that," he began, "I married a man the other day for the third time. Man in my parish. Capital cricketer when he was young enough to run. 'What's your fee?' says he.—'Licensed marriage?' says I; 'guinea, of course.' 'I've got to bring you your tithes in three weeks, sir,' says he; 'give me tick till then.'—'All right,' says I, and married him. In three weeks he comes and pays his tithes like a man. 'Now, sir,' says he, 'about this marriage-fee, sir? I do hope you'll kindly let me off at half-price, for I have married a bitter bad 'un this time. I've got a half-guinea about me, sir, if you'll only please to take it. She isn't worth a farthing more—on the word of a man, she isn't, sir!' I looked hard in his face, and saw two scratches on it, and took the half-guinea, more out of pity than anything else. Lesson to me, however. Never marry a man on credit again as long as I live. Cash on all future occasions—cash down, or no marriage."

While he was speaking, I had my eye on Miss Sticker. Thanks to the luncheon which was on the table, she was physically incapable of "con-

versing" while our reverend friend was telling
his humorous little anecdote. Just as he had
done, and just as the editor of the newspaper
was taking up the subject, she finished her
chicken and turned round from the table.

"Cash down, my dear sir, as you say," continued the editor. "You exactly describe our
great principle of action in the Press. Some of
the most extraordinary and amusing things happen with subscribers to newspapers—"

"Ah, the Press!" burst in Miss Sticker, beginning to converse. "What a wonderful en-
gine! and how grateful we ought to feel when
we get the paper so regularly every morning at
breakfast. The only question is—at least many
people think so—I mean with regard to the Press,
the only question is whether it ought to be—"

Here Miss Sticker lost the next word, and all
the company had to look for it.

"With regard to the Press, the only question
is, whether it ought to be— Oh, dear, dear,
dear me!" cried Miss Sticker, lifting both her
hands in despair, "what is the word?"

"Cheaper?" suggested our reverend friend.
"Hang it, ma'am! it can hardly be that, when
it is down to a penny already."

"Oh no; not cheaper," said Miss Sticker.

"More independent!" inquired the editor. "If
you mean that, I defy anybody to find more
fearless exposures of corruption—"

"No, no!" cried Miss Sticker, in an agony of
polite confusion. "I didn't mean that. More
independent wasn't the word."

"Better printed?" suggested the engineer.

"On better paper?" added my aunt.

"It can't be done—if you refer to the cheap press—it can't be done for the money," interposed the editor, irritably.

"Oh, but that's not it!" continued Miss Sticker, wringing her bony fingers, with horrid black mittens on them. "I didn't mean to say better printed or better paper. It was one word I meant, not two. With regard to the Press," pursued Miss Sticker, repeating her own ridiculous words carefully, as an aid to memory, "the only question is whether it ought to be— Bless my heart, how extraordinary! Well, well, never mind; I'm quite shocked, and ashamed of myself. Pray go on talking, and don't notice me."

It was all very well to say, Go on talking; but the editor's amusing story about subscribers to newspapers had been by this time fatally interrupted. As usual, Miss Sticker had stopped us in full flow. The engineer considerately broke the silence by starting another subject.

"Here are some wedding-cards on your table," he said to my aunt, "which I am very glad to see there. The bridegroom is an old friend of mine. His wife is really a beauty. You know how he first became acquainted with her? No? It was quite an adventure, I assure you. One evening he was on the Brighton Railway; last down train. A lovely girl in the carriage; our friend Dilberry immensely struck with her. Got her to talk after a long time, with great difficulty. Within half an hour of Brighton, the lovely girl smiles and says to our friend, 'Shall we be very long now, sir, before we get to Gravesend?' Case of confusion at that dreadful London Bridge terminus. Dilberry explained that she would be at Brighton in half an hour, upon which the lovely girl instantly and properly burst into tears. 'Oh, what shall I do! Oh, what will my friends think!' Second flood of tears. 'Suppose you telegraph?' says Dilberry, soothingly. 'Oh, but I don't know how!' says the lovely girl. Out comes Dilberry's pocketbook. Sly dog! he saw his way now to finding out who her friends were. 'Pray let me write the necessary message for you,' says Dilberry. 'Who shall I direct to at Gravesend?'—'My father and mother are staying there with some friends,' says the lovely girl. 'I came up with a day-ticket, and I saw a crowd of people, when I came back to the station, all going one way, and I was hurried and frightened, and nobody told me, and it was late in the evening, and the bell was ringing, and, oh heavens! what will become of me!' Third burst of tears. 'We will telegraph to your father,' says Dilberry. 'Pray don't distress yourself. Only tell me who your father is.'—'Thank you a thousand times,' says the lovely girl, 'my father is—' "

"ANONYMOUS!" shouts Miss Sticker, producing her lost word with a perfect burst of triumph. "How glad I am I remember it at last! Bless me!" exclaims the Lady-Bore, quite unconscious that she has brought the engineer's story to an abrupt conclusion, by giving his distressed damsel an anonymous father; "bless me! what are you all laughing at? I only meant to say that the question with regard to the Press was, whether it ought to be anonymous. What in the world is there to laugh at in that? I really don't see the joke."

And this woman escapes scot-free, while comparatively innocent men are held up to ridicule, in novel after novel, by dozens at a time! When will the deluded male writers see my sex in its true colors, and describe it accordingly? When will Miss Sticker take her proper place in the literature of England?

My second Lady-Bore is that hateful creature, Mrs. Tincklepaw. Where, over the whole interesting surface of male humanity (including cannibals)—where is the man to be found whom it would not be scandalous to mention in the same breath with Mrs. Tincklepaw? The great delight of this shocking woman's life is to squabble with her husband (poor man, he has my warmest sympathy and best good wishes), and then to bring the quarrel away from home with her, and to let it off again at society in general, in a series of short, spiteful hints. Mrs. Tincklepaw is the exact opposite of Miss Sticker. She is a very little woman; she is (and more shame for her, considering how she acts) young enough to be Miss Sticker's daughter; and she has a kind of snappish tact in worrying innocent people, under every possible turn of circumstances, which distinguishes her (disgracefully) from the poor feeble-minded Maid-Bore, to whom the reader has been already introduced. Here are some examples—all taken, be it observed, from my own personal observation—of the manner in which Mrs. Tincklepaw contrives to persecute her harmless fellow-creatures wherever she happens to meet with them:

Let us say I am out walking, and I happen to meet Mr. and Mrs. Tincklepaw. (By-the-by, she never lets her husband out of her sight—he is too necessary to the execution of her schemes of petty torment. And such a noble creature, to be used for so base a purpose! He stands six feet two, and is additionally distinguished by a glorious and majestic stoutness, which has no sort of connection with the comparatively comic element of fat. His nature, considering what a wife he has got, is inexcusably meek and patient. Instead of answering her, he strokes his magnificent flaxen whiskers, and looks up resignedly at the sky. I sometimes fancy that he stands too high to hear what his dwarf of a wife says. For his sake, poor man, I hope this view of the matter may be the true one.)

I am afraid I have contrived to lose myself in a long parenthesis. Where was I? Oh! out walking, and happening to meet with Mr. and Mrs. Tincklepaw. She has had a quarrel with her husband at home, and this is how she contrives to let me know it.

"Delightful weather, dear, is it not?" I say, as we shake hands.

"Charming, indeed," says Mrs. Tincklepaw.

"Do you know, love, I am so glad you made that remark to me, and not to Mr. Tincklepaw?"

"Really?" I ask. "Pray tell me why?"

"Because," answers the malicious creature, "if you had said it was a fine day to Mr. Tincklepaw, I should have been so afraid of his frowning at you directly, and saying, 'Stuff! talk of something worth listening to, if you talk at all!' What a love of a bonnet you have got on! and how Mr. Tincklepaw would have liked to be staying in your house when you were getting ready to-day to go out. He would have waited for you so patiently, dear. He would never have stamped in the passage; and no such words as, 'Deuce take the woman! is she going to keep me here all day?' would by any possibility have escaped his lips. Don't, love! don't look at the shops, while Mr. Tincklepaw is with us. He might say, 'Oh, bother! you're always wanting to buy something!' I shouldn't like that to happen. Should you, dear?"

Once more. Say I meet Mr. and Mrs. Tincklepaw at a dinner-party, given in honor of a bride and bridegroom. From the instant when she enters the house, Mrs. Tincklepaw never has her eye off the young couple. She looks at them with an expression of heart-broken curiosity. Whenever they happen to speak to each other, she instantly suspends any conversation in which she is engaged, and listens to them with a mournful eagerness. When the ladies retire, she gets the bride into a corner, appropriates her to herself for the rest of the evening,

and persecutes the wretched young woman in
this manner:

"May I ask, is this your first dinner since you
came back?"

"Oh, no! we have been in town for some
weeks."

"Indeed? I should really have thought, now,
that this was your first dinner."

"Should you? I can't imagine why."

"How very odd, when the reason is as plain as
possible! Why, I noticed you all dinner-time,
eating and drinking what you liked, without
looking at your husband for orders. I saw nothing rebellious in your face when you eat all these
nice sweet things at dessert. Dear! dear! don't
you understand? Do you really mean to say
that your husband has not begun yet? Did he
not say, as you drove here to-day, 'Now, mind,
I'm not going to have another night's rest broken, because you always choose to make yourself
ill with stuffing creams and sweets, and all that
sort of thing?' No!!! Mercy on me, what an
odd man he must be! Perhaps he waits till he
gets home again? Oh, come, come; you don't
mean to tell me that he doesn't storm at you
frightfully for having every one of your glasses
filled with wine, and then never touching a drop
of it, but asking for cold water instead, at the
very elbow of the master of the house? If he
says, 'Cursed perversity, and want of proper
tact' once, *I* know he says it a dozen times.
And as for treading on your dress in the hall,
and then bullying you before the servant for not

holding it up out of his way, it's too common a thing to be mentioned—isn't it? Did you notice Mr. Tincklepaw particularly? Ah, you did, and you thought he looked good-natured? No! no! don't say any more; don't say you know better than to trust to appearances. Please do take leave of all common sense and experience, and pray trust to appearances, without thinking of their invariable deceitfulness, this once. Do, dear, to oblige *me*."

I might fill pages with similar examples of the manners and conversation of this intolerable Lady-Bore. I might add other equally aggravating characters, to her character and to Miss Sticker's, without extending my researches an inch beyond the circle of my own acquaintance. But I am true to my unfeminine resolution to write as briefly as if I were a man; and I feel that I have said enough already, to show that I can prove my case. When a woman like me can produce, without the least hesitation, or the slightest difficulty, two such instances of Lady-Bores as I have just exhibited, the additional number which she might pick out of her list, after a little mature reflection, may be logically inferred by all impartial readers.

In the mean time, let me hope I have succeeded sufficiently well in my present purpose to induce our next great satirist to pause before he, too, attacks his harmless fellow-men, and to make him turn his withering glance in the direction of our sex. Let all rising young gentlemen who are racking their brains in search of

originality take the timely hint which 1 have
given them in these pages. Let us have a new
fictitious literature, in which not only the Bores
shall be women, but the villains too. Look at
Shakspeare—do, pray, look at Shakspeare. Who
is most in fault, in that shocking business of the
murder of King Duncan? Lady Macbeth, to be
sure! Look at King Lear, with a small family
of only three daughters, and two of the three
wretches; and even the third an aggravating
girl, who can't be commonly civil to her own
father in the first act, out of sheer contradiction,
because her elder sisters happen to have been
civil before her. Look at Desdemona, who falls
in love with a horrid, copper-colored foreigner,
and then, like a fool, instead of managing him,
aggravates him into smothering her. Ah!
Shakspeare was a great man, and knew our
sex, and was not afraid to show he knew it.
What a blessing it would be if some of his literary brethren in modern times could muster courage enough to follow his example!

I have fifty different things to say, but I shall
bring myself to a conclusion by only mentioning
one of them. If it would at all contribute toward forwarding the literary reform that I advocate, to make a present of the characters of Miss
Sticker and Mrs. Tincklepaw to modern writers
of fiction, I shall be delighted to abandon all
right of proprietorship in those two odious
women. At the same time, I think it fair to
explain that, when I speak of modern writers, 1
mean gentlemen writers only. I wish to say

nothing uncivil to the ladies who compose books, whose effusions may, by the rule of contraries, be exceedingly agreeable to male readers; but I positively forbid them to lay hands upon my two characters. I am charmed to be of use to the men, in a literary point of view, but I decline altogether to mix myself up with the women. There need be no fear of offending them by printing this candid expression of my intentions. Depend on it, they will all declare, on their sides, that they would much rather have nothing to do with *me*.

NOOKS AND CORNERS OF HISTORY.—II.

THE GREAT (FORGOTTEN) INVASION.

PREAMBLE.

IT happened some sixty years ago; it was a French invasion; and it actually took place in England. Thousands of people are alive at the present moment who ought to remember it perfectly well. And yet it has been forgotten. In these times, when the French invasion that *may* come turns up perpetually, in public and in private, as a subject of discussion, the French invasion that *did* come is not honored with so much as a passing word of notice. The new generation knows nothing about it. The old generation has carelessly forgotten it. This is discreditable, and it must be set right; this is a dangerous security, and it must be disturbed; this is a gap in the Modern History of England, and it must be filled up.

Fathers and mothers, read and be reminded; British youths and maidens, read and be informed. Here follows the true history of the great forgotten Invasion of England, at the end of the last century; divided into scenes and periods, and carefully derived from proved and written facts recorded in Kelly's History of the Wars:

I. OF THE FRENCH INVASION AS SEEN
FROM ILFRACOMBE.

On the twenty-second day of February, in the year seventeen hundred and ninety-seven, the inhabitants of North Devonshire looked toward the Bristol Channel, and saw the French invasion coming on, in four ships.

The Directory of the French Republic had been threatening these islands some time previously; but much talk and little action having characterized the proceedings of that governing body in most other matters, no great apprehension was felt of their really carrying out their expressed intention in relation to this country. The war between the two nations was, at this time, confined to naval operations, in which the English invariably got the better of the French. North Devonshire (as well as the rest of England) was aware of this, and trusted implicitly in our supremacy of the seas. North Devonshire got up on the morning of the twenty-second of February, without a thought of the invasion; North Devonshire looked out toward the Bristol Channel, and there—in spite of our supremacy of the seas—there the invasion was, as large as life.

Of the four ships which the Directory had sent to conquer England, two were frigates and two were smaller vessels. This formidable fleet sailed along, in view of a whole panicstricken, defenseless coast; and the place at which it seemed inclined to try the invading experiment first was Ilfracombe. The commander of the expedition brought his ships up before the harbor, scuttled a few coasting-vessels, prepared to destroy the rest, thought better of it, and suddenly turned his four warlike sterns on North Devonshire in the most unaccountable manner. History is silent as to the cause of this abrupt and singular change of purpose. Did the chief of the invaders act from sheer indecision? Did he distrust the hotel accommodation at Ilfracombe? Had he heard of the clotted cream of Devonshire, and did he apprehend the bilious disorganization of the whole army, if they once got within reach of that luscious delicacy? These are important questions, but no satisfactory answer can be found to them. The motives which animated the commander of the invading Frenchmen are buried in oblivion; the fact alone remains, that he spared Ilfracombe. The last that was seen of him from North Devonshire, he was sailing over ruthlessly to the devoted coast of Wales.

II. OF THE FRENCH INVASION AS SEEN BY WELSHMEN IN GENERAL.

In one respect it may be said that Wales was favored by comparison with North Devonshire. The great fact of the French invasion had burst suddenly on Ilfracombe, but it only dawned in a gradual manner on the coast of Pembrokeshire. In the course of his cruise across the Bristol Channel, it had apparently occurred to the commander of the expedition that a little diplomatic deception at the outset might prove to be of ultimate advantage to him. He decided, therefore, on concealing his true character from the eyes of the Welshmen; and when his four ships were first made out from the heights above Saint Bride's Bay, they were all sailing under British colors.

There are men in Wales, as in the rest of the world, whom it is impossible to satisfy; and there were spectators on the heights of Saint Bride's who were not satisfied with the British colors on this occasion, because they felt doubtful about the ships that bore them.   To the eyes of these skeptics all four vessels had an unpleasantly French look, and maneuvered in an unpleasantly French manner. Wise Welshmen along the coast collected together by twos and threes, and sat down on the heights, and looked out to sea, and shook their heads, and suspected. But the majority, as usual, saw nothing extraordinary where nothing extraordinary appeared to be intended, and the country was not yet alarmed; and the four ships sailed on till they doubled Saint David's Head, and sailed on again, a few miles to the northward, and then stopped, and came to single anchor in Cardigan Bay.

Here, again, another difficult question occurs, which recalcitrant History once more declines to solve. The Frenchmen had hardly been observed to cast their single anchors in Cardigan Bay before they were also observed to pull them up again and go on. Why? The commander of the expedition had doubted already at Ilfracombe

—was he doubting again in Cardigan Bay? Or
did he merely want time to mature his plans;
and was it a peculiarity of his nature that he always required to come to anchor before he could
think at his ease? To this mystery, as to the
mystery at Ilfracombe, there is no solution; and
here, as there, nothing is certainly known but
that the Frenchman paused—threatened—and
then sailed on.

III. OF ONE WELSHMAN IN PARTICULAR, AND OF WHAT HE SAW.

He was the only man in Great Britain who
saw the invading army land on our native shores,
and his name has perished.

It is known that he was a Welshman, and that
he belonged to the lower order of the population.
He may be still alive—this man, who is connected with a crisis in English History, may be
still alive—and nobody has found him out; nobody has taken his photograph; nobody has written a genial biographical notice of him; nobody
has made him into an Entertainment; nobody
has held a Commemoration of him; nobody has
presented him with a testimonial, relieved him
by a subscription, or addressed him with a speech.
In these enlightened times, this brief record can
only single him out and individually distinguish
him—as the Hero of the Invasion. Such is
Fame.

The Hero of the Invasion, then, was standing,
or sitting—for even on this important point tradition is silent—on the cliffs of the Welsh coast,

near Lanonda Church, when he saw the four ships enter the bay below him and come to anchor—this time without showing any symptoms of getting under way again. The English colors, under which the expedition had thus far attempted to deceive the population of the coast, were now hauled down, and the threatening flag of France was boldly hoisted in their stead. This done, the boats were lowered away, were filled with a ferocious soldiery, and were pointed straight for the beach.

It is on record that the Hero of the Invasion distinctly saw this; and it is *not* on record that he ran away. Honor to the unknown brave! Honor to the solitary Welshman who faced the French army!

The boats came on straight to the beach—the ferocious soldiery leaped out on English soil, and swarmed up the cliff, thirsting for the subjugation of the British Isles. The Hero of the Invasion, watching solitary on the cliffs, saw the Frenchmen crawling up below him—tossing their muskets on before them—climbing with the cool calculation of an army of chimney-sweeps—nimble as the monkey, supple as the tiger, stealthy as the cat—hungry for plunder, bloodshed, and Welsh mutton, void of all respect for the British Constitution—an army of Invaders on the Land of the Habeas Corpus!

The Welshman saw that, and vanished. Whether he waited with clinched fist till the head of the foremost Frenchman rose parallel with the cliff-side, or whether he achieved a long start by letting the army get half-way up the cliff, and then retreating inland to give the alarm —is, like every other circumstance in connection with the Hero of the Invasion, a matter of the profoundest doubt. It is only known that he got away at all, because it is *not* known that he was taken prisoner. He parts with us here, the shadow of a shade, the most impalpable of historical apparitions. Honor, nevertheless, to the crafty brave! Honor to the solitary Welshman who faced the French army without being shot, and retired from the French army without being caught.

IV. OF WHAT THE INVADERS DID WHEN THEY GOT ON SHORE.

The Art of Invasion has its routine, its laws, manners, and customs, like other arts. And the French army acted strictly in accordance with established precedents. The first thing the first men did, when they got to the top of the cliff, was to strike a light and set fire to the furze-bushes. While national feeling deplores this destruction of property, unprejudiced History looks on at her ease. Given Invasion as a cause, fire follows, according to all known rules, as an effect. If an army of Englishmen had been invading France under similar circumstances, they, on either side, would necessarily have begun by setting fire to something; and unprejudiced History would, in that case also, have looked on at her ease.

While the furze-bushes were blazing, the remainder of the invaders—assured by the sight of the flames of their companions' success so far—was disembarking and swarming up the rocks. When it was finally mustered on the top of the cliff, the army amounted to fourteen hundred men. This was the whole force which the Directory of the French Republic had thought it desirable to dispatch for the subjugation of Great Britain. History, until she is certain of results, will pronounce no opinion on the wisdom of this proceeding. She knows that nothing in politics is abstractedly rash, cruel, treacherous, or disgraceful—she knows that Success is the sole touch-stone of merit—she knows that the man who fails is contemptible, and the man who succeeds is illustrious, without any reference to the means used in either case—to the character of the men, or to the nature of the motives under which they may have proceeded to action. If the Invasion succeeds, History will applaud it as an act of heroism; if it fails, History will condemn it as an act of folly.

It has been said that the Invasion began creditably, according to the rules established in all cases of conquering. It continued to follow those rules with the most praiseworthy regularity. Having started with setting something on fire, it went on, in due course, to accomplish the other first objects of all Invasions, thieving and killing —performing much of the former, and little of the latter. Two rash Welshmen, who persisted in defending their native leeks, suffered accordingly; the rest lost nothing but their national victuals and their national flannel. On this first day of the Invasion, when the army had done marauding, the results on both sides may be thus summed up. Gains to the French; good dinners, and protection next the skin. Loss to the English: mutton, stout Welsh flannel, and two rash countrymen.

V. OF THE BRITISH DEFENSE, AND OF THE WAY IN WHICH THE WOMEN CONTRIBUTED TO IT.

The appearance of the Frenchmen on the coast, and the loss to the English, mentioned above, produced the results naturally to be expected. The country was alarmed, and started up to defend itself.

On the numbers of the invaders being known, and on its being discovered that, though they were without field-pieces, they had with them seventy cart-loads of powder and ball and a quantity of grenades, the principal men in the country bestirred themselves in setting up the defense. Before nightfall, all the available men who knew anything of the art of fighting were collected. When the ranks were drawn out, the English defense was even more ridiculous in point of numbers than the French attack. It amounted, at a time when we were at war with France, and were supposed to be prepared for any dangers that might threaten—it amounted, including militia, fencibles, and yeomanry cavalry, to just six hundred and sixty men, or, in other words, to less than half the number of the invading Frenchmen.

Fortunately for the credit of the nation, the command of this exceedingly compact force was taken by the principal grandee in the neighborhood. He turned out to be a man of considerable cunning, as well as a man of high rank, and he was known by the style and title of the Earl of Cawdor.

The one cheering circumstance in connection with the heavy responsibility which now rested on the shoulders of the Earl, consisted in this— that he had apparently no cause to dread internal treason as well as foreign invasion. The remarkably inconvenient spot which the French had selected for their landing showed, not only that they themselves knew nothing of the coast, but that none of the inhabitants, who might have led them to an easier place of disembarkation, were privy to their purpose. So far so good. But still, the great difficulty remained of facing the French with an equality of numbers, and with the appearance, at least, of an equality of discipline. The first of these requisites it was easy to fulfill. There were hosts of colliers and other laborers in the neighborhood—big, bold, lusty fellows enough; but, so far as the art of marching and using weapons was concerned, as helpless as a pack of children. The question was, how to make good use of these men for show purposes, without allowing them fatally to embarrass the proceedings of their trained and disciplined companions. In this emergency, Lord Cawdor hit on a grand idea. He boldly mixed the women up in the business—and it is

unnecessary to add that the business began to
prosper from that lucky moment.

In those days the wives of the Welsh laborers
wore, what the wives of all classes of the community have been wearing since, red petticoats.
It was Lord Cawdor's happy idea to call on these
patriot matrons to sink the question of skirts, to
forego the luxurious consideration of warmth,
and to turn the colliers into military men (so far
as external appearances, viewed at a distance,
were concerned) by taking off the wives' red petticoats and putting them over the husbands'
shoulders.   Where patriot matrons are concerned, no national appeal is made in vain,
and no personal sacrifice is refused   All the
women seized their strings, and stepped out of
their petticoats on the spot.   What man in that
make-shift military but must think of "home
and beauty," now that he had the tenderest
memento of both to grace his shoulders and jog
his memory?   In an inconceivably short space of
time every woman was shivering, and every collier was turned into a soldier.

VI. OF HOW IT ALL ENDED.

Thus recruited, Lord Cawdor marched off to
the scene of action; and the patriot women, deprived of their husbands and their petticoats,
retired, it is to be hoped and presumed, to the
friendly shelter of bed.   It was then close on
nightfall, if not actually night; and the disor-
derly marching of the transformed colliers could
not be perceived.   But when the British army

took up its position, then was the time when the
excellent stratagem of Lord Cawdor told at its
true worth. By the uncertain light of fires and
torches, the French scouts, let them venture as
near as they might, could see nothing in detail.
A man in a scarlet petticoat looked as soldier-like
as a man in a scarlet coat, under those dusky circumstances. All that the enemy could now see
were lines on lines of men in red, the famous
uniform of the English army.

The council of the French braves must have
been a perturbed assembly on that memorable
night. Behind them was the empty bay; for the
four ships, after landing the invaders, had set
sail again for France, sublimely indifferent to the
fate of the fourteen hundred. Before them there
waited in battle array an apparently formidable
force of British soldiers. Under them was the
hostile English ground, on which they were tres-
passers caught in the fact. Girt about by these
serious perils, the discreet commander of the Invasion fell back on those safeguards of caution
and deliberation of which he had already given
proofs on approaching the English shore. He
had doubted at Ilfracombe; he had doubted again
in Cardigan Bay; and now, on the eve of the first
battle, he doubted for the third time—doubted,
and gave in. If History declines to receive the
French commander as a hero, Philosophy opens
her peaceful doors to him, and welcomes him in
the character of a wise man.

At ten o'clock that night a flag of truce appeared in the English camp, and a letter was de-

livered to Lord Cawdor from the prudent chief
of the invaders. The letter set forth, with amazing gravity and dignity, that the circumstances
under which the French troops had landed, having rendered it "unnecessary" to attempt any
military operations, the commanding officer did
not object to come forward generously and propose terms of capitulation. Such a message as
this was little calculated to impose on any man,
far less on the artful nobleman who had invented
the stratagem of the red petticoats. Taking a
slightly different view of the circumstances, and
declining altogether to believe that the French
Directory had sent fourteen hundred men over
to England to divert the inhabitants by the spectacle of a capitulation, Lord Cawdor returned for
answer that he did not feel himself at liberty to
treat with the French commander, except on the
condition of his men surrendering as prisoners of
war. On receiving this reply, the Frenchman
gave an additional proof of that philosophical
turn of mind which has been already claimed for
him as one of his merits, by politely adopting the
course which Lord Cawdor suggested. By noon
the next day, the French troops were all marched
off prisoners of war, the patriot matrons had resumed their petticoats, and the short terror of the
invasion had happily passed away.

The first question that occurred to everybody
as soon as the alarm had been dissipated was,
what this extraordinary burlesque of an invasion
could possibly mean. It was asserted in some
quarters that the fourteen hundred Frenchmen

had been recruited from those insurgents of La Vendee who had enlisted in the service of the Republic, who could not be trusted at home, and who were therefore dispatched on the first desperate service that might offer itself abroad. Others represented the invading army as a mere gang of galley-slaves and criminals in general, who had been landed on our shores with the double purpose of annoying England and ridding France of a pack of rascals. The commander of the expedition, however, disposed of this latter theory by declaring that six hundred of his men were picked veterans from the French army, and by referring, for corroboration of this statement, to his large supplies of powder, ball, and hand-grenades, which would certainly not have been wasted, at a time when military stores were especially precious, on a gang of galley-slaves.

The truth seems to be that the French (who were even more densely ignorant of England and English institutions at that time than they are at this) had been so entirely deceived by false reports of the temper and sentiments of our people, as to believe that the mere appearance of the troops of the Republic on these Monarchical shores would be the signal for a revolutionary rising of all the disaffected classes from one end of Great Britain to the other. Viewed merely as materials for kindling the insurrectionary spark, the fourteen hundred Frenchmen might certainly be considered sufficient for the purpose, providing the Directory of the Republic could only have made sure beforehand that the English tinder might be depended on to catch light!

One last event must be recorded before this History can be considered complete. The disasters of the invading army on shore were matched at sea by the disasters of the vessels that had carried them. Of the four ships which had alarmed the English coast, the two largest (the frigates) were both captured, as they were standing in for Brest harbor, by Sir Harry Neale. This smart and final correction of the fractious little French invasion was administered on the ninth of March, seventeen hundred and ninety-seven.

MORAL.

This is the history of the Great (Forgotten) Invasion. It is short, it is not impressive, it is unquestionably deficient in serious interest. But there is a Moral to be drawn from it, nevertheless. If we are invaded again, and on a rather larger scale, let us not be so ill-prepared this next time as to be obliged to take refuge in our wives' red petticoats.

CURIOSITIES OF LITERATURE.—I.

THE UNKNOWN PUBLIC.

Do the customers at publishing houses, the members of book-clubs and circulating libraries, and the purchasers and borrowers of newspapers and reviews, compose altogether the great bulk of the reading public of England? There was a time when, if anybody had put this question to me, I, for one, should certainly have answered Yes.

I know better now. So far from composing the bulk of English readers, the public just mentioned represents nothing more than the minority.

This startling discovery dawned upon me gradually. I made my first approaches toward it in walking about London, more especially in the second and third rate neighborhoods. At such times, whenever I passed a small stationer's or small tobacconist's shop, I became mechanically conscious of certain publications which invariably occupied the windows. These publications all appeared to be of the same small quarto size: they seemed to consist merely of a few unbound pages; each one of them had a picture on the upper half of the front leaf, and a quantity of small print on the under. I noticed just as much

as this, for some time, and no more. None of
the gentlemen who profess to guide my taste in
literary matters had ever directed my attention
toward these mysterious publications. My favorite Review is, as 1 firmly believe, at this very
day, unconscious of their existence. My enterprising librarian—who forces all sorts of books
on my attention that I don't want to read, because he has bought whole editions of them a
great bargain—has never yet tried me with the
limp, unbound picture-quarto of the small shops.
Day after day, and week after week, the mysterious publications haunted my walks, go where 1
might; and still I was too careless to stop and
notice them in detail. I left London, and traveled
about England. The neglected publications followed me. There they were in every town, large
or small. I saw them in fruit-shops, in oyster-
shops, in cigar-shops, in lozenge-shops. Villages
even — picturesque, strong - smelling villages—
were not free from them. Wherever the speculative daring of one man could open a shop, and
the human appetites and necessities of his fellow-
mortals could keep it from shutting up again,
there, as it appeared to me, the unbound picture-
quarto instantly entered, set itself up obtrusively
in the window, and insisted on being looked at
by everybody. "Buy me, borrow me, stare at
me, steal me. Oh, inattentive stranger, do anything but pass me by!"

Under this sort of compulsion, it was not long
before I began to stop at shop-windows and look
attentively at these all-pervading specimens of

what was to me a new species of literary production. I made acquaintance with one of them among the deserts of West Cornwall; with another in a populous thoroughfare of Whitechapel; with a third in a dreary little lost town at the north of Scotland. I went into a lovely county of South Wales; the modest railway had not penetrated to it, but the audacious picture-quarto had found it out. Who could resist this perpetual, this inevitable, this magnificently unlimited appeal to notice and patronage? From looking in at the windows of the shops, I got on to entering the shops themselves—to buying specimens of this locust-flight of small publications—to making strict examination of them from the first page to the last—and finally, to instituting inquiries about them in all sorts of well-informed quarters. The result has been the discovery of an Unknown Public; a public to be counted by millions; the mysterious, the unfathomable, the universal public of the penny-novel-journals.*

I have five of these journals now before me, represented by one sample copy, bought haphazard, of each. There are many more; but these five represent the successful and well-established members of the literary family. The eldest of them is a stout lad of fifteen years' standing;

---

* It may be as well to explain that I use this awkward compound word in order to mark the distinction between a penny journal and a penny newspaper. The "journal" is what I am now writing about. The "newspaper" is an entirely different subject, with which this article has no connection.

the youngest is an infant of three months old. All
five are sold at the same price of one penny; all
five are published regularly once a week; all
five contain about the same quantity of matter.
The weekly circulation of the most successful of
the five is now publicly advertised (and, as I am
informed, without exaggeration) at half a million. Taking the other four as attaining altogether to a circulation of another half-million
(which is probably much under the right estimate)
we have a sale of a million weekly for five penny
journals. Reckoning only three readers to each
copy sold, the result is *a public of three millions*—a public unknown to the literary world;
unknown, as disciples, to the whole body of professed critics; unknown, as customers, at the
great libraries and the great publishing houses;
unknown, as an audience, to the distinguished
English writers of our own time. A reading
public of three millions which lies right out of
the pale of literary civilization is a phenomenon
worth examining—a mystery which the sharpest
man among us may not find it easy to solve.

In the first place, who are the three millions—
the Unknown Public—as I have ventured to call
them?

The known reading public—the minority already referred to—are easily discovered and classi-
fied. There is the religious public, with booksellers and literature of its own, which includes
reviews and newspapers as well as books. There
is the public which reads for information, and
devotes itself to Histories, Biographies, Essays,

Treatises, Voyages and Travels. There is the public which reads for amusement, and patronizes the Circulating Libraries and the railway bookstalls. There is, lastly, the public which reads nothing but newspapers. We all know where to lay our hands on the people who represent these various classes. We see the books they like on their tables. We meet them out at dinner, and hear them talk of their favorite authors. We know, if we are at all conversant with literary matters, even the very districts of London in which certain classes of people live who are to be depended upon beforehand as the picked readers for certain kinds of books. But what do we know of the enormous, outlawed majority—of the lost literary tribes—of the prodigious, the overwhelming three millions? Absolutely nothing.

I myself—and I say it to my sorrow—have a very large circle of acquaintance. Ever since I undertook the interesting task of exploring the Unknown Public, I have been trying to discover among my dear friends and my bitter enemies (both alike on my visiting-list), a subscriber to a penny-novel-journal—and I have never yet succeeded in the attempt. I have heard theories started as to the probable existence of penny-novel-journals in kitchen dressers, in the back parlors of Easy-shaving Shops, in the greasy seclusion of the boxes at the small Chop-houses. But I have never yet met with any man, woman or child who could answer the inquiry: "Do you subscribe to a penny journal?" plainly in the affirmative, and who could produce the periodi-

cal in question. I have learned, years ago, to
despair of ever meeting with a single woman,
after a certain age, who has not had an offer of
marriage. I have given up long since all idea
of ever discovering a man who has himself seen
a ghost, as distinguished from that other inevitable man who has had a bosom friend who has
unquestionably seen one. These are two among
many other aspirations of a wasted life which I
have definitely resigned. I have now to add one
more to the number of my vanished illusions.

In the absence, therefore, of any positive information on the subject, it is only possible to
pursue the present investigation by accepting
such negative evidence as may help us to guess,
with more or less accuracy, at the social position,
the habits, the tastes, and the average intelligence of the Unknown Public. Arguing carefully by inference, we may hope, in this matter,
to arrive at something like a safe, if not a satisfactory, conclusion.

To begin with, it may be fairly assumed—seeing that the staple commodity of each one of the
five journals before me is composed of stories—
that the Unknown Public reads for its amusement more than for its information.

Judging by my own experience, I should be
inclined to add that the Unknown Public looks
to quantity rather than quality in spending its
penny a week on literature. In buying my five
specimen copies at five different shops, I pur-
posely approached the individual behind the
counter on each occasion in the character of a

member of the Unknown Public—say, Number Three Million and One—who wished to be guided in laying out a penny entirely by the recommendation of the shop-keeper himself. I expected, by this course of proceeding, to hear a little popular criticism, and to get at what the conditions of success might be, in a branch of literature which was quite new to me. No such result rewarded my efforts in any case. The dialogue between buyer and seller always took some such practical turn as this:

Reader, Number Three Million and One. "I want to take in one of the penny journals. Which do you recommend?"

Enterprising Publisher. "Some likes one, and some likes another. They're all good pennurths. Seen this one?"

"Yes."

"Seen that one?"

"No."

"Look what a pennurth!"

"Yes—but about the stories in this one? Are they as good, now, as the stories in that one?"

"Well, you see, some likes one, and some likes another. Sometimes I sells more of one, and sometimes I sells more of another. Take 'em all the year round, and there an't a pin, as I knows of, to choose between 'em. There's just about as much in one as there is in another. All good pennurths. Bless your soul, just take 'em up and look for yourself! All good pennurths, choose where you like!"

I never got any further than this, try as I
might.   And yet I found the shop-keepers, both
men and women, ready enough to talk on other
topics.   On each occasion, so far from receiving
any practical hints that I was interrupting business, I found myself sociably delayed in the shop,
after I had made my purchase, as if I had been
an old acquaintance.   I got all sorts of curious
information on all sorts of subjects—excepting
the good pennurth of print in my pocket.   Does
the reader know the singular facts in connection
with Everton Toffey?   It is like eau de Cologne.
There is only one genuine receipt for making it in
the world.   It has been a family inheritance from
remote antiquity.   You may go here, there, and
everywhere, and buy what you think is Everton
Toffey (or eau de Cologne); but there is only one
place in London, as there is only one place in
Cologne, at which you can obtain the genuine
article.   That information was given me at one
penny journal shop.   At another, the proprietor
explained his new system of Stay-making to me.
He offered to provide my wife with something
that would support her muscles and not pinch
her flesh; and, what was more, he was not the
man to ask for his bill afterward, except in the
case of giving both of us perfect satisfaction.
This man was so talkative and intelligent; he
could tell me all about so many other things besides stays, that I took it for granted he could
give me the information of which I stood in need.
But here, again, I was disappointed.   He had a
perfect snow-drift of penny journals all over his

counter; he snatched them up by handfuls, and gesticulated with them cheerfully; he smacked and patted them, and brushed them all up in a heap, to express to me that "the whole lot would be worked off by the evening"; but he, too, when I brought him to close quarters, only repeated the one inevitable form of words: "A good pennurth; that's all I can say! Bless your soul, look at any one of them for yourself, and see what a pennurth it is!"

Having, inferentially, arrived at the two conclusions that the Unknown Public reads for amusement, and that it looks to quantity in its reading, rather than to quality, I might have found it difficult to proceed further toward the making of new discoveries but for the existence of a very remarkable aid to inquiry, which is common to all the penny-novel-journals alike.

The peculiar facilities to which I now refer are presented in the Answers to Correspondents. The page containing these is, beyond all comparison, the most interesting page in the penny journals. There is no earthly subject that it is possible to discuss, no private affair that it is possible to conceive, which the inscrutable Unknown Public will not confide to the editor in the form of a question, and which the editor will not set himself seriously and resolutely to answer. Hidden under cover of initials, or Christian names, or conventional signatures—such as Subscriber, Constant Reader, and so forth—the editor's correspondents seem, many of them, to judge by the published answers to their questions, utterly impervious to the senses of ridicule or shame. Young girls beset by perplexities which are usually supposed to be reserved for a mother's or an elder sister's ear, consult the editor. Married women who have committed little frailties, consult the editor. Male jilts in deadly fear of actions for breach of promise of marriage, consult the editor. Ladies whose complexions are on the wane, and who wish to know the best artificial means of restoring them, consult the editor. Gentlemen who want to dye their hair and get rid of their corns consult the editor. Inconceivably dense ignorance, inconceivably petty malice, and inconceivably complacent vanity, all consult the editor, and all, wonderful to relate, get serious answers from him. No mortal position is too difficult for this wonderful man; there is no change of character as general referee which he is not prepared to assume on the instant. Now he is a father, now a mother, now a schoolmaster, now a confessor, now a doctor, now a lawyer, now a young lady's confidante, now a young gentleman's bosom friend, now a lecturer on morals, and now an authority in cookery.

However, our present business is not with the editor, but with his readers. As a means of getting at the average intelligence of the Unknown Public—as a means of testing the general amount of education which they have acquired, and of ascertaining what share of taste and delicacy they have inherited from Nature—these extraordinary Answers to Correspondents may fairly be produced in detail, to serve us for a guide. I must premise that I have not maliciously hunted them up out of many numbers; I have merely looked into my five sample copies of five separate journals—all, I repeat, bought accidentally, just as they happened to catch my attention in the shop windows. I have not waited for bad specimens, or anxiously watched for good; I have impartially taken my chance. And now, just as impartially, I dip into one journal after another, on the Correspondents' page, exactly as the five happen to lie on my desk. The result is, that I have the pleasure of presenting to those ladies and gentlemen who may honor me with their attention the following members of the Unknown Public who are in a condition to speak quite unreservedly for themselves:

A reader of a penny-novel-journal who wants a recipe for gingerbread. A reader who complains of fullness in his throat. Several readers who want cures for gray hair, for warts, for sores on the head, for nervousness, and for worms. Two readers who have trifled with Woman's Affections, and who want to know if Woman can sue them for breach of promise of marriage. A reader who wants to know what the sacred initials I. H. S. mean, and how to get rid of small-pox marks. Another reader who desires to be informed what an esquire is. Another who cannot tell how to pronounce picturesque and acquiescence. Another who requires to be told that *chiaroscuro* is a term used by printers. Three readers who want to know how to soften ivory, how to get a divorce, and how to make black varnish. A reader who is not certain what the word poems means; not certain that "Mazeppa" was written by Lord Byron; not certain whether there are such things in the world as printed and published Lives of Napoleon Bonaparte.

Two afflicted readers, well worthy of a place by themselves, who want a recipe apiece for the cure of knock-knees; and who are referred (it is to be hoped, by a straight-legged editor) to a former answer, addressed to other sufferers, which contains the information they require.

Two readers, respectively, unaware, until the editor has enlightened them, that the author of "Robinson Crusoe" was Daniel Defoe, and the author of the "Irish Melodies," Thomas Moore. Another reader, a trifle denser, who requires to be told that the histories of Greece and Rome are ancient histories, and the histories of France and England modern histories.

A reader who wants to know the right hour of the day at which to visit a newly-married couple. A reader who wants a recipe for liquid blacking.

A lady reader who expresses her sentiments prettily on crinoline. Another lady reader, who wants to know how to make crumpets. Another, who has received presents from a gentleman to whom she is not engaged, and who wants the editor to tell her whether she is right or wrong. Two lady readers who require lovers, and wish the editor to provide them. Two timid girls, who are respectively afraid of a French invasion and dragon-flies.

A Don Juan of a reader, who wants the private address of a certain actress. A reader with a noble ambition who wishes to lecture, and wants to hear of an establishment at which he can buy discourses ready-made. A natty reader, who wants German polish for boots and shoes. A sore-headed reader, who is editorially advised to use soap and warm water. A virtuous reader, who writes to condemn married women for listening to compliments, and who is informed by an equally virtuous editor that his remarks are neatly expressed. A guilty (female) reader, who confides her frailties to a moral editor and shocks him. A pale-faced reader, who asks if she shall darken her skin. Another pale-faced reader, who asks if she shall put on rouge. An undecided reader, who asks if there is any inconsistency in a dancing-mistress being a teacher at a Sunday-school. A bashful reader, who has been four years in love with a lady, and has not yet mentioned it to her. A speculative reader, who wishes to know if he can sell lemonade without a license. An uncertain reader, who wants to be told whether he had better declare his feelings frankly and honorably at once. An indignant female reader, who reviles all the gentlemen in her neighborhood because they don't take the ladies out. A scorbutic reader, who wants to be cured. A pimply reader, in the same condition. A jilted reader, who writes to know what his best revenge may be, and who is advised by a wary editor to try indifference. A domestic reader, who wishes to be told the weight of a newly-born child. An inquisitive reader, who wants to know if the name of David's mother is mentioned in the Scriptures.

Here are ten editorial sentiments on things in general, which are pronounced at the express request of correspondents, and which are therefore likely to be of use in assisting us to form an estimate of the intellectual condition of the Unknown Public:

1. All months are lucky to marry in, when your union is hallowed by love.

2. When you have a sad trick of blushing on being introduced to a young lady, and when you want to correct the habit, summon to your aid a manly confidence.

3. If you want to write neatly, do not bestow too much ink on occasional strokes.

4. You should not shake hands with a lady on your first introduction to her.

5. You can sell ointment without a patent.

6. A widow should at once and most decidedly discourage the lightest attentions on the part of a married man.

7. A rash and thoughtless girl will scarcely make a steady, thoughtful wife.

8. We do not object to a moderate quantity of crinoline.

9. A sensible and honorable man never flirts himself, and ever despises flirts of the other sex.

10. A collier will not better his condition by going to Prussia.

At the risk of being wearisome, I must once more repeat that these selections from the Answers to Correspondents, incredibly absurd as they may appear, are presented *exactly as I find them.* Nothing is exaggerated for the sake of a joke; nothing is invented, or misquoted, to serve the purpose of any pet theory of my own. The sample produced of the three million penny readers is left to speak for itself; to give some idea of the social and intellectual materials of which a portion, at least, of the Unknown Public may fairly be presumed to be composed. Having so far disposed of this first part of the matter in hand, the second part follows, naturally enough, of its own accord. We have all of us formed some opinion by this time on the subject of the Public itself: the next thing to do is to find out what that Public reads.

I have already said that the staple commodity of the journals appears to be formed of stories. The five specimen copies of the five separate weekly publications now before me contain, altogether, ten serial stories, one reprint of a famous novel (to be hereafter referred to), and seven short tales, each of which begins and ends in one number. The remaining pages are filled up with miscellaneous contributions, in literature and art, drawn from every conceivable source; pickings from Punch and Plato; wood engravings, representing notorious people and views of famous places, which strongly suggest that the original blocks have seen better days in other periodicals; modern and ancient anecdotes; short memoirs; scraps of poetry; choice morsels of general information; household receipts, riddles, and extracts from moral writers—all appear in the most or-derly manner, arranged under separate heads, and cut up neatly into short paragraphs. However, the prominent feature in each journal is the serial story, which is placed in every case as the first article, and which is illustrated by the only wood-engraving that appears to have been expressly cut for the purpose. To the serial story, therefore, we may fairly devote our chief attention, because it is clearly regarded as the chief attraction of these very singular publications.

Two of my specimen copies contained, respectively, the first chapters of new stories. In the case of the other three, I found the stories in various stages of progress. The first thing that struck me, after reading the separate weekly portions of all five, was their extraordinary sameness. Each portion purported to be written (and no doubt was written) by a different author, and yet all five might have been produced by the same man. Each part of each successive story settled down in turn, as I read it, to the same dead level of the smoothest and flattest conventionality. A combination of fierce melodrama and meek domestic sentiment; short dialogues and paragraphs on the French pattern, with moral English reflections of the sort that occur on the top lines of children's copy-books; incidents and characters taken from the old exhausted mines of the circulating library, and presented as complacently and confidently as if they were original ideas; descriptions and reflections for the beginning of the number, and a "strong situation," dragged in by the neck and shoul-

ders, for the end—formed the common literary
sources from which the five authors drew their
weekly supply; all collecting it by the same
means; all carrying it in the same quantities;
all pouring it out before the attentive public in
the same way. After reading my samples of
these stories, I understood why it was that the
fictions of the regularly established writers for
the penny journals are never republished. There
is, I honestly believe, no man, woman, or child
in England, not a member of the Unknown Public, who could be got to read them. The one
thing which it is possible to advance in their
favor is, that there is apparently no wickedness
in them. There seems to be an intense indwell-
ing respectability in their dullness. If they lead
to no intellectual result, even of the humblest
kind, they may have at least this negative advantage, that they can do no harm.

If it be objected that I am condemning these
stories after having merely read one number of
each of them, I have only to ask, in return,
whether anybody ever waits to go all through a
novel before passing an opinion on the goodness
or the badness of it? In the latter case, we throw
the story down before we get through it, and
that is its condemnation. There is room enough
for promise, if not for performance, in any one
part of any one genuine work of fiction. If I
had found the smallest promise in the style, in
the dialogue, in the presentation of character, in
the arrangement of incident, in any of the five
specimens of cheap fiction before me, each one of

which extended, on the average, to ten columns of small print, I should have gone on gladly to the next number. But I discovered nothing of the kind; and I put down my weekly sample, just as an editor, under similar circumstances, puts down a manuscript, after getting through a certain number of pages, or a reader a book.

And this sort of writing appeals to a monster audience of at least three millions! Has a better sort ever been tried? It has. The former proprietor of one of these penny journals commissioned a thoroughly competent person to translate "The Count of Monte Christo" for his periodical. He knew that there was hardly a language in the civilized world into which that consummate specimen of the rare and difficult art of story-telling had not been translated. In France, in England, in America, in Russia, in Germany, in Italy, in Spain, Alexandre Dumas had held hundreds of thousands of readers breathless. The proprietor of the penny journal naturally thought that he could do as much with the Unknown Public. Strange to say, the result of this apparently certain experiment was a failure. The circulation of the journal in question seriously decreased from the time when the first of living story-tellers became a contributor to it! The same experiment was tried with the "Mysteries of Paris" and "The Wandering Jew," only to produce the same result. Another penny journal gave Dumas a commission to write a new story, expressly for translation in its columns. The speculation was tried, and once again the inscrutable Unknown

Public held back the hand of welcome from the spoiled child of a whole world of novel-readers.

How is this to be accounted for?

Does a rigid moral sense permeate the Unknown Public from one end of it to the other, and did the productions of the French novelists shock that sense from the very outset? The page containing the Answers to Correspondents would be enough in itself to dispose of this theory. But there are other and better means of arriving at the truth, which render any further reference to the Correspondents' page unnecessary. Some time since, an eminent novelist (the only living English author with a literary position who had at that time written for the Unknown Public) produced his new novel in a penny journal. No shadow of a moral objection has ever been urged by any readers against the works published by the author of "It is Never Too Late to Mend"; but even he, unless I have been greatly misinformed, failed to make the impression that had been anticipated on the impenetrable Three Millions. The great success of his novel was not obtained in its original serial form, but in its republished form, when it appealed from the Unknown to the Known Public. Clearly, the moral obstacle was not the obstacle which militated against the success of Alexandre Dumas and Eugene Sue.

What was it, then? Plainly this, as I believe. The Unknown Public is, in a literary sense, hardly beginning, as yet, to learn to read. The members of it are evidently, in the mass, from

no fault of theirs, still ignorant of almost everything which is generally known and understood
among readers whom circumstances have placed,
socially and intellectually, in the rank above
them. The mere references in "Monte Christo,"
"The Mysteries of Paris," and "White Lies" (the
scene of this last English fiction having been laid
on French ground), to foreign names, titles, manners, and customs, puzzled the Unknown Public
on the threshold. Look back at the answers to
correspondents, and then say, out of fifty subscribers to a penny journal, how many are likely
to know, for example, that mademoiselle means
miss? Besides the difficulty in appealing to the
penny audience caused at the beginning by such
simple obstacles as this, there was the great additional difficulty, in the case of all three of the
fictions just mentioned, of accustoming untried
readers to the delicacies and subtleties of literary
art. An immense public has been discovered;
the next thing to be done is, in a literary sense,
to teach that public how to read.

An attempt, to the credit of one of the penny
journals, has already been made. I have mentioned in one place a reprint of a novel, and later,
a remarkable exception to the drearily commonplace character of the rest of the stories. In both
these cases I refer to one and the same fiction—to
the "Kenilworth" of Sir Walter Scott, which is
reprinted as a new serial experiment in a penny
journal. Here is the great master of modern
fiction appealing, at this time of day, to a new
public, and (amazing anomaly!) marching in

company with writers who have the rudiments of their craft still to learn! To my mind, one result seems certain. If "Kenilworth" be appreciated by the Unknown Public, then the very best men among living English writers will one of these days be called on, as a matter of necessity, to make their appearance in the pages of the penny journals.

Meanwhile, it is perhaps hardly too much to say that the future of English fiction may rest with this Unknown Public, which is now waiting to be taught the difference between a good book and a bad. It is probably a question of time only. The largest audience for periodical literature, in this age of periodicals, must obey the universal law of progress, and must, sooner or later, learn to discriminate. When that period comes, the readers who rank by millions will be the readers who give the widest reputations, who return the richest rewards, and who will, therefore, command the service of the best writers of their time. A great, an unparalleled prospect awaits, perhaps, the coming generation of English novelists. To the penny journals of the present time belongs the credit of having discovered a new public. When that public shall discover its need of a great writer, the great writer will have such an audience as has never yet been known.*

---

* Five years have passed since this article was first published, and no signs of progress in the Unknown Public have made their appearance as yet. Patience! patience! (September, 1863).

SOCIAL GRIEVANCES.—III.

GIVE US ROOM!

[The Imperative Request of a Family Man.]

THE entertainments of the festive season of the year, so far as I am personally concerned, have at last subsided into a temporary lull. 1 and my family actually have one or two evenings to ourselves just at present. It is my purpose to take advantage of this interval of leisure to express my sentiments on the subject of evening parties and ladies' dress.

Let nobody turn over this page impatiently, alarmed at the prospect of another diatribe against Crinoline. I, for one, am not going to exhibit myself in the character of a writer who vainly opposes one of the existing institutions of this country. The Press, the Pulpit, and the Stage have been in the habit of considering themselves as three very powerful levers, capable of being used with terrible effect on the inert material of society. All three have tried to jerk that flourishing foreign plant, Crinoline, out of English earth, and have failed to stir so much as a single root of it. All three have run full tilt against the women of England, and have not moved

them an inch. Talk of the power of the Press!
what is it, compared to the power of a French
milliner? The Press has tried to abridge the
women's petticoats, and has entirely failed in the
attempt. When the right time comes, a French
milliner will abridge them at a week's notice.
The Pulpit preaches, the Stage ridicules; and
each woman of the congregation or the audience
sits, imperturbable, in the middle of her balloon,
and lets the serious words or the comic words go
in at one ear and come out at the other, precisely
as if they were spoken in an unknown tongue.
Nothing that I can remember has so effectually
crushed the pretensions of the Press, the Pulpit,
and the Stage as the utter failure of their crusade
against Crinoline.

My present object in writing is likely, I think,
to be popular—at least, with the ladies. I do
not want to put down Crinoline—I only want to
make room for it. Personally, I rather like it—
I do, indeed, though I am a man. The fact is,
I am a thoroughly well-disciplined husband and
father, and I know the value of it. The only
defect in my eldest daughter's otherwise perfect
form lies in her feet and ankles. She is married,
so I don't mind mentioning that they are decidedly
clumsy. Without Crinoline, they would be seen;
with Crinoline (except when she goes upstairs),
nobody has the slightest suspicion of them. My
wife—pray don't tell her that I ever observed it
—my wife used to waddle **before** the invention
of Crinoline. Now she swims voluptuously, and
knocks down all the light articles of furniture,

whenever she crosses the room, in a manner
which, but for the expense of repairs, would be
perfectly charming.   One of my other single
daughters used to be sadly thin, poor girl. Oh,
how plump she is now! Oh, my marriageable
young men, how ravishingly plump she is now!
Long life to the monarchy of Crinoline! Every
mother in this country who has daughters to
marry, and who is not quite so sure of their unaided personal attractions as she might wish to
be, echoes that loyal cry, I am sure, from the
bottom of her affectionate heart.   And the Press
actually thinks it can shake our devotion to our
Queen Petticoat? Pooh! pooh!

But we must have room—we must positively
have room for our petticoat at evening parties.
We wanted it before Crinoline. We want it ten
thousand times more now. I don't know how
other parents feel; but unless there is some speedy
reform in the present system of party-giving, so
far as regards health, purse, and temper, I am
a lost man.   Let me make my meaning clear on
this point by a simple and truthful process.   Let
me describe how we went to our last party, and
how we came back from it.

Doctor and Mrs. Crump, of Gloucester Place
(I mention names and places to show the respectable character of the party), kindly requested the
pleasure of our company a week ago. We accepted the invitation, and agreed to assemble in
my dining-room previous to departure at the hour
of half-past nine. It is unnecessary to say that
I and my son-in-law (who is now staying with

me on a visit) had the room entirely to ourselves at the appointed time. We waited half an hour: both ill-tempered, both longing to be in bed, and both obstinately silent. When the hall clock struck ten, a sound was heard on the stairs as if a whole gale of wind had broken into the house, and was advancing to the dining-room to blow us both into empty space. We knew what this meant, and looked at each other, and said, "Here they are!" The door opened, and Boreas swam in voluptuously, in the shape of my wife, in claret-colored velvet. She stands five feet nine, and wears—No! I have never actually counted them. Let me not mislead the public, or do injustice to my wife. Let me rest satisfied with stating her height, and adding that she is a fashionable woman. Her circumference, and the causes of it, may be left to the imagination of the reader.

She was followed by four minor winds, blowing dead in our teeth—by my married daughter in pink moire antique; by my own Julia (single) in violet tulle illusion; by my own Emily (single) in white lace over glace silk; by my own Charlotte (single) in blue gauze over glace silk. The four minor winds and the majestic maternal Boreas entirely filled the room, and overflowed on to the dining-table. It was a grand sight. My son-in-law and I—a pair of mere black tadpoles—shrank into a corner, and gazed at it helplessly.

Our corner was, unfortunately, the farthest from the door. So, when I moved to lead the

way to the carriages, I confronted a brilliant in-
termediate expanse of ninety yards of outer clothing alone (allowing only eighteen yards each to
the ladies). Being old, wily, and respected in
the house, I took care to avoid my wife, and succeeded in getting through my daughters. My
son-in-law, young, innocent, and of secondary
position in the family, was not so fortunate. I
left him helpless, looking round the corner of his
mother-in-law's claret-colored velvet, with one of
his legs lost in his wife's moire antique. There
is every reason to suppose that he never extricated
himself; for when we got into the carriages he
was not to be found; and, when ultimately recovered, he exhibited symptoms of physical and
mental exhaustion. I am afraid my son-in-law
caught it—I am very much afraid that, during
my absence, my son-in-law caught it.

We filled—no, we overflowed—two carriages.
My wife and her married daughter in one, and
I myself on the box—the front seat being very
properly wanted for the velvet and the moire antique. In the second carriage were my three
girls—crushed, as they indignantly informed me,
crushed out of all shape (didn't I tell you just
now how plump one of them was?) by the miserably inefficient accommodation which the vehicle
offered to them. They told my son-in-law, as he
meekly mounted to the box, that they would take
care not to marry a man like him, at any rate!
I have not the least idea what he had done to pro-
voke them. The worthy creature gets a great
deal of scolding in the house, without any assign-

able cause for it. Do my daughters resent his official knowledge, as a husband, of the secret of their sister's ugly feet? Oh, dear me, I hope not —I sincerely hope not!

At ten minutes past ten we drove to the hospitable abode of Doctor and Mrs. Crump. The women of my family were then perfectly dressed in the finest materials. There was not a flaw in any part of the costume of any one of the party. This is a great deal to say of ninety yards of clothing, without mentioning the streams of ribbon, and the dense thickets of flowery bushes that wantoned gracefully all over their heads and half down their backs—nevertheless, I can say it.

At forty minutes past four the next morning we were all assembled once more in my dining-room, to light our bedroom candles. Judging by costume only, I should not have known one of my daughters again—no, not one of them! The tulle illusion was illusion no longer. My daughter's gorgeous substratum of gros de Naples bulged through it in half a dozen places. The pink moire antique was torn into a draggle-tailed pink train. The white lace was in tatters, and the blue gauze was in shreds.

"A charming party!" cried my daughters, in melodious chorus, as I surveyed this scene of ruin. Charming, indeed! If I had dressed up my four girls, and sent them to Greenwich Fair, with strict orders to get drunk and assault the police, and if they had carefully followed my directions, could they have come home to me in a much worse condition than the condition in which

I see them now? Could any man not acquainted with the present monstrous system of party-giving look at my four young women and believe that they had been spending the evening, under the eyes of their parents, at a respectable house? If the party had been at a linen-draper's, I could understand the object of this wanton destruction of property. But Doctor Crump is not interested in making me buy new gowns. What have I done to him that he should ask me and my family to his house, and all but tear my children's gowns off their backs, in return for our friendly readiness to accept his invitation?

But my daughters danced all the evening, and these little accidents will happen in private ballrooms. Indeed? I did not dance, my wife did not dance, my son-in-law did not dance. Have we escaped injury on that account? Decidedly not. Velvet is not an easy thing to tear, so I have no rents to deplore in my wife's dress. But I apprehend that a spoonful of trifle does not reach its destination properly when it is deposited in a lady's lap; and I altogether deny that there is any necessary connection between the charms of society and the wearing of crushed macaroons adhesively dotted over the back part of a respectable matron's dress. I picked three off my wife's gown, as she swam out of the dining-room, on her way upstairs; and I am informed that two new breadths will be wanted in front, in consequence of her lap having been turned into a plate for trifle. As for my son-in-law, his trousers are saturated with spilled Champagne; and he took, in my presence, nearly a handful of flabby lobster salad out of the cavity between his shirt-front and his waistcoat. For myself, I have had my elbow in a game pie, and I see with disgust a slimy path of extinct custard meandering down the left hand lappel of my coat. Altogether, this party, on the lowest calculation, casts me in damages to the tune of ten pounds eighteen shillings and six-pence.*

In damages for spoiled garments only. I have still to find out what the results may be of the suffocating heat in the rooms, and the freezing draughts in the passages and on the stairs—I have still to face the possible doctor's bills for treating our influenzas and our rheumatisms. And to what cause is all this destruction and dis-comfort attributable? Plainly and simply, to this. When Doctor and Mrs. Crump issued their invitations, they followed the example of the rest of the world, and asked to their house five times as many people as their rooms would comfortably

---

* For the information of ignorant young men who are beginning life, I subjoin the lamentable particulars of this calculation:

	£.	s.	d.
A Tulle Illusion spoiled	2	0	0
Repairing gathers of Moiré Antique . . .	0	5	0
Cheap white lace dress spoiled	3	0	0
Do. blue gauze do.	1	6	0
Two new breadths of velvet for Mamma .	4	0	0
Cleaning my son-in-law's trousers . . .	0	2	6
Cleaning my own coat	0	5	0
Total	10	18	6

hold. Hence, jostling, bumping, and tearing among the dancers, and jostling, bumping, and spilling in the supper-room. Hence, a scene of barbarous crowding and confusion, in which the successful dancers are the heaviest and rudest couples in the company, and the successful guests at the supper-table the people who have the least regard for the restraints of politeness and the wants of their neighbors.

Is there no remedy for this great social nuisance? for a nuisance it certainly is. There is a remedy in every district in London, in the shape of a spacious and comfortable public room, which may be had for the hiring. The rooms to which I allude are never used for doubtful purposes. They are mainly devoted to Lectures, Concerts, and Meetings. When used for a private object, they might be kept private by giving each guest a card to present at the door, just as cards are presented at the opera. The expense of the hiring, when set against the expense of preparing a private house for a party, and the expense of the injuries whcih crowding causes, would prove to be next to nothing. The supper might be sent into the large room as it is sent into the small house. And what benefit would be gained by all this? The first and greatest of all benefits, in such cases—room. Room for the dancers to exercise their art in perfect comfort; room for the spectators to move about and talk to each other at their ease; room for the musicians in a comfortable gallery; room for eating and drinking; room for agreeable equal ventilation. In one word, all the acknowledged advantages of a public ball, with all the pleasant social freedom of a private entertainment.

And what hinders the adopting of this sensible reform? Nothing but the domestic vanity of my beloved countrymen.

I suggested the hiring of a room the other day to an excellent friend of mine who thought of giving a party, and who inhumanly contemplated asking at least a hundred people into his trumpery little ten-roomed house. He absolutely shuddered when I mentioned my idea; all his insular prejudices bristled up in an instant. "If I can't receive my friends under my own roof, on my own hearth, sir, and in my own home, I won't receive them at all. Take a room, indeed! Do you call that an Englishman's hospitality? I don't." It was quite useless to suggest to this gentleman that an Englishman's hospitality, or any man's hospitality, is unworthy of the name unless it fulfills the first great requisite of making his guests comfortable. We don't take that far-fetched view of the case in this domestic country. We stand on our own floor (no matter whether it is only twelve feet square or not); we make a fine show in our houses (no matter whether they are large enough for the purpose or not); never mind the women's dresses; never mind the dancers being in perpetual collision; never mind the supper being a comfortless, barbarous scramble; never mind the ventilation alternating between unbearable heat and unbearable cold — an Englishman's house is his castle, even when you

can't get up his staircase, and can't turn round
in his rooms.   If I lived in the Black Hole at Cal-
cutta, sir, I would see my friends *there* because
I lived there, and would turn up my nose at the
finest marble palace in the whole city, because it
was a palace that could be had for the hiring!

And yet the innovation on a senseless established custom which I now propose is not without precedent, even in this country.   When I was
a young man, I and some of my friends used to
give a Bachelors' Ball once a year.   We hired a
respectable public room for the purpose.   Nobody
ever had admission to our entertainment who was
not perfectly fit to be asked into any gentleman's
house.   Nobody wanted room to dance in; nobody's dress was injured; nobody was uncomfortable at supper.   Our ball was looked forward
to every year by the young ladies as the especial
dance of the season, at which they were sure to
enjoy themselves.   They talked rapturously of
the charming music, and the brilliant lighting,
and the pretty decorations, and the nice supper.
Old ladies and gentlemen used to beg piteously
that they might not be left out on account of
their years.   People of all ages and tastes found
something to please them at the Bachelors' Ball,
and never had a recollection in connection with
it which was not of the happiest nature.   What
prevents us, now we are married, from following
the sensible proceeding of our younger days?
The stupid assumption that my house must be
big enough to hold all my friends comfortably,
because it is my house.   I did not reason in that

way when I had lodgings, although my bachelor sitting-room was, within a few feet each way, as large as my householder's drawing-room at the present time.

However, I have really some hopes of seeing the sensible reform which I have ventured to propose practically and generally carried out before I die. Not because l advocate it, not because it is in itself essentially reasonable; but merely because the course of Time is likely, before long, to leave obstinate Prejudice no choice of alternatives and no power of resistance. Party-giving is on the increase, party-goers are on the increase, petticoats are on the increase; but private houses remain exactly as they were. It is evidently only a question of time. The guests already overflow on to the staircase. Give us a ten years' increase of the population, and they will overflow into the street. When the door of the Englishman's nonsensical castle cannot be shut, on account of the number of his guests who are squeezed out to the threshold, then he will concede to necessity what he will not now concede to any strength of reasoning, or to any gentleness of persuasion. The only cogent argument with obstinate people is Main Force; and Time, in the case now under consideration, is sooner or later sure to employ it.

CURIOSITIES OF LITERATURE.—II.

PORTRAIT OF AN AUTHOR, PAINTED BY HIS PUBLISHER.

I.

THE Author was born a Frenchman, and died in the year 1850. Over the whole continent of Europe, wherever the literature of France has penetrated, his readers are numbered by tens of thousands. Women of all ranks and orders have singled him out, long since, as the marked man, among modern writers of fiction, who most profoundly knows and most subtly appreciates their sex in its strength and in its weakness. Men whose critical judgment is widely and worthily respected have declared that he is the deepest and truest observer of human nature whom France has produced since the time of Molière. Unquestionably he ranks as one of the few great geniuses who appear by ones and twos, in century after century of authorship, and who leave their mark ineffaceably on the literature of their age. And yet, in spite of this widely-extended continental fame, and this indisputable right and title to enjoy it, there is probably no civilized country in the Old World in which he is so little

known as in England. Among all the readers
—a large class in these islands—who are, from
various causes, unaccustomed to study French
literature in its native language, there are probably very many who have never even heard of
the name of HONORÉ DE BALZAC.

Unaccountable as it may appear at first sight,
the reason why the illustrious author of "Eugenie Grandet," "Le Pere Goriot," and "La
Recherche de l'Absolu" happens to be so little
known to the general public of England is, on
the surface of it, easy enough to discover. Balzac is little known, because he has been little
translated. An English version of "Eugenie
Grandet" was advertised lately as one of a
cheap series of novels. And the present writer
has some indistinct recollection of meeting, many
years since, with a translation of "La Peau de
Chagrin." But so far as he knows, excepting
the instances of these two books, not one other
work out of the whole number of ninety-seven
fictions, long and short, which proceeded from
the same fertile pen, has been offered to our own
readers in our own language. Immense help has
been given in this country to the reputations of
Alexandre Dumas, Victor Hugo, and Eugene
Sue; no help whatever, or next to none, has
been given to Balzac, although he is regarded in
France (and rightly regarded, in some respects)
as a writer of fiction superior to all three.

Many causes, too numerous to be elaborately
traced within the compass of a single article,
have probably contributed to produce this singu-

lar instance of literary neglect. It is not to be denied, for example, that serious difficulties stand in the way of translating Balzac, which are caused by his own peculiarities of style and treatment. His French is not the clear, graceful, neatly-turned French of Voltaire and Rousseau. It is a strong, harsh, solidly vigorous language of his own; now flashing into the most exquisite felicities of expression, and now again involved in an obscurity which only the closest attention can hope to penetrate. A special man, not hurried for time, and not easily brought to the end of his patience, might give the English equivalent of Balzac with admirable effect. But ordinary translating of him by average workmen would only lead, through the means of feeble parody, to the result of utter failure.*

The difficulties, again, caused by his style of treatment are not to be lightly estimated, in considering the question of presenting this author to our own general public. The peculiarity of Balzac's literary execution is, that he never compro-

---

* This sentence has unfortunately proved prophetic. Cheap translations of "Le Père Goriot" and "Le Recherche de l'Absolu" were published soon after the present article appeared in print, with extracts from the opinions here expressed on Balzac's writings appended by way of advertisement. Critical remonstrance in relation to such productions as these would be remonstrance thrown away. It will be enough to say here, by way of warning to the reader, that the experiment of rendering the French of Balzac into its fair English equivalent still remains to be tried.

mises the subtleties and delicacies of Art for any consideration of temporary effect. The frame-work in which his idea is set is always wrought with a loving minuteness which leaves nothing out. Everything which in this writer's mind can even remotely illustrate the characters that he depicts, must be elaborately conveyed to the minds of his readers before the characters themselves start into action. This quality of minute finish, of reiterated refining, which is one of Balzac's great merits, so far as foreign audiences are concerned, is another of the hinderances, so far as an English audience is concerned, in the way of translating him.

Allowing all due weight to the force of these obstacles; and further admitting that Balzac lays himself open to grave objection (on the part of that unhappily large section of the English public which obstinately protests against the truth wherever the truth is painful) as a writer who sternly insists on presenting the dreary aspects of human life, literally, exactly, nakedly, as he finds them—making these allowances, and many more if more be needful—it is still impossible not to regret, for the sake of readers themselves, that worthy English versions of the best works of this great writer are not added to the national library of translated literature. Toward the latter part of his career, Balzac's own taste in selection of subject seems to have become vitiated. His later novels, consummately excellent as some of them were in a literary sense, are assuredly, in a moral sense, not to be defended against the grave accu-

sation of being needlessly and even horribly re-
pulsive. But no objections of this sort apply to
the majority of the works which he produced
when he was in the prime of his life and his faculties. The conception of the character of "Eugenie Grandet" is one of the purest, tenderest,
and most beautiful things in the whole range of
fiction, and the execution of it is even worthy of
the idea. If the translation already accomplished
of this book be only creditably executed, it may
be left to speak for itself. But there are other
fictions of the writer which deserve the same
privilege, and which have not yet obtained it.
"La Recherche de l'Absolu"—a family picture
which, for truth, delicacy, and pathos, has been
surpassed by no novelist of any nation or any
time; a literary achievement in which a new and
an imperishable character (the exquisitely beautiful character of the wife) has been added to the
great gallery of fiction—remains still unknown
to the general public of England. "Le Pere
Goriot"—which, though it unveils some of the
hidden corruptions of Parisian life, unveils them
nobly in the interests of that highest morality belonging to no one nation and no one sect—"Le
Pere Goriot," which stands first and foremost
among all the writer's works, which has drawn
the tears of thousands from the purest sources,
has its appeal still left to make to the sympathies
of English readers. Other shorter stories, scattered about the "Scenes de la Vie Privee," the
"Scenes de la Vie de Province," and the "Scenes
de la Vie Parisienne," are as completely un-

known to a certain circle of readers in this country, and as unquestionably deserve careful and competent translation, as the longer and more elaborate productions of Balzac's inexhaustible pen. Reckoning these shorter stories, there are at least a dozen of his highest achievements in fiction which might be safely rendered into English; which might form a series by themselves; and which no sensible Englishwoman could read and be, either intellectually or morally, the worse for them.

Thus much, in the way of necessary preliminary comment on the works of this author, and on their present position in reference to the English public. Readers who may be sufficiently interested in the subject to desire to know something next about the man himself may now derive this information from a singular, and even from a unique source. The Life of Balzac has been lately written by his publisher, of all the people in the world! This is a phenomenon in itself; and the oddity of it is still further increased by the fact that the publisher was brought to the brink of ruin by the author, that he mentions this circumstance in writing his life, and that it does not detract one iota from his evidently sincere admiration for the great man with whom he was once so disastrously connected in business. Here is surely an original book, in an age when originality grows harder and harder to meet with—a book containing disclosures which will perplex and dismay every admirer of Balzac who cannot separate the man from his works—a

book which presents one of the most singular
records of human eccentricity, so far as the hero
of it is concerned, and of human credulity so far
as the biographer is concerned, which has probably ever been published for the amusement and
bewilderment of the reading world.

The title of this singular work is, "Portrait
Intime De Balzac; sa Vie, son Humeur et son
Caractere. Par Edmond Werdet, son ancien
Libraire-Editeur." Before, however, we allow
Monsieur Werdet to relate his own personal experience ·of the celebrated writer, it will be ad-
visable to introduce the subject by giving an
outline of the struggles, the privations, and the
disappointments which marked the early life of
Balzac, and which, doubtless, influenced his after-
character for the worse. These particulars are
given by Monsieur Werdet in the form of an
episode, and are principally derived, on his part,
from information afforded by the author's sister.

Honore de Balzac was born in the city of
Tours, on the sixteenth of May, seventeen hundred and ninety-nine. His parents were people
of rank and position in the world. His father
held a legal appointment in the council-chamber
of Louis XVI. His mother was the daughter
of one of the directors of the public hospital of
Paris. She was much younger than her husband, and brought him a rich dowry. Honore
was her first-born; and he retained throughout
life his first feeling of childish reverence for his
mother. That mother suffered the unspeakable

affliction of seeing her illustrious son taken from her by death at the age of fifty years. Balzac breathed his last in the kind arms which had first caressed him on the day of his birth.

His father, from whom he evidently inherited much of the eccentricity of his character, is described as a compound of Montaigne, Rabelais, and Uncle Toby—a man in manners, conversation, and disposition generally, of the quaintly original sort. On the breaking out of the Revolution, he lost his court situation, and obtained a place in the commissariat department of the Army of the North. This appointment he held for some years. It was of the greater importance to him, in consequence of the change for the worse produced in the pecuniary circumstances of the family by the convulsion of the Revolution.

At the age of seven years, Balzac was sent to the College of Vendome; and for seven years more there he remained. This period of his life was never a pleasant one in his remembrance. The reduced circumstances of his family exposed him to much sordid persecution and ridicule from the other boys, and he got on but little better with the masters. They reported him as idle and incapable—or, in other words, as ready enough to devour all sorts of books on his own desultory plan, but hopelessly obstinate in resisting the educational discipline of the school. This time of his life he has reproduced in one of the strangest and the most mystical of all his novels, "La Vie Intellectuelle de Louis Lambert."

On reaching the critical age of fourteen, his intellect appears to have suffered under a species of eclipse, which occurred very suddenly and mysteriously, and the cause of which neither his masters nor the medical men were able to explain. He himself always declared in after-life, with a touch of his father's quaintness, that his brain had been attacked by "a congestion of ideas." Whatever the cause might be, the effect was so serious that the progress of his education had to be stopped, and his removal from the college followed as a matter of course. Time, care, quiet, and breathing his native air, gradually restored him to himself, and he was ultimately enabled to complete his studies at two private schools. Here again, however, he did nothing to distinguish himself among his fellow-pupils. He read incessantly, and preserved the fruits of his reading with marvelous power of memory; but the school-teaching, which did well enough for ordinary boys, was exactly the species of teaching from which the essentially original mind of Balzac recoiled in disgust. All that he felt and did at this period has been carefully reproduced by his own pen in the earlier pages of "Le Lys dans la Vallee."

Badly as he got on at school, he managed to imibe a sufficient quantity of conventional learning to entitle him, at the age of eighteen, to his degree of Bachelor of Arts. He was destined for the law; and after attending the legal lectures in the various Institutions of Paris, he passed his examination by the time he was twenty, and then entered a notary's office in the capacity of clerk. There were two other clerks to keep him company, who hated the drudgery of the law as heartily as he hated it himself. One of them was the future author of "The Mysteries of Paris," Eugène Sue; the other was the famous critic, Jules Janin.

After he had been engaged in this office and in another for more than three years, a legal friend, who was under great obligations to Balzac the father, offered to give up his business as a notary to Balzac the son. To the great scandal of the family, Honore resolutely refused the offer—for the one sufficient reason that he had determined to be the greatest writer in France. His relations began by laughing at him, and ended by growing angry with him. But nothing moved Honore. His vanity was of the calm, settled sort; and his own conviction that his business in life was simply to be a famous man, proved too strong to be shaken by anybody.

While he and his family were at war on this point, a change for the worse occurred in the elder Balzac's official circumstances. He was superannuated. The diminution of income thus produced was followed by a pecuniary catastrophe. He had embarked almost the whole of his own little remaining property and his wife's in two speculations, and they both failed. No resource was now left him but to retire to a small country house in the neighborhood of Paris, which he had purchased in his prosperous days, and to live there as well as might be on the wreck of his lost fort-

une. Honore, sticking fast to the hopeless business of becoming a great man, was, by his own
desire, left alone in a Paris garret, with an allowance of five pounds English a month, which was
all the kind father could spare to feed, clothe, and
lodge the wrong-headed son.

And now, without a literary friend to help him
in all Paris; alone in his wretched attic, with his
deal table and his truckle-bed, his dog-eared
books, his bescrawled papers, his wild vanity,
and his ravenous hunger for fame, Balzac stripped
resolutely for the great fight. He was then twenty-
three years old—a sturdy fellow to look at, with
a big, jovial face, and a strong, square forehead
topped by a very untidy and superfluous allowance of long, tangled hair. His only difficulty
at starting was what to begin upon. After con-
suming many lonely months in sketching out
comedies, operas, and novels, he finally obeyed
the one disastrous rule which seems to admit of
no exception in the early lives of men of letters,
and fixed the whole bent of his industry and his
genius on the production of a tragedy. After
infinite pains and long labor, the great work was
completed. The subject was Cromwell; and the
treatment, in Balzac's hands, appears to have
been so inconceivably bad, that even his own
family—to say nothing of other judicious friends
—told him in the plainest terms, when he read
it to them, that he had perpetrated a signal failure. Modest men might have been discouraged by
this. Balzac took his manuscript back to his garret, standing higher in his own estimation than

ever. "I will give up being a great dramatist," he told his parents at parting, "and I will be a great novelist instead." The vanity of the man expressed itself with this sublime disregard of ridicule all through his life. It was a precious quality to him—it is surely (however unquestionably offensive it may be to our friends) a precious quality to all of us. What man ever yet did anything great without beginning with a profound belief in his own untried powers?

Confident as ever, therefore, in his own resources, Balzac now took up the pen once more —this time in the character of a novelist. But another and a serious check awaited him at the outset. Fifteen months of solitude, privation, and reckless hard writing—months which are recorded in the pages of "La Peau de Chagrin" with a fearful and pathetic truth, drawn straight from the bitterest of all experiences, the experience of studious poverty—had reduced him to a condition of bodily weakness which made all present exertion of his mental powers simply hopeless, and which obliged him to take refuge—a worn-out, wasted man, in his twenty-fifth year, in his father's quiet little country house. Here, under his mother's care, his exhausted energies slowly revived; and here, in the first days of his convalescence, he returned, with the grim resolution of despair, to working out the old dream in the garret, to resuming the old hopeless business of making himself a great man.

It was under his father's roof, during the time of his slow recovery, that the youthful fictions of

Balzac were produced. The strength of his belief in his own resources and his own future gave
him also the strength, in relation to these first
efforts, to rise above his own vanity, and to see
plainly that he had not yet learned to do himself
full justice. His early novels bore on their title
pages a variety of feigned names; for the starving, struggling author was too proud to acknowledge them, so long as they failed to satisfy his
own conception of what his own powers could
accomplish. These first efforts—now included
in the Belgian editions of his collected works,
and comprising among them two stories, "Jane
la Pâle" and "Le Vicaire des Ardennes," which
show unquestionable dawnings of the genius of
a great writer—were originally published by the
lower and more rapacious order of booksellers,
and did as little toward increasing his means as
toward establishing his reputation. Still, he
forced his way slowly and resolutely through
poverty, obscurity, and disappointment, nearer
and nearer to the promised land which no eye
saw but his own—a greater man, by far, at this
hard period of his adversity than at the more trying after-time of his prosperity and his fame. One
by one the heavy years rolled on, till he was a
man of thirty; and then the great prize which
he had so long toiled for dropped within his reach
at last. In the year eighteen hundred and twenty-
nine, the famous "Physiologie du Mariage" was
published; and the starveling of the Paris garret
became a name and a power in French literature.

In England this book would have been universally condemned as an unpardonable exposure of the most sacred secrets of domestic life. It unveils the whole social side of Marriage in its innermost recesses, and exhibits it alternately in its bright and dark aspects with a marvelous minuteness of observation, a profound knowledge of human nature, and a daring eccentricity of style and arrangement which amply justify the extraordinary success of the book on its first appearance in France. It may be more than questionable, judging from the English point of view, whether such a subject should ever have been selected for any other than the most serious, reverent, and forbearing treatment. Setting this objection aside, however, in consideration of the French point of view, it cannot be denied that the merits of the "Physiology of Marriage," as a piece of writing, were by no means overestimated by the public to which it was addressed. In a literary sense, the book would have done credit to a man in the maturity of his powers. As the work of a man whose intellectual life was only beginning, it was such an achievement as is not often recorded in the history of modern literature.

This first triumph of the future novelist—obtained, curiously enough, by a book which was not a novel—failed to smooth the way onward and upward for Balzac as speedily and pleasantly as might have been supposed. He had another stumble on that hard road of his before he fairly started on the career of success. Soon after the publication of "The Physiology of Marriage" an unlucky idea of strengthening his resources by trading in literature, as well as by writing books, seems to have occurred to him. He tried book-selling and printing; proved himself to be, in both cases, probably the very worst man of business who ever lived and breathed in this world; failed in the most hopeless way, with the most extraordinary rapidity; and so learned at last, by the cruel teaching of experience, that his one fair chance of getting money lay in sticking fast to his pen for the rest of his days. In the next ten years of his life that pen produced the noble series of fictions which influenced French literature far and wide, and which will last in public remembrance long after the miserable errors and inconsistencies of the writer's personal character are forgotten. This was the period when Balzac was in the full enjoyment of his matured intellectual powers and his enviable public celebrity; and this was also the golden time when his publisher and biographer first became acquainted with him. Now, therefore, Monsieur Werdet may be encouraged to come forward and take the post of honor as narrator of the strange story that is still to be told; for now he is placed in the fit position to address himself intelligibly, as well as amusingly, to an English audience.

The story opens with the starting of Monsieur Werdet as a publisher in Paris on his own account. The modest capital at his command amounted to just one hundred and twenty pounds

English; and his leading idea, on beginning business, was to become the publisher of Balzac.

He had already entered into transactions on a large scale with his favorite author, in the character of agent for a publishing house of high standing. He had been very well received, on that first occasion, as a man representing undeniable capital and a great commercial position. On the second occasion, however, of his representing nobody but himself, and nothing but the smallest of existing capitals, he very wisely secured the protection of an intimate friend of Balzac's, to introduce him as favorably as might be for the second time. Accompanied by this gentleman, whose name was Monsieur Barbier, and carrying his capital in his pocketbook, the embryo publisher nervously presented himself in the sanctum sanctorum of the great man.

Monsieur Barbier having carefully explained the business on which they came, Balzac addressed himself, with an indescribable suavity and grandeur of manner, to anxious Monsieur Werdet.

"Just so," said the eminent man. "You are doubtless possessed, sir, of considerable capital? You are probably aware that no man can hope to publish for ME who is not prepared to assert himself magnificently in the matter of cash? I sell high—high—very high. And, not to deceive you—for I am incapable of suppressing the truth—I am a man who requires to be dealt with on the principle of considerable advances. Proceed, sir—I am prepared to listen to you."

But Monsieur Werdet was too cautious to proceed without strengthening his position before starting. He intrenched himself instantly behind his pocketbook.

One by one the notes of the Bank of France which formed the poor publisher's small capital were drawn out of their snug hiding-place. Monsieur Werdet produced six of them, representing five hundred francs each (or, as before mentioned, a hundred and twenty pounds sterling), arranged them neatly and impressively in a circle on the table, and then cast himself on the author's mercy in an agitated voice, and in these words:

"Sir, behold my capital. There lies my whole fortune. It is yours in exchange for any book you please to write for me—"

At that point, to the horror and astonishment of Monsieur Werdet, his further progress was cut short by roars of laughter—formidable roars, as he himself expressly states—bursting from the lungs of the highly-diverted Balzac.

"What astonishing simplicity!" exclaimed the great man. "Do you actually believe, sir, that I—De Balzac—can so entirely forget what is due to myself as to sell you any conceivable species of fiction which is the product of MY PEN for the sum of three thousand francs? You have come here, Monsieur Werdet, to address an offer to me, without preparing yourself by previous reflection. If I felt so disposed, I should have every right to consider your conduct as unbecoming in the highest degree. But I don't feel so disposed. On the contrary, I can even allow your honest ignorance, your innocent confidence, to excuse you in my estimation. Don't be alarmed, sir. Consider yourself excused to a certain extent."

Between disappointment, indignation, and astonishment, Monsieur Werdet was struck dumb. His friend, Monsieur Barbier, therefore spoke for him, urging every possible consideration; and finally proposing that Balzac, if he was determined not to write a new story for three thousand francs, should at least sell one edition of an old one for that sum. Monsieur Barbier's arguments were admirably put; they lasted a long time; and when they had come to an end, they received this reply:

"Gentlemen!" cried Balzac, pushing back his long hair from his heated temples, and taking a fresh dip of ink, "you have wasted an hour of MY TIME in talking of trifles. I rate the pecuniary loss thus occasioned to me at two hundred francs. My time is my capital. I must work. Gentlemen! leave me." Having expressed himself in these hospitable terms, the great man immediately resumed the process of composition.

Monsieur Werdet, naturally and properly indignant, immediately left the room. He was overtaken, after he had proceeded a little distance in the street, by his friend Barbier, who had remained behind to remonstrate.

"You have every reason to be offended," said Barbier. "His conduct is inexcusable. But pray don't suppose that your negotiation is broken off. I know him better than you do; and I tell you that you have nailed Balzac. He wants money, and before three days are over your head he will return your visit."

"If he does," replied Werdet, "I'll pitch him out window."

"No, you won't," said Barbier. "In the first place, it is an extremely uncivil proceeding to pitch a man out of window; and, as a naturally polite gentleman, you are incapable of committing a breach of good manners. In the second place, rude as he has been to you, Balzac is not the less a man of genius; and as such, he is just the man of whom you, as a publisher, stand in need. Wait patiently; and in a day or two you will see him, or hear from him again."

Barbier was right. Three days afterward, the following satisfactory communication was received by Monsieur Werdet:

"My brain, sir, was so prodigiously preoccupied by work uncongenial to my fancy, when you visited me the other day, that I was incapable of comprehending otherwise than imperfectly what it was that you wanted of me.

"To-day my brain is not preoccupied. Do me the favor to come and see me at four o'clock.

"A thousand civilities.   DE BALZAC."

Monsieur Werdet viewed this singular note in the light of a fresh impertinence. On consideration, however, he acknowledged it, and curtly added that important business would prevent his accepting the appointment proposed to him.

In two days more friend Barbier came with a second invitation from the great man. But Monsieur Werdet steadily refused it. "Balzac has already been playing his game with me," he said. "Now it is my turn to play my game with Balzac. I mean to keep him waiting four days longer."

At the end of that time Monsieur Werdet once more entered the sanctum sanctorum. On this second occasion, Balzac's graceful politeness was indescribable. He deplored the rarity of intelligent publishers. He declared his deep sense of the importance of an intelligent publisher's appearance on the literary horizon. He expressed himself as quite enchanted to be now enabled to remark that appearance, to welcome it, and even to deal with it. Polite as he was by nature, Monsieur Werdet had no chance this time against Monsieur De Balzac. In the race of civility the publisher was now nowhere, and the author made all the running.

The interview, thus happily begun, terminated in a most agreeable transaction on both sides. Balzac cheerfully locked up the six bank-notes in his strong-box. Werdet as cheerfully retired, with a written agreement in his empty pocket-book, authorizing him to publish the second edition of "Le Medecin de Campagne"—hardly, it may be remarked in parenthesis, one of the best to select of the novels of Balzac.

II.

Once started in business as the happy proprietor and hopeful publisher of the second edition of
"Le Medecin de Campagne," Monsieur Werdet
was too wise a man not to avail himself of the
only certain means of success in modern times.
He puffed magnificently.   Every newspaper in
Paris was inundated with a deluge of advertise-
ments, announcing the forthcoming work in terms
of eulogy such as the wonderstruck reader had
never met with before.   The result, aided by
Balzac's celebrity, was a phenomenon in the
commercial history of French literature at that
time.   Every copy of the second edition of "Le
Medecin de Campagne" was sold in eight days.

This success established Monsieur Werdet's
reputation.   Young authors crowded to him
with their manuscripts, all declaring piteously
that they wrote in the style of Balzac.   But
Monsieur Werdet flew at higher game.   He received the imitators politely, and even published
for one or two of them; but the high business
aspirations which now glowed within him were
all concentrated on the great original.   He had
conceived the sublime idea of becoming Balzac's
sole publisher; of buying up all his copyrights
held by other houses, and of issuing all his new
works that were yet to be written.   Balzac himself welcomed this proposal with superb indulgence.   "Walter Scott," he said in his grandest
way, "had only one publisher—Archibald Constable.   Work out your idea.   I authorize it; I

support it. I will be Scott, and you shall be Constable!"

Fired by the prodigious future thus disclosed to him, Monsieur Werdet assumed forthwith the character of a French Constable, and opened negotiations with no less than six publishers who held among them the much-desired copyrights. His own enthusiasm did something for him; his excellent previous character in the trade, and his remarkable success at starting, did much more. The houses he dealt with took his bills in all directions, without troubling him for security. After innumerable interviews and immense exercise of diplomacy, he raised himself at last to the pinnacle of his ambition; he became sole proprietor and publisher of the works of Balzac.

The next question—a sordid, but, unhappily, a necessary question also—was how to turn this precious acquisition to the best pecuniary account. Some of the works, such as "La Physiologie du Mariage" and "La Peau de Chagrin," had produced, and were still producing, large sums. Others, on the contrary, such as the "Contes Philosophiques" (which were a little too profound for the public) and "Louis Lambert" (which was intended to popularize the mysticism of Swedenborg), had not yet succeeded in paying their expenses. Estimating his speculation by what he had in hand, Monsieur Werdet had not much chance of seeing his way speedily to quick returns. Estimating it, however, by what was coming in the future—that is to say, by the promised privilege of issuing all the writer's

contemplated works—he had every reason to
look happily and hopefully at his commercial
prospects.   At this crisis of the narrative, when
the publisher's credit and fortune depended
wholly on the pen of one man, the history of
that man's habits of literary composition assumes
a special interest and importance.   Monsieur
Werdet's description of Balzac at his writing-
desk presents by no means the least extraordinary of the many singular revelations which
compose the story of the author's life.

When he had once made up his mind to produce a new book, Balzac's first proceeding was
to think it out thoroughly before he put pen to
paper.   He was not satisfied with possessing himself of the main idea only; he followed it mentally into its minutest ramifications, devoting to the
process just that amount of patient hard labor
and self-sacrifice which no inferior writer ever
has the common sense or the courage to bestow
on his work.   With his note-book ready in his
hand, Balzac studied his scenes and characters
straight from life.   General knowledge of what
he wanted to describe was not enough for this
determined realist.   If he found himself in the
least at fault, he would not hesitate to take a
long journey merely to insure truth to nature in
describing the street of a country town, or in
painting some minor peculiarity of rustic character.   In Paris he was perpetually about the
streets, perpetually penetrating into all classes
of society, to study the human nature about him
in its minutest varieties.   Day by day, and week

by week, his note-book and his brains were hard
at work together, before he thought of sitting
down to his desk to begin. When he had finally
amassed his materials in this laborious manner,
he at last retired to his study; and from that
time till his book had gone to press society saw
him no more.

His house door was now closed to everybody
except the publisher and the printer, and his costume was changed to a loose white robe, of the
sort which is worn by the Dominican monks.
This singular writing-dress was fastened round
the waist by a chain of Venetian gold, to which
hung little pliers and scissors of the same precious metal. White Turkish trousers, and red
morocco slippers, embroidered with gold, covered his legs and feet. On the day when he sat
down to his desk the light of heaven was shut
out, and he worked by the light of candles in
superb silver sconces. Even letters were not allowed to reach him. They were all thrown, as
they came, into a japan vase, and not opened, no
matter how important they might be, [till his
work was all over. He rose to begin writing at
two in the morning, continued with extraordinary rapidity, till six; then took his warm bath,
and stopped in it, thinking, for an hour or more.
At eight o'clock his servant brought him up a
cup of coffee. Before nine his publisher was admitted to carry away what he had done. From
nine till noon he wrote on again, always at the
top of his speed. At noon he breakfasted on
eggs, with a glass of water and a second cup of

coffee. From one o'clock to six he returned to work. At six he dined lightly, only allowing himself one glass of wine. From seven to eight he received his publisher again: and at eight o'clock he went to bed. This life he led, while he was writing his books, for two months together, without intermission. Its effect on his health was such that, when he appeared once more among his friends, he looked, in the popular phrase, like his own ghost. Chance acquaintances would hardly have known him again.

It must not be supposed that this life of resolute seclusion and fierce hard toil ended with the complexion of the first draught of his manuscript. At the point where, in the instances of most men, the serious part of the work would have come to an end, it had only begun for Balzac.

In spite of all the preliminary studying and thinking, when his pen had scrambled its way straight through to the end of the book, the leaves were all turned back again, and the first manuscript was altered into a second with inconceivable patience and care. Innumerable corrections and interlinings, to begin with, led, in the end, to transpositions and expansions which metamorphosed the entire work. Happy thoughts were picked out of the beginning of the manuscript, and inserted where they might have a better effect at the end. Others at the end would be moved to the beginning, or the middle. In one place, chapters would be expanded to three or four times their original length; in another, abridged to a few paragraphs; in a third, taken out alto-

gether or shifted to new positions. With all this
mass of alterations in every page, the manuscript
was at last ready for the printer. Even to the
experienced eyes in the printing-office, it was
now all but illegible. The deciphering it, and
setting it up in a moderately correct form, cost
an amount of patience and pains which wearied
out all the best men in the office, one after another, before the first series of proofs could be
submitted to the author's eye. When these were
at last complete, they were sent in on large slips,
and the indefatigable Balzac immediately set to
work to rewrite the whole book for the third
time!

He now covered with fresh corrections, fresh
alterations, fresh expansions of this passage, and
fresh abridgments of that, not only the margins
of the proofs all round, but even the little intervals of white space between the paragraphs.
Lines crossing each other in indescribable con
fusion were supposed to show the bewildered
printer the various places at which the multitude of new insertions were to be slipped in.
Illegible as Balzac's original manuscripts were,
his corrected proofs were more hopelessly puz-
zling still. The picked men in the office, to
whom alone they could be intrusted, shuddered
at the very name of Balzac, and relieved each
other at intervals of an hour, beyond which time
no one printer could be got to continue at work
on the universally execrated and universally unintelligible proofs. The "revises"—that is to
say, the proofs embodying the new alterations—

were next pulled to pieces in their turn. Two, three, and sometimes four, separate sets of them were required before the author's leave could be got to send the perpetually rewritten book to press at last, and so have done with it. He was literally the terror of all printers and editors; and he himself described his process of work as a misfortune, to be the more deplored, because it was, in his case, an intellectual necessity. "I toil sixteen hours out of the twenty-four," he said, "over the elaboration of my unhappy style; and I am never satisfied myself when all is done."

Looking back to the school-days of Balzac, when his mind suffered under the sudden and mysterious shock which has already been described in its place; remembering that his father's character was notorious for its eccentricity; observing the prodigious toil, the torture almost of mind which the act of literary production seems to have cost him all through life, it is impossible not to arrive at the conclusion that in his case there must have been a fatal incompleteness somewhere in the mysterious intellectual machine. Magnificently as it was endowed, the balance of faculties in his mind seems to have been even more than ordinarily imperfect. On this theory, his unparalleled difficulties in expressing himself as a writer, and his errors, inconsistencies, and meannesses of character as a man, become, at least, not wholly unintelligible. On any other theory, all explanation both of his personal life and his literary life appears to be simply impossible.

Such was the perilous pen on which Monsieur Werdet's prospects in life all depended. If Balzac failed to perform his engagements punctually, or if his health broke down under his severe literary exertions, the commercial decease of his unfortunate publisher followed either disaster, purely as a matter of course.

At the outset, however, the posture of affairs looked encouragingly enough. On its completion in the *Revue de Paris*, "Le Lys dans la Vallee" was republished by Monsieur Werdet, who had secured his interest in the work by a timely advance of six thousand francs. Of this novel (the most highly valued in France of all the writer's fictions) but two hundred copies of the first edition were left unsold within two hours after its publication. This unparalleled success kept Monsieur Werdet's head above water, and encouraged him to hope great things from the next novel, "Seraphita," which was also begun periodically in the *Revue de Paris*. Before it was finished, however, Balzac and the editor of the Review quarreled. The long-suffering publisher was obliged to step in and pay the author's forfeit-money, obtaining the incomplete novel in return, and with it Balzac's promise to finish the work offhand. Months passed, however, and not a page of manuscript was produced. One morning at eight o'clock, to Monsieur Werdet's horror and astonishment, Balzac burst in on him in a condition of sublime despair, to announce that he and his genius had to all appearance parted company forever.

"My brain is empty!" cried the great man. "My imagination is dried up! Hundreds of cups of coffee and two warm baths a day have done nothing for me. Werdet, I am a lost man!"

The publisher thought of his empty cash-box, and was petrified. The author proceeded:

"I must travel!" he exclaimed, distractedly. "My genius has run away from me—I must pursue it over mountains and valleys. Werdet! I must catch my genius up!"

Poor Monsieur Werdet faintly suggested a little turn in the immediate neighborhood of Paris —something equivalent to a nice airy ride to Hampstead on the top of an omnibus. But Balzac's runaway genius had, in the estimation of its bereaved proprietor, got as far as Vienna already; and he coolly announced his intention of traveling after it to the Austrian capital.

"And who is to finish 'Seraphita'?" inquired the unhappy publisher. "My illustrious friend, you are ruining me!"

"On the contrary," remarked Balzac, persuasively, "I am making your fortune. At Vienna I shall find my genius. At Vienna I shall finish 'Seraphita,' and a new book besides. At Vienna I shall meet with an angelic woman who admires me—she permits me to call her 'Carissima'—she has written to invite me to Vienna. I ought, I must, I will, accept the invitation."

Here an ordinary acquaintance would have had an excellent opportunity of saying something smart. But poor Monsieur Werdet was not in a position to be witty; and, moreover, he knew but too well what was coming next. All he ventured to say was:

"But I am afraid you have no money."

"You can raise some," replied his illustrious friend. "Borrow—deposit stock in trade—get me two thousand francs. Everything else I can do for myself. Werdet, I will hire a post-chaise —I will dine with my dear sister—I will set off after dinner—I will not be later than eight o'clock—click-clack!" And the great man executed an admirable imitation of the cracking of a postilion's whip.

There was no resource for Monsieur Werdet but to throw the good money after the bad. He raised the two thousand francs; and away went Balzac to catch his runaway genius, to bask in the society of a female angel, and to coin money in the form of manuscripts.

Eighteen days afterward a perfumed letter from the author reached the publisher. He had caught his genius at Vienna; he had been magnificently received by the aristocracy; he had finished "Seraphita," and nearly completed the other book; his angelic friend, Carissima, already loved Werdet from Balzac's description of him; Balzac himself was Werdet's friend till death; Werdet was his Archibald Constable; Werdet should see him again in fifteen days; Werdet should ride in his carriage in the Bois de Boulogne, and meet Balzac riding in his carriage, and see the enemies of both parties looking on at the magnificent spectacle and bursting with spite. Finally, Werdet would have the goodness to remark (in a postscript) that Balzac had provided himself with another little advance of fifteen hundred francs, received from Rothschild in Vienna, and had given in exchange a bill at ten days' sight on his excellent publisher, on his admirable and devoted Archibald Constable.

While Monsieur Werdet was still prostrate under the effect of this audacious postscript, a clerk entered his office with the identical bill. It was drawn at one day's sight instead of ten; and the money was wanted immediately. The publisher was the most long-suffering of men; but there were limits even to his patient endurance. He took Balzac's letter with him, and went at once to the office of the Parisian Rothschild. The great financier received him kindly, admitted that there must have been some mistake, granted the ten days' grace, and dismissed his visitor with this excellent and sententious piece of advice:

"1 recommend you to mind what you are about, sir, with Monsieur De Balzac. He is a highly inconsequent man."

It was too late for Monsieur Werdet to mind what he was about. He had no choice but to lose his credit, or pay at the end of the ten days. He paid; and ten days later Balzac returned, considerately bringing with him some charming little Viennese curiosities for his esteemed publisher. Monsieur Werdet expressed his acknowledgments, and then politely inquired for the conclusion of "Seraphita," and the manuscript of the new novel.

Not a single line of either had been committed to paper.

The farce (undoubtedly a most disgraceful performance, so far as Balzac was concerned) was not played out even yet. The publisher's reproaches seem at last to have awakened the author to something remotely resembling a sense of shame. He promised that "Seraphita," which had been waiting at press a whole year, should be finished in one night. There were just two sheets of sixteen pages each to write. They might have been completed either at the author's house or at the publisher's, which was close to the printer's. But no—it was not in Balzac's character to miss the smallest chance of producing a sensation anywhere. His last caprice was a determination to astonish the printers. Twenty-five compositors were called together at eleven at night, a truckle-bed and table were set up for the author—or, to speak more correctly, for the literary mountebank—in the workshop; Balzac arrived, in a high state of inspiration, to stagger the sleepy journeymen by showing them how fast he could write; and the two sheets were completed magnificently on the spot. By way of fit and proper climax to this ridiculous exhibition of literary quackery, it is only necessary to add that, on Balzac's own confession, the two concluding sheets of "Seraphita" had been mentally composed and carefully committed to memory, two years before he affected to write them impromptu in the printer's office. It seems impossible to deny that the man who could act in this outrageously puerile

manner must have been simply mad. But what
becomes of the imputation when we remember that
this very madman has produced books which, for
depth of thought and marvelous knowledge of
human nature, are counted deservedly among the
glories of French literature, and which were never
more living and more lasting works than they are
at this moment!

"Seraphita" was published three days after the
author's absurd exhibition of himself at the printer's office. In this novel, as in its predecessor—
"Louis Lambert" — Balzac left his own firm
ground of reality, and soared, on the wings of
Swedenborg, into an atmosphere of transcenden-
tal obscurity impervious to all ordinary eyes.
What the book meant the editor of the periodical in which part of it originally appeared never
could explain. Monsieur Werdet, who published
it, confesses that he was in the same mystified
condition; and the present writer, who has vainly
attempted to read it through, desires to add in this
place his own modest acknowledgment of inability to enlighten English readers in the smallest
degree on the subject of "Seraphita." Luckily
for Monsieur Werdet, the author's reputation
stood so high with the public that the book sold
prodigiously, merely because it was a book by
Balzac. The proceeds of the sale, and the profits
derived from new editions of the old novels, kept
the sinking publisher from absolute submersion,
and might even have brought him safely to
land, but for the ever-increasing dead-weight
of the author's perpetual borrowings on the

security of forthcoming works which he never produced.

No commercial success, no generous self-sacrifice could keep pace with the demands of Balzac's insatiate vanity and love of show, at this period of his life. He had two establishments, to begin with, btoh splendidly furnished, and one adorned with a valuable gallery of pictures. He had his box at the French Opera, and his box at the Italian Opera. He had a chariot and horses, and an establishment of men-servants. The panels of the carriage were decorated with the arms, and the bodies of the footmen were adorned with the liveries, of the noble family of D'Entragues, to which Balzac persisted in declaring that he was allied, although he never could produce the smallest proof in support of the statement. When he could add no more to the sumptuous magnificence of his houses, his dinners, his carriage, and his servants; when he had filled his rooms with every species of expensive knickknack; when he had lavished money on all the known extravagances which extravagant Paris can supply to the spendthrift's inventory, he hit on the entirely new idea of providing himself with such a walking-stick as the world had never yet beheld.

His first proceeding was to procure a splendid cane, which was sent to the jeweler's, and was grandly topped by a huge gold knob. The inside of the knob was occupied by a lock of hair presented to the author by an unknown lady admirer. The outside was studded with all the jewels he had bought, and with all the jewels he had received as presents. With this cane, nearly as big as a drum-major's staff, and all ablaze at the top with rubies, diamonds, emeralds, and sapphires, Balzac exhibited himself, in a rapture of satisfied vanity, at the theaters and in the public promenades. The cane became as celebrated in Paris as the author. Madame de Girardin wrote a sparkling little book all about the wonderful walking-stick. Balzac was in the seventh heaven of happiness; Balzac's friends were either disgusted or diverted, according to their tempers. One unfortunate man alone suffered the inevitable penalty of this insane extravagance: need it be added that his name was Werdet?

The end of the connection between the author and the publisher was now fast approaching. All entreaties or reproaches addressed to Balzac failed in producing the slightest result. Even confinement in a sponging-house, when creditors discovered, in course of time, that they could wait no longer, passed unheeded as a warning. Balzac only borrowed more money the moment the key was turned on him, gave a magnificent dinner in prison, and left the poor publisher, as usual, to pay the bill. He was extricated from the sponging-house before he had been there quite three days; and in that time he had spent over twenty guineas on luxuries which he had not a farthing of his own to purchase. It is useless, it is even exasperating, to go on accumulating instances of this sort of mad and cruel prodigality; let us advance rapidly to the end. One morning Monsieur Werdet balanced accounts with his author

from the beginning, and found, in spite of the
large profits produced by the majority of the
works, that fifty-eight thousand francs were (to
use his own expression) paralyzed in his hands
by the life Balzac persisted in leading; and that
fifty-eight thousand more might soon be in the
same condition, if he had possessed them to advance. A rich publisher might have contrived
to keep his footing in such a crisis as this, and
to deal, for the time to come, on purely commercial grounds. But Monsieur Werdet was a
poor man; he had relied on Balzac's verbal prom-
ises when he ought to have exacted his written
engagements; and he had no means of appealing
to the author's love of money by dazzling prospects of bank-notes awaiting him in the future,
if he chose honestly to earn his right to them. In
short, there was but one alternative left, the alternative of giving up the whole purpose and
ambition of the bookseller's life, and resolutely
breaking off his ruinous connection with Balzac.

Reduced to this situation, driven to bay by the
prospect of engagements falling due which he
had no apparent means of meeting, Monsieur
Werdet answered the next application for an advance by a flat refusal, and followed up that un-
exampled act of self-defense by speaking his mind
at last, in no measured terms, to his illustrious
friend. Balzac turned crimson with suppressed
anger, and left the room. A series of business
formalities followed, initiated by Balzac, with the
view of breaking off the connection between his
publisher and himself, now that he found there

was no more money to be had; Monsieur Werdet
being, on his side, perfectly ready to "sign, seal,
and deliver," as soon as his claims were properly
satisfied in due form of law.

Balzac had now but one means of meeting his
liabilities. His personal reputation was gone;
but his literary reputation remained as high as
ever, and he soon found a publisher, with large
capital at command, who was ready to treat for
his copyrights. Monsieur Werdet had no resource but to sell or be bankrupt. He parted
with all the valuable copyrights for a sum of sixty
thousand and odd francs, which sufficed to meet
his most pressing engagements. Some of the less
popular and less valuable books he kept, to help
him, if possible, through his daily and personal
liabilities. As for gaining any absolute profit, or
even holding his position as a publisher, the bare
idea of securing either advantage was dismissed
as an idle dream. The purpose for which he had
toiled so hard and suffered so patiently was sacrificed forever, and he was reduced to beginning
life again as a country traveler for a prosperous
publishing house. So far as his main object in
existence was concerned, Balzac had plainly and
literally ruined him. It is impossible to part with
Monsieur Werdet, imprudent and credulous as he
appears to have been, without a strong feeling of
sympathy, which becomes strengthened to something like positive admiration when we discover
that he cherished, in after life, no unfriendly sentiments toward the man who had treated him so
shamefully; and when we find him, in the Me-

moir now under notice, still trying hard to make the best of Balzac's conduct, and still writing of him in terms of affection and esteem to the very end of the book.

The remainder of Balzac's life was, in substance, merely the lamentable repetition of the personal faults and follies, and the literary merits and triumphs, which have already found their record in these pages. The extremes of idle vanity and unprincipled extravagance still alternated, to the last, with the extremes of hard mental labor and amazing mental productiveness. Though he found new victims among new men, he never again met with so generous and forbearing a friend as the poor publisher whose fortunes he had destroyed. The women, whose impulses in his favor were kept alive by their admiration of his books, clung to their spoiled darling to the last—one of their number even stepping forward to save him from a debtors' prison, at the heavy sacrifice of paying the whole demand against him out of her own purse. In all cases of this sort, even where men were concerned as well as women, his personal means of attraction, when he chose to exert them, strengthened immensely his literary claims on the sympathy and good-will of others. He appears to have possessed in the highest degree those powers of fascination which are quite independent of mere beauty of face and form, and which are perversely and inexplicably bestowed in the most lavish abundance on the most unprincipled of mankind. Poor Monsieur Werdet can only account for half his own acts of indiscretion by declaring that his eminent friend wheedled him into committing them. Other and wiser men kept out of Balzac's way through sheer distrust of themselves. Virtuous friends who tried hard to reform him retreated from his presence, declaring that the reprobate whom they had gone to convert had all but upset their moral balance in a morning's conversation. An eminent literary gentleman, who went to spend the day with him to talk over a proposed work, rushed out of the house after a two hours' interview, exclaiming, piteously: "The man's imagination is in a state of delirium—his talk has set my brain in a whirl—he would have driven me mad if I had spent the day with him!" If men were influenced in this way, it is not wonderful that women (whose self-esteem was delicately flattered by the prominent and fascinating position which they hold in all his books) should have worshiped a man who publicly and privately worshiped them.

His personal appearance would have recalled to English minds the popular idea of Friar Tuck —he was the very model of the conventional fat, sturdy, red-faced, jolly monk. But he had the eye of a man of genius, and the tongue of a certain infernal personage, who may be broadly hinted at, but who must on no account be plainly named. The Balzac candlestick might be clumsy enough; but when once the Balzac candle was lit, the moths flew into it, only too readily, from all points of the compass.

The last important act of his life was, in a worldly point of view, one of the wisest things

he ever did. The lady who had invited him to
Vienna, and whom he called Carissima, was the
wife of a wealthy Russian nobleman. On the
death of her husband, she practically asserted her
admiration of her favorite author by offering him
her hand and fortune. Balzac accepted both;
and returned to Paris (from which respect for his
creditors had latterly kept him absent) a married
man, and an enviable member of the wealthy
class of society. A splendid future now opened
before him—but it opened too late. Arrived at
the end of his old course, he just saw the new
career beyond him, and dropped on the threshold
of it. The strong constitution which he had re-
morselessly wasted for more than twenty years
past gave way at length, at the very time when
his social chances looked most brightly. Three
months after his marriage, Honore de Balzac
died, after unspeakable suffering, of disease of
the heart. He was then but fifty years of age.
His fond, proud, heart-broken old mother held
him in her arms. On that loving bosom he had
drawn his first breath. On that loving bosom
the weary head sank to rest again, when the
wild, wayward, miserable, glorious life was over.

The sensation produced in Paris by his death
was something akin to the sensation produced in
London by the death of Byron. Mr. Carlyle has
admirably said that there is something touching
in the loyalty of men to their Sovereign Man.
That loyalty most tenderly declared itself when
Balzac was no more. Men of all ranks and par-

ties, who had been shocked by his want of principle and disgusted by his inordinate vanity while he was alive, now accepted universally the atonement of his untimely death, and remembered nothing but the loss that had happened to the literature of France. A great writer was no more; and a great people rose with one accord to take him reverently and gloriously to his grave. The French Institute, the University, the scientific societies, the Association of Dramatic Authors, the Schools of Law and Medicine, sent their representatives to walk in the funeral procession. English readers, American readers, German readers, and Russian readers, swelled the immense assembly of Frenchmen that followed the coffin. Victor Hugo and Alexandre Dumas were among the mourners who supported the pall. The first of these two celebrated men pronounced the funeral oration over Balzac's grave, and eloquently characterized the whole series of the dead writer's works as forming, in truth, but one grand book, the text-book of contemporary civilization. With that just and generous tribute to the genius of Balzac, offered by the most illustrious of his literary rivals, these few pages may fitly and gracefully come to an end. Of the miserable frailties of the man, enough has been recorded to serve the first of all interests, the interest of truth. The better and nobler part of him calls for no further comment at any writer's hands. It remains to us in his works, and it speaks with deathless eloquence for itself.

FRAGMENTS OF PERSONAL EXPERIENCE.—II.

MY BLACK MIRROR.

HAS everybody heard of Doctor Dee, the magician, and of the black speculum or mirror of cannel-coal, in which he could see at will everything in the wide world, and many things beyond it? If so, I may introduce myself to my readers in the easiest manner possible. Although I cannot claim to be a descendant of Doctor Dee, I profess the occult art to the extent of keeping a black mirror, made exactly after the model of that possessed by the old astrologer. My speculum, like his, is constructed of an oval piece of cannel-coal, highly polished, and set on a wooden back with a handle to hold it by. Nothing can be simpler than its appearance; nothing more marvelous than its capacities—provided always that the person using it be a true adept. Any man who disbelieves nothing is a true adept. Let him get a piece of cannel-coal, polish it highly, clean it before use with a white cambric handkerchief, retire to a private sitting-room, invoke the name of Doctor Dee, shut both eyes for a moment, and open them

again suddenly on the black mirror. If he does
not see anything he likes, after that—past, present, or future—then let him depend on it there is
some speck or flaw of incredulity in his nature;
and the sad termination of his career may be
considered certain. Sooner or later, he will end
in being nothing but a rational man.

1, who have not one morsel of rationality about
me; I, who am as true an adept as if I had lived
in the good old times ("The Ages of Faith," as
another adept has very properly called them), find
unceasing interest and occupation in my black
mirror. For everything I want to know, and
for everything I want to do, I consult it. This
very day, for instance (being in the position of
most of the other inhabitants of London at the
present season), I am thinking of soon going out
of town. My time for being away is so limited,
and my wanderings have extended, at home and
abroad, in so many directions, that I can hardly
hope to visit any really beautiful scenes, or gather
any really interesting experiences that are absolutely new to me. I must go to some place that
I have visited before; and I must, in common
regard to my own holiday interests, take care
that it is a place where I have already thoroughly enjoyed myself, without a single drawback to
my pleasure that is worth mentioning.

Under these circumstances, if I were a mere
rational man, what should I do? Weary my
memory to help me to decide on a destination, by
giving me my past traveling recollections in one
long panorama—although I can tell by experi-

ence that of all my faculties memory is the least serviceable at the very time when I most want to employ it. As a true adept, I know better than to give myself any useless trouble of this sort. I retire to my private sitting-room, take up my black mirror, mention what I want—and, behold! on the surface of the cannel-coal the image of my former travels passes before me, in a succession of dream-scenes. I revive my past experiences, and I make my present choice out of them, by the evidence of my own eyes; and I may add, by that of my own ears also—for the figures in my magic landscapes move and speak!

Shall I go on the Continent again? Yes. To what part of it? Suppose I revisit Austrian Italy, for the sake of renewing my familiarity with certain views, buildings, and pictures which once delighted me? But let me first ascertain whether I had any serious drawbacks to complain of on making acquaintance with that part of the world. Black mirror! show me my first evening in Austrian Italy.

A cloud rises on the magic surface—rests on it a little while—slowly disappears. My eyes are fixed on the cannel-coal. I see nothing, hear nothing of the world about me. The first of the magic scenes grows visible. I behold it, as in a dream. Away with the ignorant Present. 1 am in Italy again.

The darkness is just coming on. I see myself looking out of the side widow of a carriage. The hollow roll of the wheels has changed to a sharp rattle, and we have entered a town. We cross a vast square, illuminated by two lamps and **a** glimmer of reflected light from a coffee-shop window. We get on into a long street, with heavy stone arcades for foot-passengers to walk under. Everything looks dark and confused; grim visions of cloaked men flit by, all smoking; shrill female voices rise above the clatter of our wheels, then subside again in a moment. We stop. The bells on the horses' necks ring their last tiny peal for the night. A greasy hand opens the carriage door, and helps me down the steps. I am under an archway, with blank darkness before me, with a smiling man holding a flaming tallow-candle by my side, with street spectators silently looking on behind me. They wear high-crowned hats and brown cloaks, mysteriously muffling them up to the chin. Brigands, evidently. Pass, Scene! I am a peaceable man, and I don't like the suspicion of a stiletto, even in a dream.

Show me my sitting-room. Where did I dine, and how, on my first evening in Austrian Italy?

I am in the presence of two cheerful waiters, with two flaring candles. One is lighting lamps; the other is setting brush-wood and logs in a blaze in a perfect cavern of a hearth. Where am I, now that there is plenty of light to see by? Apparently in a banqueting hall, fifty feet long by forty wide. This is my private sitting-room, and I am to eat my little bit of dinner in it all alone. Let me look about observantly while the meal is preparing. Above me is an arched painted ceiling, all alive with Cupids rolling about on clouds, and scattering perpetual roses on the heads of travelers beneath. Around me are classical landscapes of the school which treats the spectator to umbrella-shaped trees, calm green oceans, and foregrounds rampant with dancing goddesses. Beneath me is something elastic to tread upon, smelling very like old straw, which indeed it is, covered with a thin drugget. This is humanely intended to protect me against the cold of the stone or brick floor, and is a concession to English prejudices on the subject of comfort. May I be grateful for it, and take no unfriendly notice of the fleas, though they are crawling up my legs from the straw and the drugget already!

What do I see next? Dinner on table. Drab-colored soup, which will take a great deal of thickening with grated Parmesan cheese, and five dishs all around it. Trout fried in oil, rolled beef steeped in succulent brown gravy, roast chicken with water-cresses, square pastry cakes with mince-meat inside them, fried potatoes—all excellent. This is really good Italian cookery; it is more fanciful than the English and more solid than the French. It is not greasy, and none of the fried dishes taste in the slightest degree of lamp-oil. The wine is good, too—effervescent, smacking of the Muscatel grape, and only eighteen-pence a bottle. The second course more than sustains the character of the first. Small browned birds that look like larks, their plump breasts clothed succulently with a counterpane of fat bacon, their tender

backs reposing on beds of savory toast—stewed
pigeon—a sponge-cake pudding—baked pears.
Where could one find a better dinner or a pleasanter waiter to serve at table? He is neither
servile nor familiar, and is always ready to oc
cupy any superfluous attention I have to spare
with all the small-talk that is in him. He has,
in fact, but one fault, and that consists in his
very vexatious and unaccountable manner of
varying the language in which he communi
cates with me.

I speak French and Italian, and he can speak
French also as well as his own tongue. I naturally, however, choose Italian on first addressing
him, because it is his native language. He understands what I say to him perfectly, but he
answers me in French. I bethink myself, upon
this, that he may be wishing, like the rest of us,
to show off any little morsel of learning that he
has picked up, or that he may fancy I understand French better than I do Italian, and may
be politely anxious to make our colloquy as easy
as possible to me. Accordingly I humor him,
and change to French when I next speak. No
sooner are the words out of my mouth than, with
inexplicable perversity, he answers me in Italian.
All through the dinner I try hard to make him
talk the same language that I do; yet, excepting
now and then a few insignificant phrases, I never
succeed. What is the meaning of his playing
this game of philological see-saw with me? Do
the people here actually carry the national politeness so far as to flatter the stranger by according

him an undisturbed monopoly of the language in
which he chooses to talk to them? I cannot explain it, and dessert surprises me in the midst of
my perplexities. Four dishes again! Parmesan
cheese, macaroons, pears and green figs. With
these and another bottle of the effervescent wine,
how brightly the evening will pass away by the
blazing wood-fire! Surely I cannot do better
than go to Austrian Italy again, after having
met with such a first welcome to the country as
this. Shall I put down the cannel-coal, and determine without any more ado on paying a second visit to the land that is cheered by my comfortable inn? No, not too hastily. Let me try
the effect of one or two more scenes from my past
traveling experience in this particular division of
the Italian peninsula before I decide.

Black Mirror! how did I end my evening at
the comfortable inn?

The cloud passes again, heavily and thickly
this time, over the surface of the mirror—clears
away slowly—shows me myself dozing luxuriously by the red embers with an empty bottle at
my side. A suddenly opening door wakes me
up; the landlord of the inn approaches, places a
long, official-looking book on the table, and hands
me pen and ink. I inquire peevishly what I am
wanted to write at that time of night, when I am
just digesting my dinner. The landlord answers
respectfully that I am required to give the police
a full, true, and particular account of myself. I
approach the table, thinking this demand rather
absurd, for my passport is already in the hands

of the authorities   However, as 1 am in a despotic country, I keep my thoughts to myself, open a blank page in the official-looking book, see that it is divided into columns, with printed headings, and find that I no more understand what they mean than I understand an assessed tax-paper at home, to which, by-the-by, the blank page bears a striking general resemblance. The headings are technical official words, which I now meet with as parts of Italian speech for the first time. I am obliged to appeal to the polite landlord, and by his assistance, I get gradually to understand what it is the Austrian police want of me.

The police require to know, before they will let me go on peaceably to-morrow, first, What my name is in full? (Answered easily enough.) Second, What is my nation? (British, and delighted to cast it in the teeth of continental tyrants.) Third, Where was I born? (In London—parish of Marylebone—and I wish my native vestry knew how the Austrian authorities were using me.) Fourth, Where do I live? (In London, again, and I have half a mind to write to the *Times* about this nuisance before I go to bed.) Fifth, How old am I? (My age is what it has been for the last seven years, and what it will remain till further notice —twenty-five exactly.) What next? By all that is inquisitive, here are the police wanting to know (Sixth) whether I am married or single! Landlord, what is the Italian for Bachelor? "Write Nubile, signor." Nubile? That means Marriageable. Permit me to remark, my good sir, that this is a woman's definition of a bachelor—

not a man's. No matter, let it pass. What next? (Oh, distrustful despots! what next?) Seventh, What is my condition? (First-rate condition, to be sure—full of rolled beef, toasted larks, and effervescent wine. Condition! What do they mean by that? Profession, is it? I have not got one. What shall I write? "Write Proprietor, signor." Very well; but I don't know that I am proprietor of anything except the clothes I stand up in; even my trunk was borrowed of a friend.) Eighth, Where do I come from? Ninth, Where am I going to? Tenth, When did I get my passport? Eleventh, Where did I get my passport? Twelfth, Who gave me my passport? Was there ever such a monstrous string of questions to address to a harmless, idle man, who only wants to potter about Italy quietly in a post-chaise? Do they catch Mazzini, landlord, with all these precautions? No; they only catch *me*. There! there! take your Travelers' Book back to the police. Surely, such unfounded distrust of my character as the production of that volume at my dinner-table implies, forms a serious drawback to the pleasure of traveling in Austrian Italy. Shall I give up at once all idea of going there, in my own innocent character, again? No; let me be deliberate in arriving at a decision—let me patiently try the experiment of looking at one more scene from the past.

Black Mirror! how did I travel in Austrian Italy after I had paid my bill in the morning, and had left my comfortable inn?

The new dream-scene shows me evening again.

I have joined another English traveler in taking a vehicle that they call a calèche. It is a frowzy kind of sedan-chair on wheels, with greasy leather curtains and cushions. In the days of its prosperity and youth it might have been a state coach, and might have carried Sir Robert Walpole to court, or the Abbe Dubois to a supper with the Regent Orleans. It is driven by a tall, cadaverous, ruffianly postilion, with his clothes all in rags, and without a spark of mercy for his miserable horses. It smells badly, looks badly, goes badly; and jerks, and cracks, and totters as if it would break down altogether—when it is suddenly stopped on a rough stone pavement in front of a lonely post house, just as the sun is sinking and the night is setting in.

The postmaster comes out to superintend the harnessing of fresh horses. He is tipsy, familiar, and confidential; he first apostrophizes the calèche with contemptuous curses, then takes me mysteriously aside, and declares that the whole highroad onward to our morning's destination swarms with thieves. It seems, then, that the Austrian police reserve all their vigilance for innocent travelers, and leave local rogues entirely unmolested. I make this reflection and ask the postmaster what he recommends us to do for the protection of our portmanteaus, which are tied on to the roof of the calèche. He answers that, unless we take special precautions, the thieves will get up behind, on our crazy foot-board, and will cut the trunks off the top of our frowzy traveling-carriage, under cover of the night, while we are quietly seated inside, seeing and suspecting nothing. We instantly express our readiness to take any precautions that any one may be kind enough to suggest. The postmaster winks, lays his finger archly on the side of his nose, and gives an unintelligible order in the patois of the district. Before I have time to ask what he is going to do, every idler about the post-house who can climb scales the summit of the calèche, and every idler who cannot stands roaring and gesticulating below with a lighted candle in his hand.

While the hubbub is at its loudest, a rival traveling-carriage suddenly drives into the midst of us, in the shape of a huge barrel-organ on wheels, and bursts out awfully in the darkness with the grand march in "Semiramide," played with the utmost fury of the drum, cymbal and trumpet-stops. The noise is so bewildering that my traveling companion and I take refuge inside our carriage, and shut our eyes, and stop our ears, and abandon ourselves to despair. After a time, our elbows are jogged and a string apiece is given to us through each window. We are informed in shouts, accompanied fiercely by the grand march, that the strings are fastened to our portmanteaus above; that we are to keep the loose ends round our forefingers all night; and that the moment we feel a tug, we may be quite certain the thieves are at work, and may feel justified in stopping the carriage and fighting for our baggage without any more ado. Under these agreeable auspices, we start again, with our strings round our forefingers. We feel like men about

to ring the bell—or like men engaged in deep-sea
fishing—or like men on the point of pulling the
string of a shower-bath. Fifty times at least,
during the next stage, each of us is certain that
he feels a tug, and pops his head agitatedly
out of window, and sees absolutely nothing,
and falls back again exhausted with excitement
in a corner of the calèche. All through the
night this wear and tear of our nerves goes on;
and all through the night (thanks, probably, to
the ceaseless popping of our heads out of the windows) not the ghost of a thief comes near us. We
begin, at last, almost to feel that it would be a
relief to be robbed—almost to doubt the policy of
resisting any mercifully larcenous hands stretched
forth to rescue us from the incubus of our own
baggage. The morning dawn finds us languid
and haggard, with the accursed portmanteau
strings dangling unregarded in the bottom of
the calèche. And this is taking our pleasure!
This is an incident of travel in Austrian Italy!
Faithful Black Mirror, accept my thanks. The
warning of the two last dream-scenes that you
have shown me shall not be disregarded. Whatever other direction I may take when I go out of
town for the present season, one road at least I
know that I shall avoid—the road that leads to
Austrian Italy.

Shall I keep on the northern side of the Alps,
and travel a little, let us say, in German Switzerland? Black Mirror! how did I get on when I
was last in that country? Did I like my introductory experience at my first inn?

The vision changes, and takes me again to the outside of a house of public entertainment; a great white, clean, smooth-fronted, opulent-looking hotel —a very different building from my dingy, cavernous Italian inn. At the street door stands the landlord. He is a little, lean, rosy man, dressed all in black, and looking like a master-undertaker. I observe that he neither steps forward nor smiles when I get out of the carriage and ask for a bedroom. He gives me the shortest possible answer, growls guttural instructions to a waiter, then looks out into the street again, and, before I have so much as turned my back on him, forgets my existence immediately. The vision changes again, and takes me inside the hotel. I am following a waiter upstairs—the man looks unaffectedly sorry to see me. In the bedroom corridor we find a chambermaid asleep, with her head on a table. She is woke up; opens a door with a groan, and scowls at me reproachfully when I say that the room will do. I descend to dinner. Two waiters attend on me, under protest, and look as if they were on the point of giving warning every time I require them to change my plate. At the second course the landlord comes in, and stands and stares at me intently and silently with his hands in his pockets. This may be his way of seeing that my dinner is well-served; but it looks much more like his way of seeing that I do not abstract any spoons from his table.

I become irritated by the boorish staring and frowning of everybody about me, and express myself strongly on the subject of my reception at the hotel to an English traveler dining near me.

The English traveler is one of those exasperating men who are always ready to put up with injuries, and he coolly accounts for the behavior of which I complain, by telling me that it is the result of the blunt honesty of the natives, who cannot pretend to take an interest in me which they do not really feel. What do I care about the feelings of the stolid landlord and the sulky waiters? I require the comforting outward show from them—the inward substance is not of the smallest consequence to me. When I travel in civilized countries, I want such a reception at my inn as shall genially amuse and gently tickle all the region round about my organ of self-esteem. Blunt honesty, which is too offensively truthful to pretend to be glad to see me, shows no corresponding integrity—as my own experience informs me at this very hotel— about the capacities of its wine-bottles, but gives me a pint and charges me for a quart in the bill, like the rest of the world. Blunt honesty, although it is too brutally sincere to look civilly distressed and sympathetic when I say that I am tired after my journey, does not hesitate to warm up, and present before me as newly dressed, a Methuselah of a duck that has been cooked several times over, several days ago, and paid for, though not eaten, by my traveling predecessors. Blunt honesty fleeces me according to every established predatory law of the landlord's code, yet shrinks from the amiable duplicity of fawn-

ing affectionately before me all the way upstairs
when I first present myself to be swindled.
Away with such detestable sincerity as this!
Away with the honesty which brutalizes a landlord's manners without reforming his bottles or
his bills! Away with my German-Swiss hotel,
and the extortionate cynic who keeps it! Let
others pay tribute if they will to that boor in
innkeeper's clothing, the color of my money he
shall never see again.

Suppose I avoid German Switzerland, and try
Switzerland Proper? Mirror! how did I travel
when I last found myself on the Swiss side of the
Alps?

The new vision removes me even from the
most distant view of a hotel of any kind, and
places me in a wild mountain country where the
end of a rough road is lost in the dry bed of a
torrent. I am seated in a queer little box on
wheels, called a Char, drawn by a mule and a
mare, and driven by a jovial coachman in a blue
blouse. I have hardly time to look down alarm-
edly at the dry bed of the torrent, before the
Char plunges into it. Rapidly and recklessly we
thump along over rocks and stones, acclivities
and declivities that would shake down the stout-
est English traveling-carriage, knock up the
best-bred English horses, nonplus the most
knowing English coachman. Jovial Blue Blouse,
singing like a nightingale, drives ahead regard-
less of every obstacle—the mule and mare tear
along as if the journey was the great enjoyment
of the day to them—the Char cracks, rends,

sways, bumps and totters, but scorns, as becomes a hardy little mountain vehicle, to over-
turn or come to pieces.   When we are not among
the rocks we are rolling and heaving in sloughs
of black mud and sand, like a Dutch-herring-
boat in a groundswell. It is all one to Blue
Blouse and the mule and mare. They are just
as ready to drag through sloughs as to jolt over
rocks; and when we do come occasionally to a bit
of unencumbered ground, they always indemnify
themselves for past hardship and fatigue by gal-
loping like mad. As for my own sensations in
the character of passenger in the Char, they are
not, physically speaking, of the pleasantest possible kind. I can only keep myself inside my vehicle
by dint of holding tight with both hands by anything I can find to grasp at; and I am so shaken
throughout my whole anatomy that my very jaws
clatter again, and my feet play a perpetual tattoo
on the bottom of the Char. Did I hit on no
method of traveling more composed and deliberate than this, I wonder, when I was last in
Switzerland? Must I make up my mind to be
half shaken to pieces if I am bold enough to
venture on going there again?

The surface of the Black Mirror is once more
clouded over. It clears, and the vision is now
of a path along the side of a precipice. A mule
is following the path, and I am the adventurous
traveler who is astride on the beast's back. The
first observation that occurs to me in my new
position is, that mules thoroughly deserve their
reputation for obstinacy, and that, in regard to

the particular animal on which I am riding, the less I interfere with him and the more I conduct myself as if I was a pack-saddle on his back, the better we are sure to get on together.

Carrying pack-saddles is his main business in life; and though he saw me get on his back, he persists in treating me as if I was a bale of goods, by walking on the extreme edge of the precipice, so as not to run any risk of rubbing his load against the safe, or mountain, side of the path. In this and in other things I find that he is the victim of routine, and the slave of habit. He has a way of stopping short, placing himself in a slanting position, and falling into a profound meditation at some of the most awkward turns in the wild mountain roads. I imagine at first that he may be halting in this abrupt and inconvenient manner to take breath; but then he never exerts himself so as to tax his lungs in the smallest degree, and he stops on the most unreasonable, irregular principles, sometimes twice in ten minutes—sometimes not more than twice in two hours—evidently just as his new ideas happen to absorb his attention or not. It is part of his exasperating character at these times always to become immersed in reflection where the muleteer's staff has not room to reach him with the smallest effect; and where loading him with blows being out of the question, loading him with abusive language is the only other available process for getting him on. I find that he generally turns out to be susceptible to the influence of injurious epithets after he has heard himself insulted five

or six times. Once his obdurate nature gives
way, even at the third appeal. He has just
stopped with me on his back, to amuse himself,
at a dangerous part of the road, with a little
hard thinking in a steeply slanting position;
and it becomes, therefore, urgently necessary to
abuse him into proceeding forthwith. First, the
muleteer calls him a Serpent—he never stirs an
inch. Secondly, the muleteer calls him a Frog
—he goes on imperturbably with his meditation.
Thirdly, the muleteer roars out indignantly, *Ah
sacre nom d'un Butor!* (which, interpreted by
the help of my Anglo-French dictionary, means
apparently, Ah, sacred name of a Muddlehead!);
and at this extraordinary adjuration the beast instantly jerks up his nose, shakes his ears, and
goes on his way indignantly.

Mule-riding, under these circumstances, is certainly an adventurous and amusing method of
traveling, and well worth trying for once in a
way; but I am not at all sure that I should enjoy
a second experience of it, and I have my doubts
on this account—to say nothing of my dread of a
second jolting journey in a Char—about the propriety of undertaking another journey to Switzerland during the present sultry season. It will be
wisest, perhaps, to try the effect of a new scene
from the past, representing some former visit to
some other locality, before I venture on arriving
at a decision. I have rejected Austrian Italy
and German Switzerland, and I am doubtful
about Switzerland Proper. Suppose I do my
duty as a patriot, and give the attractions of my

own country a fair chance of appealing to any
past influences of the agreeable kind which they
may have exercised over me? Black Mirror!
when 1 was last a tourist at home, how did I
travel about from place to place?

The cloud on the magic surface rises slowly
and grandly, like the lifting of a fog at sea, and
discloses a tiny drawing-room, with a skylight
window, and a rose-colored curtain drawn over
it to keep out the sun. A bright bookshelf runs
all round this little fairy chamber, just below the
ceiling, where the cornice would be in loftier
rooms. Sofas extend along the wall on either
side, and mahogany cupboards full of good things
ensconce themselves snugly in the four corners.
The table is brightened with nosegays; the man-
tle-shelf has a smart railing all round it; and the
looking-glass above is just large enough to reflect
becomingly the face and shoulders of any lady
who will give herself the trouble of looking into
it. The present inhabitants of the room are three
gentlemen with novels and newspapers in their
hands, taking their ease in blouses, dressing-
gowns, and slippers. They are reposing on the
sofas with fruit and wine within easy reach—and
one of the party looks to me very much like the
enviable possessor of the Black Mirror. They
exhibit a spectacle of luxury which would make
an ancient Spartan shudder with disgust; and,
in an adjoining apartment, their band is attending on them, in the shape of a musical box which
is just now playing the last scene in "Lucia di
Lammermoor."

Hark! what sounds are those mingling with the notes of Donizetti's lovely music—now rising over it sublimely, now dying away under it, gently and more gently still? Our sweet opera air shall come to its close, our music shall play for its short destined time, and then be silent again; but those more glorious sounds shall go on with us day and night, shall still swell and sink inexhaustibly, long after we and all who know and love and remember us have passed from this earth forever. It is the wash of the waves that now travels along with us grandly wherever we go. We are at sea in a schooner-yacht, and are taking our pleasure along the southern shores of the English coast.

Yes, this to every man who can be certain of his own stomach, this is the true luxury of traveling, the true secret for thoroughly enjoying all the attractions of moving about from place to place. Wherever we now go, we carry our elegant and comfortable home along with us. We can stop where we like, see what we like, and always come back to our favorite corner on the sofa, always carry on our favorite occupations and amusements, and still be traveling, still be getting forward to new scenes all the time. Here is no hurrying to accommodate yourself to other people's hours for starting, no scrambling for places, no wearisome watchfulness over baggage. Here are no anxieties about strange beds—for have we not each of us our own sweet little cabin to nestle in at night?—no agitating dependence at the dinner-hour upon the vagaries of strange cooks—for have we not our own sumptuous larder always to return to, our own accomplished and faithful culinary artist always waiting to minister to our special tastes? We can walk and sleep, stand up or lie down just as we please, in our floating traveling-carriage. We can make our own road, and trespass nowhere. The bores we dread, the letters we don't want to answer, cannot follow and annoy us. We are the freest travelers under heaven; and we find something to interest and attract us through every hour of the day. The ships we meet, the trimming of our sails, the varying of the weather, the everlasting innumerable changes of the ocean, afford constant occupation for eye and ear. Sick, indeed, must that libelous traveler have been who first called the sea monotonous—sick to death, and perhaps, born brother also to that other traveler of evil renown, the first man who journeyed from Dan to Beersheba, and found all barren.

Rest, then, a while unemployed, my faithful Black Mirror! The last scene you have shown me is sufficient to answer the purpose for which I took you up. Toward what point of the compass I may turn after leaving London is more than I can tell; but this I know, that my next post-horses shall be the winds, my next stages coast towns, my next road over the open waves. I will be a sea traveler once more, and will put off resuming my land journeyings until the arrival of that most obliging of all convenient periods of time—a future opportunity.

SKETCHES OF CHARACTER.—III.

MRS. BADGERY.

[Drawn from Life. By a Gentleman with No Sensibilities.]

Is there any law in England which will protect me from Mrs. Badgery?

I am a bachelor, and Mrs. Badgery is a widow. Don't suppose she wants to marry me! She wants nothing of the sort. She has not attempted to marry me; she would not think of marrying me, even if I asked her. Understand, if you please, at the outset, that my grievance in relation to this widow lady is a grievance of an entirely new kind.

Let me begin again. I am a bachelor of a certain age. I have a large circle of acquaintance; but I solemnly declare that the late Mr. Badgery was never numbered on the list of my friends. I never heard of him in my life; I never knew that he had left a relict; I never sat eyes on Mrs. Badgery until one fatal morning when I went to see if the fixtures were all right in my new house.

My new house is in the suburbs of London. I looked at it, liked it, took it. Three times I

visited it before I sent my furniture in. Once
with a friend, once with a surveyor, once by myself, to throw a sharp eye, as I have already intimated, over the fixtures. The third visit marked
the fatal occasion on which I first saw Mrs. Badgery. A deep interest attaches to this event, and
I shall go into details in describing it.

I rang at the bell of the garden door. The
old woman appointed to keep the house answered it. I directly saw something strange and
confused in her face and manner. Some men
would have pondered a little and questioned her.
I am by nature impetuous and a rusher at conclusions. "Drunk," I said to myself, and walked
on into the house perfectly satisfied.

I looked into the front parlor. Grate all right,
curtain-pole all right, gas chandelier all right. I
looked into the back parlor—ditto, ditto, ditto, as
we men of business say. I mounted the stairs.
Blind on back window right? Yes; blind on
back window right. I opened the door of the
front drawing-room—and there, sitting in the
middle of the bare floor, was a large woman
on a little camp-stool! She was dressed in the
deepest mourning; her face was hidden by the
thickest crape veil I ever saw; and she was
groaning softly to herself in the desolate solitude
of my new unfurnished house.

What did I do? Do! I bounced back into the
landing as if I had been shot, uttering the national exclamation of terror and astonishment,
"Hullo!" (And here I particularly beg, in parenthesis, that the printer will follow my spelling

of the word, and not put Hillo or Halloo instead, both of which are senseless compromises which represent no sound that ever yet issued from an Englishman's lips.) I said, "Hullo!" and then I turned round fiercely upon the old woman who kept the house, and said "Hullo!" again.

She understood the irresistible appeal that I had made to her feelings, and courtesied, and looked toward the drawing-room, and humbly hoped that I was not startled or put out. I asked who the crape-covered woman on the camp-stool was, and what she wanted there. Before the old woman could answer, the soft groaning in the drawing-room ceased, and a muffled voice, speaking from behind the crape veil, addressed me reproachfully, and said:

"I am the widow of the late Mr. Badgery."

What do you think I said in answer? Exactly the words which I flatter myself any other sensible man in my situation would have said. And what words were they? These two:

"Oh, indeed?"

"Mr. Badgery and myself were the last tenants who inhabited this house," continued the muffled voice. "Mr. Badgery died here." The voice ceased, and the soft groans began again.

It was perhaps not necessary to answer this; but I did answer it. How? In two words again:

"Did he?"

"Our house has been long empty," resumed the voice, choked by sobs. "Our establishment has been broken up. Being left in reduced circumstances, I now live in a cottage near; but it is not home to me. This is home. However long I live, wherever I go, whatever changes may happen to this beloved house, nothing can ever prevent me from looking on it as *my* home. I came here, sir, with Mr. Badgery after our honeymoon. All the brief happiness of my life was once contained within these four walls. Every dear remembrance that I fondly cherish is shut up in these sacred rooms."

Again the voice ceased, and again the soft groans echoed round my empty walls, and oozed out past me down my uncarpeted staircase.

I reflected. Mrs. Badgery's brief happiness and dear remembrances were not included in the list of fixtures. Why could she not take them away with her? Why should she leave them littered about in the way of my furniture? I was just thinking how I could put this view of the case strongly to Mrs. Badgery, when she suddenly left off groaning and addressed me once more.

"While this house has been empty," she said, "I have been in the habit of looking in from time to time, and renewing my tender associations with the place. I have lived, as it were, in the sacred memories of Mr. Badgery and of the past, which these dear, these priceless rooms call up, dismantled and dusty as they are at the present moment. It has been my practice to give a remuneration to the attendant for any slight trouble that I might occasion—"

"Only sixpence, sir," whispered the old woman, close at my ear.

"And to ask nothing in return," continued Mrs. Badgery, "but the permission to bring my camp-stool with me, and to meditate on Mr. Badgery in the empty rooms, with every one of which some happy thought, or eloquent word, or tender action of his, is everlastingly associated. I came here on my usual errand to-day. I am discovered, I presume, by the new proprietor of the house—discovered, I am quite ready to admit, as an intruder. I am willing to go, if you wish it after hearing my explanation. My heart is full, sir; I am quite incapable of contending with you. You would hardly think it, but I am sitting on the spot once occupied by *our* ottoman. I am looking toward the window in which *my* flower-stand once stood. In this very place Mr. Badgery first sat down and clasped me to his heart, when we came back from our honeymoon trip. 'Matilda,' he said, 'your drawing - room has been expensively papered, carpeted, and furnished for a month; but it has only been adorned, love, since you entered it.' If you have no sympathy, sir, for such remembrances as these; if you see nothing pitiable in my position, taken in connection with my presence here; if you cannot enter into my feelings, and thoroughly understand that this is not a house, but a Shrine—you have only to say so, and I am quite willing to go."

She spoke with the air of a martyr—a martyr to my insensibility. If she had been the proprietor and I had been the intruder, she could not have been more mournfully magnanimous.

All this time, too, she never raised her veil—she never has raised it, in my presence, from that time to this. I have no idea whether she is young or old, dark or fair, handsome or ugly: my impression is, that she is in every respect a finished and perfect Gorgon; but I have no basis of fact on which I can support that horrible idea. A moving mass of crape and a muffled voice—that, if you drive me to it, is all I know, in a personal point of view, of Mrs. Badgery.

"Ever since my irreparable loss, this has been the shrine of my pilgrimage, and the altar of my worship," proceeded the voice. "One man may call himself a landlord, and say that he will let it; another man may call himself a tenant, and say that he will take it. I don't blame either of those two men; I don't wish to intrude on either of those two men; I only tell them that this is my home; that my heart is still in possession, and that no mortal laws, landlords, or tenants can ever turn it out. If you don't understand this, sir; if the holiest feelings that do honor to our common nature have no particular sanctity in your estimation, pray do not scruple to say so; pray tell me to go."

"I don't wish to do anything uncivil, ma'am," said I. "But I am a single man, and I am not sentimental." (Mrs. Badgery groaned.) "Nobody told me I was coming into a Shrine when I took this house; nobody warned me, when I first went over it, that there was a Heart in possession. I regret to have disturbed your meditations, and I am sorry to hear that Mr. Badgery

is dead. That is all I have to say about it; and
now, with your kind permission, I will do myself
the honor of wishing you good-morning, and will
go upstairs to look after the fixtures on the second
floor."

Could I have given a gentler hint than this?
Could I have spoken more compassionately to
a woman whom I sincerely believe to be old and
ugly? Where is the man to be found who can
lay his hand on his heart and honestly say that
he ever really pitied the sorrows of a Gorgon?
Search through the whole surface of the globe,
and you will discover human phenomena of all
sorts; but you will not find that man.

To resume. I made her a bow, and left her
on the camp-stool in the middle of the drawing-
room floor, exactly as I had found her. I ascended
to the second floor, walked into the back room
first, and inspected the grate. It appeared to be
a little out of repair, so I stooped down to look
at it closer. While I was kneeling over the bars,
I was violently startled by the fall of one large
drop of Warm Water, from a great height, exactly in the middle of a bald place, which has
been widening a great deal of late years on the
top of my head. I turned on my knees, and
looked round. Heaven and earth! the crape-
covered woman had followed me upstairs—the
source from which the drop of warm water had
fallen was Mrs. Badgery's eye!

"I wish you could contrive not to cry over the
top of my head, ma'am," I remarked. My patience was becoming exhausted, and I spoke with

considerable asperity. The curly-headed youth of the present age may not be able to sympathize with my feelings on this occasion; but my bald brethren know as well as I do that the most unpardonable of all liberties is a liberty taken with the unguarded top of the human head.

Mrs. Badgery did not seem to hear me. When she had dropped the tear, she was standing exactly over me, looking down at the grate; and she never stirred an inch after I had spoken. "Don't cry over my head, ma'am," I repeated, more irritably than before.

"This was his dressing - room," said Mrs. Badgery, indulging in muffled soliloquy. "He was singularly particular about his shaving-water. He always liked to have it in a little tin pot, and he invariably desired that it might be placed on this hob." She groaned again, and tapped one side of the grate with the leg of her camp-stool.

If I had been a woman, or if Mrs. Badgery had been a man, I should now have proceeded to extremities, and should have vindicated my right to my own house by an appeal to physical force. Under existing circumstances, all that I could do was to express my indignation by a glance. The glance produced not the slightest result—and no wonder. Who can look at a woman with any effect through a crape veil?

I retreated into the second-floor front room, and instantly shut the door after me. The next moment I heard the rustling of the crape garments outside, and the muffled voice of Mrs.

Badgery poured lamentably through the keyhole.
"Do you mean to make that your bedroom?"
asked the voice on the other side of the door.
"Oh, don't, don't make that your bedroom! I
am going away directly—but, oh pray, pray let
that one room be sacred! Don't sleep there! If
you can possibly help it, don't sleep there!"

I opened the window, and looked up and down
the road. If I had seen a policeman within hail
I should certainly have called him in. No such
person was visible. I shut the window again,
and warned Mrs. Badgery, through the door, in
my sternest tones, not to interfere with my domestic arrangements. "I mean to have my own
iron bedstead put up here," I said. "And what
is more, I mean to sleep here. And what is
more, I mean to snore here!" Severe, I think,
that last sentence? It completely crushed Mrs.
Badgery for the moment. I heard the crape garments rustling away from the door; I heard the
muffled groans going slowly and solemnly down
the stairs again.

In due course of time I also descended to the
ground-floor. Had Mrs. Badgery really left the
premises? I looked into the front parlor—empty.
Back parlor—empty. Any other room on the
ground-floor? Yes; a long room at the end of
the passage. The door was closed. I opened it
cautiously, and peeped in. A faint scream, and
a smack of two distractedly clasped hands saluted
my appearance. There she was, again on the
camp stool, again sitting exactly in the middle
of the floor.

"Don't, don't look in, in that way!" cried Mrs. Badgery, wringing her hands. "I could bear it in any other room, but I can't bear it in this. Every Monday morning I looked out the things for the wash in this room. He was difficult to please about his linen; the washerwoman never put starch enough into his collars to satisfy him. Oh, how often and often has he popped his head in here, as you popped yours just now; and said, in his amusing way, 'More starch!' Oh, how droll he always was—how very, very droll in this dear little back room!"

I said nothing. The situation had now got beyond words. I stood with the door in my hand, looking down the passage toward the garden, and waiting doggedly for Mrs. Badgery to go out. My plan succeeded. She rose, sighed, shut up the camp-stool, stalked along the passage, paused on the hall mat, said to herself, "Sweet, sweet spot!" descended the steps, groaned along the gravel-walk, and disappeared from view at last through the garden door.

"Let her in again at your peril!" said I to the woman who kept the house. She courtesied and trembled. I left the premises, satisfied with my own conduct under very trying circumstances; delusively convinced also that I had done with Mrs. Badgery.

The next day I sent in the furniture. The most unprotected object on the face of this earth is a house when the furniture is going in. The doors must be kept open; and employ as many servants as you may, nobody can be depended on as a domestic sentry so long as the van is at the gate. The confusion of "moving in" demoralizes the steadiest disposition, and there is no such thing as a properly guarded post from the top of the house to the bottom. How the invasion was managed, how the surprise was effected, I know not; but it is certainly the fact that, when my furniture went in, the inevitable Mrs. Badgery went in along with it.

I have some very choice engravings, after the old masters; and I was first awakened to a consciousness of Mrs. Badgery's presence in the house while I was hanging up my proof impression of Titian's Venus over the front-parlor fireplace. "Not there!" cried the muffled voice, imploringly. "*His* portrait used to hang there. Oh, what a print—what a dreadful, dreadful print to put where *his* dear portrait used to be!"

I turned round in a fury. There she was, still muffled up in crape, still carrying her abominable camp-stool. Before I could say a word in remonstrance, six men in green baize aprons staggered in with my sideboard, and Mrs. Badgery suddenly disappeared. Had they trampled her under foot or crushed her in the doorway? Though not an inhuman man by nature, I asked myself those questions quite composedly. No very long time elapsed before they were practically answered in the negative by the re-appearance of Mrs. Badgery herself, in a perfectly unruffled condition of chronic grief. In the course of the day I had my toes trodden on, I was knocked about by

my own furniture, the six men in baize aprons
dropped all sorts of small articles over me in going up and down stairs; but Mrs. Badgery escaped
unscathed.   Every time I thought she had been
turned out of the house she proved, on the contrary, to be groaning close behind me.   She wept
over Mr. Badgery's memory in every room, perfectly undisturbed to the last by the chaotic confusion of moving in.   I am not sure, but I think
she brought a tin box of sandwiches with her, and
celebrated a tearful picnic of her own in the groves
of my front garden.   I say I am not sure of this;
but I am positively certain that I never entirely
got rid of her all day; and I know to my cost
that she insisted on making me as well acquainted
with Mr. Badgery's favorite notions and habits
as I am with my own.   It may interest the reader
if I report that my taste in carpets is not equal
to Mr. Badgery's; that my ideas on the subject
of servants' wages are not so generous as Mr.
Badgery's; and that I ignorantly persisted in
placing a sofa in the position which Mr. Badgery, in his time, considered to be particularly
fitted for an armchair.   I could go nowhere, look
nowhere, do nothing, say nothing, all that day,
without bringing the widowed incubus in the
crape garments down upon me immediately.   I
tried civil remonstrances, I tried rude speeches,
I tried sulky silence—nothing had the least effect
on her.   The memory of Mr. Badgery was the
shield of proof with which she warded off my
fiercest attacks.   Not till the last article of furniture had been moved in did I lose sight of her;

and even then she had not really left the house.
One of my six men in green baize aprons routed
her out of the back-garden area, where she was
telling my servants, with floods of tears, of Mr.
Badgery's virtuous strictness with his housemaid
in the matter of followers. My admirable man
in green baize courageously saw her out, and
shut the garden door after her. I gave him half
a crown on the spot; and if anything happens to
him, I am ready to make the future prosperity of
his fatherless family my own peculiar care.

The next day was Sunday, and I attended
morning service at my new parish church.

A popular preacher had been announced, and
the building was crowded. I advanced a little
way up the nave, and looked to my right, and
saw no room. Before I could look to my left, I
felt a hand laid persuasively on my arm. I
turned round—and there was Mrs. Badgery,
with her pew door open, solemnly beckoning me
in. The crowd had closed up behind me; the
eyes of a dozen members of the congregation, at
least, were fixed on me. I had no choice but to
save appearances, and accept the dreadful invitation. There was a vacant place next to the door
of the pew. I tried to drop into it, but Mrs.
Badgery stopped me. "*His* seat," she whispered, and signed to me to place myself on the
other side of her. It is unnecessary to say that I
had to climb over a hassock, and that I knocked
down all Mrs. Badgery's devotional books before
I succeeded in passing between her and the front
of the pew. She cried uninterruptedly through

the service; composed herself when it was over; and began to tell me what Mr. Badgery's opinions had been on points of abstract theology. Fortunately there was great confusion and crowding at the door of the church; and I escaped, at the hazard of my life, by running round the back of the carriages. I passed the interval between the services alone in the fields, being deterred from going home by the fear that Mrs. Badgery might have got there before me.

Monday came. I positively ordered my servants to let no lady in deep mourning pass inside the garden door without first consulting me. After that, feeling tolerably secure, I occupied myself in arranging my books and prints.

I had not pursued this employment much more than an hour, when one of the servants burst excitably into the room, and informed me that a lady in deep mourning had been taken faint just outside my door, and had requested leave to come in and sit down for a few moments. I ran down the garden path to bolt the door, and arrived just in time to see it violently pushed open by an officious and sympathizing crowd. They drew away on either side as they saw me. There she was, leaning on the grocer's shoulder, with the butcher's boy in attendance, carrying her camp-stool! Leaving my servants to do what they liked with her, I ran back and locked myself up in my bed-room. When she evacuated the premises some hours afterward, I received a message of apology, informing me that this particular Monday was the sad anniversary of her wedding-day, and that

she had been taken faint, in consequence, at the
sight of her lost husband's house.

Tuesday forenoon passed away happily, without any new invasion. After lunch I thought I
would go out and take a walk. My garden door
has a sort of peep-hole in it, covered with a wire
grating. As I got close to this grating, I thought
I saw something mysteriously dark on the outer
side of it. I bent my head down to look through,
and instantly found myself face to face with the
crape veil. "Sweet, sweet spot!" said the muffled
voice, speaking straight into my eyes through the
grating. The usual groans followed, and the
name of Mr. Badgery was plaintively pronounced
before I could recover myself sufficiently to retreat
to the house.

Wednesday is the day on which I am writing
this narrative. It is not twelve o'clock yet, and
there is every probability that some new form of
sentimental persecution is in store for me before
the evening. Thus far, these lines contain a perfectly true statement of Mrs. Badgery's conduct
toward me since I entered on the possession of
my house and *her* shrine. What am I to do—
that is the point I wish to insist on—what am I
to do? How am I to get away from the memory
of Mr. Badgery, and the unappeasable grief of
his disconsolate widow? Any other species of
invasion it is possible to resist; but how is a man
placed in my unhappy and unparalleled circumstances to defend himself? I can't keep a dog
ready to fly at Mrs. Badgery. I can't charge her
at a police court with being oppressively fond of

the house in which her husband died. I can't set man-traps for a woman, or prosecute a weeping widow as a trespasser and a nuisance. I am helplessly involved in the unrelaxing folds of Mrs. Badgery's crape veil. Surely there was no exaggeration in my language when I said that I was a sufferer under a perfectly new grievance! Can anybody advise me? Has anybody had even the remotest experience of the peculiar form of persecution which I am now enduring? If nobody has, is there any legal gentleman in the United Kingdom who can answer the all-important question which appears at the head of this narrative? I began by asking that question because it was uppermost in my mind. It is uppermost in my mind still, and I therefore beg leave to conclude appropriately by asking it again:

Is there any law in England which will protect me from Mrs. Badgery?

CASES WORTH LOOKING AT.—I.

MEMOIRS OF AN ADOPTED SON.*

I.—CIRCUMSTANCES WHICH PRECEDED HIS BIRTH.

TOWARD the beginning of the eighteenth century there stood on a rock in the sea, near a fishing village on the coast of Brittany, a ruined tower with a very bad reputation. No mortal was known to have inhabited it within the memory of living man. The one tenant whom Tradition associated with the occupation of the place at a remote period had moved into it from the infernal regions nobody knew why—had lived in

---

* The curious legend connected with the birth of this "Adopted Son," and the facts relating to his extraordinary career in after-life, are derived from the "Records" of the French Police of the period. In this instance, and in the instances of those other papers in the present collection which deal with foreign incidents and characters, while the facts of each narrative exist in print, the form in which the narrative is cast is of my own devising. If these facts had been readily accessible to readers in general, the papers in question would not have been reprinted. But the scarce and curious books from which my materials are derived have been long since out of print, and are, in all human probability, never likely to be published again.

it nobody knew how long—and had quitted possession nobody knew when. Under such circumstances, nothing was more natural than that his unearthly Individual should give a name to this residence; for which reason, the building was thereafter known to all the neighborhood round as Satanstower.

Early in the year seventeen hundred, the inhabitants of the village were startled one night by seeing the red gleam of a fire in the tower, and by smelling, in the same direction, a preternaturally strong odor of fried fish. The next morning the fishermen who passed by the building in their boats were amazed to find that a stranger had taken up his abode in it. Judging of him at a distance, he seemed to be a fine tall, stout fellow; he was dressed in fisherman's costume, and he had a new boat of his own, moored comfortably in a cleft of the rock. If he had inhabited a place of decent reputation, his neighbors would have immediately made his acquaintance; but, as things were, all they could venture to do was to watch him in silence.

The first day passed, and, though it was fine weather, he made no use of his boat. The second day followed, with a continuance of the fine weather, and still he was as idle as before. On the third day, when a violent storm kept all the boats of the village on the beach—on the third day, in the midst of the tempest, away went the man of the tower to make his first fishing experiment in strange waters! He and his boat came back safe and sound, in a lull of the storm;

and the villagers watching on the cliff above
saw him carrying the fish up, by great basketfuls, to his tower. No such haul had ever fallen
to the lot of any one of them, and the stranger
had taken it in a whole gale of wind.

Upon this the inhabitants of the village called
a council. The lead in the debate was assumed
by a smart young fellow, a fisherman named
Poulailler, who stoutly declared that the stranger
at the tower was of infernal origin. "The rest
of you may call him what you like," said Poulailler; "I call him The Fiend-Fisherman!"

The opinion thus expressed proved to be the
opinion of the entire audience—with the one exception of the village priest. The priest said,
"Gently, my sons. Don't make sure about the
man of the tower before Sunday. Wait and see
if he comes to church."

"And if he doesn't come to church?" asked
all the fishermen, in a breath.

"In that case," replied the priest, "1 will ex-
communicate him; and then, my children, you
may call him what you like."

Sunday came, and no sign of the stranger darkened the church doors. He was excommunicated
accordingly. The whole village forthwith adopted Poulailler's idea, and called the man of the
tower by the name which Poulailler had given
him—"The Fiend-Fisherman."

These strong proceedings produced not the
slightest apparent effect on the diabolical personage who had occasioned them. He persisted
in remaining idle when the weather was fine, in

going out to fish when no other boat in the place
dare put to sea, and in coming back again to his
solitary dwelling-place with his nets full, his boat
uninjured, and himself alive and hearty. He
made no attempts to buy and sell with anybody,
he kept steadily away from the village, he lived
on fish of his own preternaturally strong frying,
and he never spoke to a living soul—with the
solitary exception of Poulailler himself. One
fine evening, when the young man was rowing
home past the tower, the Fiend-Fisherman darted
out on to the rock, said, "Thank you, Poulailler,
for giving me a name," bowed politely, and darted
in again. The young fisherman felt the words
run cold down the marrow of his back; and
whenever he was at sea again, he gave the tower
a wide berth from that day forth.

Time went on, and an important event occurred in Poulailler's life. He was engaged to
be married. On the day when his betrothal was
publicly made known, his friends clustered noisily about him on the fishing-jetty of the village to
offer their congratulations. While they were all
in full cry, a strange voice suddenly made itself
heard through the confusion, which silenced
everybody in an instant. The crowd fell back,
and disclosed the Fiend-Fisherman, sauntering
up the jetty. It was the first time he had ever
set foot—cloven foot—within the precincts of the
village.

"Gentlemen," said the Fiend-Fisherman,
"where is my friend Poulailler?" He put the
question with perfect politeness; he looked re-

markably well in his fisherman's costume; he exhaled a relishing odor of fried fish; he had a cordial nod for the men, and a sweet smile for the women; but, with all these personal advantages, everybody fell back from him, and nobody answered his question. The coldness of the popular reception, however, did not in any way abash him. He looked about for Poulailler with searching eyes, discovered the place in which he was standing, and addressed him in the friendliest manner.

"So you are going to be married?" remarked the Fiend-Fisherman.

"What's that to you?" said Poulailler. He was inwardly terrified, but outwardly gruff—not an uncommon combination of circumstances with men of his class in his mental situation.

"My friend," pursued the Fiend-Fisherman, "I have not forgotten your polite attention in giving me a name, and I come here to requite it. You will have a family, Poulailler, and your first child will be a boy. I propose to make that boy my adopted son."

The marrow of Poulailler's back became awfully cold; but he grew gruffer than ever, in spite of his back.

"You won't do anything of the sort," he replied. "If I have the largest family in France, no child of mine shall ever go near you."

"I shall adopt your first-born for all that," persisted the Fiend-Fisherman. "Poulailler, I wish you good-morning. Ladies and gentlemen, the same to all of you."

With those words, he withdrew from the jetty, and the marrow of Poulailler's back recovered its temperature.

The next morning was stormy, and all the village expected to see the boat from the tower put out, as usual, to sea. Not a sign of it appeared. Later in the day the rock on which the building stood was examined from a distance. Neither boat nor nets were in their customary places. At night the red gleam of the fire was missed for the first time. The Fiend-Fisherman had gone! He had announced his intentions on the jetty, and had disappeared. What did this mean? Nobody knew.

On Poulailler's wedding-day, a portentous circumstance recalled the memory of the diabolical stranger, and, as a matter of course, seriously discomposed the bridegroom's back. At the moment when the marriage ceremony was complete, a relishing odor of fried fish stole into the nostrils of the company, and a voice from invisible lips said, "Keep up your spirits, Poulailler; I have not forgotten my promise!"

A year later, Madame Poulailler was in the hands of the midwife of the district, and a repetition of the portentous circumstance took place. Poulailler was waiting in the kitchen to hear how matters ended upstairs. The nurse came in with a baby. "Which is it?" asked the happy father; "girl or boy?" Before the nurse could answer, an odor of supernaturally fried fish filled the kitchen, and a voice from invisible lips replied, "A boy, Poulailler, *and I've got him!*"

Such were the circumstances under which the subject of this Memoir was introduced to the joys and sorrows of mortal existence.

II.—HIS BOYHOOD AND EARLY LIFE.

When a boy is born under auspices which lead his parents to suppose that, while the bodily part of him is safe at home, the spiritual part is subjected to a course of infernal tuition elsewhere, what are his father and mother to do with him? They must do the best they can—which was exactly what Poulailler and his wife did with the hero of these pages.

In the first place, they had him christened instantly. It was observed with horror that his infant face was distorted with grimaces, and that his infant voice roared with a preternatural lustiness of tone the moment the priest touched him. The first thing he asked for, when he learned to speak, was "fried fish"; and the first place he wanted to go to, when he learned to walk, was the diabolical tower on the rock. "He won't learn anything," said the master, when he was old enough to go to school. "Thrash him," said Poulailler; and the master thrashed him. "He won't come to his first communion," said the priest. "Thrash him," said Poulailler; and the priest thrashed him. The farmers' orchards were robbed; the neighboring rabbit-warrens were depopulated; linen was stolen from the gardens, and nets were torn on the beach. "The deuce take Poulailler's boy," was the general cry. "The deuce has got him," was Poulailler's

answer. "And yet he is a nice-looking boy,"
said Madame Poulailler. And he was—as tall,
as strong, as handsome a young fellow as could
be seen in all France. "Let us pray for him,"
said Madame Poulailler. "Let us thrash him,"
said her husband. "Our son has been thrashed
till all the sticks in the neighborhood are broken," pleaded his mother. "We will try him
with the rope's-end next," retorted his father;
"he shall go to sea, and live in an atmosphere
of thrashing. Our son shall be a cabin-boy."
It was all one to Poulailler Junior; he knew who
had adopted him, as well as his father; he had
been instinctively conscious from infancy of the
Fiend-Fisherman's interest in his welfare; he
cared for no earthly discipline; and a cabin-boy
he became at ten years old.

After two years of the rope's-end (applied quite
ineffectually), the subject of this Memo'r robbed
his captain, and ran away in an English port.
London became the next scene of his adventures.
At twelve years old he persuaded society in the
metropolis that he was the forsaken natural son
of a French duke. British benevolence, after
blindly providing for him for four years, opened
its eyes and found him out at the age of sixteen;
upon which he returned to France, and entered
the army in the capacity of drummer. At eighteen he deserted, and had a turn with the gypsies.
He told fortunes, he conjured, he danced on the
tight-rope, he acted, he sold quack medicines,
he altered his mind again, and returned to the
army. Here he fell in love with the vivandiere

of his new regiment. The sergeant-major of the company, touched by the same amiable weakness, naturally resented his attentions to the lady. Poulailler (perhaps unjustifiably) asserted himself by boxing his officer's ears. Out flashed the swords on both sides, and in went Poulailler's blade through and through the tender heart of the sergeant-major. The frontier was close at hand. Poulailler wiped his sword, and crossed it.

Sentence of death was recorded against him in his absence. When society has condemned us to die, if we are men of any spirit, how are we to return the compliment? By condemning society to keep us alive—or, in other words, by robbing right and left for a living. Poulailler's destiny was now accomplished. He was picked out to be the greatest thief of his age; and when Fate summoned him to his place in the world, he stepped forward and took it. His life hitherto had been merely the life of a young scamp; he was now to do justice to the diabolical father who had adopted him, and to expand to the proportions of a full-grown robber.

His first exploits were performed in Germany. They showed such a novelty of combination, such daring, such dexterity, and, even in his most homicidal moments, such irresistible gayety and good humor, that a band of congenial spirits gathered about him in no time. As commander-in-chief of the thieves' army, his popularity never wavered. His weaknesses—and what illustrious man is without them?—were three in number. First weakness: he was extravagantly susceptible to the charms of the fair sex.   Second weakness: he was perilously fond of practical jokes. Third weakness (inherited from his adopted parent): his appetite was insatiable in the matter of fried fish.   As for the merits to set against these defects, some have been noticed already, and others will appear immediately.   Let it merely be premised in this place that he was one of the handsomest men of his time, that he dressed superbly, and that he was capable of the most exalted acts of generosity wherever a handsome woman was concerned—let this be understood, to begin with; and let us now enter on the narrative of his last exploit in Germany before he returned to France.   This adventure is something more than a mere specimen of his method of workmanship; it proved, in the future, to be the fatal event of his life.

On a Monday in the week he had stopped on the highway, and robbed of all his valuables and all his papers an Italian nobleman—the Marquis Petrucci, of Sienna.   On Tuesday he was ready for another stroke of business.   Posted on the top of a steep hill, he watched the road which wound up to the summit on one side, while his followers were ensconced on the road which led down from it on the other.   The prize expected in this case was the traveling-carriage (with a large sum of money inside) of the Baron De Kirbergen.

Before long Poulailler discerned the carriage afar off at the bottom of the hill, and in advance of it, ascending the eminence, two ladies on foot.

They were the Baron's daughters—Wilhelmina,
a fair beauty; Frederica, a brunette—both lovely,
both accomplished, both susceptible, both young.
Poulailler sauntered down the hill to meet the
fascinating travelers.   He looked, bowed, introduced himself, and fell in love with Wilhelmina
on the spot.   Both the charming girls acknowledged in the most artless manner that confinement to the carriage had given them the fidgets,
and that they were walking up the hill to try the
remedy of gentle exercise.   Poulailler's heart was
touched, and Poulailler's generosity to the sex
was roused in the nick of time.   With a polite
apology to the young ladies, he ran back, by a
short cut, to the ambush on the other side of the
hill in which his men were posted.

"Gentlemen!" cried the generous thief, "in
the charming name of Wilhelmina de Kirbergen,
I charge you all, let the Baron's carriage pass
free."   The band was not susceptible; the band
demurred.   Poulailler knew them.   He had appealed to their hearts in vain; he now appealed
to their pockets.   "Gentlemen!" he resumed,
"excuse my momentary misconception of your
sentiments.   Here is my one-half share of the
Marquis Petrucci's property.   If I divide it among
you, will you let the carriage pass free?"   The
band knew the value of money, and accepted the
terms.   Poulailler rushed back up the hill, and
arrived at the top just in time to hand the young
ladies into the carriage.   "Charming man!" said
the white Wilhelmina to the brown Frederica, as
they drove off.   Innocent soul! what would she

have said if she had known that her personal attractions had saved her father's property? Was
she ever to see the charming man again? Yes;
she was to see him the next day—and, more than
that, Fate was hereafter to link her fast to the
robber's life and the robber's doom.

Confiding the direction of the band to his first
lieutenant, Poulailler followed the carriage on
horseback, and ascertained the place of the
Baron's residence that night.

The next morning a superbly-dressed stranger
knocked at the door. "What name, sir?" said
the servant. "The Marquis Petrucci, of Sienna,"
replied Poulailler. "How are the young ladies
after their journey?" The Marquis was shown
in, and introduced to the Baron. The Baron
was naturally delighted to receive a brother nobleman; Miss Wilhelmina was modestly happy to
see the charming man again; Miss Frederica
was affectionately pleased on her sister's account.
Not being of a disposition to lose time where his
affections were concerned, Poulailler expressed
his sentiments to the beloved object that evening.
The next morning he had an interview with the
Baron, at which he produced the papers which
proved him to be the Marquis. Nothing could
be more satisfactory to the mind of the most anxious parent—the two noblemen embraced. They
were still in each other's arms, when a second
stranger knocked at the door. "What name,
sir?" said the servant. "The Marquis Petrucci,
of Sienna," replied the stranger. "Impossible!"
said the servant; "his lordship is now in the

house." "Show me in, scoundrel," cried the visitor. The servant submitted, and the two Marquises stood face to face. Poulailler's composure was not shaken in the least; he had come first to the house, and he had got the papers. "You are the villain who robbed me!" cried the true Petrucci. "You are drunk, mad, or an impostor," retorted the false Petrucci. "Send to Florence, where I am known," exclaimed one of the Marquises, apostrophizing the Baron. "Send to Florence by all means," echoed the other, addressing himself to the Baron also. "Gentlemen," replied the noble Kirbergen, "I will do myself the honor of taking your advice" —and he sent to Florence accordingly.

Before the messenger had advanced ten miles on his journey, Poulailler had said two words in private to the susceptible Wilhelmina, and the pair eloped from the baronial residence that night. Once more the subject of this Memoir crossed the frontier, and re-entered France. Indifferent to the attractions of rural life, he forthwith established himself with the beloved object in Paris. In that superb city he met with his strangest adventures, performed his boldest achievements, committed his most prodigious robberies, and, in a word, did himself and his infernal patron the fullest justice in the character of the Fiend-Fisher-man's adopted son.

III.—HIS CAREER IN PARIS.

Once established in the French metropolis, Poulailler planned and executed that vast system

of perpetual robbery and occasional homicide
which made him the terror and astonishment of
all Paris. Indoors as well as out his good fortune befriended him. No domestic anxieties ha-
rassed his mind, and diverted him from the pursuit of his distinguished public career. The
attachment of the charming creature with whom
he had eloped from Germany survived the discovery that the Marquis Petrucci was Poulailler
the robber. True to the man of her choice, the
devoted Wilhelmina shared his fortunes, and
kept his house. And why not, if she loved him
—in the all-conquering name of Cupid, why not?

Joined by picked men from his German followers, and by new recruits gathered together in
Paris, Poulailler now set society and its safeguards
at flat defiance. Cartouche himself was his inferior in audacity and cunning. In course of
time, the whole city was panic-stricken by the
new robber and his band—the very Boulevards
were deserted after nightfall. Monsieur Hérault, lieutenant of police of the period, in
despair of laying hands on Poulailler by any
other means, at last offered a reward of a hundred pistoles and a place in his office worth two
thousand livres a year to any one who would apprehend the robber alive. The bills were posted
all over Paris, and the next morning they produced the very last result in the world which the
lieutenant of police could possibly have anticipated.

While Monsieur Hérault was at breakfast in
his study, the Count de Villeneuve was an-

nounced as wishing to speak to him. Knowing
the Count by name only, as belonging to an ancient
family in Provence or in Languedoc, Monsieur
Hérault ordered him to be shown in. A perfect
gentleman appeared, dressed with an admirable
mixture of magnificence and good taste. "I
have something for your private ear, sir," said
the Count. "Will you give orders that no one
must be allowed to disturb us?"

Monsieur Herault gave the orders.

"May I inquire, Count, what your business
is?" he asked when the door was closed.

"To earn the reward you offer for taking
Poulailler," answered the Count. "I am Poulailler."

Before Monsieur Herault could open his lips,
the robber produced a pretty little dagger and
some rose-colored silk cord. "The point of this
dagger is poisoned," he observed; "and one
scratch of it, my dear sir, would be the death of
you." With these words Poulailler gagged the
lieutenant of police, bound him to his chair with
the rose-colored cord, and lightened his writing-
desk of one thousand pistoles. "I'll take money,
instead of taking the place in the office which
you kindly offer," said Poulailler. "Don't
trouble yourself to see me to the door. Good-
morning."

A few weeks later, while Monsieur Herault
was still the popular subject of ridicule throughout Paris, business took Poulailler on the road
to Lille and Cambrai. The only inside passenger in the coach besides himself was the vener-

able Dean Potter, of Brussels. They fell into talk on the one interesting subject of the time— not the weather, but Poulailler.

"It's a disgrace, sir, to the police," said the Dean, "that such a miscreant is still at large. I shall be returning to Paris by this road in ten days' time, and I shall call on Monsieur Herault to suggest a plan of my own for catching the scoundrel."

"May I ask what it is?" said Poulailler.

"Excuse me," replied the Dean; "you are a stranger, sir, and moreover I wish to keep the merit of suggesting the plan to myself."

"Do you think the lieutenant of police will see you?" asked Poulailler; "he is not accessible to strangers, since the miscreant you speak of played him that trick at his own breakfast-table."

"He will see Dean Potter, of Brussels," was the reply, delivered with the slightest possible tinge of offended dignity.

"Oh, unquestionably!" said Poulailler; "pray pardon me."

"Willingly, sir," said the Dean; and the conversation flowed into other channels.

Nine days later the wounded pride of Monsieur Herault was soothed by a very remarkable letter. It was signed by one of Poulailler's band, who offered himself as king's evidence, in the hope of obtaining a pardon. The letter stated that the venerable Dean Potter had been waylaid and murdered by Poulailler, and that the robber, with his customary audacity, was about to re-enter Paris by the Lisle coach the next day, disguised

in the Dean's own clothes, and furnished with
the Dean's own papers. Monsieur Herault took
his precautions without losing a moment. Picked
men were stationed, with their orders, at the
barrier through which the coach must pass to
enter Paris, while the lieutenant of police waited
at his office, in the company of two French gentlemen who could speak to the Dean's identity,
in the event of Poulailler's impudently persisting
in the assumption of his victim's name.

At the appointed hour the coach appeared, and
out of it got a man in the Dean's costume. He
was arrested in spite of his protestations; the
papers of the murdered Potter were found on
him, and he was dragged off to the police-office
in triumph. The door opened and the *posse comitatus* entered with the prisoner. Instantly the
two witnesses burst out with a cry of recognition, and turned indignantly on the lieutenant of
police. "Gracious Heaven, sir, what have you
done!" they exclaimed in horror; "this is not
Poulailler—here is our venerable friend; here is
the Dean himself!" At the same moment a servant entered with a letter. "Dean Potter. To the
care of Monsieur Herault, Lieutenant of Police."
The letter was expressed in these words: "Venerable Sir—Profit by the lesson I have given you.
Be a Christian for the future, and never again try
to injure a man unless he tries to injure you. Entirely yours—Poulailler."

These feats of cool audacity were matched by
others, in which his generosity to the sex asserted
itself as magnanimously as ever.

Hearing one day that large sums of money were kept in the house of a great lady, one Madame De Brienne, whose door was guarded, in anticipation of a visit from the famous thief, by a porter of approved trustworthiness and courage, Poulailler undertook to rob her in spite of her precautions, and succeeded. With a stout pair of leather straps and buckles in his pocket, and with two of his band disguised as a coachman and a footman, he followed Madame De Brienne one night to the theater. Just before the close of the performance, the lady's coachman and footman were tempted away for five minutes by Poulailler's disguised subordinates to have a glass of wine. No attempt was made to detain them, or to drug their liquor. But in their absence Poulailler had slipped under the carriage, had hung his leather straps round the pole—one to hold by, and one to support his feet—and, with these simple preparations, was now ready to wait for events. Madame De Brienne entered the carriage—the footman got up behind—Poulailler hung himself horizontally under the pole, and was driven home with them under those singular circumstances. He was strong enough to keep his position after the carriage had been taken into the coach-house, and he only left it when the doors were locked for the night. Provided with food beforehand, he waited patiently, hidden in the coach-house, for two days and nights, watching his opportunity of getting into Madame De Brienne's boudoir.

On the third night the lady went to a grand

ball; the servants relaxed in their vigilance
while her back was turned, and Poulailler slipped
into the room. He found two thousand louis
d'ors, which was nothing like the sum he expected, and a pocketbook, which he took away
with him to open at home. It contained some
stock warrants for a comparatively trifling
amount. Poulailler was far too well off to care
about taking them, and far too polite, where a
lady was concerned, not to send them back
again, under those circumstances. Accordingly,
Madame De Brienne received her warrants, with
a note of apology from the polite thief.

"Pray excuse my visit to your charming boudoir," wrote Poulailler, "in consideration of the
false reports of your wealth, which alone induced
me to enter it. If I had known what your
pecuniary circumstances really were, on the
honor of a gentleman, madame, I should have
been incapable of robbing you. I cannot return
your two thousand louis d'ors by post, as I return your warrants. But if you are at all
pressed for money in future, I shall be proud
to assist so distinguished a lady by lending her,
from my own ample resources, double the sum
of which I regret to have deprived her on the
present occasion." This letter was shown to
royalty at Versailles. It excited the highest admiration of the Court—especially of the ladies.
Whenever the robber's name was mentioned,
they indulgently referred to him as the Chevalier
De Poulailler. Ah! that was the age of politeness, when good-breeding was recognized, even

in the thief. Under similar circumstances, who would recognize it now? O tempora! O mores!

On another occasion Poulailler was out one night taking the air, and watching his opportunities on the roofs of the houses, a member of the band being posted in the street below to assist him in case of necessity. While in this position, sobs and groans proceeding from an open back-garret window caught his ear. A parapet rose before the window, which enabled him to climb down and look in. Starving children surrounding a helpless mother, and clamoring for food, was the picture that met his eye. The mother was young and beautiful, and Poulailler's hand impulsively clutched his purse, as a necessary consequence. Before the charitable thief could enter by the window, a man rushed in by the door with a face of horror, and cast a handful of gold into the lovely mother's lap. "My honor is gone," he cried, "but our children are saved! Listen to the circumstances. I met a man in the street below; he was tall and thin; he had a green patch over one eye; he was looking up suspiciously at this house, apparently waiting for somebody. I thought of you—I thought of the children—I seized the suspicious stranger by the collar. Terror overwhelmed him on the spot. 'Take my watch, my money, and my two valuable gold snuff-boxes,' he said, 'but spare my life.' I took them." "Noble-hearted man!" cried Poulailler, appearing at the window. The husband started; the wife screamed; the children hid themselves. "Let me entreat you to be composed," continued Poulailler. "Sir! I enter on the scene for the purpose of soothing your uneasy conscience. From your vivid description, I recognize the man whose property is now in your wife's lap. Resume your mental tranquillity. You have robbed a robber—in other words, you have vindicated society. Accept my congratulations on your restored innocence. The miserable coward whose collar you seized is one of Poulailler's band. He has lost his stolen property as the fit punishment for his disgraceful want of spirit."

"Who are you?" exclaimed the husband.

"I am Poulailler," replied the illustrious man, with the simplicity of an ancient hero. "Take this purse, and set up in business with the contents. There is a prejudice, sir, in favor of honesty. Give that prejudice a chance. There was a time when I felt it myself; I regret to feel it no longer. Under all varieties of misfortune, an honest man has his consolation still left. Where is it left? Here!" He struck his heart, and the family fell on their knees before him.

"Benefactor of your species!" cried the husband; "how can I show my gratitude?"

"You can permit me to kiss the hand of madame," answered Poulailler.

Madame started to her feet and embraced the generous stranger. "What more can I do?" exclaimed this lovely woman, eagerly; "oh heavens! what more?"

"You can beg your husband to light me downstairs," replied Poulailler. He spoke, pressed their hands, dropped a generous tear, and departed. At that touching moment his own adopted father would not have known him.

This last anecdote closes the record of Poulailler's career in Paris. The lighter and more agreeable aspects of that career have hitherto been designedly presented, in discreet remembrance of the contrast which the tragic side of the picture must now present. Comedy and Sentiment, twin sisters of French extraction, farewell! Horror enters next on the stage, and enters welcome, in the name of the Fiend-Fisherman's adopted son.

IV.—HIS EXIT FROM THE SCENE.

The nature of Poulailler's more serious achievements in the art of robbery may be realized by reference to one terrible fact. In the police records of the period, more than one hundred and fifty men and women are reckoned up as having met their deaths at the hands of Poulailler and his band. It was not the practice of this formidable robber to take life as well as property, unless life happened to stand directly in his way — in which case he immediately swept off the obstacle without hesitation and without remorse. His deadly determination to rob, which was thus felt by the population in general, was matched by his deadly determination to be obeyed, which was felt by his followers in particular. One of their number, for example, having withdrawn from his allegiance, and having afterward attempted to betray his leader, was tracked to his hiding-place in a cellar, and was there walled up alive in Poulailler's presence, the robber composing the unfortunate wretch's epitaph, and scratching it on the wet plaster with his own hand. Years afterward the inscription was noticed when the house fell into the possession of a new tenant, and was supposed to be nothing more than one of the many jests which the famous robber had practiced in his time. When the plaster was removed, the skeleton fell out, and testified that Poulailler was in earnest.

To attempt the arrest of such a man as this by tampering with his followers was practically impossible. No sum of money that could be offered would induce any one of the members of his band to risk the fatal chance of his vengeance. Other means of getting possession of him had been tried, and tried in vain. Five times over the police had succeeded in tracking him to different hiding-places; and on all five occasions, the women—who adored him for his gallantry, his generosity, and his good looks—had helped him to escape. If he had not unconsciously paved the way to his own capture, first by eloping with Mademoiselle Wilhelmina de Kirbergen, and secondly by maltreating her, it is more than doubtful whether the long arm of the law would ever have reached far enough to fasten its grasp on him. As it was, the extremes of love and hatred met at last in the bosom of the devoted Wilhelmina, and the vengeance of a neglected woman accomplished what the whole police force of Paris had been powerless to achieve.

Poulailler, never famous for the constancy of his attachments, had wearied, at an early period, of the companion of his flight from Germany; but Wilhelmina was one of those women whose affections, once aroused, will not take No for an answer. She persisted in attaching herself to a man who had ceased to love her. Poulailler's patience became exhausted; he tried twice to rid himself of his unhappy mistress—once by the knife, and once by poison—and failed on both occasions. For the third and last time, by way of attempting an experiment of another kind, he established a rival, to drive the German woman out of the house. From that moment his fate was sealed. Maddened by jealous rage, Wilhelmina cast the last fragments of her fondness to the winds. She secretly communicated with the police, and Poulailler met his doom.

A night was appointed with the authorities, and the robber was invited by his discarded mistress to a farewell interview. His contemptuous confidence in her fidelity rendered him careless of his customary precautions. He accepted the appointment, and the two supped together, on the understanding that they were henceforth to be friends and nothing more. Toward the close of the meal Poulailler was startled by a ghastly change in the face of his companion.

"What is wrong with you?" he asked.

"A mere trifle," she answered, looking at her glass of wine. "I can't help loving you still, badly as you have treated me. You are a dead man, Poulailler, and I shall not survive you."

The robber started to his feet, and seized a knife on the table.

"You have poisoned me!" he exclaimed.

"No," she replied. "Poison is my vengeance on myself; not my vengeance on *you*. You will rise from this table as you sat down to it. But your evening will be finished in prison, and your life will be ended on the wheel."

As she spoke the words, the door was burst open by the police and Poulailler was secured. The same night the poison did its fatal work, and his mistress made atonement with her life for the first, last act of treachery which had revenged her on the man she loved.

Once safely lodged in the hands of justice, the robber tried to gain time to escape in, by promising to make important disclosures. The maneuver availed him nothing. In those days the Laws of the Land had not yet made acquaintance with the Laws of Humanity. Poulailler was put to the torture—was suffered to recover—was publicly broken on the wheel—and was taken off it alive, to be cast into a blazing fire. By those murderous means Society rid itself of a murderous man, and the idlers on the Boulevards took their evening stroll again in recovered security.

.   .   .   .

Paris had seen the execution of Poulailler; but if legends are to be trusted, our old friends, the people of the fishing village in Brittany, saw the end of him afterward. On the day and hour when he perished, the heavens darkened, and a terrible storm arose. Once more, and for a moment only, the gleam of the unearthly fire reddened the windows of the old tower. Thunder pealed, and struck the building into fragments. Lightning flashed incessantly over the ruins; and, in the scorching glare of it, the boat which, in former years, had put off to sea whenever the storm rose highest, was seen to shoot out into the raging ocean from the cleft in the rock, and was discovered on this final occasion to be doubly manned. The Fiend-Fisherman sat at the helm; his adopted son tugged at the oars; and a clamor of diabolical voices, roaring awfully through the roaring storm, wished the pair of them a prosperous voyage.

SKETCHES OF CHARACTER.—IV.

THE BACHELOR BEDROOM.

THE great merit of this subject is that it starts itself.

The Bachelor Bedroom is familiar to everybody who owns a country house, and to everybody who has stayed in a country house. It is the one especial sleeping apartment, in all civilized residences used for the reception of company which preserves a character of its own. Married people and young ladies may be shifted about from bedroom to bedroom as their own caprice or the domestic convenience of the host may suggest. But the bachelor guest, when he has once had his room set apart for him, contrives to dedicate it to the perpetual occupation of single men from that moment. Who else is to have the room afterward, when the very atmosphere of it is altered by tobacco-smoke? Who can venture to throw it open to nervous spinsters, or respectable married couples, when the footman is certain, from mere force of habit, to make his appearance at the door with contraband bottles and glasses, after the rest of the family have retired for the night? Where, even if these difficulties could be got over, is any second sleeping

apartment to be found, in any house of ordinary
construction, isolated enough to secure the so-
berly reposing portion of the guests from being
disturbed by the regular midnight party which
the bachelor persists in giving in his bedroom?
Dining-rooms and breakfast-rooms may change
places; double-bedded rooms and single-bedded
rooms may shift their respective characters backward and forward amicably among each other—
but the Bachelor Bedroom remains immovably
in its own place; sticks immutably to its own
bad character; stands out victoriously whether
the house is full or whether the house is empty,
the one hospitable institution that no repentant
after-thoughts of host or hostess can ever hope to
suppress.

Such a social phenomenon as this, taken with
its surrounding circumstances, deserves more
notice than it has yet obtained. The bachelor
has been profusely served up on all sorts of literary tables; but the presentation of him has been
hitherto remarkable for a singularly monotonous
flavor of matrimonial sauce. We have heard of
his loneliness, and its remedy; of his solitary
position in illness, and its remedy; of the miserable neglect of his linen, and its remedy. But
what have we heard of him in connection with
his remarkable bedroom at those periods of his
existence when he, like the rest of the world, is
a visitor at his friend's country house? Who
has presented him, in his relation to married society, under those peculiar circumstances of his
life, when he is away from his solitary cham-

bers, and is thrown straight into the sacred center of that home circle from which his ordinary
habits are so universally supposed to exclude
him? Here, surely, is a new aspect of the
bachelor still left to be presented; and here is a
new subject for worn-out readers of the nine-
teenth century, whose fountain of literary novelty has become exhausted at the source.

Let me sketch the history—in anticipation of
a large and serious work which I intend to produce, one of these days, on the same subject—of
the Bachelor Bedroom, in a certain comfortable
country house, whose hospitable doors fly open
to me with the beginning of summer, and close
no more until the autumn is ended. I must beg
permission to treat this interesting topic from
the purely human point of view. In other words,
I propose describing, not the Bedroom itself, but
the succession of remarkable bachelors who have
passed through it in my time.

The hospitable country-seat to which I refer is
Coolcup House, the residence of that enterprising
gentleman-farmer and respected chairman of
Quarter Sessions, Sir John Giles. Sir John's
Bachelor Bedroom has been wisely fitted up on
the ground-floor. It is the one solitary sleeping
apartment in that part of the house. Fidgety
bachelors can jump out on to the lawn at night,
through the bow-window, without troubling anybody to unlock the front door; and can communicate with the presiding genius of the cellar
by merely crossing the hall. For the rest, the
room is delightfully airy and spacious, and fitted

up with all possible luxury. It started in life, under Sir John's careful auspices, the perfection of neatness and tidiness. But the Bachelors have corrupted it long since. However carefully the servants may clean and alter and arrange it, the room loses its respectability again, and gets slovenly and unpresentable the moment their backs are turned. Sir John himself, the tidiest man in existence, has given up all hope of reforming it. He peeps in occasionally, and sighs and shakes his head, and puts a chair in its place, and straightens a print on the wall, and looks about him at the general litter and confusion, and gives it up and goes out again. He is a rigid man and a resolute in the matter of order, and has his way all over the rest of the house— but the Bachelor Bedroom is too much for him.

The first bachelor who inhabited the room when 1 began to be a guest at Coolcup House, was Mr. Bigg.

Mr. Bigg is, in the strictest sense of the word, what you call a fine man. He stands over six feet, is rather more than stout enough for his height, holds his head up nobly, and dresses in a style of mingled gayety and grandeur which impresses everybody. The morning shirts of Mr. Bigg are of so large a pattern that nobody but his haberdasher knows what that pattern really is. You see a bit of it on one side of his collar which looks square, and a bit of it on the other side which looks round. 1t goes up his arm on one of his wristbands, and down his arm on the other. Men who have seen his shirts off (if such a

statement may be permitted), and scattered
loosely, to Sir John's horror, over all the chairs
in the Bedroom, have been questioned, and have
not been found able to state that their eyes ever
followed out the patterns of any one of them
fairly to the end. In the mattter of beautiful
and expensive clothing for the neck, Mr. Bigg is
simply inexhaustible. Every morning he appears at breakfast in a fresh scarf, and taps his
egg magnificently with a daily blaze of new color
glowing on his capacious chest, to charm the
eyes of the young ladies who sit opposite to him.
All the other component parts of Mr. Bigg's costume are of an equally grand and attractive
kind, and are set off by Mr. Bigg's enviable figure to equal advantage. Outside the Bachelor
Bedroom, he is altogether an irreproachable
character in the article of dress. Outside the
Bachelor Bedroom, he is essentially a man of the
world, who can be depended on to perform any
part allotted to him in any society assembled at
Coolcup House; who has lived among all ranks
and sorts of people; who has filled a public situation with great breadth and dignity, and has sat
at table with crowned heads, and played his part
there with distinction; who can talk of these experiences, and of others akin to them, with curious fluency and ease, and can shift about to
other subjects, and pass the bottle, and carve,
and draw out modest people, and take all other
social responsibilities on his own shoulders complacently, at the largest and dreariest county
dinner-party that Sir John, to his own great dis-

comfiture, can be obliged to give. Such is Mr.
Bigg in the society of the house, when the door
of the Bachelor Bedroom has closed behind him.

But what is Mr. Bigg, when he has courte-
ously wished the ladies good-night, when he has
secretly summoned the footman with the surreptitious tray, and when he has deluded the unprincipled married men of the party into having
half an hour's cozy chat with him before they go
upstairs? Another being—a being unknown to
the ladies, and unsuspected by the respectable
guests. Inside the Bedroom, the outward aspect
of Mr. Bigg changes as if by magic; and a kind
of gorgeous slovenliness pervades him from top to
toe. Buttons which have rigidly restrained him
within distinct physical boundaries, slip exhausted out of their button-holes; and the figure
of Mr. Bigg suddenly expands and asserts itself
for the first time as a protuberant fact. His
neckcloth flies on to the nearest chair, his rigid
shirt-collar yawns open, his wiry under-whiskers
ooze multitudinously into view, his coat, waistcoat, and braces drop off his shoulders. If the
two young ladies who sleep in the room above,
and who most unreasonably complain of the
ceaseless nocturnal croaking and growling of
voices in the Bachelor Bedroom, could look down
through the ceiling now, they would not know
Mr. Bigg again, and would suspect that a dissipated artisan had intruded himself into Sir
John's house.

In the same way, the company who have sat
in Mr. Bigg's neighborhood at the dinner-table

at seven o'clock, would find it impossible to recognize his conversation at midnight. Outside
the Bachelor Bedroom, if his talk has shown
him to be anything at all, it has shown him to
be the exact reverse of an enthusiast. Inside the
Bachelor Bedroom, after all due attention has
been paid to the cigar-box and the footman's
tray, it becomes unaccountably manifest to
everybody that Mr. Bigg is, after all, a fanati-
cal character, a man possessed of one fixed idea.
Then, and then only, does he mysteriously confide to his fellow-revelers that he is the one
remarkable man in Great Britain who has discovered the real authorship of Junius's Letters.
In the general society of the house, nobody ever
hears him refer to the subject; nobody ever sus-
pects that he takes more than the most ordinary
interest in literary matters. In the select society
of the Bedroom, inspired by the surreptitious
tray and the midnight secrecy, wrapped in
clouds of tobacco-smoke, and freed from the
restraint of his own magnificent garments, the
truth flies out of Mr. Bigg, and the authorship
of Junius's Letters becomes the one dreary subject which this otherwise variously gifted man
persists in dilating on for hours together. But
for the Bachelor Bedroom, nobody alive would ever
have discovered that the true key to unlock Mr.
Bigg's character is Junius. If the subject is referred to the next day by his companions of the
night, he declines to notice it; but, once in the
Bedroom again, he takes it up briskly, as if the
attempted reference to it had been made but the

moment before. The last time I saw him was in the Bachelor Bedroom. It was three o'clock in the morning; two tumblers were broken; half a lemon was in a soap-dish, and the soap itself was on the chimney-piece; restless married rakes, who were desperately afraid of waking up their wives when they left us, were walking to and fro absently, and crunching knobs of loaf-sugar under foot at every step; Mr. Bigg was standing, with his fourth cigar in his mouth, before the fire; one of his hands was in the tumbled bosom of his shirt, the other was grasping mine, while he pathetically appointed me his literary executor, and generously bequeathed to me his great discovery of the authorship of Junius's Letters. Upon the whole, Mr. Bigg is the most incorrigible bachelor on record in the annals of the Bedroom; he has consumed more candles, ordered more footman's trays, seen more early daylight, and produced more pale faces among the gentlemen at breakfast-time than any other single visitor at Coolcup House.

The next bachelor in the order of succession, and the completest contrast conceivable to Mr. Bigg, is Mr. Jeremy.

Mr. Jeremy is, perhaps, the most miserable-looking little man that ever tottered under the form of humanity. Wear what clothes he may, he invariably looks shabby in them. He is the victim of perpetual accidents and perpetual ill health; and the Bachelor Bedroom, when he in-habits it, is turned into a doctor's shop, and bristles all over with bottles and pills. Mr. Jeremy's personal tribute to the hospitalities of Coolcup House is always paid in the same singularly unsatisfactory manner to his host. On one day in the week, he gorges himself gayly with food and drink, and soars into the seventh heaven of convivial beatitude. On the other six, he is invariably ill in consequence, is reduced to the utmost rigors of starvation and physic, sinks into the lowest depths of depression, and takes the bitterest imaginable views of human life. Hardly a single accident has happened at Coolcup House in which he has not been personally and chiefly concerned; hardly a single malady can occur to the human frame the ravages of which he has not practically exemplified in his own person under Sir John's roof. If any one guest, in the fruit season, terrifies the rest by writhing under the internal penalties in such cases made and provided by the laws of Nature, it is Mr. Jeremy. If any one tumbles upstairs, or downstairs, or off a horse, or out of a dog-cart, it is Mr. Jeremy. If you want a case of sprained ankle, a case of suppressed gout, a case of complicated earache, toothache, headache, and sore throat, all in one, a case of liver, a case of chest, a case of nerves, or a case of low fever, go to Coolcup House while Mr. Jeremy is staying there, and he will supply you, on demand, at the shortest notice and to any extent. It is conjectured by the intimate friends of this extremely wretched bachelor, that he has but two sources of consolation to draw on, as a set-off against his innumerable

troubles. The first is the luxury of twisting his
nose on one side, and stopping up his air passages and Eustachian tubes with inconceivably
large quantities of strong snuff. The second is
the oleaginous gratification of incessantly anoint-
ing his miserable little beard and mustache with
cheap bear's grease, which always turns rancid
on the premises before he has half done with it.
When Mr. Jeremy gives a party in the Bachelor
Bedroom, his guests have the unexpected pleasure of seeing him take his physic, and hearing
him describe his maladies and recount his accidents. In other respects, the moral influence of
the Bedroom over the characters of those who
occupy it, which exhibits Mr. Bigg in the unexpected literary aspect of a commentator on
Junius, is found to tempt Mr. Jeremy into betraying a horrible triumph and interest in the
maladies of others, of which nobody would suspect him in the general society of the house.

"I noticed you, after dinner to-day," says this
invalid bachelor, on such occasions, to any one of
the Bedroom guests who may be rash enough
to complain of the slightest uneasiness in his
presence; "I saw the corners of your mouth get
green, and the whites of your eyes look yellow.
You have got a pain here," says Mr. Jeremy,
gayly indicating the place to which he refers on
his own shattered frame, with an appearance of
extreme relish—"a pain *here*, and a sensation
like having a cannon-ball inside you, *there*.
You will be parched with thirst and racked with
fidgets all to-night; and to-morrow morning you

will get up with a splitting headache, and a
dark-brown tongue, and another cannon-ball in
your inside. My dear fellow, I'm a veteran at
this sort of thing; and I know exactly the state
you will be in next week, and the week after,
and when you will have to try the seaside, and
how many pounds' weight you will lose to a
dead certainty, before you can expect to get over
this attack. Suppose we look under his ribs, on
the right side of him?" continues Mr. Jeremy,
addressing himself confidentially to the company
in general. "I lay anybody five to one we find
an alarming lump under the skin. And that
lump will be his liver!"

Thus, while Mr. Bigg always astonishes the
Bedroom guests on the subject of Junius, Mr.
Jeremy always alarms them on the subject of
themselves. Mr. Smart, the next, and third
bachelor, placed in a similar situation, displays
himself under a more agreeable aspect, and
makes the society that surrounds him, for the
night at least, supremely happy.

On the first day of his arrival at Coolcup
House Mr. Smart deceived us all. When he
was first presented to us, we were deeply impressed by the serene solemnity of this gentleman's voice, look, manner, and costume. He
was as carefully dressed as Mr. Bigg himself,
but on totally different principles. Mr. Smart
was fearfully and wonderfully gentlemanly in
his avoidance of anything approaching to bright
color on any part of his body. Quakerish drabs

and grays clothed him in the morning. Dismal black, unrelieved by an atom of jewelry, undisturbed even by so much as a flower in his button-hole, incased him grimly in the evening. He moved about the room and the garden with a ghostly and solemn stalk. When the ladies got brilliant in their conversation, he smiled upon them with a deferential modesty and polite Grandisonian admiration that froze the blood of "us youth" in our veins. When he spoke, it was like reading a passage from an elegant moral writer—the words were so beautifully arranged, the sentences were turned so musically, the sentiment conveyed was so delightfully well regulated, so virtuously appropriate to nothing in particular. At such times he always spoke in a slow, deep, and gentle drawl, with a thrillingly clear emphasis on every individual syllable. His speech sounded occasionally like a kind of highly-bred foreign English, spoken by a distinguished stranger who had mastered the language to such an extent that he had got beyond the natives altogether. We watched enviously all day for any signs of human infirmity in this surprising individual. The men detected him in nothing. Even the sharper eyes of the women only discovered that he was addicted to looking at himself affectionately in every glass in the house, when he thought that nobody was noticing him. At dinner-time we all pinned our faith on Sir John's excellent wine, and waited anxiously for its legitimate effect on the superb and icy stranger. Nothing came of it; Mr. Smart was as carefully guarded with the bottle as he was with the English language. All through the evening he behaved himself so dreadfully well that we quite began to hate him. When the company parted for the night, and when Mr. Smart (who was just mortal enough to be a bachelor) invited us to a cigar in the Bedroom, his highly-bred foreign English was still in full perfection; his drawl had reached its elocutionary climax of rich and gentle slowness; and his Grandisonian smile was more exasperatingly settled and composed than ever.

The Bedroom door closed on us. We took off our coats, tore open our waistcoats, rushed in a body on the new bachelor's cigar-box, and summoned the evil genius of the footman's tray.

At the first round of the tumblers, the false Mr. Smart began to disappear, and the true Mr. Smart approached, as it were, from a visionary distance, and took his place among us. He chuckled—Grandison chuckled—within the hearing of every man in the room! We were surprised at that; but what were our sensations when, in less than ten minutes afterward, the highly-bred English and the gentle drawl mysteriously disappeared, and there came bursting out upon us, from the ambush of Mr. Smart's previous elocution, the jolliest, broadest, and richest Irish brogue we had ever heard in our lives! The mystery was explained now. Mr. Smart had a coat of the smoothest English varnish laid over him, for highly-bred county society, which nothing mortal could peel off but bachelor com-

pany and whisky-and-water. He slipped out of
his close-fitting English envelope, in the loose
atmosphere of the Bachelor Bedroom, as glibly as
a tightly-laced young lady slips out of her stays
when the admiring eyes of the world are off her
waist for the night. Never was man so changed
as Mr. Smart was now. His moral sentiments
melted like the sugar in his grog; his grammar
disappeared with his white cravat. Wild and
lavish generosity suddenly became the leading
characteristic of this once reticent man. We
tried all sorts of subjects, and were obliged to
drop every one of them, because Mr. Smart
would promise to make us a present of whatever
we talked about. The family mansion in Ire-
land contained everything that this world can
supply; and Mr. Smart was resolved to dissipate
that priceless store in gifts distributed to the
much-esteemed company. He promised me a
schooner-yacht, and made a memorandum of the
exact tonnage in his pocketbook. He promised
my neighbor, on one side, a horse, and, on the
other, a unique autograph letter of Shakespeare's.
We had all three been talking respectively of
sailing, hunting, and the British drama; and we
now held our tongues for fear of getting new
presents if we tried new subjects. Other members of the festive assembly took up the ball of
conversation, and were prostrated forthwith by
showers of presents for their pains. When we
all parted in the dewy morning, we left Mr.
Smart with disheveled hair, checking off his voluminous memoranda of gifts with an unsteady

pencil, and piteously entreating us, in the richest Irish-English, to correct him instantly if we detected the slightest omission anywhere.

The next morning, at breakfast, we rather wondered which nation our friend would turn out to belong to. He set all doubts at rest the moment he opened the door, by entering the room with the old majestic stalk; saluting the ladies with the serene Grandison smile; trusting we had all rested well during the night, in a succession of elegantly turned sentences; and enunciating the highly-bred English with the imperturbably gentle drawl which we all imagined, the night before, that we had lost forever. He stayed more than a fortnight at Coolcup House; and, in all that time, nobody ever knew the true Mr. Smart except the guests in the Bachelor Bedroom.

The fourth Bachelor on the list deserves especial consideration and attention. In the first place, because he presents himself to the reader in the character of a distinguished foreigner. In the second place, because he contrived, in the most amiable manner imaginable, to upset all the established arrangements of Coolcup House—inside the Bachelor Bedroom, as well as outside it —from the moment when he entered its doors, to the moment when he left them behind him on his auspicious return to his native country. This, ladies and gentlemen, is a rare, probably a unique, species of bachelor; and Mr. Bigg, Mr. Jeremy, and Mr. Smart have no claim whatever to stand in the faintest light of comparison with him.

When I mention that the distinguished guest now introduced to notice is Herr von Muffe, it will be unnecessary for me to add that I refer to the distinguished German poet, whose far-famed Songs Without Sense have aided so immeasurably in thickening the lyric obscurities of his country's harp. On his arrival in London, Herr von Muffe forwarded his letter of introduction to Sir John by post, and immediately received, in return, the usual hospitable invitation to Coolcup House.

The eminent poet arrived barely in time to dress for dinner; and made his first appearance in our circle while we were waiting in the drawing-room for the welcome signal of the bell. He waddled in among us softly and suddenly, in the form of a very short, puffy, florid, roundabout old gentleman, with flowing gray hair and a pair of huge circular spectacles. The extreme shabbiness and dinginess of his costume was so singularly set off by the quantity of foreign orders of merit which he wore all over the upper part of it, that a sarcastic literary gentleman among the guests defined him to me, in a whisper, as a compound of "decorations and dirt." Sir John advanced to greet his distinguished guest, with friendly right hand extended as usual. Herr von Muffe, without saying a word, took the hand carefully in both his own, and expressed affectionate recognition of English hospitality, by transferring it forthwith to that vacant space

between his shirt and his waistcoat which extended over the region of the heart. Sir John
turned scarlet, and tried vainly to extricate his
hand from the poet's too affectionate bosom.
The dinner-bell rang, but Herr von Muffe still
held fast. The principal lady in the company
half rose, and looked perplexedly at her host—
Sir John made another and a desperate effort to
escape—failed again—and was marched into the
dining-room, in full view of his servants and his
guests, with his hand sentimentally imprisoned
in his foreign visitor's waistcoat.

After this romantic beginning, Herr von Muffe
rather surprised us by showing that he was decidedly the reverse of a sentimentalist in the
matter of eating and drinking.

Neither dish nor bottle passed the poet, without paying heavy tribute, all through the repast.
He mixed his liquors, especially, with the most
sovereign contempt for all sanitary considerations; drinking Champagne and beer, the sweet-
est Constantia and the tawniest port, all together,
with every appearance of the extremest relish.
Conversation with Herr von Muffe, both at dinner, and all through the evening, was found to
be next to impossible, in consequence of his knowing all languages (his own included) equally in-
correctly. His German was pronounced to be a
dialect never heard before; his French was inscrutable; his English was a philological riddle
which all of us guessed at and none of us found
out. He talked, in spite of these difficulties, incessantly; and, seeing that he shed tears several

times in the course of the evening, the ladies assumed that his topics were mostly of a pathetic nature, while the coarser men compared notes with each other, and all agreed that the distinguished guest was drunk. When the time came for retiring, we had to invite ourselves into the Bachelor Bedroom; Herr von Muffe having no suspicion of our customary midnight orgies, and apparently feeling no desire to entertain us, until we informed him of the institution of the footman's tray—when he became hospitable on a sudden, and unreasonably fond of his gay young English friends.

While we were settling ourselves in our places round the bed, a member of the company kicked over one of the poet's capacious Wellington boots. To the astonishment of every one, there instantly ensued a tinkling of coin, and some sovereigns and shillings rolled surprisingly out on the floor from the innermost recesses of the boot. On receiving his money back, Herr von Muffe informed us, without the slightest appearance of embarrassment, that he had not had time before dinner, to take more than his watch, rings, and decorations out of his boots. Seeing us all stare at this incomprehensible explanation, our distinguished friend kindly endeavored to enlighten us further by a long personal statement in his own polyglot language. From what we could understand of this narrative (which was not much), we gathered that Herr von Muffe had started at noon that day, as a total stranger in our metropolis, to reach the London Bridge station in a cab;

and that the driver had taken him as usual across Waterloo Bridge. On going through the Borough, the narrow streets, miserable houses, and squalid population had struck the lively imagination of Herr von Muffe, and had started in his mind a horrible suspicion that the cabman was driving him into a low neighborhood, with the object of murdering a helpless foreign fare in perfect security, for the sake of the valuables he carried on his person. Chilled to the very marrow of his bones by this idea, the poet raised the ends of his trousers stealthily in the cab, slipped his watch, rings, orders, and money into the legs of his Wellington boots, arrived at the station quaking with mortal terror, and screamed "Help!" at the top of his voice, when the railway policeman opened the cab door. The immediate starting of the train had left him no time to alter the singular traveling arrangements he had made in the Borough; and he arrived at Coolcup House, the only individual who had ever yet entered that mansion with his property in his boots.

Amusing as it was in itself, this anecdote failed a little in its effect on us at the time, in consequence of the stifling atmosphere in which we were condemned to hear it.

Although it was then the sultry middle of summer, and we were all smoking, Herr von Muffe insisted on keeping the windows of the Bachelor Bedroom fast closed, because it was one of his peculiarities to distrust the cooling effect of the night air. We were more than half inclined to go, under these circumstances; and we were alto-

gether determined to remove, when the tray came
in, and when we found our German friend madly
mixing his liquors again by pouring gin and
sherry together into the same tumbler. We
warned him, with a shuddering prevision of consequences, that he was mistaking gin for water;
and he blandly assured us in return that he was
doing nothing of the kind. "It is good for
My—" said Herr von Muffe, supplying his
ignorance of the word stomach by laying his
chubby forefinger on the organ in question, with
a sentimental smile. "It is bad for Our—" retorted the wag of the party, imitating the poet's
action, and turning quickly to the door. We all
followed him—and, for the first time in the annals of Coolcup House, the Bachelor Bedroom
was emptied of company before midnight.

Early the next morning, one of Sir John's
younger sons burst into my room in a state of
violent excitement.

"I say, what's to be done with Muffe?" inquired the young gentleman, with wildly staring
eyes.

"Open his windows, and fetch the doctor," I
answered, inspired by the recollections of the past
night.

"Doctor!" cried the boy; "the doctor won't
do—it's the barber."

"Barber?" I repeated.

"He's been asking me *to shave him!*" roared
my young friend, with vehement comic indignation. "He rang his bell, and asked for 'the Son
of the House'—and they made me go; and there

he was, grinning in the big armchair, with his mangy little shaving-brush in his hand, and a towel over his shoulder. 'Good-morning, my dear. Can you shave My—' says he, and taps his quivering old double chin with his infernal shaving-brush. Curse his impudence! What's to be done with him?"

I arranged to explain to Herr von Muffe, at the first convenient opportunity, that it was not the custom in England, whatever it might be in Germany, for "the Son of the House" to shave his father's guests; and undertook, at the same time, to direct the poet to the residence of the village barber. When the German guest joined us at breakfast, his unshaven chin, and the external results of his mixed potations and his seclusion from fresh air, by no means tended to improve his personal appearance. In plain words, he looked the picture of dyspeptic wretchedness.

"I am afraid, sir, you are hardly so well this morning as we could all wish!" said Sir John, kindly.

Herr von Muffe looked at his host affectionately, surveyed the company all round the table, smiled faintly, laid the chubby forefinger once more on the organ whose name he did not know, and answered with the most enchanting innocence and simplicity:

"I am *so* sick!"

There was no harm—upon my word, there was no harm in Herr von Muffe. On the contrary, there was a great deal of good nature and

genuine simplicity in his composition. But he
was a man naturally destitute of all power of
adapting himself to new persons and new circumstances; and he became amiably insupporta-
ble, in consequence, to everybody in the house
throughout the whole term of his visit. He
could not join one of us in any country diver-
sions. He hung about the house and garden in
a weak, pottering, aimless manner, always turning up at the wrong moment, and always attaching himself to the wrong person. He was
dexterous in a perfectly childish way at cutting
out little figures of shepherds and shepherdesses
in paper; and he was perpetually presenting
these frail tributes of admiration to the ladies,
who always tore them up and threw them away
in secret the moment his back was turned. When
he was not occupied with his paper figures, he
was out in the garden, gathering countless little
nosegays, and sentimentally presenting them to
everybody; not to the ladies only, but to lusty
agricultural gentlemen as well, who accepted
them with blank amazement; and to school-
boys, home for the holidays, who took them,
bursting with internal laughter at the "molly-
coddle" gentleman from foreign parts. As for
poor Sir John, he suffered more than any of us;
for Herr von Muffe was always trying to kiss
him. In short, with the best intentions in the
world, this unhappy foreign bachelor wearied
out the patience of everybody in the house; and,
to our shame be it said, we celebrated his departure, when he left us at last, by a festival meet-

ing in the Bachelor Bedroom, in honor of the welcome absence of Herr von Muffe.

I cannot say in what spirit my fellow-revelers have reflected on our behavior since that time; but I know, for my own part, that 1 now look back at my personal share in our proceedings with rather an uneasy conscience. I am afraid we were all of us a little hard on Herr von Muffe; and I hereby desire to offer him my own individual tribute of tardy atonement, by leaving him to figure as the last and crowning type of the Bachelor species presented in these pages. If he has produced anything approaching to a pleasing effect on the reader's mind, that effect shall not be weakened by the appearance of any more single men, native or foreign.   Let the door of the Bachelor Bedroom close with our final glimpse of the German guest; and permit the present chronicler to lay down the pen when it has traced penitently, for the last time, the name of Herr von Muffe.

NOOKS AND CORNERS OF HISTORY.—III.

A REMARKABLE REVOLUTION.

A REVOLUTION which is serious enough to overthrow a reigning sovereign—which is short enough to last only nine hours—and which is peaceable enough to begin and end without the taking of a single life or the shedding of a drop of blood, is certainly a phenomenon in the history of human affairs which is worth being carefully investigated. Such a revolution actually happened, in the empire of Russia, little more than a century and a quarter ago. The narrative here attempted of its rise, its progress, and its end may be trusted throughout as faithful to the truth. Extraordinary as they may appear, the events described in this fragment of history are matters of fact from first to last.

We start with a famous Russian character—Peter the Great. His son, who may be not unfairly distinguished as Peter the Small, died in the year seventeen hundred and thirty. With the death of this last personage the political difficulties arose which ended in the easy pulling down of one sovereign ruler at midnight, and the easy setting up of another by nine o'clock the next morning.

Besides the son whom he left to succeed him, Peter the Great had a daughter, whose title was princess, and whose name was Elizabeth. Peter's widow, the famous Empress Catherine, being a far-seeing woman, made a will which contained the expression of her wishes in regard to the succession to the throne, and which plainly and properly designated the Princess Elizabeth (there being no Salic law in Russia) as the reigning sovereign to be chosen after the death of her brother, Peter the Small. Nothing, apparently, could be more straightforward than the course to be followed at that time in appointing a new ruler over the Russian people.

But there happened to be living at Court two noblemen—Prince D'Olgorowki and Count Osterman—who had an interest of their own in complicating the affairs connected with the succession.

These two distinguished personages had possessed considerable power and authority under the feeble reign of Peter the Small, and they knew enough of his sister's resolute and self-reliant character to doubt what might become of their court position and their political privileges after the Princess Elizabeth was seated on the throne. Accordingly they lost no time in nominating a rival candidate of their own choosing, whom they dexterously raised to the imperial dignity, before there was time for the partisans of the Princess Elizabeth to dispute the authority under which they acted. The new sovereign,

thus unjustly invested with power, was a woman
—Anne, Dowager Duchess of Courland—and the
pretense under which Prince D'Olgorowki and
Count Osterman proclaimed her Empress of Russia was that Peter the Small had confidentially
communicated to them, on his death-bed, a desire
that the Dowager Duchess should be chosen as
the sovereign to succeed him.

The main result of the Dowager Duchess's occupation of the throne was the additional compli-
cation of the confused political affairs of Russia.
The new Empress had an eye to the advancement
of her family; and among the other relatives for
whom she provided was a niece, named Catherine, whom she married to the Prince of Bruns-
wick, brother-in-law of the King of Prussia.
The first child born of the marriage was a boy,
named Ivan. Before he had reached the age of
two years, the new Empress died; and, when
her will was opened, it was discovered, to the
amazement of every one, that she had appointed
this child to succeed her on the throne of Russia.

The private motive which led the Empress to
take this extraordinary course was her desire to
place the sovereign power in the hands of one of
her favorites, the Duke De Biren, by nominating
that nobleman as the guardian of the infant
Ivan. To accomplish this purpose, she had not
only slighted the legitimate claims of Peter the
Great's daughter, the Princess Elizabeth, but
had also entirely overlooked the interests of
Ivan's mother, who naturally felt that she had
a right to ascend the throne, as the nearest rela-

tion of the deceased empress, and the mother of
the child who was designated to be the future
emperor.   To the bewilderment and dissatisfaction thus produced, a further element of confusion was added by the total incapacity of the
Duke De Biren to occupy creditably the post of
authority which had been assigned to him.   Before he had been long in office, he gave way altogether under the double responsibility of guiding
the affairs of Russia and directing the education
of the future emperor.   Ivan's mother saw the
chance of asserting her rights which the weakness of the duke afforded to her.   She was a
resolute woman; and she seized her opportunity
by banishing Biren to Siberia, and taking his
place as regent of the empire and guardian of
her infant son.

Such was the result, thus far, of the great
scramble for the crown which began with the
death of the son of Peter the Great.   Such was
the position of affairs in Russia at the time when
the revolution broke out.

Through all the contentions which distracted
the country, the Princess Elizabeth lived in the
retirement of her own palace, waiting secretly,
patiently, and vigilantly for the fit opportunity
of asserting her rights.   She was, in every sense
of the word, a remarkable woman, and she numbered two remarkable men among the adherents
of her cause.   One was the French embassador
at the court of Russia, the Marquis De la Chetardie.   The other was the surgeon of Elizabeth's
household, a German, named Lestoc.   The

Frenchman had money to spend; the German had brains to plot. Both were men of tried courage and resolute will; and both were destined to take the foremost places in the coming struggle. It is certainly not the least curious circumstance in the extraordinary revolution which we are now about to describe, that it was planned and carried out by two foreigners. In the struggle for the Russian throne, the natives of the Russian soil were used only as instruments to be handled and directed at the pleasure of the French embassador and the German surgeon.

The Marquis and Lestoc, watching the signs of the times, arrived at the conclusion that the period of the banishment of the Duke De Biren and of the assumption of the supreme power by the mother of Ivan, was also the period for effecting the revolution which was to place the Princess Elizabeth on the throne of her ancestors. The dissatisfaction in Russia had, by this time, spread widely among all classes. The people chafed under a despotism inflicted on them by foreigners. The native nobility felt outraged by their exclusion from privileges which had been conceded to their order under former reigns, before the aliens from Courland had seized on power. The army was for the most part to be depended on to answer any bold appeal that might be made to it in favor of the daughter of Peter the Great. With these chances in their favor, the Frenchman and the German set themselves to the work of organizing the scattered elements of discontent. The Marquis opened his

well-filled purse; and Surgeon Lestoc prowled
about the city and the palace with watchful
eyes, with persuasive tongue, with delicately
bribing hands. The great point to be achieved
was to tamper successfully with the regiment on
duty at the palace; and this was skillfully and
quickly accomplished by Lestoc. In the course of
a few days only, he contrived to make sure of all
the considerable officers of the regiment, and of
certain picked men from the ranks besides. On
counting heads, the members of the military conspiracy thus organized came to thirty-three.
Exactly the same number of men had once plot-
ted the overthrow of Julius Cæsar, and had succeeded in the attempt.

Matters had proceeded thus far when the suspicions of the Duchess Regent (that being the
title which Ivan's mother had now assumed)
were suddenly excited, without the slightest apparent cause to arouse them. Nothing dangerous had been openly attempted as yet, and not
one of the conspirators had betrayed the secret.
Nevertheless, the Duchess Regent began to
doubt; and one morning she astonished and
alarmed the Marquis and Lestoc by sending,
without any previous warning, for the Princess
Elizabeth, and by addressing a series of searching questions to her at a private interview.
Fortunately for the success of the plot, the
daughter of Peter the Great was more than a
match for the Duchess Regent. From first to
last Elizabeth proved herself equal to the dangerous situation in which she was placed. The

Duchess discovered nothing; and the heads of the thirty-three conspirators remained safe on their shoulders.

This piece of good fortune operated on the cunning and resolute Lestoc as a warning to make haste. Between the danger of waiting to mature the conspiracy and the risk of letting it break out abruptly before the organization of it was complete, he chose the latter alternative. The Marquis agreed with him that it was best to venture everything before there was time for the suspicions of the Duchess to be renewed; and the Princess Elizabeth, on her part, was perfectly ready to be guided by the advice of her two trusty adherents. The fifteenth of January, seventeen hundred and forty-one, had been the day originally fixed for the breaking out of the revolution. Lestoc now advanced the period for making the great attempt by nine days. On the night of the sixth of January the Duchess Regent and the Princess Elizabeth were to change places, and the throne of Russia was to become once more the inheritance of the family of Peter the Great.

Between nine and ten o'clock, on the night of the sixth, Surgeon Lestoc strolled out, with careless serenity on his face, and devouring anxiety at his heart, to play his accustomed game of billiards at a French coffee-house. The stakes were ten ducats, and Lestoc did not play quite so well as usual that evening. When the clock of the coffee-house struck ten, he stopped, in the middle of the game, and drew out his watch.

"I beg ten thousand pardons," he said to the gentleman with whom he was playing; "but I am afraid I must ask you to let me go before the game is done. I have a patient to see at ten o'clock, and the hour has just struck. Here is a friend of mine," he continued, bringing forward one of the by-standers by the arm, "who will, with your permission, play in my place. It is quite immaterial to me whether he loses or whether he wins; I am merely anxious that your game should not be interrupted. Ten thousand pardons again. Nothing but the necessity of seeing a patient could have induced me to be guilty of this apparent rudeness. I wish you much pleasure, gentlemen, and I most unwillingly bid you good-night."

With that polite farewell he departed. The patient whom he was going to cure was the sick Russian empire.

He got into his sledge, and drove off to the palace of the Princess Elizabeth. She trembled a little when he told her quietly that the hour had come for possessing herself of the throne; but, soon recovering her spirits, dressed to go out, concealed a knife about her in case of emergency, and took her place by the side of Lestoc in the sledge. The two then set forth together for the French embassy to pick up the second leader of the conspiracy.

They found the Marquis alone, cool, smiling, humming a gay French tune and quietly amusing himself by making a drawing. Elizabeth and Lestoc looked over his shoulder, and the former started a little when she saw what the subject of the drawing was. In the background appeared a large monastery, a grim, prison-like building, with barred windows and jealously closed gates; in the foreground were two high gibbets, and two wheels of the sort used to break criminals on. The drawing was touched in with extraordinary neatness and steadiness of hand; and the Marquis laughed gayly when he saw how seriously the subject represented had startled and amazed the Princess Elizabeth.

"Courage, madam!" he said. "I was only amusing myself by making a sketch illustrative of the future which we may all three expect if we fail in our enterprise. In an hour from this time you will be on the throne, or on your way to this ugly building." (He touched the monastery in the background of the drawing lightly with the point of his pencil.) "In an hour from this time, also, our worthy Lestoc and myself will either be the two luckiest men in Russia, or the two miserable criminals who are bound on these" (he touched the wheels) "and hung up afterward on those" (he touched the gibbets). "You will pardon me, madam, for indulging in this ghastly fancy! I was always eccentric from childhood. My good Lestoc, as we seem to be quite ready, perhaps you will kindly precede us to the door, and allow me the honor of handing the Princess to the sledge?"

They left the house, laughing and chatting as carelessly as if they were a party going to the theater. Lestoc took the reins. "To the palace

of the Duchess Regent, coachman!" said the
Marquis, pleasantly. And to the palace they
went.

They made no attempt to slip in by back doors,
but boldly drove up to the grand entrance, inside
of which the guard-house was situated.

"Who goes there?" cried the sentinel, as they
left the sledge and passed in.

The Marquis took a pinch of snuff.

"Don't you see, my good fellow?" he said.
"A lady and two gentlemen."

The slightest irregularity was serious enough
to alarm the guard at the imperial palace in those
critical times. The sentinel presented his mus-
ket at the Marquis, and a drummer-boy who was
standing near, ran to his instrument and caught
up his drum-sticks to beat the alarm.

Before the sentinel could fire he was surrounded by the thirty-three conspirators, and
was disarmed in an instant. Before the drummer-boy could beat the alarm, the Princess Elizabeth had drawn out her knife, and had stabbed
—not the boy, but—the drum! These slight
preliminary obstacles being thus disposed of,
Lestoc and the Marquis, having the Princess
between them, and being followed by their
thirty-three adherents, marched resolutely into
the great hall of the palace, and there confronted
the entire guard.

"Gentlemen," said the Marquis, "I have the
honor of presenting you to your future Empress,
the daughter of Peter the Great."

Half the guard had been bribed by the cun-

ning Lestoc. The other half, seeing their com-
rades advance and pay homage to the Princess,
followed the example of loyalty. Elizabeth was
escorted into a room on the ground-floor by a
military court formed in the course of five minutes. The Marquis and the faithful thirty-three
went upstairs to the sleeping apartments of the
palace. Lestoc ran out and ordered a carriage
to be got ready—then joined the Marquis and the
conspirators. The Duchess Regent and her child
were just retiring for the night, when the German surgeon and the French embassador politely informed them that they were prisoners.
Entreaties were of no avail, resistance was out
of the question. Both mother and son were led
down to the carriage that Lestoc had ordered,
and were driven off, under a strong guard, to
the fortress of Riga.

The palace was secured, and the Duchess was
imprisoned, but Lestoc and the Marquis had not
done their night's work yet. It was necessary to
make sure of three powerful personages connected with the Government. Three more carriages were ordered out when the Duchess's
carriage had been driven off; and three noblemen
—among them Count Osterman, the original
cause of the troubles in Russia—were woke out
of their first sleep with the information that they
were State prisoners, and were started before
daylight on their way to Siberia. At the same
time, the thity-three conspirators were scattered
about in every barrack-room in St. Petersburg,
proclaiming Elizabeth Empress, in right of her

illustrious parentage, and in the name of the Russian people. Soon after daylight, the moment the working population was beginning to be astir, the churches were occupied by trusty men under Lestoc's orders, and the oaths of fidelity to Elizabeth were administered to the willing populace as fast as they came in to morning prayers. By nine o'clock the work was done; the people were satisfied; the army was gained over; Elizabeth sat on her father's throne, unopposed, unquestioned, unstained by the shedding of a drop of blood; and Lestoc and the Marquis could rest from their labors at last, and could say to each other with literal truth, "The Government of Russia has been changed in nine hours, and we two foreigners are the men who have worked the miracle!"

This was the Russian revolution of seventeen hundred and forty-one. It was not the less effectual because it had lasted but a few hours, and had been accomplished without the sacrifice of a single life. The imperial inheritance which it had placed in the hands of Elizabeth was not snatched from them again. The daughter of the great Czar lived and died Empress of Russia.

And what became of the two men who had won the throne for her? The story of the after-conduct of the Marquis and Lestoc must answer that question. The events of the revolution itself are hardly more strange than the events in the lives of the French embassador and the German surgeon, when the brief struggle was over, and the change in the dynasty was accomplished.

To begin with the Marquis. He had laid the Princess Elizabeth under serious obligations to his courage and fidelity; and his services were repaid by such a reward as, in his vainest moments, he could never have dared to hope for. His fidelity had excited Elizabeth's gratitude, but his personal qualities had done more—they had touched her heart. As soon as she was settled quietly on the throne, she proved her admiration of his merits, his services, and himself by offering to marry him.

This proposal, which conferred on the Marquis the highest distinction in Russia, fairly turned his brain. The imperturbable man, who had preserved his coolness in a situation of the deadliest danger, lost all control over himself the moment he rose to the climax of prosperity. Having obtained leave of absence from his imperial mistress, he returned to France to ask leave from his own sovereign to marry the Empress. This permission was readily granted. After receiving it, any man of ordinary discretion would have kept the fact of the Empress's partiality for him as strictly secret as possible, until it could be openly avowed on the marriage-day. Far from this, the Marquis's vanity led him to proclaim the brilliant destiny in store for him all over Paris. He commissioned the king's genealogist to construct a pedigree which should be made to show that he was not unworthy to contract a royal alliance. When the pedigree was com-

pleted, he had the incredible folly to exhibit it
publicly, along with the keepsakes which the
Empress had given to him, and the rich presents
which he intended to bestow as marks of his favor on the lords and ladies of the Russian court.
Nor did his imprudence end even here. When
he returned to St. Petersburg, he took back with
him, among the other persons comprising his
train, a woman of loose character, dressed in the
disguise of a page. The persons about the Russian court, whose prejudices he had never attempted to conciliate—whose envy at his success waited only for the slightest opportunity to
effect his ruin—suspected the sex of the pre-
tended page, and took good care that the report
of their suspicions should penetrate gradually to
the foot of the throne. It seems barely credible,
but it is, nevertheless, unquestionably the fact
that the infatuated Marquis absolutely allowed
the Empress an opportunity of seeing his page.
Elizabeth's eye, sharpened by jealousy, penetrated instantly to the truth. Any less disgraceful insult she would probably have forgiven, but
such an outrage as this no woman—especially no
woman in her position—could pardon. With one
momentary glance of anger and disdain, she dismissed the Marquis from her presence, and never,
from that moment, saw him again.

The same evening his papers were seized, all
the presents that he had received from the Empress were taken from him, and he was ordered
to leave the Russian dominions forever, within
eight days' time. He was not allowed to write,

or take any other means of attempting to justify himself; and, on his way back to his native country, he was followed to the frontier by certain officers of the Russian army, and there stripped, with every mark of ignominy, of all the orders of nobility which he had received from the imperial court. He returned to Paris a disgraced man, lived there in solitude, obscurity, and neglect for some years, and died in a state of positive want —the unknown inhabitant of one of the meanest dwellings in the whole city.

The end of Lestoc is hardly less remarkable than the end of the Marquis.

In their weak points, as in their strong, the characters of these two men seem to have been singularly alike. Making due allowance for the difference in station between the German surgeon and the French embassador, it is undeniable that Elizabeth showed her sense of the services of Lestoc as gratefully and generously as she had shown her sense of the services of the Marquis. The ex-surgeon was raised at once to the position of the chief favorite and the most powerful man about the court. Besides the privileges which he shared equally with the highest nobles of the period, he was allowed access to the Empress on all private as well as on all public occasions. He had a perpetual right of entry into her domestic circle, which was conceded to no one else; and he held a place, on days of public reception, that placed him on an eminence to which no other man in Russia could hope to attain. Such was his position; and, strange to say, it had precisely the same maddening effect on his vanity which the prospect of an imperial alliance had exercised over the vanity of the Marquis. Lestoc's audacity became ungovernable, his insolence knew no bounds. He abused the privileges conferred upon him by Elizabeth's grateful regard, with such baseness and such indelicacy, that the Empress, after repeatedly cautioning him in the friendliest possible terms, found herself obliged, out of regard to her own reputation and to the remonstrances which assailed her from all the persons of her court, to deprive him of the privilege of entry into her private apartments.

This check, instead of operating as a timely warning to Lestoc, irritated him into the commission of fresh acts of insolence, so wanton in their nature that Elizabeth at last lost all patience, and angrily reproached him with the audacious ingratitude of his behavior. The reproach was retorted by Lestoc, who fiercely accused the Empress of forgetting the great services that he had rendered her, and declared that he would turn his back on her and her dominions, after first resenting the contumely with which he had been treated by an act of revenge that she would remember to the day of her death.

The vengeance which he had threatened proved to be the vengeance of a forger and a cheat. The banker in St. Petersburg who was charged with the duty of disbursing the sums of State money which were set apart for the Empress's use, received an order, one day, to pay four hundred thousand ducats to a certain person who was not mentioned by name, but who, it was stated, would call with the proper credentials, to receive the money. The banker was struck by this irregular method of performing the preliminaries of an important matter of business, and he considered it to be his duty to show the document which he had received to one of the ministers. Secret inquiries were immediately set on foot, and they ended in the discovery that the order was a false one, and that the man who had forged it was no other than Lestoc.

For a crime of this kind the punishment was death. But the Empress had declared on her accession that she would sign no warrant for the taking away of life during her reign, and, moreover, she still generously remembered what she had owed in former times to Lestoc. Accordingly, she changed his punishment to a sentence of exile to Siberia, with special orders that the life of the banished man should be made as easy to him as possible. He had not passed many years in the wildernesses of Siberia before Elizabeth's strong sense of past obligation to him induced her still further to lighten his punishment by ordering that he should be brought back to St. Petersburg, and confined in the fortress there, where her own eyes might assure her that he was treated with mercy and consideration. It is probable that she only intended this change as a prelude to the restoration of his liberty; but the future occasion for pardoning him never came. Shortly after his return to St. Petersburg, Lestoc ended his days in the prison of the fortress.

So the two leaders of the Russian revolution lived, and so they died. It has been said, and said well, that the only sure proof of a man's strength of mind is to be discovered by observing the manner in which he bears success. History shows few such remarkable examples of the truth of this axiom as are afforded by the lives of the Marquis De la Chetardie and the German surgeon, Lestoc. Two stronger men in the hour of peril, and two weaker men in the hour of security, have not often appeared in this world to vanquish adverse circumstances like heroes, and to be conquered like cowards afterward by nothing but success.

DOUGLAS JERROLD.*

SOME seventy years ago, there lived a poor country player, named Samuel Jerrold. His principal claim to a prominent position among the strolling company to which he was attached consisted in the possession of a pair of shoes once belonging to the great Garrick himself. Samuel Jerrold always appeared on the stage in these invaluable "properties"—a man, surely, who deserves the regard of posterity, as the only actor of modern times who has shown himself capable of standing in Garrick's shoes.

Samuel Jerrold was twice married—the second time to a wife so much his junior that he was older than his own mother-in-law. Partly, perhaps, in virtue of this last great advantage on the part of the husband, the marriage was a

---

* The biographical facts mentioned in this little sketch are derived from Mr. Blanchard Jerrold's interesting narrative of his father's Life and Labors. For the rest —that is to say, for the opinions here expressed on Jerrold's works, and for the estimate attempted of his personal character—I am responsible. This is the only instance of a reprinted article in the present collection, any part of which is founded on a modern and an accessible book. The reader will perhaps excuse and understand my making an exception here to my own rules, when I add that Douglas Jerrold was one of the first and the dearest friends of my literary life.

very happy one. The second Mrs. Samuel was a clever, good-tempered, notable woman; and helped her husband materially in his theatrical affairs, when he rose in time (and in Garrick's shoes) to be a manager of country theaters. Young Mrs. Samuel brought her husband a family—two girls to begin with; and, on the third of January, eighteen hundred and three, while she was staying in London, a boy, who was christened Douglas William, and who was destined, in after-life, to make the name of the obscure country manager a household word on the lips of English readers.

In the year eighteen hundred and seven, Samuel Jerrold became the lessee of the Sheerness Theater; and little Douglas was there turned to professional account, as a stage-child. He appeared in "The Stranger" as one of the little cherubs of the frail and interesting Mrs. Haller; and he was "carried on" by Edmund Kean, as the child in "Rolla." These early theatrical experiences (whatever influence they might have had, at a later time, in forming his instincts as a dramatist) do not appear to have at all inclined him toward his father's profession when he grew older. The world of ships and sailors amid which he lived at Sheerness seems to have formed his first tastes and influenced his first longings. As soon as he could speak for himself on the matter of his future prospects, he chose the life of a sailor; and at ten years old he entered on board the guardship *Namur* as a first-class volunteer.

Up to this time the father had given the son as

good an education as it lay within his means to
command. Douglas had been noted as a studious boy at school; and he brought with him a
taste for reading and for quiet pursuits when he
entered on board the *Namur*. Beginning his
apprenticeship to the sea as a Midshipman, in
December, eighteen hundred and thirteen, he
was not transferred from the guardship to active
service until April, eighteen hundred and fifteen,
when he was drafted off, with forty-six men, to
his Majesty's gunbrig *Ernest*.

Those were stirring times. The fierce struggle
of Waterloo was at hand; and Douglas's first
cruise was across the Channel to Ostend, at the
head of a fleet of transports carrying troops and
stores to the battlefield. Singularly enough, his
last cruise connected him with the results of the
great fight, as his first had connected him with
the preparations for it. In the July of the Waterloo year, the *Ernest* brought her share of the
wounded back to Sheerness. On the deck of
that brig Jerrold first stood face to face with the
horror of war. In after-life, when other pens
were writing glibly enough of the glory of war,
his pen traced the dark reverse of the picture,
and set the terrible consequences of all victories,
righteous as well as wicked, in their true light.

The great peace was proclaimed, and the nations rested at last. In October, eighteen hundred and fifteen, the *Ernest* was "paid off."
Jerrold stepped on shore, and never returned to
the service. He was without interest; and the
peace virtually closed his professional prospects.

To the last day of his life he had a genuinely English love for the sea and sailors; and, short as his naval experience had been, neither he nor his countrymen were altogether losers by it. If the Midshipman of the *Ernest* had risen to be an Admiral, what would have become then of the author of "Black-eyed Susan"?

Douglas's prospects were far from cheering when he returned to his home on shore. The affairs of Samuel Jerrold (through no fault of his own) had fallen into sad confusion. In his old age his vocation of manager sank from under him; his theater was sold; and, at the end of the Waterloo year, he and his family found themselves compelled to leave Sheerness. On the first day of eighteen hundred and sixteen they sailed away in the Chatham boat, to try their fortune in London.

The first refuge of the Jerrolds was at Broad Court, Bow Street. Poor old Samuel was now past his work; and the chief dependence of the ruined family rested on Douglas and his mother. Mrs. Samuel contrived to get some theatrical employment in London; and Douglas, after beginning life as an officer in the navy, was apprenticed to a printer, in Northumberland Street, Strand.

He accepted his new position with admirable cheerfulness and resolution; honestly earning his money, and affectionately devoting it to the necessities of his parents. A delightful anecdote of him, at this time of his life, is told by his son. On one of the occasions when his mother and

sister were absent in the country, the little domestic responsibility of comforting the poor worn-
out old father with a good dinner rested on
Douglas's shoulders. With the small proceeds
of his work he bought all the necessary materials
for a good beefsteak pie—made the pie himself,
succeeded brilliantly with the crust—himself took
it to the bake-house—and himself brought it back,
with one of Sir Walter Scott's novels, which the
dinner left him just money enough to hire from
a library, for the purpose of reading a story to
his father in the evening, by way of dessert.
For our own parts, we shall henceforth always
rank that beefsteak pie as one among the many
other works of Douglas Jerrold which have established his claim to remembrance and to regard. The clew to the bright, affectionate nature of the man—sometimes lost by those who
knew him imperfectly, in after-life—could hardly
be found in any pleasanter or better place, now
that he is gone from among us, than on the poor
dinner-table in Broad Court.

Although he was occupied for twelve hours out
of the twenty-four at the printing-office, he contrived to steal time enough from the few idle intervals allowed for rest and meals to store his
mind with all the reading that lay within his
reach. As early as at the age of fourteen, the
literary faculty that was in him seems to have
struggled to develop itself in short papers and
scraps of verse. Only a year later, he made his
first effort at dramatic composition, producing a
little farce, with a part in it for an old friend

of the family, the late Mr. Wilkinson, the come-
dian. Although Samuel Jerrold was well remembered among many London actors as an
honest country manager; and although Douglas
could easily secure from his father's friends his
admission to the theater whenever he was able to
go to it, he does not appear to have possessed interest enough to gain a reading for his piece when
it was first sent in to the English Opera-house.
After three years had elapsed, however, Mr.
Wilkinson contrived to get the lad's farce produced at Sadler's Wells, under the title of "More
Frightened than Hurt." It was not only successful on its first representation, but it also won
the rare honor of being translated for the French
stage. More than this, it was afterward translated back again, by a dramatist who was ignorant of its original history, for the stage of the
Olympic Theater; where it figured in the bills
under the new title of "Fighting by Proxy,"
with Liston in the part of the hero. Such is the
history of Douglas Jerrold's first contribution
to the English drama. When it was produced
on the boards of Sadler's Wells, its author's age
was eighteen years.

He had appeared in public, however, as an
author before this time, having composed some
verses which were printed in a forgotten periodical called *Arliss's Magazine*. The loss of
his first situation, through the bankruptcy of his
master, obliged him to seek employment anew
in the printing-office of one Mr. Bigg, who was
also the editor of a newspaper called the *Sunday*

Monitor. In this journal appeared his first article—a critical paper on "Der Freischütz." He had gone to the theater with an order to see the opera; and had been so struck by the supernatural drama and the wonderful music to which it was set, that he noted down his impressions of the performance, and afterward dropped what he had written, anonymously, into the editor's box. The next morning his own article was handed to him to set up in type for the forthcoming number of the *Sunday Monitor.*

After this first encouragement, he began to use his pen frequently in the minor periodicals of the time; still sticking to the printer's work, however, and still living at home with his family. The success of his little farce at Sadler's Wells led to his writing three more pieces for that theater. They all succeeded; and the managers of some of the other minor theaters began to look after the new man. Just at this time, when his career as dramatist and journalist was beginning to open before him, his father died. After that loss, the next important event in his life was his marriage. In the year eighteen hundred and twenty-four, when he was twenty-one years of age, he married his "first love," Miss Mary Swann, the daughter of a gentleman who held an appointment in the Post-office. He and his bride settled, with his mother and sister and a kind old friend of his boyish days, in Holborn; and here—devoting his days to the newspapers, and his evenings to the drama—the newly-married man started as author by profession, and met the world and its cares bravely at the point of the pen.

The struggle at starting was a hard one. His principal permanent source of income was a small weekly salary paid to him as dramatist to the establishment, by one Davidge, manager of the Coburg (now the Victoria) Theater. This man appears to have treated Jerrold, whose dramas brought both money and reputation to his theater, with an utter want of common consideration and common gratitude. He worked his poor author pitilessly; and it is, on that account, highly satisfactory to know that he overreached himself in the end, by quarreling with his dramatist, at the very time when Jerrold had a theatrical fortune (so far as managers' interests were concerned) lying in his desk, in the shape of "Black-Eyed Susan." With that renowned play (the most popular of all nautical dramas) in his hand, Douglas left the Coburg to seek employment at the Surrey Theater—then under the management of Mr. Elliston. This last tradesman in plays—who subsequently showed himself to be a worthy contemporary of the other tradesman at the Coburg —bid rather higher for Jerrold's services, and estimated the sole monopoly of the fancy, invention, and humor of a man who had already proved to be a popular, money-bringing dramatist at the magnificent rate of five pounds a week. The bargain was struck; and Jerrold's first play produced at the Surrey Theater was "Black-Eyed Susan."

He had achieved many enviable dramatic successes before this time. He had written domestic dramas—such as "Fifteen Years of a Drunkard's Life," and "Ambrose Gwinett"—the popularity of which is still well remembered by playgoers of the old generation; but the reception of "Black-Eyed Susan" eclipsed all previous successes of his or of any other dramatist's in that line. Mr. T. P. Cooke, who, as the French say, "created" the part of William, not only found half London flocking into the Borough to see him; but was actually called upon, after acting in the play, as a first piece, at the Surrey Theater, to drive off in his sailor's dress, and act in it again on the same night, as the last piece, at Covent Garden Theater. Its first "run" mounted to three hundred nights; it afterward drew money into the empty treasury of Drury Lane: it remains, to this day, a "stock-piece" on which managers and actors know that they can depend; and, strangest phenomenon of all, it is impossible to see the play now without feeling that its great and well deserved dramatic success has been obtained with the least possible amount of assistance from the subtleties and refinements of dramatic art. The piece is indebted for its hold on the public sympathy solely to the simple force, the irresistible directness, of its appeal to some of the strongest affections in our nature. It has succeeded, and it will succeed, not because the dialogue is well, or, as to some passages of it, even naturally written; not because the story is neatly told, for it is (especially in the first act) full of faults in construction; but solely

344 WORKS OF WILKIE COLLINS.

because the situations in which the characters
are placed appeal to the hearts of every husband
and every wife in the theater. In this aspect of
it, and in this only, the play is a study to any
young writer; for it shows on what amazingly
simple foundations rest the main conditions of
the longest, the surest, and the widest dramatic
success.

It is sad, it is almost humiliating, to be obliged
to add, in reference to the early history of Jerrold's first dramatic triumph, that his share of
the gains which "Black-Eyed Susan" poured into
the pockets of managers on both sides of the water
was just seventy pounds. Mr. Elliston, whose
theater the play had raised from a state of something like bankruptcy to a condition of prosperity
which, in the Surrey annals, has not since been
paralleled, not only abstained from presenting
Jerrold with the smallest fragment of anything
in the shape of a token of gratitude, but actually
had the pitiless insolence to say to him, after
"Black-Eyed Susan" had run its three hundred
nights, "My dear boy, why don't you get your
friends to present you with a bit of plate?"*

* When this article was first published in *Household
Words*, a son of Mr. Elliston wrote to the conductor to
protest against the epithets which I had attached to his
father's name. In the present reprint I have removed
the epithets; not because I think them undeserved, but
because they merely represented my own angry sense of
Mr. Elliston's treatment of Jerrold—a sense which I have
no wish needlessly to gratify at the expense of a son's
regard for his father's memory. But the facts of the

The extraordinary success of "Black-Eyed Susan" opened the doors of the great theaters to Jerrold, as a matter of course. He made admirable use of the chances in his favor which he had so well deserved, and for which he had waited so long. At the Adelphi, at Drury Lane, and at the Haymarket, drama after drama flowed in quick succession from his pen. The "Devil's Ducat," the "Bride of Ludgate," the "Rent Day," "Nell Gwynne," the "Housekeeper"—this last the best of his plays in point of construction—date, with many other dramatic works, from the period of his life now under review. The one slight check to his career of prosperity occurred in eighteen hundred and thirty-six, when he and his brother-in-law took the Strand Theater, and when Jerrold acted a character in one of his own plays. Neither the theatrical speculation nor the theatrical appearance proved to be successful; and he wisely abandoned, from that time, all professional connection with the stage, except in his old and ever-welcome character of dramatist. In the other branches of his art—to which he devoted himself, at this turn-

---

case as they were originally related, and as I heard them from Jerrold himself, remain untouched—exactly as my own opinion of Mr. Elliston's conduct remains to this day unaltered. If the "impartial" reader wishes to have more facts to decide on than those given in the text, he is referred to Raymond's "Life of Elliston"—in which work he will find the clear profits put into the manager's pocket by "Black-Eyed Susan," estimated at one hundred and fifty pounds a week.

ing-point of his career, as faithfully as he devoted himself to the theatrical branch—his progress was not less remarkable. As journalist and essayist, he rose steadily toward the distinguished place which was his due among the writers of his time. This middle term of his literary exertions produced, among other noticeable results, the series of social studies called "Men of Character," originally begun in *Blackwood's Magazine*, and since republished among his collected works.

He had now advanced, in a social as well as in a literary point of view, beyond that period in the lives of self-made men which may be termed the adventurous period. Whatever difficulties and anxieties henceforth oppressed him were caused by the trials and troubles which more or less beset the exceptional lives of all men of letters. The struggle for a hearing, the fight for a fair field in which to show himself, had now been bravely and creditably accomplished; and all that remains to be related of the life of Douglas Jerrold is best told in the history of his works.

Taking his peculiar literary gifts into consideration, the first great opportunity of his life, as a periodical writer, was offered to him, unquestionably, by the starting of *Punch*. The brilliant impromptu faculty which gave him a place apart, as thinker, writer, and talker, among the remarkable men of his time, was exactly the faculty which such a journal as *Punch* was calculated to develop to the utmost. The day on which Jerrold was secured as a contributor would

have been a fortunate day for that periodical, if
he had written nothing in it but the far-famed
"Caudle Lectures," and the delightful "Story of
a Feather." But the service that he rendered to
Punch must by no means be associated only with
the more elaborate contributions to its pages
which are publicly connected with his name.
His wit often flashed out at its brightest, his
sarcasm often cut with its keenest edge, in those
well-timed paragraphs and short articles which
hit the passing event of the day, and which, so
far as their temporary purpose with the public is
concerned, are all-important ingredients in the
success of such a periodical as *Punch.* A contributor who can strike out new ideas from the
original resources of his own mind is one man,
and a contributor who can be depended on for
the small workaday emergencies which are felt
one week and forgotten the next, is generally another. Jerrold united these two characters in
himself; and the value of him to *Punch,* on that
account only, can never be too highly estimated.

At this period of his life the fertility of his
mental resources showed itself most conspicu-
ously. While he was working for *Punch,* he
was also editing and largely contributing to *The
Illuminated Magazine.* In this publication appeared, among a host of shorter papers, the
series called "The Chronicles of Clovernook,"
which he himself always considered to be one of
his happiest efforts, and which does indeed contain, in detached passages, some of the best
things that ever fell from his pen. On the cessa-

tion of *The Illuminated Magazine*, he started *The Shilling Magazine*, and contributed to it his well-known novel, "Saint Giles and Saint James." These accumulated literary occupations and responsibilities would have been enough for most men; but Jerrold's inexhaustible energy and variety carried him on through more work still. Theatrical audiences now found their old favorite addressing them again, and occupying new ground as a writer of five-act and three-act comedies. "Bubbles of the Day," "Time Works Wonders," "The Cat's-paw," "Retired from Business," "Saint Cupid," were all produced, with other plays, after the period when he became a regular writer in *Punch*.

Judged from the literary point of view, these comedies were all original and striking contributions to the library of the stage. From the dramatic point of view, however, it must not be concealed that they were less satisfactory; and that some of them were scarcely so successful with audiences as their author's earlier and humbler efforts. The one solid critical reason which it is possible to assign for this, implies in itself a compliment which could be paid to no other dramatist of modern times. The perpetual glitter of Jerrold's wit seems to have blinded him to some of the more sober requirements of the dramatic art. When Charles Kemble said, and said truly, that there was wit enough for three comedies in "Bubbles of the Day," he implied that this brilliant overflow left little or no room for the indispensable resources of story and situation to display

themselves fairly on the stage. The comedies
themselves, examined with reference to their success in representation, as well as to their intrinsic
merits, help to support this view. "Time Works
Wonders" was the most prosperous of all, and it
is that comedy precisely which has the most story
and the most situation in it. The idea and the
management of the charming love-tale out of
which the events of this play spring, show what
Jerrold might have achieved in the construction
of other plots, if his own superabundant wit had
not dazzled him and led him astray. As it is,
the readers of these comedies, who can appreciate
the rich fancy, the delicate subtleties of thought,
the masterly terseness of expression, and the exquisite play and sparkle of wit scattered over
every page, may rest assured that they rather
gain than lose—especially in the present condition of theatrical companies—by not seeing the
last dramatic works of Douglas Jerrold represented on the stage.

The next, and, sad to say, the final achievement of his life, connected him most honorably
and profitably with the newspaper press. Many
readers will remember the starting of *Douglas
Jerrold's Weekly Newspaper*—its great temporary success—and then its sudden decline,
through defects in management, to which it is
not now necessary to refer at length. The signal ability with which the editorial articles in
the paper were written, the remarkable aptitude
which they displayed in striking straight at the
sympathies of large masses of readers, did not

escape the notice of men who were well fitted to judge of the more solid qualifications which go to the production of a popular journalist. In the spring of the year eighteen hundred and fifty-two, the proprietor of *Lloyd's Weekly Newspaper* proposed the editorship to Jerrold, on terms of such wise liberality as to insure the ready acceptance of his offer. From the spring of eighteen hundred and fifty-two, to the spring of eighteen hundred and fifty-seven—the last he was ever to see—Jerrold conducted the paper, with such extraordinary success as is rare in the history of journalism. Under his supervision, and with the regular assistance of his pen, *Lloyd's Newspaper* rose, by thousands and thousands a week, to the great circulation which it now enjoys. Of the many successful labors of Jerrold's life, none had been so substantially prosperous as the labor that was destined to close it.

His health had shown signs of breaking, and his heart was known to be affected, for some little time before his last brief illness; but the unconquerable energy and spirit of the man upheld him through all bodily trials, until the first day of June, eighteen hundred and fifty-seven. Even his medical attendant did not abandon all hope when his strength first gave way. But he sank rapidly—so rapidly, that in one short week the struggle was over. On the eighth day of June, surrounded by his family and his friends, preserving all his faculties to the last, passing away calmly, resignedly, affectionately, Douglas Jerrold closed his eyes on the world which it had been the long and noble purpose of his life to inform and to improve.

It is too early yet to attempt any estimate of the place which his writings will ultimately occupy in English literature. So long as honesty, energy, and variety are held to be the prominent qualities which should distinguish a genuine writer, there can be no doubt of the vitality of Douglas Jerrold's reputation. The one objection urged against the works, which, feeble and ignorant though it was, often went to the heart of the writer, was the objection of bitterness. Calling to mind many of the passages in his books in which this bitterness most sharply appears, and seeing plainly in those passages what the cause was that provoked it, we venture to speak out our own opinion boldly, and to acknowledge at once that we admire this so-called bitterness as one of the great and valuable qualities of Douglas Jerrold's writings; because we can see for ourselves that it springs from the uncompromising earnestness and honesty of the author. In an age when it is becoming unfashionable to have a positive opinion about anything; when the detestable burlesque element scatters its profanation with impunity on all beautiful and all serious things; when much, far too much, of the current literature of the day vibrates contemptibly between unbelieving banter and unblushing claptrap, that element of bitterness in Jerrold's writings—which never stands alone in them; which is never disassociated from the kind word that goes before, or the generous thought that comes after—is in our opinion an essentially wholesome element, breathing that admiration of truth, and that hatred of falsehood, which is the chiefest and brightest jewel in the crown of any writer, living or dead.

This same cry of bitterness, which assailed him in his literary character, assailed him in his social character also. Absurd as the bare idea of bitterness must appear in connection with such a nature as his, to those who really knew him, the reason why strangers so often and so ridiculously misunderstood him, is not difficult to discover. That marvelous brightness and quickness of perception which has distinguished him far and wide as the sayer of some of the wittiest, and often some of the wisest things also, in the English language, expressed itself almost with the suddenness of lightning. This absence of all appearance of artifice or preparation, this flash and readiness which made the great charm of his wit, rendered him, at the same time, quite incapable of suppressing a good thing from prudential considerations. It sparkled off his tongue before he was aware of it. It was always a bright surprise to himself; and it never occurred to him that it could be anything but a bright surprise to others. All his so-called bitter things were said with a burst of hearty school-boy laughter, which showed how far he was himself from attaching a serious importance to them. Strangers apparently failed to draw this inference, plain as it was; and often mistook him accordingly. If they had seen him in the society of children; if they had surprised him in the house of any one of his literary brethren who was in difficulty and distress; if they had met him by the bedside of a sick friend, how simply and how irresistibly the gentle, generous, affectionate nature of the man would then have disclosed itself to the most careless chance acquaintance who ever misunderstood him! Very few men have won the loving regard of so many friends so rapidly, and have kept that regard so enduringly to the last day of their lives, as Douglas Jerrold.

SKETCHES OF CHARACTER.—V.

PRAY EMPLOY MAJOR NAMBY!

[A Privileged Communication from a Lady in Distress.]

I HAVE such an extremely difficult subject to write about, that I really don't know how to begin. The fact is, I am a single lady—single, you will please to understand, entirely because I have refused many excellent offers. Pray don't imagine from this that I am old. Some women's offers come at long intervals, and other women's offers come close together. Mine came remarkably close together—so, of course, I cannot possibly be old. Not that I presume to describe myself as absolutely young either; so much depends on people's points of view. I have heard female children of the ages of eighteen or nineteen called young ladies. This seems to me to be ridiculous —and I have held that opinion, without once wavering from it, for more than ten years past. It is, after all, a question of feeling; and, shall I confess it? I feel so young!

Dear, dear me! this is dreadfully egotistical; and, besides, it is not in the least what I want. May I be kindly permitted to begin again?

Is there any chance of our going to war with somebody before long? This is such a dreadful question for a lady to put, that I feel called upon to apologize and explain myself. I don't rejoice in bloodshed—I don't, indeed. The smell of gunpowder is horrible to me; and the going off of the smallest imaginable gun invariably makes me scream. But if on some future occasion we —of course, I mean the Government—find it quite impossible to avoid plunging into the horrors of war—then, what I want to know is whether my next door neighbor, Major Namby, will be taken from his home by the Horse Guards, and presented with his fit post of command in the English army? It will come out sooner or later; so there is no harm in my acknowledging at once that it would add immeasurably to my comfort and happiness if the major were ordered off on any service which would take him away from his own house.

I am really very sorry, but I must leave off beginning already, and go back again to the part before the beginning (if there is such a thing) in order to explain the nature of my objection to Major Namby, and why it would be such a great relief to me (supposing we are unfortunate enough to plunge into the horrors of war), if he happened to be one of the first officers called out for the service of his Queen and country.

I live in the suburbs, and I have bought my house. The major lives in the suburbs, next door to me, and *he* has bought his house. I don't object to this, of course. I merely mention it to make things straight.

Major Namby has been twice married. His first wife—dear, dear! how can I express it? Shall I say, with vulgar abruptness, that his first wife had a family? And must I descend into particulars, and add that they are four in number, and that two of them are twins? Well, the words are written; and if they will do over again for the same purpose, I beg to repeat them in reference to the second Mrs. Namby (still alive), who has also had a family, and is—no, I really cannot say, is likely to go on having one. There are certain limits in a case of this kind, and I think I have reached them. Permit me simply to state that the second Mrs. Namby has three children at present. These, with the first Mrs. Namby's four, make a total of seven. The seven are composed of five girls and two boys. And the first Mrs. Namby's family all have one particular kind of constitution, and the second Mrs. Namby's family all have another particular kind of constitution. Let me explain once more that I merely mention these little matters, and that I don't object to them.

Now pray be patient; I am coming fast to the point—I am, indeed. But please let me say a little word or two about Major Namby himself.

In the first place, I have looked out his name in the Army List, and I cannot find that he was ever engaged in battle anywhere. He appears to have entered the army, most unfortunately for his own renown, just after, instead of just before, the battle of Waterloo. He has been at all sorts of foreign stations, at the very time, in each case, when there was no military work to do—except once at some West Indian island, where he seems to have assisted in putting down a few poor unfortunate negroes who tried to get up a riot. This is the only active service that he has ever performed; so I suppose it is all owing to his being well off, and to those dreadful abuses of ours, that he has been made a major for not having done a major's work. So far as looks go, however, he is military enough in appearance to take the command of the British army at five minutes' notice. He is very tall and upright, and carries a martial cane, and wears short martial whiskers, and has an awfully loud martial voice. His face is very pink, and his eyes are extremely round and staring, and he has that singularly disagreeable-looking roll of fat red flesh at the back of his neck, between the bottom of his short gray hair and the top of his stiff black stock which seems to be peculiar to all hearty old officers who are remarkably well to do in the world. He is certainly not more than sixty years of age; and, if a lady may presume to judge of such a thing, I should say decidedly that he had an immense amount of undeveloped energy still left in him at the service of the Horse Guards.

This undeveloped energy—and here, at length, I come to the point—not having any employment in the right direction, has run wild in the wrong direction, and has driven the major to devote the

whole of his otherwise idle time to his domestic
affairs. He manages his children instead of his
regiment, and establishes discipline in the servants' hall instead of in the barrack-yard. Have
I any right to object to this? None whatever, I
readily admit. I may hear (most unwillingly)
that Major Namby has upset the house by going
into the kitchen and objecting to the smartness
of the servants' caps; but as I am not, thank
Heaven, one of those unfortunate servants, I am
not called on to express my opinion of such un-
manly meddling, much as I scorn it. I may be
informed (entirely against my own will) that
Mrs. Namby's husband has dared to regulate,
not only the size and substance, but even the
number, of certain lower and inner articles of
Mrs. Namby's dress, which no earthly consideration will induce me particularly to describe; but
as I do not (I thank Heaven again) occupy the
degraded position of the major's wife, I am not
justified in expressing my indignation at domestic
prying and pettifogging, though I feel it all over
me, at this very moment, from head to foot.
What Major Namby does and says inside his
own house is his business, and not mine. But
what he does and says outside his own house, on
the gravel-walk of his front garden—under my
own eyes and close to my own ears, as I sit at
work at the window—is as much my affair as the
major's, and more; for it is I who suffer by it.

Pardon me a momentary pause for relief, a
momentary thrill of self-congratulation. I have
got to my destination at last—I have taken the

right literary turning at the end of the preceding paragraph; and the fair high-road of plain narrative now spreads engagingly before me.

My complaint against Major Namby is, in plain terms, that he transacts the whole of his domestic business in his front garden. Whether it arises from natural weakness of memory, from total want of a sense of propriety, or from a condition of mind which is closely allied to madness of the eccentric sort, I cannot say—but the major certainly does sometimes partially, and sometimes entirely, forget his private family matters, and the necessary directions connected with them, while he is inside the house; and does habitually remember them, and repair all omissions, by bawling through his windows, at the top of his voice, as soon as he gets outside the house. It never seems to occur to him that he might advantageously return indoors, and there mention what he has forgotten in a private and proper way. The instant the lost idea strikes him—which it invariably does, either in his front garden or in the roadway outside his house—he roars for his wife, either from the gravel-walk or over the low wall; and (if I may use so strong an expression) empties his mind to her in public, without appearing to care whose ears he wearies, whose delicacy he shocks, or whose ridicule he invites. If the man is not mad, his own small family fusses have taken such complete possession of all his senses, that he is quite incapable of noticing anything else, and perfectly impenetrable to the opinions of his neighbors. Let me

show that the grievance of which I complain is
no slight one, by giving a few examples of the
general persecution that I suffer, and the occasional shocks that are administered to my delicacy, at the coarse hands of Major Namby.

We will say it is a fine warm morning. I am
sitting in my front room, with the window open,
absorbed over a deeply interesting book. I hear
the door of the next house bang; I look up, and
see the major descending the steps into his front
garden.

He walks—no, he marches—half-way down
the front garden path, with his head high in the
air, and his chest stuck out, and his military
cane fiercely flourished in his right hand. Suddenly he stops, stamps with one foot, knocks up
the hinder part of the brim of his extremely
curly hat with his left hand, and begins to
scratch at that singularly disagreeable-looking
roll of fat red flesh in the back of his neck
(which scratching, I may observe, in parenthesis, is always a sure sign, in the case of this horrid man, that a lost domestic idea has suddenly
come back to him). He waits a moment in the
ridiculous position just described, then wheels
round on his heel, looks up at the first-floor window, and instead of going back into the house to
mention what he has forgotten, bawls out fiercely
from the middle of the walk:

"Matilda!"

I hear his wife's voice—a shockingly shrill
one; but what can you expect of a woman who
has been seen over and over again in a slatternly

striped wrapper as late as two o'clock in the afternoon?—I hear his wife's voice answer from inside the house:

"Yes, dear."

"I said it was a south wind."

"Yes, dear."

"It isn't a south wind."

"Lor', dear!"

"It's southeast. I won't have Georgina taken out to-day." (Georgina is one of the first Mrs. Namby's family, and they are all weak in the chest.) "Where's nurse?"

"Here, sir!"

"Nurse, I won't have Jack allowed to run. Whenever that boy perspires, he catches cold. Hang up his hoop. If he cries, take him into my dressing-room and show him the birch rod. Matilda!"

"Yes, dear."

"What the devil do they mean by daubing all that grease over Mary's hair? It's beastly to see it—do you hear?—beastly! Where's Pamby?" (Pamby is the unfortunate work-woman who makes and mends the family linen.)

"Here, sir."

"Pamby, what are you about now?"

No answer. Pamby, or somebody else, giggles faintly. The major flourishes his cane in a fury.

"Why the devil don't you answer me? I give you three seconds to answer me, or leave the house. One—two—three. Pamby! what are you about now?"

"If you please, sir, I'm doing something—"

"What?"

"Something particular for baby, sir."

"Drop it directly, whatever it is. Matilda! how many pair of trousers has Katie got?"

"Only three, dear."

"Pamby!"

"Yes, sir."

"Shorten all Miss Katie's trousers directly, including the pair she's got on. I've said, over and over again, that I won't have those frills of hers any lower down than her knees. Don't let me see them at the middle of her shins again. Nurse!"

"Yes, sir."

"Mind the crossings. Don't let the children sit down if they're hot. Don't let them speak to other children. Don't let them get playing with strange dogs. Don't let them mess their things. And, above all, don't bring Master Jack back in a perspiration. Is there anything more, before I go out?"

"No, sir."

"Matilda! Is there anything more?"

"No, dear."

"Pamby! Is there anything more?"

"No, sir."

Here the domestic colloquy ends, for the time being. Will any sensitive person—especially a person of my own sex—please to imagine what I must suffer, as a delicate single lady, at having all these family details obtruded on my attention, whether I like it or not, in the major's rasping

martial voice, and in the shrill answering screams
of the women inside?   It is bad enough to be submitted to this sort of persecution when one is
alone; but it is far worse to be also exposed to it
—as I am constantly—in the presence of visitors,
whose conversation is necessarily interrupted,
whose ears are necessarily shocked, whose very
stay in my house is necessarily shortened, by
Major Namby's unendurably public way of managing his private concerns.

Only the other day, my old, dear, and most
valued friend, Lady Malkinshaw, was sitting
with me, and was entering at great length into
the interesting story of her second daughter's unhappy marriage-engagement, and of the dignified
manner in which the family ultimately broke it
off.   For a quarter of an hour or so our interview
continued to be delightfully uninterrupted.   At
the end of that time, however, just as Lady Malkinshaw, with the tears in her eyes, was beginning to describe the effect of her daughter's
dreadful disappointment on the poor dear girl's
mind and looks, I heard the door of the major's
house bang as usual; and, looking out of the
window in despair, saw the major himself strut
half-way down the walk, stop, scratch violently
at his roll of red flesh, wheel round so as to face
the house, consider a little, pull his tablets out of
his waistcoat-pocket, shake his head over them,
and then look up at the front windows, prepara-
tory to bawling as usual at the degraded female
members of his household.   Lady Malkinshaw,
quite ignorant of what was coming, happened at

the same moment to be proceeding with her pathetic story in these terms:

"I do assure you my poor dear girl behaved throughout with the heroism of a martyr.   When I had told her of the vile wretch's behavior, breaking it to her as gently as I possibly could; and when she had a little recovered, I said to her—"

("Matilda!")

The major's rasping voice sounded louder than ever as he bawled out that dreadful name, just at the wrong moment.   Lady Malkinshaw started as if she had been shot.   I put down the window in despair; but the glass was no protection to our ears—Major Namby can roar through a brick wall.   I apologized—I declared solemnly that my next-door neighbor was mad—I entreated Lady Malkinshaw to take no notice, and to go on.   That sweet woman immediately complied. I burn with indignation when I think of what followed.   Every word from the Namby's garden (which I distinguish below by parentheses) came, very slightly muffled by the window, straight into my room, and mixed itself up with her ladyship's story in this inexpressibly ridiculous and impertinent manner:

"Well," my kind and valued friend proceeded, "as I was telling you, when the first natural burst of sorrow was over, I said to her—"

"Yes, dear Lady Malkinshaw?" I murmured, encouragingly.

"I said to her—"

("By jingo, I've forgotten something!   Matilda! when I made my memorandum of errands, how many had I to do?")

" 'My dearest, darling child,' I said—"

("Pamby! how many errands did your mistress give me to do?")

"I said, 'My dearest, darling child—' "

("Nurse! how many errands did your mistress give me to do?")

" 'My own love,' I said—"

("Pooh! pooh! I tell you, I had four errands to do, and I've only got three of 'em written down. Check me off, all of you—I'm going to read my errands.")

" 'Your own proper pride, love,' I said, 'will suggest to you—' "

("Gray powder for baby.")

—" 'the necessity of making up your mind, my angel, to—' "

("Row the plumber for infamous condition of back-kitchen sink.")

—" 'to return all the wretch's letters, and—' "

("Speak to the haberdasher about patching Jack's shirts.")

—" 'all his letters and presents, darling. You need only make them up into a parcel, and write inside—' "

("Matilda! is that all?")

—" 'and write inside—' "

("Pamby! is that all?")

—" 'and write inside—' "

("Nurse! is that all?")

" 'I have my mother's sanction for making one last request to you. It is this—' "

("What have the children got for dinner to-day?")

—" 'it is this: Return me my letters, as I have returned yours. You will find inside—' "

("A shoulder of mutton and onion sauce? And a devilish good dinner, too.")

The coarse wretch roared out those last shocking words cheerfully, at the top of his voice. Hitherto Lady Malkinshaw had preserved her temper with the patience of an angel; but she began—and who can wonder?—to lose it at last.

"It is really impossible, my dear," she said, rising from her chair, "to continue any conversation while that very intolerable person persists in talking to his family from his front garden. No! I really cannot go on—I cannot, indeed."

Just as I was apologizing to my sweet friend for the second time, I observed, to my great relief (having my eye still on the window), that the odious major had apparently come to the end of his domestic business for that morning, and had made up his mind at last to relieve us of his presence. I distinctly saw him put his tablets back in his pocket, wheel round again on his heel, and march straight to the garden gate. I waited until he had his hand on the lock to open it, and then, when I felt that we were quite safe, I informed dear Lady Malkinshaw that my detestable neighbor had at last taken himself off, and, throwing open the window again to get a little air, begged and entreated her to oblige me by resuming her charming narrative.

"Where was I?" inquired my distinguished friend.

"You were telling me what you recommended your poor darling to write inside her inclosure," I answered.

"Ah, yes—so I was. Well, my dear, she controlled herself by an admirable effort, and wrote exactly what I told her. You will excuse a mother's partiality, I am sure; but I think I never saw her look so lovely—so mournfully lovely, I should say—as when she was writing those last lines to the man who had so basely trifled with her. The tears came into my eyes as I looked at her sweet pale cheeks; and I thought to myself—"

("Nurse, which of the children was sick, last time, after eating onion sauce?")

He had come back again—the monster had come back again, from the very threshold of the garden gate—to shout that unwarrantably atrocious question in at his nursery window!

Lady Malkinshaw bounced off her chair at the first note of his horrible voice, and changed toward me instantly—as if it had been *my* fault—in the most alarming and unexpected manner. Her ladyship's face became awfully red; her ladyship's head trembled excessively; her ladyship's eyes looked straight into mine with an indescribable fierceness.

"Why am I thus insulted?" inquired Lady Malkinshaw, with a slow and dignified sternness which froze the blood in my veins. "What do you mean by it?" continued her ladyship, with a sudden rapidity of utterance that quite took my breath away.

Before I could remonstrate with my friend for visiting her natural irritation on poor innocent me; before I could declare that I had seen the major actually open his garden gate to go away, the provoking brute's voice burst in on us again.

"Ha! yes," we heard him growl to himself, in a kind of shameless domestic soliloquy. "Yes, yes, yes—Sophy was sick, to be sure. Curious. All Mrs. Namby's stepchildren have weak chests and strong stomachs. All Mrs. Namby's own children have weak stomachs and strong chests. *I* have a strong stomach *and* a strong chest. Pamby!"

"I consider this," continued Lady Malkinshaw, literally glaring at me, in the fullness of her indiscriminate exasperation—"I consider this to be unwarrantable and unlady-like. I beg to know—"

"Where's Bill?" burst in the major, from below, before her ladyship could add another word. "Matilda! Nurse! Pamby! where's Bill? I didn't bid Bill good-by—hold him up at the window, one of you!"

"My dear Lady Malkinshaw," I remonstrated, "why blame *me?* What have I done?"

"Done!" repeated her ladyship. "Done!!!— all that is most unfriendly, most unwarrantable, most unlady-like—"

"Ha, ha, ha-a-a-a!" roared the major, shouting her ladyship down, and stamping about the garden in fits of fond, paternal laughter. "Bill,

my boy, how are you? There's a young Turk
for you! Pull up his frock—I want to see his
jolly legs—"

Lady Malkinshaw screamed, and rushed to the
door. I sank into a chair, and clasped my hands
in despair.

"Ha, ha, ha-a-a-a! What calves the dog's
got! Pamby, look at his calves. Aha! bless
his heart, his legs are the model of his father's!
The Namby build, Matilda—the Namby build,
every inch of him. Kick again, Bill—kick out,
like mad. I say, ma'am! I beg your pardon,
ma'am—"

Ma'am? I ran to the window. Was the
major actually daring to address Lady Malkinshaw, as she passed, indignantly, on her way
out, down my front garden? He was! The
odious monster was pointing out his—his, what
shall I say?—his *undraped* offspring to the notice of my outraged visitor.

"Look at him, ma'am. If you're a judge of
children, look at him. There's a two-year-older
for you! Ha, ha, ha-a-a-a! Show the lady your
legs, Bill—kick out for the lady, you dog, kick
out!"

I can write no more: I have done great violence to myself in writing so much. Further
specimens of the daily outrages inflicted on me
by my next-door neighbor (though I could add
them by dozens) could do but little more to illustrate the intolerable nature of the grievance
of which I complain. Although Lady Malkin-

shaw's naturally fine sense of justice suffered me to call and remonstrate the day after she left my house; although we are now faster friends than ever, how can I expect her ladyship to visit me again, after the reiterated insults to which she was exposed on the last occasion of her esteemed presence under my roof? How can I ask my niece—a young person who has been most carefully brought up—to come and stay with me, when I know that she will be taken into the major's closest domestic confidence on the first morning of her arrival, whether she likes it or not? Of all the dreary prospects stretching before all the single ladies in the world, mine seems the most hopeless. My neighbors can't help me, and I can't help myself. The law of the land contains no provision against the habitual management of a wife and family in a front garden. Private remonstrance, addressed to a man so densely impenetrable to a sense of propriety as the major, would only expose me to ridicule and perhaps to insult. I can't leave my house, for it exactly suits me, and I have bought it. The major can't leave his house, for it exactly suits him, and he has bought it. There is actually no remedy possible but the forcible removal of my military neighbor from his home; and there is but one power in the country which is strong enough to accomplish that removal—the Horse Guards, infuriated by the horrors of war

CASES WORTH LOOKING AT.—II.

THE POISONED MEAL.

[From the Records of the French Courts.]

CHAPTER I.   THE POCKETS.

THIS case takes us across the Channel to Normandy; and introduces us to a young French girl, named Marie Françoise Victoire Salmon.

Her father was a poor Norman laborer. Her mother died while she was a child. From an early age Marie had learned to get her own living by going out to service. Three different mistresses tried her while she was a very young girl, and found every reason to be satisfied with her conduct. She entered her fourth place, in the family of one Monsieur Dumesnil, when she was twenty years of age. This was the turning-point in her career; and here the strange story of her life properly begins.

Among the persons who often visited Monsieur Dumesnil and his wife was a certain Monsieur Revel, a relation of Madame Dumesnil's. He was a man of some note in his part of the country, holding a responsible legal appointment at the town of Caen, in Normandy; and he honored Marie, when he first saw her at her master's

house, with his special attention and approval.
She had an innocent face and a winning manner; and Monsieur Revel became almost oppressively anxious, in a strictly paternal way, that she should better her condition, by seeking service at Caen, where places were plentiful and wages higher than in the country, and where, it is also necessary to remember, Monsieur Revel himself happened to live.

Marie's own idea, however, of the best means of improving her condition was a little at variance with the idea of her disinterested adviser. Her ambition was to gain her living independently, if she could, by being a seamstress. She left the service of Monsieur Dumesnil of her own accord, without so much as the shadow of a stain on her character, and went to the old town of Bayeux to try what she could do by taking in needlework. As a means of subsistence, needlework soon proved itself to be insufficient; and she found herself thrown back again on the old resource of going out to service. Most unfortunately, as events afterward turned out, she now called to mind Monsieur Revel's paternal advice, and resolved to seek employment as a maid of all work at Caen.

She left Bayeux with the little bundle of clothes which represented all the property she had in the world, on the first of August, seventeen hundred and eighty-one. It will be well to notice this date particularly, and to remember—in case some of the events of Marie's story should seem almost incredible—that it marks the period which immediately preceded the first outbreak of the French Revolution.

Among the few articles of the maid's apparel which the bundle contained, and to which it is necessary to direct attention at the outset, were *two pairs of pockets*, one of them being still in an unfinished condition. She had a third pair which she wore on her journey. In the last century, a country girl's pockets were an important and prominent part of her costume. They hung on each side of her, ready to her hand. They were sometimes very prettily embroidered, and they were almost always large and of a bright color.

On the first of August, seventeen hundred and eighty-one, Marie left Bayeux, and early on the same day she reached Caen. Her good manners, her excellent character, and the modesty of her demands in the matter of wages, rendered it easy for her to find a situation. On the very evening of her arrival she was suited with a place; and her first night at Caen was passed under the roof of her new employers.

The family consisted of Marie's master and mistress, Monsieur and Madame Huet Duparc (both highly respectable people); of two sons, aged respectively twenty-one and eleven years; of their sister, aged seventeen years; and of Monsieur and Madame De Beaulieu, the father and mother of Madame Duparc, one eighty-eight years old, the other eighty-six.

Madame Duparc explained to Marie the various duties which she was expected to perform,

on the evening when she entered the house. She
was to begin the day by fetching some milk—
that being one of the ingredients used in preparing the hasty-pudding which formed the favorite
morning meal of the old gentleman, Monsieur De
Beaulieu. The hasty-pudding was always to be
got ready by seven o'clock exactly. When this
had been done, Marie was next required to take
the infirm old lady, Madame De Beaulieu, every
morning to mass. She was then to go to market,
and get all the provisions that were wanted for
the daily use of the family; and she was, finally,
to look to the cooking of the food, and to make
herself additionally useful (with some occasional
assistance from Madame Duparc and her daughter) in every remaining branch of household
work. The yearly wages she was to receive for
performing all these conflicting duties amounted
to precisely two pounds sterling of English
money.

She had entered her new place on a Wednesday. On Thursday she took her first lesson in
preparing the old gentleman's morning meal.
One point which her mistress then particularly
impressed on her was, that she was *not* to put
any salt in the hasty-pudding.

On the Saturday following, when she went out
to buy milk, she made a little purchase on her
own account. Of course the purchase was an
article of dress—a piece of fine bright orange-
colored stuff, for which she paid nearly the
whole price on the spot, out of her small savings. The sum of two sous six deniers (about a

penny English) was all that Marie took credit
for. On her return to the house she showed the
piece of stuff to Madame Duparc, and asked to
be advised whether she should make an apron or
a jacket of it.

The next day being Sunday, Marie marked the
occasion by putting on all the little finery she
had. Her pair of festive pockets, striped with
blue and white, came out of her bundle along
with other things. When she had put them on,
she hung the old workaday pockets which she
had worn on leaving Bayeux to the back of a
chair in her bed-chamber. This was a little
room on the ground floor, situated close to the
dining-room, and perfectly easy of access to
every one in the house. Long afterward, Marie
remembered how pleasantly and quietly that
Sunday passed. It was the last day of happiness the poor creature was to enjoy in the house
of Madame Duparc.

On the Monday morning, she went to fetch the
milk as usual. But the milk-woman was not in
the shop to serve her. After returning to the
house, she proposed making a second attempt;
but her mistress stopped her, saying that the
milk would doubtless be sent before long. This
turned out to be the case, and Marie, having
cleaned the saucepan for Monsieur De Beaulieu's
hasty-pudding, received from the hands of Madame Duparc the earthen vessel containing the
meal used in the house. She mixed this flour
and put it into the saucepan in the presence of
Madame Duparc and her daughter. She had

just set the saucepan on the fire, when her mistress said, with a very remarkable abruptness:

"Have you put any salt in it?"

"Certainly not, ma'am," answered Marie, amazed by the question. "You told me yourself that I was never to put salt in it."

Upon this, Madame Duparc snatched up the saucepan without saying another word, turned to the dresser, stretched out her hand toward one of four salt-cellars which always stood there, and sprinkled salt into the saucepan—or (to speak with extreme correctness, the matter being important), if not salt something which she took for salt.

The hasty-pudding made, Marie poured it from the saucepan into a soup-plate which her mistress held. Madame Duparc herself then took it to Monsieur De Beaulieu. She and her daughter, and one of her sons, remained with the old man while he was eating his breakfast. Marie, left in the kitchen, prepared to clean the saucepan; but, before she could do so, she was suddenly called in two different directions by Madame De Beaulieu and Madame Duparc. The old lady wished to be taken to mass, and her mistress wanted to send her on a number of errands. Marie did not stop even to pour some clean water, as usual, into the saucepan. She went at once to get her instructions from Madame Duparc, and to attend on Madame De Beaulieu. Taking the old lady to church, and then running on her mistress's errands, kept her so long away from the house, that it was half-past eleven in the forenoon before she got back to the kitchen.

The first news that met her on her return was that Monsieur De Beaulieu had been suffering, ever since nine o'clock, from a violent attack of vomiting and colic. Madame Duparc ordered her to help the old man to bed immediately; and inquired, when these directions had been followed, whether Marie felt capable of looking after him herself, or whether she would prefer that a nurse should be sent for. Being a kind-hearted, willing girl, always anxious to make herself useful, Marie replied that she would gladly undertake the nursing of the old man; and thereupon her bed was moved at once into Monsieur De Beaulieu's room.

Meanwhile Madame Duparc fetched from a neighboring apothecary's one of the apprentices of the shop to see her father. The lad was quite unfit to meet the emergency of the case, which was certainly serious enough to require the atten tion of his master, if not of a regularly qualified physician. Instead of applying any internal remedies, the apprentice stupidly tried blister-ing. This course of treatment proved utterly useless; but no better advice was called in. After he had suffered for hours without relief, Monsieur De Beaulieu began to sink rapidly to-ward the afternoon. At half-past five o'clock he had ceased to exist.

This shocking catastrophe, startling and sus-picious as it was, did not appear to discompose the nerves of Madame Duparc. While her eld-

est son immediately left the house to inform his
father (who had been absent in the country all
day) of what had happened, she lost no time in
sending for the nearest nurse to lay out the
corpse of Monsieur De Beaulieu. On entering
the chamber of death, the nurse found Marie
there alone, praying by the old man's bedside.

"He died suddenly, did he not?" said the nurse.

"Very suddenly," answered Marie. "He was
walking about only yesterday in perfect health."

Soon afterward the time came when it was customary to prepare supper. Marie went into the
kitchen mechanically, to get the meal ready.
Madame Duparc, her daughter, and her youngest son, sat down to it as usual. Madame De
Beaulieu, overwhelmed by the dreadful death of
her husband, was incapable of joining them.

When supper was over, Marie assisted the old
lady to bed. Then, worn out though she was
with fatigue, she went back to the nurse to keep
her company in watching by the dead body.
Monsieur De Beaulieu had been kind to Marie,
and had spoken gratefully of the little attentions
she had shown him. She remembered this tenderly now that he was no more; and she could
not find it in her heart to leave a hired mourner
to be the only watcher by his death-bed. All
that night she remained in the room, entirely
ignorant of what was passing the while in every
other part of the house—her own little bedroom
included, as a matter of course.

About seven o'clock the next morning, after
sitting up all night, she went back again wearily

to the kitchen to begin her day's work. Her mistress joined her there, and saluted her instantly with a scolding.

"You are the most careless, slovenly girl I ever met with," said Madame Duparc. "Look at your dress; how can you expect to be decent on a Sunday, if you wear your best pair of pockets on week-days?"

Surely Madame Duparc's grief for the loss of her father must have been slight enough, if it did not prevent her from paying the strictest attention to her servant's pockets! Although Marie had only known the old man for a few days, she had been too deeply impressed by his illness and its fatal end to be able to think of such a trifle as the condition of her dress. And now, of all the people in the world, it was Monsieur De Beaulieu's daughter who reminded her that she had never thought of changing her pockets only the day after the old man's dreadful death.

"Put on your old pockets directl y, you untidy girl!" said Madame Duparc.

The old pockets were of course hanging where Marie had left them, at the back of the chair in her own room—the room which was open to any one who chose to go into it—the room which she herself had not entered during the past night. She left the kitchen to obey her mistress; and taking the old pair of pockets off the chair, tied them on as quickly as possible. From that fatal moment the friendless maid of all work was a ruined girl.

CHAPTER II.   THE ARSENIC.

On returning to the kitchen to go on with her
work, the exhaustion against which Marie had
hitherto fought successfully, overpowered her the
moment she sat down; her heavy head drooped,
her eyes closed in spite of her, and she fell into a
broken, uneasy slumber. Madame Duparc and
her daughter, seeing the condition she was in,
undertook the preparation of the day's dinner
themselves. Among the dishes which they got
ready, and which they salted from the cellars on
the dresser, were two different kinds of soup—
one kind for themselves, made from fresh "stock"
—the other, for Marie and the nurse, made from
old "stock." They were engaged over their
cookery, when Monsieur Duparc arrived from
the country; and Marie was awakened to take
the horse he had ridden to the stables, to unsad-
dle the animal, and to give him his feed of corn.

While she was thus engaged, Madame Duparc
and her daughter remained alone in the kitchen.
When she left the stable, it was time for her to
lay the cloth. She was told to put plates for
seven persons. Only six, however, sat down to
dinner. Those six were, Madame De Beaulieu,
Monsieur and Madame Duparc, the youngest of
their two sons, Madame Beauguillot (sister of
Madame Duparc), and Monsieur Beauguillot
(her son). Mademoiselle Duparc remained in the
kitchen to help Marie in serving up the dinner,
and only took her place at table after the soup

had been put on. Her elder brother, after summoning his father home, had not returned to the house.

After the soup had been taken away, and while Marie was waiting at table during the eating of the second course, young Duparc complained that he felt something gritty between his teeth. His mother made precisely the same remark. Nobody else, however, agreed with them, and the subject was allowed to drop. When the second course was done with, the dessert followed, consisting of a plate of cherries. With the dessert there arrived a visitor, Monsieur Fergant, a relation of Madame Duparc's. This gentleman placed himself at table with the rest of the company.

Meanwhile, the nurse and Marie were making their dinner in the kitchen off the soup which had been specially provided for them—Marie having previously placed the dirty plates and the empty soup-tureen from the dining-room, in the scullery, as usual, to be washed at the proper time. While she and her companion were still engaged over their soup, young Duparc and his mother suddenly burst into the kitchen, followed by the other persons who had partaken of dinner.

"We are all poisoned!" cried Madame Duparc, in the greatest terror. "Good heavens! I smell burned arsenic in the kitchen!"

Monsieur Fergant, the visitor, hearing these last words, politely stepped forward to echo them.

"Burned arsenic, beyond a doubt," said Monsieur Fergant. When this gentleman was subsequently questioned on the subject, it may not be amiss to mention that he was quite unable to say what burned arsenic smelled like. Neither is it altogether out of place to inquire how Madame Duparc happened to be so amazingly apt at discovering the smell of burned arsenic? The answer to the question does not seem easy to discover.

Having settled that they were all poisoned, and having even found out (thanks to those two intelligent amateur chemists, Madame Duparc and Monsieur Fergant) the very nature of the deadly drug that had been used to destroy them, the next thing the company naturally thought of was the necessity of summoning medical help. Young Monsieur Beauguillot obligingly ran off (it was apparently a very mild case of poisoning, so far as he was concerned) to the apothecary's shop, and fetched, not the apprentice this time, but the master. The master, Monsieur Thierry, arrived in great haste, and found the dinner-eaters all complaining of nausea and pains in the stomach. He naturally asked what they had eaten. The reply was, that they had eaten nothing but soup.

This was, to say the least of it, rather an unaccountable answer. The company had had for dinner, besides soup, a second course of boiled meat, and ragout of beef, and a dessert of cherries. Why was this plain fact concealed? Why was the apothecary's attention to be fixed exclusively on the soup? Was it because the tureen was empty, and because the alleged smell of burned arsenic might be accounted for on the theory that the remains of the soup brought from the dining-room had been thrown on the kitchen fire? But no remains of soup came down—it had been all consumed by the guests. And what is still more remarkable, the only person in the kitchen (excepting Marie and the nurse) who could not discover the smell of burned arsenic, was the person of all others who was professionally qualified to find it out first—the apothecary himself.

After examining the tureen and the plates, and stirring up the wood-ashes on the fire, and making no sort of discovery, Monsieur Thierry turned to Marie, and asked if she could account for what had happened. She simply replied that she knew nothing at all about it; and thereupon her mistress and the rest of the persons present all overwhelmed her together with a perfect torrent of questions. The poor girl, terrified by the hubbub, worn out by a sleepless night and by the hard work and agitation of the day preceding it, burst into an hysterical fit of tears, and was ordered out of the kitchen to lie down and recover herself. The only person who showed her the least pity and offered her the slightest attention, was a servant-girl like herself, who lived next door, and who stole up to the room in which she was weeping alone, with a cup of warm milk-and-water to comfort her.

Meanwhile the report had spread in the town that the old man, Monsieur De Beaulieu, and the whole Duparc family had been poisoned by their servant. Madame Duparc did her best to

give the rumor the widest possible circulation.
Entirely forgetting, as it would seem, that she
was on her own showing a poisoned woman, she
roamed excitably all over the house with an audience of agitated female friends at her heels; telling the burned-arsenic story over and over again
to every fresh detachment of visitors that arrived
to hear it; and finally leading the whole troop of
women into the room where Marie was trying to
recover herself. The poor girl was surrounded
in a moment; angry faces and shrill voices met
her on every side; the most insolent questions,
the most extravagant accusations, assailed her;
and not one word that she could say in her own
defense was listened to for an instant. She had
sprung up in the bed, on her knees, and was
frantically entreating for permission to speak in
her own defense, when a new personage appeared
on the scene, and stilled the clamor by his pres·
ence. This individual was a surgeon named
Hébert, a friend of Madame Duparc's, who announced that he had arrived to give the amily
the benefit of his assistance, and who proposed
to commence operations by searching the servant's pockets without further delay.

The instant Marie heard him make this proposal she untied her pockets, and gave them to
Surgeon Hebert with her own hands. He examined them on the spot. In one he found some
copper money and a thimble. In the other (to
use his own words, given in evidence) he discovered "various fragments of bread, sprinkled over
with some minute substance which was white

and shining. He kept the fragments of bread, and left the room immediately without saying a word." By this course of proceeding he gave Marie no chance of stating at the outset whether she knew of the fragments of bread being in her pocket, or whether she was totally ignorant how they came there. Setting aside, for the present, the question, whether there was really any arsenic on the crumbs at all, it would clearly have been showing the unfortunate maid of all work no more than common justice to have allowed her the opportunity of speaking before the bread was carried away.

It was now seven o'clock in the evening. The next event was the arrival of another officious visitor. The new friend in need belonged to the legal profession—he was an advocate named Friley. Monsieur Friley's legal instincts led him straightway to a conclusion which seriously advanced the progress of events. Having heard the statement of Madame Duparc and her daughter, he decided that it was his duty to lodge an information against Marie before the Procurator of the king, at Caen.

The Procurator of the king is, by this time, no stranger to the reader. He was the same Monsieur Revel who had taken such an amazingly strong interest in Marie's fortunes, and who had strongly advised her to try her luck at Caen. Here then, surely, was a friend found at last for the forlorn maid of all work. We shall see how Monsieur Revel acted, after Friley's information had been duly lodged.

The French law of the period, and, it may be
added, the commonest principles of justice also,
required the Procurator to perform certain plain
duties as soon as the accusation against Marie
had reached his ears.

He was, in the first place, bound to proceed
immediately, accompanied by his official colleague, to the spot where the alleged crime 'of
poisoning was supposed to have taken place.
Arrived there, it was his business to ascertain
for himself the condition of the persons attacked
with illness; to hear their statements; to examine the rooms, the kitchen utensils, and the family medicine-chest, if there happened to be one in
the house; to receive any statement the accused
person might wish to make; to take down her
answers to his questions; and, lastly, to keep
anything found on the servant (the bread-crumbs,
for instance, of which Surgeon Hebert had coolly
taken possession), or anything found about the
house which it might be necessary to produce in
evidence, in a position of absolute security, under
the hand and seal of justice.

These were the plain duties which Monsieur
Revel, the Procurator, was officially bound to
fulfill. In the case of Marie, he not only neglected to perform any one of them, but actually
sanctioned a scheme for entrapping her into
prison, by sending a commissary of police to
the house, in plain clothes, with an order to
place her in solitary confinement. To what motive could this scandalous violation of his duties
and of justice be attributed? The last we saw

of Monsieur Revel, he was so benevolently disposed toward Marie that he condescended to advise her about her prospects in life, and even went the length of recommending her to seek for a situation in the very town in which he lived himself. And now we find him so suddenly and bitterly hostile toward the former object of his patronage, that he actually lends the assistance of his high official position to sanction an accusation against her, into the truth or falsehood of which he had not made a single inquiry! Can it be that Monsieur Revel's interest in Marie was, after all, not of the purest possible kind, and that the unfortunate girl proved too stubbornly virtuous to be taught what the real end was toward which the attentions of her over-benevolent adviser privately pointed? There is no evidence attaching to the case (as how should there be?) to prove this. But is there any other explanation of Monsieur Revel's conduct which at all tends to account for the extraordinary inconsistency of it?

Having received his secret instructions, the Commissary of Police—a man named Bertot—proceeded to the house of Monsieur and Madame Duparc, disguised in plain clothes. His first proceeding was to order Marie to produce the various plates, dishes, and kitchen utensils which had been used at the dinner of Tuesday, the seventh of August (that being the day on which the poisoning of the company was alleged to have taken place). Marie produced a saucepan, an earthen vessel, a stew-pan, and several plates piled on each other, in one of which there were the remains of some soup. These articles Bertot locked up in the kitchen cupboard, and took away the key with him. He ought to have taken the additional precaution of placing a seal on the cupboard, so as to prevent any tampering with the lock, or any treachery with a duplicate key. But this he neglected to do.

His next proceeding was to tell Marie that the Procurator Revel wished to speak to her, and to propose that she should accompany him to the presence of that gentleman forthwith. Not having the slightest suspicion of any treachery, she willingly consented, and left the house with the Commissary. A friend of the Duparcs, named Vassol, accompanied them.

Once out of the house, Bertot led his unsuspecting prisoner straight to the jail. As soon as she was inside the gates, he informed her that she was arrested, and proceeded to search her person in the presence of Vassol, of the jailer of the prison, and of a woman named Dujardin. The first thing found on her was a little linen bag, sewn to her petticoat, and containing a species of religious charm, in the shape of a morsel of the sacramental wafer. Her pockets came next under review (the pockets which Surgeon Hebert had previously searched). A little dust was discovered at the bottom of them, which was shaken out on paper, wrapped up along with the linen bag, sealed in one packet, and taken to the Procurator's office. Finally, the woman Dujardin found in Marie's bosom a little key, which she readily admitted to be the key of her own cupboard.

The search over, one last act of cruelty and injustice was all that remained to be committed for that day. The unfortunate girl was placed at once in solitary confinement.

CHAPTER III.   THE EVIDENCE.

Thus far the case is one of suspicion only. Waiting until the end of the trial before we decide on whom that suspicion ought to rest, let us now hear the evidence by which the Duparcs and their adherents proceeded to justify their conspiracy against the liberty and the life of a friendless girl.

Having secured Marie in solitary confinement, and having thus left the house and all that it contained for a whole night at the free disposal of the Duparcs, the Procurator Revel bethought himself, the morning after the arrest of his prisoner, of the necessity of proceeding with something like official regularity. He accordingly issued his requisition to the Lieutenant-Criminel to accompany him to the house of Monsieur Duparc, attended by the medical officers and the clerk, to inquire into the circumstances under which the suspected death by poisoning of Monsieur De Beaulieu had taken place. Marie had been imprisoned on the evening of the seventh of August, and this requisition is dated on the morning of the eighth. The document betrays one remarkable informality. It mentions the death of Monsieur De Beaulieu; but is absolute-

ly silent on the subject of the alleged poisoning
of seven persons at dinner the next day. And
yet it was this latter circumstance only which
first directed suspicion against Marie, and which
induced Friley to lodge the information against
her on which the Procurator was now acting.
Probably Monsieur Revel's legal acumen convinced him, at the outset, that the story of the
poisoned dinner was too weak to be relied on.

The officers of the law, accompanied by the
doctors, proceeded to the house of the Duparcs
on the eighth of August. After viewing the
body of Monsieur De Beaulieu, the medical men
were directed to open and examine it. They reported the discovery in the stomach of a reddish,
brick-colored liquid, somewhat resembling the lees
of wine. The mucous membrane was detached
in some places, and its internal surface was cor-
roded. On examining the reddish liquid, they
found it to contain a crystallized sediment, which,
on analyzation, proved to be arsenic. Upon this,
the doctors delivered it as their opinion that Monsieur De Beaulieu had been poisoned, and that
poison had been the cause of his death.

The event having taken this serious turn, the
first duty of the Lieutenant-Criminel (according
to the French law) was to send for the servant
on whom suspicion rested, to question her, and
to confront her with the Duparcs. He did nothing of the kind; he made no inquiry after the
servant (being probably unwilling to expose his
colleague, the Procurator, who had illegally arrested and illegally imprisoned her); he never

examined the kitchen utensils which the Commissary had locked up; he never opened the servant's cupboard with the key that had been taken from her when she was searched in prison. All he did was to reduce the report of the doctors to writing, and to return to his office with his posse comitatus at his heels.

It was necessary to summon the witnesses and examine them. But the Procurator Revel now conveniently remembered the story of the poisoned dinner, and he sent the Lieutenant-Criminel to examine the Duparcs and their friends at the private residence of the family, in consideration of the sickly condition of the eaters of the adulterated meal. It may be as well to observe, here as elsewhere, that these highly indulged personages had none of them been sufficiently inconvenienced even to go to bed, or in any way to alter their ordinary habits.

On the afternoon of the eighth, the Lieutenant-Criminel betook himself to the house of Monsieur Duparc, to collect evidence touching the death by poison of Monsieur De Beaulieu. The first witness called was Monsieur Duparc.

This gentleman, it will be remembered, was away from home on Monday, the sixth, when Monsieur De Beaulieu died, and only returned, at the summons of his eldest son, at half-past eleven on the forenoon of the seventh. He had nothing to depose connected with the death of his father-in-law. or with the events which might have taken place in the house on the night of the sixth and the morning of the seventh. On the

other hand, he had a great deal to say about
the state of his own stomach after the dinner of
the seventh—a species of information not calculated to throw much light on the subject of inquiry, which was the poisoning of Monsieur De
Beaulieu.

The old lady, Madame De Beaulieu, was next
examined. She could give no evidence of the
slightest importance touching the matter in hand;
but, like Monsieur Duparc, she had something to
say on the topic of the poisoned dinner.

Madame Duparc followed on the list of witnesses. The report of her examination—so thoroughly had she recovered from the effects of the
dinner of the seventh—ran to a prodigious length.
Five-sixths of it related entirely to her own sensations and suspicions, and the sensations and
suspicions of her relatives and friends, after they
had risen from the table. As to the point at
issue, the point which affected the liberty, and
perhaps the life, of her unfortunate servant, she
had so little to say that her testimony may be
repeated here in her own words:

"The witness (Madame Duparc) deposed, that
after Marie had helped Monsieur De Beaulieu to
get up, she (Marie) hastened out for the milk,
and, on her return with it, prepared the hasty-pudding, took it herself off the fire, and herself poured
it out into the plate—then left the kitchen to accompany Madame De Beaulieu to mass. Four
or five minutes after Monsieur De Beaulieu had
eaten the hasty-pudding, he was seized with violent illness."

Short as it is, this statement contains several distinct suppressions of the truth.

First, Madame Duparc is wrong in stating that Marie fetched the milk, for it was the milk-woman who brought it to the house. Secondly, Madame Duparc conceals the fact that she handed the flour to the servant to make the hasty-pudding. Thirdly, Madame Duparc does not mention that she held the plate for the pudding to be poured into, and took it to her father. Fourthly, and most important of all, Madame Duparc altogether omits to state that she sprinkled salt, with her own hands, over the hasty-pudding—although she had expressly informed her servant, a day or two before, that salt was never to be mixed with it. At a subsequent stage of the proceedings she was charged with having salted the hasty-pudding herself, and she could not, and did not, deny it.

The examination of Madame Duparc ended the business of the day of the eighth. The next morning the Lieutenant-Criminel, as politely attentive as before, returned to resume his inquiry at the private residence of Monsieur Duparc.

The first witness examined on the second day was Mademoiselle Duparc. She carefully followed her mother's lead—saying as little as possible about the preparation of the hasty-pudding on the morning of Monday, and as much as possible about the pain suffered by everybody after the dinner of Tuesday. Madame Beauguillot, the next witness, added her testimony, as to the state of her own digestive organs, after partak-

ing of the same meal—speaking at such prodigious length that the poison would appear, in her
case, to have produced its principal effect (and
that of a stimulating kind) on her tongue.   Her
son, Monsieur De Beauguillot, was next examined, quite uselessly in relation to the death
by poison, which was the object of inquiry.   The
last witness was Madame Duparc's younger son
—the same who had complained of feeling a
gritty substance between his teeth at dinner.   In
one important respect, his evidence flatly contradicted his mother's.   Madame Duparc had
adroitly connected Monsieur De Beaulieu's illness with the hasty-pudding, by describing the
old man as having been taken ill four or five
minutes after eating it.   Young Duparc, on the
contrary, declared that his grandfather first felt
ill at nine o'clock—exactly two hours after he
had partaken of his morning meal.

With the evidence of this last witness, the ex-
aminations at the private residence of Monsieur
Duparc ended.   Thus far, out of the seven persons, all related to each other, who had been
called as witnesses, three (Monsieur Duparc himself, Madame Beauguillot, and her son) had not
been in the house on the day when Monsieur De
Beaulieu died.   Of the other four, who had been
present (Madame De Beaulieu, Madame Duparc,
her son and her daughter), not one deposed to a
single fact tending to fix on Marie any reasonable suspicion of having administered poison to
Monsieur De Beaulieu.

The remaining witnesses, called before the

Lieutenant-Criminel, were twenty-nine in number. Not one of them had been in the house on the Monday which was the day of the old man's death. Twenty-six of them had nothing to offer but hearsay evidence on the subject of the events which had taken place at, and after, the dinner of Tuesday. The testimony of the remaining three; namely, of Friley, who had lodged the information against Marie; of Surgeon Hebert, who had searched her pockets in the house; and of Commissary Bertot, who had searched her for the second time, after taking her to prison— was the testimony on which the girl's enemies mainly relied for substantiating their charges by positively associating her with the possession of arsenic.

Let us see what amount of credit can be attached to the evidence of these three witnesses.

Friley was the first to be examined. After stating what share he had taken in bringing Marie to justice (it will be remembered that he lodged his information against her at the instance of Madame Duparc, without allowing her to say a word in her own defense), he proceeded to depose that he hunted about the bed on which the girl had lain down to recover herself, and that he discovered on the mattress seven or eight scattered grains of some substance which resembled the powder reported to have been found on the crumbs in her pockets. He added further, that on the next day, about two hours before the body of Monsieur De Beaulieu was examined, he returned to the house, searched under the bed, with

Monsieur Duparc and a soldier named Cauvin,
and found there four or five grains more of the
same substance which he had discovered on the
mattress.

Here were two separate portions of poison
found, then. What did Friley do with them?
Did he seal them up immediately in the presence
of witnesses, and take them to the legal authorities? Nothing of the sort. On being asked
what he did with the first portion, he replied that
he gave it to young Monsieur Beauguillot. Beauguillot's evidence was thereupon referred to, and
it was found that he had never mentioned receiving the packet of powder from Friley. He had
made himself extremely officious in examining
the kitchen utensils; he had been as anxious as
any one to promote the discovery of arsenic; and
when he had the opportunity of producing it, if
Friley were to be believed, he held it back, and
said not one word about the matter. So much
for the first portion of the mysterious powder,
and for the credibility of Friley's evidence thus
far!

On being questioned as to what he had done
with the second portion, alleged to have been
found under the bed, Friley replied that he had
handed it to the doctors who opened the body,
and that they had tried to discover what it was
by burning it between two copper pieces. A witness who had been present at this proceeding declared, on being questioned, that the experiment
had been made with some remains of hasty-pudding scraped out of the saucepan. Here again

was a contradiction, and here, once more, Friley's evidence was, to say the least of it, not to be depended on.

Sergeant Hebert followed. What had he done with the crumbs of bread scattered over with white powder which he had found in Marie's pocket? He had, after showing them to the company in the drawing-room, exhibited them next to the apothecary, and handed them afterward to another medical man. Being finally assured that there was arsenic on the bread, he had sealed up the crumbs, and given the packet to the legal authorities. When had he done that? On the day of his examination as a witness—the fourteenth of August. When did he find the crumbs? On the seventh. Here was the arsenic in this case, then, passing about from hand to hand, and not sealed up, for seven days. Had Surgeon Hebert anything more to say? Yes, he had another little lot of arsenic to hand in, which a lady-friend of his had told him she had found on Marie's bed, and which, like the first lot, had been passed about privately for seven days, from hand to hand, before it was sealed up. To us, in these later and better days, it seems hardly credible that the judge should have admitted these two packets in evidence. It is, nevertheless, the disgraceful fact that he did so receive them.

Commissary Bertot came next. He and the man named Vassol, who had helped him to entrap Marie into prison, and to search her before she was placed in solitary confinement, were ex-

amined in succession, and contradicted each other
on oath in the flattest manner.

Bertot stated that he had discovered the dust at
the bottom of her pockets; had shaken it out on
paper; had placed with it the little linen bag,
containing a morsel of the sacramental wafer,
which had been sewn to her petticoat; had sealed
the two up in one packet; and had taken the
packet to the proper office. Vassol, on the other
hand, swore that *he* had shaken out the pockets,
and had made up the packet; and that Bertot
had done nothing in the matter but lend his seal.
Contradicting each other in these details, both
agreed that what they had found on the girl was
inclosed and sealed up in *one* packet, which they
had left at the office, neglecting to take such a
receipt for it as might have established its identity in writing. At this stage of the proceedings
the packet was sent for. Three packets appeared
instead of one! Two were composed of paper,
and contained dust and a little white powder.
The third was the linen bag, presented without
any covering at all. Vassol, bewildered by the
change, declared that of these three separate objects he could only identify one—the linen bag.
In this case, it was as clear as daylight that somebody must have tampered with the single sealed
packet which Bertot and Vassol swore to having
left at the office. No attempt, however, was
made to investigate this circumstance; and the
case for the prosecution—so far as the accusation
of poisoning was concerned—closed with the examination of Bertot and Vassol.

Such was the evidence produced in support of a charge which involved nothing less than the life or death of a human being.

CHAPTER IV.   THE SENTENCE.

While the inquiry was in course of progress, various details connected with it found their way out-of-doors.   The natural sense of justice among the people which had survived the corruptions of the time was aroused to assert itself on behalf of the maid of all work.   The public voice spoke as loudly as it dared, in those days, in Marie's favor, and in condemnation of the conspiracy against her.

People persisted, from the first, in inquiring how it was that arsenic had got into the house of Monsieur Duparc; and rumor answered, in more than one direction, that a member of the family had purchased the poison a short time since, and that there were persons in the town who could prove it.   To the astonishment of every one, no steps were taken by the legal authorities to clear up this report, and to establish the truth or the falsehood of it, before the trial.   Another circumstance, of which also no explanation was attempted, filled the public mind with natural suspicion.   This was the disappearance of the eldest son of Monsieur and Madame Duparc.   On the day of his grandfather's sudden death, he had been sent, as may be remembered, to bring his father back from the country; and, from that time forth, he had never reappeared at the house, and nobody could say what had become of him.   Was

400 WORKS OF WILKIE COLLINS.

it not natural to connect together the rumors of purchased poison and the mysterious disappearance of this young man? Was it not utterly inconsistent with any proceedings conducted in the name of justice to let these suspicious circumstances exist, without making the slightest attempt to investigate and to explain them?

But, apart from all other considerations, the charge against Marie was, on the face of it, preposterously incredible. A friendless young girl arrives at a strange town, possessing excellent testimonials to her character, and gets a situation in a family every member of which is utterly unknown to her until she enters the house. Established in her new place, she instantly conceives the project of poisoning the whole family, and carries it out in five days from the time when she first took her situation, by killing one member of the household, and producing suspicious symptoms of illness in the cases of all the rest. She commits this crime having nothing to gain by it; and she is so inconceivably reckless of detection that she scatters poison about the bed on which she lies down, leaves poison sticking to the crumbs in her pockets, puts those pockets on when her mistress tells her to do so, and hands them over without a moment's hesitation to the first person who asks permission to search them. What mortal evidence could substantiate such a wild charge as this? How does the evidence actually presented substantiate it? No shadow of proof that she had purchased arsenic is offered, to begin with. The evidence against her is evidence which attempts to associate her with the actual possession of poison. What is it worth? In the first place, the witnesses contradict each other. In the second place, in no one case in which powdered substances were produced in evidence against her had those powdered substances been so preserved as to prevent their being tampered with. Two packets of the powder pass about from hand to hand for seven days; two have been given to witnesses who can't produce them, or account for what has become of them; and one, which the witnesses who made it up swear to as a single packet, suddenly expands into three when it is called for in evidence!

· Careless as they were of assuming even the external decencies of justice, the legal authorities, and their friends the Duparcs, felt that there would be some risk in trying their victim for her life on such evidence as this, in a large town like Caen. It was impossible to shift their ground and charge her with poisoning accidentally; for they either could not, or would not, account on ordinary grounds for the presence of arsenic in the house. And, even if this difficulty were overcome, and if it were alleged that arsenic purchased for killing vermin had been carelessly placed in one of the salt-cellars on the dresser, Madame Duparc could not deny that her own hands had salted the hasty-pudding on the Monday, and that her servant had been too ill through exhaustion to cook the dinner on the Tuesday. Even supposing there were no serious interests of the vilest kind at stake, which made the girl's destruction a matter of necessity, it was clearly impossible to modify the charge against her. One other alternative remained—the alternative of adding a second accusation which might help to strengthen the first, and to degrade Marie in the estimation of those inhabitants of the town who were now disposed to sympathize with her.

The poor girl's character was so good, her previous country life had been so harmless, that no hint or suggestion for a second charge against her could be found in her past history. If her enemies were to succeed, it was necessary to rely on pure invention. Having hesitated before no extremes of baseness and falsehood, thus far, they were true to themselves in regard to any vile venture which remained to be tried.

A day or two after the examination of the witnesses called to prove the poisoning had been considered complete, the public of Caen were amazed to hear that certain disclosures had taken place which would render it necessary to try Marie on a charge of theft as well as of poisoning. She was now not only accused of the murder of Monsieur De Beaulieu, but of robbing her former mistress Madame Dumesnil (a relation, be it remembered, of Monsieur Revel's), in the situation she occupied before she came to Caen; of robbing Madame Duparc; and of robbing the shop-woman from whom she had bought the piece of orange-colored stuff, the purchase of which is mentioned in an early part of this narrative.

There is no need to hinder the progress of this story by entering into details in relation to this second atrocious charge. When the reader is informed that the so-called evidence in support of the accusation of theft was got up by Procurator Revel, by Commissary Bertot, and by Madame Duparc, he will know beforehand what importance to attach to it, and what opinion to entertain on the question of the prisoner's innocence or guilt.

The preliminary proceedings were now considered to be complete. During their progress Marie had been formally interrogated, in her prison, by the legal authorities. Fearful as her situation was, the poor girl seems to have maintained self-possession enough to declare her innocence of poisoning, and her innocence of theft, firmly. Her answers, it is needless to say, availed her nothing. No legal help was assigned to her; no such institution as a jury was in existence in France. Procurator Revel collected the evidence, Procurator Revel tried the case, Procurator Revel delivered the sentence. Need the reader be told that Marie's irresponsible judge and unscrupulous enemy had no difficulty whatever in finding her guilty? She had been arrested on the seventh of August, seventeen hundred and eighty-one. Her doom was pronounced on the seventeenth of April, seventeen hundred and eighty-two. Throughout the whole of that interval she remained in prison.

The sentence was delivered in the following terms. It was written, printed, and placarded in Caen; and it is here translated from the original French:

"The Procurator Royal of the Bailiwick and
civil and criminal Bench and Presidency of
Caen, having taken cognizance of the documents concerning the trial specially instituted
against Marie Françoise Victoire Salmon accused of poisoning; the said documents consisting of an official report of the capture of the said
Marie Françoise Victoire Salmon on the seventh
of August last, together with other official reports, etc.

"Requires that the prisoner shall be declared
duly convicted:

"I. Of having, on the Monday morning of the
sixth of August last, cooked some hasty-pudding
for Monsieur Paisant De Beaulieu, father-in-law
of Monsieur Huet Duparc, in whose house the
prisoner had lived in the capacity of servant from
the first day of the said month of August; and
of having put arsenic in the said hasty-pudding
while cooking it, by which arsenic the said Monsieur De Beaulieu died poisoned, about six o'clock
on the same evening.

"II. Of having on the next day, Tuesday, the
seventh of August last, put arsenic into the soup
which was served, at noon, at the table of Monsieur and Madame Duparc, her employers, in
consequence of which all those persons who sat
at table and ate of the said soup were poisoned
and made dangerously ill, to the number of seven.

"III. Of having been discovered with arsenic
in her possession, which arsenic was found on the
said Tuesday, in the afternoon, not only in the
pockets of the prisoner, but upon the mattress

of the bed on which she was resting; the said arsenic having been recognized as being of the same nature and precisely similar to that which the guests discovered to have been put into their soup, as also to that which was found the next day, in the body of the aforesaid Monsieur De Beaulieu, and in the saucepan in which the hasty-pudding had been cooked, of which the aforesaid Monsieur De Beaulieu had eaten.

"IV. Of being *strongly suspected* of having put some of the same arsenic into a plate of cherries which she served to Madame De Beaulieu, on the same Tuesday morning, and again on the afternoon of the same day at the table of Monsieur and Madame Duparc.

"V. Of having, at the period of Michaelmas, seventeen hundred and eighty, committed different robberies at the house of Monsieur Dumesnil, where she lived in the capacity of servant, and notably of stealing a sheet, of which she made herself a petticoat and an apron.

"VI. Of having, at the beginning of the month of August last, stolen, in the house of Monsieur Huet Duparc, the different articles enumerated at the trial, and which were found locked up in her cupboard.

"VII. Of being *strongly suspected* of stealing, at the beginning of the said month of August, from the woman Lefevre, a piece of orange-colored stuff.

"For punishment and reparation of which offenses she, the said Marie Françoise Victoire Salmon, shall be condemned to make atonement, in her shift, with a halter round her neck, holding in her hands a burning wax-candle of the weight of two pounds, before the principal gate and entrance of the church of St. Peter, to which she shall be taken and led by the executioner of criminal sentences, who will tie in front of her and behind her back a placard, on which shall be written in large characters these words: *Poisoner and Domestic Thief.* And there, being on her knees, she shall declare that she has wickedly committed the said robberies and poisonings, for which she repents and asks pardon of God and justice. This done, she shall be led by the said executioner to the square of the market of Saint Saviour's, to be there fastened to a stake with a chain of iron, and to be burned alive; her body to be reduced to ashes, and the ashes to be cast to the winds; her goods to be acquired and confiscated to the King, or to whomsoever else they may belong. Said goods to be charged with a fine of ten livres to the King, in the event of the confiscation not turning to the profit of his Majesty.

"Required, additionally, that the said prisoner shall be previously submitted to the Ordinary and Extraordinary torture, to obtain information of her accomplices, and notably of those who either sold to her or gave to her the arsenic found in her possession. Order hereby given for the printing and placarding of this sentence in such places as shall be judged fit. Deliberated at the bar, this seventeenth April, seventeen hundred and eighty-two. (Signed) REVEL."

On the next day, the eighteenth, this frightful sentence was formally confirmed.

The matter had now become public, and no one could prevent the unfortunate prisoner from claiming whatever rights the law still allowed her. She had the privilege of appealing against her sentence before the Parliament of Rouen. And she appealed accordingly; being transferred, as directed by the law in such cases, from the prison at Caen to the prison at Rouen, to await the decision of the higher tribunal.

On the seventeenth of May the Rouen Parliament delivered its judgment, and confirmed the original sentence.

There was some difficulty, at first, in making the unhappy girl understand that her last chance for life had failed her. When the fact that her sentence was ordered to be carried out was at length impressed on her mind, she sank down with her face on the prison floor—then started up on her knees, passionately shrieking to Heaven to have pity on her, and to grant her the justice and the protection which men denied. Her agitation at the frightful prospect before her was so violent, her screams of terror were so shrill and piercing, that all the persons connected with the management of the prison hurried together to her cell. Among the number were three priests, who were accustomed to visit the prisoners and to administer spiritual consolation to them. These three men mercifully set themselves to soothe the mental agony from which the poor creature was suffering. When they had par-

tially quieted her, they soon found her willing
and anxious to answer their questions. They
inquired carefully into the main particulars of
her sad story; and all three came to the same
conclusion, that she was innocent. Seeing the
impression she had produced on them, she
caught, in her despair, at the idea that they
might be able to preserve her life; and the
dreadful duty devolved on them of depriving
her of this last hope. After the confirmation
of the sentence, all that they could do was to
prove their compassion by preparing her for
eternity.

On the 26th of May, the priests spoke their last
words of comfort to her soul. She was taken
back again, to await the execution of her sentence in the prison of Caen. The day was at
last fixed for her death by burning, and the
morning came when the torture-chamber was
opened to receive her.

CHAPTER V.   HUSHED UP.

The saddest part of Marie's sad story now remains to be told.

One resource was left her, by employing which
it was possible, at the last moment, to avert for a
few months the frightful prospect of the torture
and the stake. The unfortunate girl might stoop,
on her side, to use the weapons of deception
against her enemies, and might defame her own
character by pleading pregnancy. That one miserable alternative was all that now remained;
and, in the extremity of mortal terror, with the

shadow of the executioner on her prison, and
with the agony of approaching torment and death
at her heart, the forlorn creature accepted it.   If
the law of strict morality must judge her in this
matter without consideration, and condemn her
without appeal, the spirit of Christian mercy—
remembering how sorely she was tried, remembering the frailty of our common humanity, remembering the warning word which forbade us
to judge one another—may open its sanctuary of
tenderness to a sister in affliction, and may offer
her the tribute of its pity, without limit and
without blame.

The plea of pregnancy was admitted, and, at
the eleventh hour, the period of the execution
was deferred.   On the day when her ashes were
to have been cast to the winds, she was still in
her prison, a living, breathing woman.   Her
limbs were spared from the torture, her body
was released from the stake, until the twenty-
ninth of July, seventeen hundred and eighty-
two.   On that day her reprieve was to end, and
the execution of her sentence was absolutely to
take place.

During the short period of grace which was
now to elapse, the situation of the friendless girl,
accused of such incredible crimes and condemned
to so awful a doom, was discussed far and wide
in French society.   The case became notorious
beyond the limits of Caen.   The report of it
spread by way of Rouen, from mouth to mouth,
till it reached Paris; and from Paris it penetrated
into the palace of the King at Versailles.   That

unhappy man, whose dreadful destiny it was to
pay the penalty which the long and noble endurance of the French people had too mercifully abstained from inflicting on his guilty predecessors,
had then lately mounted the fatal steps of the
throne. Louis the Sixteenth was sovereign of
France when the story of the poor servant-girl
obtained its first court circulation at Versailles.

The conduct of the King, when the main facts
of Marie's case came to his ears, did all honor to
his sense of duty and his sense of justice. He
instantly dispatched his royal order to suspend
the execution of the sentence. The report of
Marie's fearful situation had reached him so
short a time before the period appointed for her
death, that the royal mandate was only delivered
to the Parliament of Rouen on the twenty-sixth
of July.

The girl's life now hung literally on a thread.
An accident happening to the courier, any delay
in fulfilling the wearisome official formalities
proper to the occasion—and the execution might
have taken its course. The authorities at Rouen,
feeling that the King's interference implied a re-
buke of their inconsiderate confirmation of the
Caen sentence, did their best to set themselves
right for the future by registering the royal order
on the day when they received it. The next
morning, the twenty-seventh, it was sent to
Caen; and it reached the authorities there on
the twenty-eighth.

That twenty-eighth of July, seventeen hundred
and eighty-two, fell on a Sunday. Throughout

the day and night the order lay in the office un-
opened. Sunday was a holiday, and Procurator
Revel was not disposed to occupy it by so much
as five minutes' performance of week-day work.

On Monday, the twenty-ninth, the crowd assembled to see the execution. The stake was set
up, the soldiers were called out, the executioner
was ready. All the preliminary horror of the
torturing and burning was suffered to darken
round the miserable prisoner, before the wretches
in authority saw fit to open the message of mercy
and to deliver it at the prison-gate.

She was now saved, as if by a miracle, for the
second time! But the cell door was still closed
on her. The only chance of ever opening it—the
only hope of publicly asserting her innocence, lay
in appealing to the King's justice by means of a
written statement of her case, presenting it exactly as it stood in all its details, from the beginning at Madame Duparc's to the end in the prison
of Caen. The production of such a document as
this was beset with obstacles; the chief of them
being the difficulty of gaining access to the voluminous reports of the evidence given at the trial,
which were only accessible in those days to persons professionally connected with the courts of
law. If Marie's case was to be placed before the
King, no man in France but a lawyer could undertake the duty with the slightest chance of
serving the interests of the prisoner and the interests of truth.

In this disgraceful emergency a man was found
to plead the girl's cause, whose profession se-

cured to him the privilege of examining the evidence against her.   This man—a barrister, named Lecauchois—not only undertook to prepare a statement of the case from the records of the court— but further devoted himself to collecting money for Marie, from all the charitably disposed inhabitants of the town.   It is to be said to his credit that he honestly faced the difficulties of his task, and industriously completed the document which he had engaged to furnish.   On the other hand, it must be recorded to his shame, that his motives were interested throughout, and that with almost incredible meanness he paid himself for the employment of his time by putting the greater part of the sum which he had collected for his client in his own pocket.   With her one friend, no less than with all her enemies, it seems to have been Marie's hard fate to see the worst side of human nature, on every occasion when she was brought into contact with her fellow-creatures.

The statement pleading for the revision of Marie's trial was sent to Paris.   An eminent barrister at the Court of Requests framed a petition from it, the prayer of which was granted by the King.   Acting under the royal order, the judges of the Court of Requests furnished themselves with the reports of the evidence as drawn up at Caen; and after examining the whole case, unanimously decided that there was good and sufficient reason for the revision of the trial. The order to that effect was not issued to the Parliament of Rouen before the twenty-fourth of May, seventeen hundred and eighty-four—nearly

two years after the King's mercy had saved
Marie from the executioner. Who can say how
slowly that long, long time must have passed to
the poor girl who was still languishing in her
prison?

The Rouen Parliament, feeling that it was held
accountable for its proceedings to a high court of
judicature, acting under the direct authority of
the King himself, recognized at last, readily
enough, that the interests of its own reputation
and the interests of rigid justice were now inti-
mately bound up together; and applied itself
impartially, on this occasion at least, to the consideration of Marie's case.

As a necessary consequence of this change of
course, the authorities of Caen began, for the
first time, to feel seriously alarmed for themselves. If the Parliament of Rouen dealt fairly
by the prisoner, a fatal exposure of the whole
party would be the certain result. Under these
circumstances, Procurator Revel and his friends
sent a private requisition to the authorities at
Rouen, conjuring them to remember that the respectability of their professional brethren was at
stake, and suggesting that the legal establishment of Marie's innocence was the error of all
others which it was now most urgently necessary
to avoid. The Parliament of Rouen was, however, far too cautious, if not too honest, to commit itself to such an atrocious proceeding as was
here plainly indicated. After gaining as much
time as possible by prolonging their deliberations
to the utmost, the authorities resolved on adopt-

ing a middle course, which, on the one hand, should not actually establish the prisoner's innocence, and, on the other, should not publicly expose the disgraceful conduct of the prosecution at Caen. Their decree, not issued until the twelfth of March, seventeen hundred and eighty-five, annulled the sentence of Procurator Revel on technical grounds; suppressed the further publication of the statement of Marie's case, which had been drawn out by the advocate Lecauchois, as libelous toward Monsieur Revel and Madame Duparc; and announced that the prisoner was ordered to remain in confinement until more ample information could be collected relating to the doubtful question of her innocence or her guilt. No such information was at all likely to present itself (more especially after the only existing narrative of the case had been suppressed); and the practical effect of the decree, therefore, was to keep Marie in prison for an indefinite period, after she had been illegally deprived of her liberty already from August, seventeen hundred and eighty-one, to March, seventeen hundred and eighty-five. Who shall say that the respectable classes did not take good care of their respectability on the eve of the French Revolution!

Marie's only hope of recovering her freedom, and exposing her unscrupulous enemies to the obliquy and the punishment which they richly deserved, lay in calling the attention of the higher tribunals of the capital to the cruelly cunning decree of the Parliament of Rouen. According-

ly, she once more petitioned the throne. The
King referred the document to his council; and
the council issued an order submitting the Rouen
decree to the final investigation of the Parliament
of Paris.

At last, then, after more than three miserable
years of imprisonment, the victim of Madame
Duparc and Procurator Revel had burst her way
through all intervening obstacles of law and in-
tricacies of office, to the judgment-seat of that
highest law court in the country, which had the
final power of ending her long sufferings and of
doing her signal justice on her adversaries of all
degrees.   The Parliament of Paris was now to
estimate the unutterable wrong that had been inflicted on her; and the eloquent tongue of one of
the first advocates of that famous bar was to plead
her cause openly before God, the King, and the
country.

The pleading of Monsieur Fournel (Marie's
counsel) before the Parliament of Paris, remains
on record.   At the outset, he assumes the highest ground for the prisoner. He disclaims all
intention of gaining her liberty by taking the
obvious technical objections to the illegal and
irregular sentences of Caen and Rouen.   He
insists on the necessity of vindicating her innocence legally and morally before the world, and
of obtaining the fullest compensation that the
law allows for the merciless injuries which the
original prosecution had inflicted on his client.
In pursuance of this design, he then proceeds to
examine the evidence of the alleged poisoning

and the alleged robbery, step by step, pointing
out in the fullest detail the monstrous contradic-
tions and improbabilities which have been already
briefly indicated in this narrative. The course
thus pursued, with signal clearness and ability,
leads, as every one who has followed the particulars of the case from the beginning will readily
understand, to a very serious result. The arguments for the defense cannot assert Marie's innocence without shifting the whole weight of suspicion, in the matter of Monsieur De Beaulieu's
death by poisoning, on to the shoulders of her
mistress, Madame Duparc.

It is necessary, in order to prepare the reader
for the extraordinary termination of the proceedings, to examine this question of suspicion in
some of its most striking details.

The poisoning of Monsieur De Beaulieu may
be accepted, in consideration of the medical evidence, as a proved fact, to begin with. The
question that remains is, whether that poisoning
was accidental or premeditated. In either case,
the evidence points directly at Madame Duparc,
and leads to the conclusion that she tried to shift
the blame of the poisoning (if accidental), and
the guilt of it (if premeditated), from herself to
her servant.

Suppose the poisoning to have been accidental.
Suppose arsenic to have been purchased for some
legitimate domestic purpose, and to have been
carelessly left, in one of the salt-cellars, on the
dresser—who salts the hasty-pudding? Madame
Duparc. Who—assuming that the dinner next

day really contained some small portion of poison, just enough to swear by—prepared that dinner? Madame Duparc and her daughter, while the servant was asleep. Having caused the death of her father, and having produced symptoms of illness in herself and her guests, by a dreadful accident, how does the circumstantial evidence further show that Madame Duparc tried to fix the responsibility of that accident on her servant before she openly charged the girl with poisoning.

In the first place, Madame Duparc is the only one of the dinner-party who attributes the general uneasiness to poison. She not only does this, but she indicates the kind of poison used, and declares in the kitchen that it is burned—so as to lead to the inference that the servant, who has removed the dishes, has thrown some of the poisoned food on the fire. Here is a foregone conclusion on the subject of arsenic in Madame Duparc's mind, and an inference in connection with it, directed at the servant by Madame Duparc's lips. In the second place, if any trust at all is to be put in the evidence touching the finding of arsenic on or about Marie's person, that trust must be reposed in the testimony of Surgeon Hebert, who first searched the girl. Where does he find the arsenic and the bread-crumbs? In Marie's pockets. Who takes the most inexplicably officious notice of such a trifle as Marie's dress, at the most shockingly inappropriate time, when the father of Madame Duparc lies dead in the house? Madame Duparc herself. Who tells Marie to take off her Sunday pockets, and sends her into her own room (which she herself has not entered during the night, and which has been open to the intrusion of any one else in the house) to tie on the very pockets in which the arsenic is found? Madame Duparc. Who put the arsenic into the pockets? Is it jumping to a conclusion to answer once more—Madame Duparc?

Thus far we have assumed that the mistress attempted to shift the blame of a fatal accident on to the shoulders of the servant. Do the facts bear out that theory, or do they lead to the suspicion that the woman was a parricide, and that she tried to fix on the friendless country girl the guilt of her dreadful crime?

If the poisoning of the hasty-pudding (to begin with) was accidental, the salting of it, through which the poisoning was, to all appearance, effected, must have been a part of the habitual cookery of the dish. So far, however, from this being the case, Madame Duparc had expressly warned her servant not to use salt; and only used the salt (or the arsenic) herself, after asking a question which implied a direct contradiction of her own directions, and the inconsistency of which she made no attempt whatever to explain. Again, when her father was taken ill, if Madame Duparc had been only the victim of an accident, would she have remained content with no better help than that of an apothecary's boy? would she not have sent, as her father grew worse, for the best medical assistance which the town afforded? The facts show that she summoned just help enough barely to save appearances, and no more.

The facts show that she betrayed a singular anxiety to have the body laid out as soon as possible after life was extinct. The facts show that she maintained an unnatural composure on the day of the death. These are significant circumstances. They speak for themselves independently of the evidence given afterward, in which she and her child contradicted each other as to the time that elapsed when the old man had eaten his fatal meal before he was taken ill. Add to these serious facts the mysterious disappearance from the house of the eldest son, which was never accounted for; and the rumor of purchased poison, which was never investigated. Consider, besides, whether the attempt to sacrifice the servant's life be not more consistent with the ruthless determination of a criminal, than with the terror of an innocent woman who shrinks from accepting the responsibility of a frightful accident—and determine, at the same time, whether the infinitesimal amount of injury done by the poisoned dinner can be most probably attributed to lucky accident, or to premeditated doctoring of the dishes with just arsenic enough to preserve appearances, and to implicate the servant without too seriously injuring the company on whom she waited. Give all these serious considerations their due weight; then look back to the day of Monsieur De Beaulieu's death, and say if Madame Duparc was the victim of a dreadful accident, or the perpetrator of an atrocious crime!

That she was·one or the other, and that, in either case, she was the originator of the vile

conspiracy against her servant which these pages
disclose, was the conclusion to which Monsieur
Fournel's pleading on his client's behalf inevi-
tably led. That pleading satisfactorily demon-
strated Marie's innocence of poisoning and theft,
and her fair claim to the fullest legal compensation for the wrong inflicted on her. On the
twenty - third of May, seventeen hundred and
eighty-six, the Parliament of Paris issued its decree, discharging her from the remotest suspicion
of guilt, releasing her from her long imprisonment, and authorizing her to bring an action for
damages against the person or persons who had
falsely accused her of murder and theft. The
truth had triumphed, and the poor servant-girl
had found laws to protect her at last.

Under these altered circumstances, what happened to Madame Duparc? What happened to
Procurator Revel and his fellow-conspirators?
What happened to the authorities of the Parliament of Rouen?

Nothing.

The premonitory rumblings of that great earth-
quake of nations which history calls the French
Revolution were, at this time, already beginning
to make themselves heard; and any public scandal which affected the wealthier and higher classes
involved a serious social risk, the importance of
which no man in France could then venture to
estimate. If Marie claimed the privilege which
a sense of justice, or rather a sense of decency,
had forced the Parliament of Paris to concede to
her—and, through her counsel, she did claim it

—the consequences of the legal inquiry into her case which her demand for damages necessarily involved would probably be the trying of Madame Duparc, either for parricide or for homicide by misadventure; the dismissal of Procurator Revel from the functions which he had disgracefully abused; and the suspension from office of the authorities at Caen and Rouen, who had in various ways forfeited public confidence by aiding and abetting him.

Here, then, was no less a prospect in view than the disgrace of a respectable family, and the dishonoring of the highest legal functionaries of two important provincial towns! And for what end was the dangerous exposure to be made? Merely to do justice to the daughter of a common day-laborer, who had been illegally sentenced to torture and burning, and illegally confined in prison for nearly five years. To make a wholesale sacrifice of her superiors, no matter how wicked they might be, for the sake of giving a mere servant-girl compensation for the undeserved obloquy and misery of many years, was too preposterous and too suicidal an act of justice to be thought of for a moment. Accordingly, when Marie was prepared to bring her action for damages, the lawyers laid their heads together in the interests of society. It was found possible to put her out of court at once and forever, by taking a technical objection to the proceedings in which she was plaintiff at the very outset. This disgraceful means of escape once discovered, the girl's guilty persecutors instantly took advantage of it. She was formally put out of court, without the possibility of any further appeal. Procurator Revel and the other authorities retained their distinguished legal positions; and the question of the guilt or innocence of Madame Duparc, in the matter of her father's death, remains a mystery which no man can solve to this day.

After recording this scandalous termination of the legal proceedings, it is gratifying to be able to conclude the story of Marie's unmerited sufferings with a picture of her after-life which leaves an agreeable impression on the mind.

If popular sympathy, after the servant-girl's release from prison, could console her for the hard measure of injustice under which she had suffered so long and so unavailingly, that sympathy was now offered to her heartily and without limit. She became quite a public character in Paris. The people followed her in crowds wherever she went. A subscription was set on foot, which, for the time at least, secured her a comfortable independence. Friends rose up in all directions to show her such attention as might be in their power; and the simple country girl, when she was taken to see the sights of Paris, actually beheld her own name placarded in the showmen's bills, and her presence advertised as the greatest attraction that could be offered to the public. When, in due course of time, all this excitement had evaporated, Marie married prosperously, and the Government granted her its license to open a shop for the sale of stamped papers. The last we hear of her is, that she was a happy wife and mother, and that she performed every duty of life in such a manner as to justify the deep interest which had been universally felt for her by the people of France.

Her story is related here, not only because it seemed to contain some elements of interest in itself, but also because the facts of which it is composed may claim to be of some little historical importance, as helping to expose the unendurable corruptions of society in France before the Revolution. It may not be amiss for those persons whose historical point of view obstinately contracts its range to the Reign of Terror, to look a little further back—to remember that the hard case of oppression here related had been, for something like one hundred years, the case (with minor changes of circumstance) of the forlorn many against the powerful few all over France—and then to consider whether there was not a reason and a necessity, a dreadful last necessity, for the French Revolution. That Revolution has expiated, and is still expiating, its excesses, by political failures, which all the world can see. But the social good which it indisputably effected remains to this day. Take, as an example, the administration of justice in France at the present time. Whatever its shortcomings may still be, no innocent Frenchwoman could be treated now as an innocent Frenchwoman was once treated at a period so little remote from our own time as the end of the last century.

SKETCHES OF CHARACTER.—VI.

MY SPINSTERS.

[Introduced by an Innocent Old Man.]

My young bachelor friends, suspend your ordinary avocations for a few minutes and listen to me. I am a benevolent old gentleman, residing in a small country town, possessing a comfortable property, a devoted housekeeper, and some charming domestic animals. I have no wife, no children, no poor relations, no cares, and nothing to do. I am a nice, harmless, idle old man; and I want to have a word with you in confidence, my worthy young bachelor friends.

I have a mania. Is it saving money? No. Good living? No. Music? Smoking? Angling? Pottery? Pictures? No, no, no—nothing of the selfish sort. My mania is as amiable as myself: it contemplates nothing less than the future happiness of all the single ladies of my acquaintance. I call them My Spinsters; and the one industrious object of my idle existence is to help them to a matrimonial settlement in life. In my own youth I missed the chance of getting a wife, as I have always firmly believed, for want of meeting with a tender - hearted old gentleman like myself to help me to the necessary spinster.

It is possibly this reflection which originally led to the formation of the benevolent mania that now possesses me. Perhaps sheer idleness, a gallant turn of mind, and living in a small country town, have had something to do with it also. You see I shirk nothing. I do not attempt any deception as to the motive which induces me to call you together. I appear before you in the character of an amateur matrimonial agent having a few choice spinsters to dispose of; and I can wait patiently, my brisk young bachelor friends, until I find that you are ready to make me a bid.

Shall we proceed at once to business? Shall we try some soft and sentimental spinsters to begin with? I am anxious to avoid mistakes at the outset, and I think softness and sentiment are perhaps the safest attractions to start upon. Let us begin with the six unmarried sisters of my friend Mr. Bettifer.

I became acquainted, gentlemen, with Mr. Bettifer in our local reading-rooms, immediately after he came to settle in my neighborhood. He was then a very young man, in delicate health, with a tendency to melancholy and a turn for metaphysics. I profited by his invitation as soon as he was kind enough to ask me to call on him; and I found that he lived with his six sisters, under the following agreeable circumstances.

On the morning of my visit I was shown into a very long room, with a piano at one end of it and an easel at another. Mr. Bettifer was alone at his writing-desk when I came in. I apologized

for interrupting him, but he very politely assured
me that my presence acted as an inestimable relief to his mind, which had been stretched—to
use his own strong language—on the metaphysical rack all the morning. He gave his forehead
a violent rub as he mentioned this circumstance,
and we sat down and looked seriously at one another in silence. Though not at all a bashful old
man, I began, nevertheless, to feel a little confused at this period of the interview.

"I know no question so embarrassing," began
Mr. Bettifer, by way of starting the talk pleasantly, "as the question on which I have been engaged this morning—I refer to the subject of our
own Personality. Here am I, and there are you
—let us say two Personalities. Are we a permanent, or are we a transient thing? There is the
problem, my dear sir, which I have been vainly
trying to solve since breakfast-time. Can you
(metaphysically speaking) be one and the same
person, for example, for two moments together,
any more than two successive moments can be
one and the same moment?—My sister Kitty."

The door opened as my host propounded this
alarming dilemma, and a tall young lady glided
serenely into the room. I rose and bowed. The
tall young lady sank softly into a chair opposite
me. Mr. Bettifer went on:

"You may tell me that our substance is constantly changing. I grant you that; but do you
get me out of the difficulty? Not the least in the
world. For it is not substance, but—My sister
Maria."

The door opened again. A second tall young lady glided in, and sank into a chair by her sister's side. Mr. Bettifer went on:

"As I was about to remark, it is not substance, but consciousness, which constitutes Personality. Now, what is the nature of consciousness?—My sisters Emily and Jane."

The door opened for the third time, and two tall young ladies glided in, and sank into two chairs by the sides of their two sisters. Mr. Bettifer went on:

"The nature of consciousness I take to be that it cannot be the same in any two moments, nor, consequently, the personality constituted by it. Do you grant me that?"

Lost in metaphysical bewilderment, I granted it directly. Just as I said yes, the door opened again; a fifth tall young lady glided in, and assisted in lengthening the charming row formed by her sisters. Mr. Bettifer murmured indicatively, "My sister Elizabeth," and made a note of what I had granted him on the manuscript by his side.

"What lovely weather," I remarked, to change the conversation.

"Beautiful!" answered five melodious voices.

The door opened again.

"Beautiful, indeed!" said a sixth melodious voice.

"My sister Harriet," said Mr. Bettifer, finishing his note of my metaphysical admission.

They all sat in one fascinating row. It was like being at a party. I felt uncomfortable in my colored trousers—more uncomfortable still, when Mr. Bettifer's sixth sister begged that she might not interrupt our previous conversation.

"We are so fond of metaphysical subjects," said Miss Elizabeth.

"Except that we think them rather exhausting for dear Alfred," said Miss Jane.

"Dear Alfred!" repeated the Misses Emily, Maria and Kitty, in mellifluous chorus.

Not having a heart of stone, I was so profoundly touched that I would have tried to resume the subject. But Mr. Bettifer waved his hand impatiently, and declared that my admission had increased the difficulties of the original question until they had become quite insuperable. I had, it apppared, innocently driven him to the conclusion that our present self was not our yesterday's self, but another self mistaken for it, which, in its turn, had no connection with the self of to-morrow. As this certainly sounded rather unsatisfactory, I agreed with Mr. Bettifer that we had exhausted that particular view of the subject, and that we had better defer starting another until a future opportunity. An embarrassing pause followed our renunciation of metaphysics for the day. Miss Elizabeth broke the silence by asking me if I was fond of pictures; and before I could say Yes, Miss Harriet followed her by asking me if I was fond of music.

"Will you show your picture, dear?" said Miss Elizabeth to Miss Harriet.

"Will you sing, dear?" said Miss Harriet to Miss Elizabeth.

"Do, dear!" said the Misses Jane and Emily to Miss Elizabeth.

"Do, dear!" said the Misses Maria and Kitty to Miss Harriet.

There was an artless symmetry and balance of affection in all that these six sensitive creatures said and did. The fair Elizabeth was followed to the end of the room where the piano was, by Jane and Emily. The lovely Harriet was attended in the direction of the easel by Maria and Kitty. I went to see the picture first.

The scene was the bottom of the sea; and the subject, "A Forsaken Mermaid." The unsentimental, or fishy lower half of the sea-nymph was dexterously hidden in a coral grove before which she was sitting, in an atmosphere of limpid blue water. She had beautiful long green hair, and was shedding those solid tears which we always see in pictures and never in real life. Groups of pet fishes circled around her with their eyes fixed mournfully on their forlorn mistress. A line at the top of the picture, and a strip of blue above it, represented the surface of the ocean and the sky; the monotony of this part of the composition being artfully broken by a receding golden galley with a purple sail, containing the fickle fisher-youth who had forsaken the mermaid. I had hardly had time to say what a beautiful picture it was, before Miss Maria put her handkerchief to her eyes, and, overcome by the pathetic nature of the scene portrayed, hurriedly left the room. Miss Kitty followed, to attend on and console her; and Miss Harriet, after covering up her picture with a sigh, followed to assist Miss Kitty. I began to doubt whether I ought not to have gone out next, to support all three; but Mr. Bettifer, who had hitherto remained in the background, lost in metaphysical speculation, came forward to remind me that the music was waiting to claim my admiration next.

"Excuse their excessive sensibility," he said. "I have done my best to harden them and make them worldly; but it is not of the slightest use. Will you come to the piano?"

Miss Elizabeth began to sing immediately, with the attendant sylphs, Jane and Emily, on either side of her, to turn over the music.

The song was a ballad composition—music and words by the lovely singer herself. A lady was dreaming in an ancient castle; a dog was howling in a ruined courtyard; an owl was hooting in a neighboring forest; a tyrant was striding in an echoing hall; and a page was singing among moonlit flowers. First five verses. Pause—and mournful symphony on the piano, in the minor key. Ballad resumed: The lady wakes with a scream. The tyrant loads his arquebus. The faithful page, hearing the scream among the moonlit flowers, advances to the castle. The dog gives a warning bark. The tyrant fires a chance shot in the darkness. The page welters in his blood. The lady dies of a broken heart. Miss Jane is so affected by the catastrophe that Miss Emily is obliged to lead her from the room; and Miss Elizabeth is so anxious about them both as to be forced to shut up the piano, and hasten after them, with a smelling bottle in her hand. Conclusion of the performance, and final exit of the six Miss Bettifers.

Tell yourselves off, my fortunate young bachelor friends, to the corresponding number of half a dozen, with your offers ready on your tongues, and your hearts thrown open to tender investigation, while favorable circumstances yet give you a chance. My boys, my eager boys, do you want pale cheeks, limpid eyes, swan-like necks, low waists, tall forms, and no money? You do—I know you do. Go, then, enviable youths—go tenderly—go immediately—go by sixes at a time, and try your luck with the Misses Bettifer!

Let me now appeal to other, and possibly to fewer tastes, by trying a sample of a new kind. It shall be something neither soft, yielding, nor hysterical this time. You who agree with the poet that

"Discourse may want an animated No,
To brush the surface and to make it flow—"

you who like girls to have opinions of their own, and to play their parts spiritedly in the give and take of conversation, do me the favor to approach, and permit me to introduce you to the three Misses Cruttwell. At the same time, gentlemen, I must inform you, with my usual candor, that these spinsters are short, sharp, and on occasion, shrill. You must have a talent for arguing, and a knack at instantaneous definition, or you will find the Misses Cruttwell too much for you, and had better wait for my next sample.

And yet for a certain peculiar class of customer these are really very choice spinsters. For instance, any unmarried legal gentleman, who would like to have his wits kept sharp for his profession by constant disputation, could not do better than address himself (as logically as possible) to one of the Misses Cruttwell. Perhaps my legal bachelor will be so obliging as to accompany me on a morning call?

It is a fine spring day, with a light air and plenty of round white clouds flying over the blue sky, when we pay our visit. We find the three young ladies in the morning-room. Miss Martha Cruttwell is fond of statistical subjects, and is annotating a pamphlet. Miss Barbara Cruttwell likes geology, and is filling a cabinet with ticketed bits of stone. Miss Charlotte Cruttwell has a manly taste for dogs, and is nursing two fat puppies on her lap. All three have florid complexions; all three have a habit of winking both eyes incessantly, and a way of wearing their hair very tight, and very far off their faces. All three acknowledge my young legal friend's bow in—what may seem to him—a very short, sharp manner; and modestly refrain from helping him by saying a word to begin the conversation. He is, perhaps, unreasonably disconcerted by this, and therefore starts the talk weakly by saying that it is a fine day.

"Fine!" exclaims Miss Martha, with a look of amazement at her sister. "Fine!" with a stare of perplexity at my young legal friend. "Dear me! what do you mean, now, by a fine day?"

"We were just saying how cold it was," says Miss Barbara.

"And how very like rain," says Miss Charlotte, with a look at the white clouds outside, which happen to be obscuring the sun for a few minutes.

"But what do you mean, now, by a fine day?" persists Miss Martha.

My young legal friend is put on his mettle by this time, and answers with professional readiness:

"At this uncertain spring season, my definition of a fine day is a day on which you do not feel the want of your great-coat, your galoches, or your umbrella."

"Oh, no," says Miss Martha, "surely not! At least, that does not appear to me to be at all a definition of a fine day. Barbara? Charlotte?"

"We think it quite impossible to call a day— when the sun is not shining—a fine day," says Miss Barbara.

"We think that when clouds are in the sky there is always a chance of rain; and, when there is a chance of rain, we think it is very extraordinary to say that it is a fine day," adds Miss Charlotte.

My legal bachelor starts another topic, and finds his faculty for impromptu definition exercised by the three Misses Cruttwell, always in the same briskly disputatious manner. He goes away—as I hope and trust—thinking what an excellent lawyer's wife any one of the three young ladies would make. If he could only be

present in the spirit, after leaving the abode of
the Misses Cruttwell in the body, his admiration
of my three disputatious spinsters would, I think,
be greatly increased.   He would find that, though
they could all agree to a miracle in differing with
him while he was present, they would begin to
vary in opinion the moment their visitor's subjects of conversation were referred to in his absence. He would, probably, for example, hear
them take up the topic of the weather again, the
instant the house door had closed after him, in
these terms:

"Do you know," he might hear Miss Martha
say, "I am not so sure after all, Charlotte, that
you were right in saying that it could not be a
fine day, because there were clouds in the sky?"

"You only say that," Miss Charlotte would be
sure to reply, "because the sun happens to be
peeping out, just now, for a minute or two.   If
it rains in half an hour, which is more than likely, who would be right then?"

"On reflection," Miss Barbara might remark
next, "I don't agree with either of you, and I
also dispute the opinion of the gentleman who
has just left us.   It is neither a fine day nor a
bad day."

"But it must be one or the other."

"No, it needn't.   It may be an indifferent
day."

"What do you mean by an indifferent day?"

So they go on, these clever girls of mine, these
mistresses in the art of fencing applied to the
tongue. I have not presented this sample from

my collection, as one which is likely to suit any
great number. But there are peculiarly constituted bachelors in this world; and 1 like to be
able to show that my assortment of spinsters is
various enough to warrant me in addressing even
the most alarming eccentricities of taste. Will
nobody offer for this disputatious sample—not
even for the dog-fancying Miss Charlotte, with
the two fat puppies thrown in? No? Take
away the Misses Cruttwell, and let us try what
we can do, thirdly and lastly, with the Misses
Ducksey produced in their place.

I confidently anticipate a brisk competition and
a ready market for the spinsters now about to be
submitted to inspection. You have already had
a sentimental sample, gentlemen, and a disputatious sample. In now offering a domestic sample, I have but one regret, which is, that my
spinsters on the present occasion are unhappily
limited to two in number. I wish I had a dozen
to produce of the same interesting texture and
the same unimpeachable quality.

The whole world, gentlemen, at the present
writing, means, in the estimation of the two Misses
Ducksey, papa, mamma, and brother George.
This loving sample can be warranted never yet
to have looked beyond the sacred precincts of the
family circle. All their innocent powers of admiration and appreciation have been hitherto
limited within the boundaries of home. If Miss
Violet Ducksey wants to see a lovely girl, she
looks at Miss Rose Ducksey, and *vice versa;* if
both want to behold manly dignity, matronly

sweetness, and youthful beauty, both look immediately at papa, mamma, and brother George. I have been admitted into the unparalleled family circle of which I now speak. I have seen—to say nothing, for the present, of papa and mamma —I have seen brother George come in from business, and sit down by the fireside, and be welcomed by Miss Violet and Miss Rose, as if he had just returned, after having been reported dead, from the other end of the world. I have seen those two devoted sisters race across the room, in fond contention which should sit first on brother George's knee. I have even seen both sit upon him together, each taking a knee, when he has been half an hour later than usual at the office. I have never beheld their lovely arms tired of clasping brother George's neck, never heard their rosy lips cease kissing brother George's cheeks, except when they were otherwise occupied for the moment in calling him "Dear!" On the word of honor of a harmless spinster - fancying old man, I declare that I have seen brother George fondled to such an extent by his sisters that, although a lusty and long-suffering youth, he has fallen asleep under it from sheer exhaustion. Even then, I have observed Miss Rose and Miss Violet contending (in each other's arms) which should have the privilege of casting her handkerchief over his face. And that touching contest concluded, I have quitted the house at a late hour, leaving Violet on papa's bosom, and Rose entwined round mamma's waist. Beautiful! beautiful!

Am I exaggerating? Go and judge for yourselves, my bachelor friends. Go, if you like, and meet my domestic sample at a ball.

My bachelor is introduced to Miss Violet, and takes his place with her in a quadrille. He begins a lively conversation, and finds her attention wandering. She has not heard a word that he has been saying, and she interrupts him in the middle of a sentence with a question which has not the slightest relation to anything that he has hitherto offered by way of a remark.

"Have you ever met my sister Rose before?"

"No, I have not had the honor—"

"She is standing there, at the other end, in a blue dress. Now, do tell me, does she not look charming?"

My bachelor makes the necessary answer, and goes on to another subject. Miss Violet's attention wanders again, and she asks another abrupt question:

"What did you think of mamma when you were introduced to her?"

My bachelor friend makes another necessary answer. Miss Violet, without appearing to be at all impressed by it, looks into the distance in search of her maternal parent, and then addresses her partner again:

"It is not a pleasant thing for young people to confess," she says, with the most artless candor, "but I really do think that mamma is the handsomest woman in the room. There she is, taking an ice, next to the old lady with the diamonds. Is she not beautiful? Do you know, when we were dressing to-night, Rose and I begged and prayed her not to wear a cap. We said, 'Don't, mamma; please don't. Put it off for another year.' And mamma said, in her sweet way, 'Nonsense, my loves! I am an old woman. You must accustom yourselves to that idea, and you must let me wear a cap; you must, darlings, indeed.' And we said—what do you think we said?"

(Another necessary answer.)

"We said, 'You are studying papa's feelings, dear—you are afraid of being taken for our youngest sister if you go in your hair—and it is on papa's account that you wear a cap. Sly mamma!'— Have you been introduced to papa?"

Later in the evening my bachelor friend is presented to Miss Rose. He asks for the honor of dancing with her. She inquires if it is for the waltz, and hearing that it is, draws back and courtesies apologetically.

"Thank you, I must keep the waltz for my brother George. My sister and I always keep waltzes for our brother George."

My bachelor draws back. The dance proceeds. He hears a soft voice behind him. It is Miss Violet who is speaking.

"You are a judge of waltzing?" she says, in tones of the gentlest insinuation. "Do pray look at George and Rose. No, thank you; I never dance when George and Rose are waltzing. It is a much greater treat to me to look on. I always look on. I do, indeed."

Perhaps my bachelor does not frequent balls.

It is of no consequence. Let him be a diner-out; let him meet my domestic sample at the social board; and he will only witness fresh instances of that all-absorbing interest in each other which is the remarkable peculiarity of the whole Ducksey family, and of the young ladies in particular. He will find them admiring one another with the same touching and demonstrative affection over the dishes on the dinner-table as amid the mazes of the dance. He will hear from the venerable Mr. Ducksey that George never gave him a moment's uneasiness from the hour of his birth. He will hear from Mrs. Ducksey that her one regret in this life is, that she can never be thankful enough for her daughters. And (to return to the young ladies, who are the main objects of these remarks) he will find, by some such fragments of dialogue as the following, that no general subjects of conversation whatever have the power of alluring the minds of the two Miss Duckseys from the contemplation of their own domestic interests, and the faithful remembrance of their own particular friends.

It is the interval, let us say, between the removal of the fish and the appearance of the meat. The most brilliant man in the company has been talking with great sprightliness and effect; has paused for a moment to collect his ideas before telling one of the good stories for which he is famous; and is just ready to begin—when Miss Rose stops him and silences all her neighbors by anxiously addressing her sister, who sits opposite to her at the table.

"Violet, dear?"

"Yes, dear."

(Profound silence follows. The next course fails to make its appearance. Nobody wanting to take any wine. The brilliant guest sits back in his chair, dogged and speechless. The host and hostess look at each other nervously. Miss Rose goes on with the happy artlessness of a child, as if nobody but her sister was present.)

"Do you know I have made up my mind what I shall give mamma's Susan when she is married?"

"Not a silk dress? That's my present."

"What do you think, dear, of a locket with our hair in it?"

"Sweet."

(The silence of the tomb falls on the dinner-table. The host and hostess begin to get angry. The guests look at each other. The second course persists in not coming in. The brilliant guest suffers from a dry cough. Miss Violet, in her turn, addresses Miss Rose across the table.)

"Rose, I met Ellen Davis to-day."

"Has she heard from Clara?"

"Yes; Clara's uncle and aunt won't let her come."

"Tiresome people! Did you go on to Brompton? Did you see Jane? Is Jane to be depended on?"

"If Jane's cold gets better, she and that odious cousin of hers are sure to come. Uncle Frank, of course, makes his usual excuse."

So the simple - hearted sisters prattle on in

public; so do they carry their own innocent affections and interests about with them into the society they adorn; so do they cast the extinguishing sunshine of their young hearts over the temporary flashes of worldly merriment, and the short-lived blaze of dinner eloquence. Without another word of preliminary recommendation, I confidently submit the Misses Ducksey to brisk public competition. I can promise the two fortunate youths who may woo and win them plenty of difficulties in weaning their affections from the family hearth, with showers of tears and poignant bursts of anguish on the wedding-day. All properly-constituted bridegrooms feel, as I have been given to understand, inexpressibly comforted and encouraged by a display of violent grief on the part of the bride when she is starting on her wedding tour. And, besides, in the particular case of the Misses Ducksey, there would always be the special resource of taking brother George into the carriage, as a sure palliative, during the first few stages of the honeymoon trip.

DRAMATIC GRUB STREET.*

EXPLORED IN TWO LETTERS.

LETTER THE FIRST.   FROM MR. READER TO MR. AUTHOR.

MY DEAR SIR—I am sufficiently well-educated, and sufficiently refined in my tastes and habits, to be a member of the large class of persons usually honored by literary courtesy with the title

---

* This paper, and the paper on Art, entitled "To Think, or Be Thought For," which immediately follows it, provoked, at the time of their first appearance, some remonstrance both of the public and the private sort. I was blamed—so far as I could understand the objections —for letting out the truth about the Drama, and for speaking my mind (instead of keeping it to myself, as other people did) on the subject of the Old Masters. Finding, however, that my positions remained practically unrefuted, and that my views were largely shared by readers with no professional interest in theaters, and no vested critical rights in old pictures—and knowing, besides, that I had not written without some previous inquiry and consideration—I held steadily to my own convictions; and I hold to them still. These articles are now reprinted (as they were originally produced) to serve two objects which I persist in thinking of some importance: Freedom of inquiry into the debased condition of the English Theater; and freedom of thought on the subject of the Fine Arts.

of the Intelligent Public. In the interests of the order to which 1 belong, I have a little complaint to make against the managers of our theaters, and a question to put afterward, which you, as a literary man, will, 1 have no doubt, be both able and willing to answer.

Like many thousands of other people, I am fond of reading and fond of going to the theater. In regard to my reading, 1 have no complaint to make—for the press supplies me abundantly with English poems, histories, biographies, novels, essays, travels, criticisms, all of modern production. But, in regard to going to the theater, 1 write with something like a sense of injury— for nobody supplies me with a good play. There is living literature of a genuine sort in the English libraries of the present time. Why (I beg to inquire) is there no living literature of a genuine sort in the English theater of the present time also?

Say I am a Frenchman, fond of the imaginative literature of my country, well-read in all the best specimens of it—I mean, best in a literary point of view, for I am not touching moral questions now. When I shut up Balzac, Victor Hugo, Dumas, and Soulie, and go to the theater—what do I find? Balzac, Victor Hugo, Dumas, and Soulie again. The men who have been interesting me in my armchair, interesting me once more in my stall. The men who can really invent and observe for the reader, inventing and observing for the spectator also. What is the necessary consequence? The literary standard of the stage is raised; and the dramatist by profession must be as clever a man, in his way, as good an inventor, as correct a writer, as the novelist. And what, in my case, follows that consequence? Clearly this: the managers of theaters get my money at night as the publishers of books get it in the day.

Do the managers get my money from me in England? By no manner of means. For they hardly ever condescend to address me.

I get up from reading the best works of our best living writers, and go to the theater, here. What do I see? The play that I have seen before in Paris. This may do very well for my servant, who does not understand French, or for my tradesman, who has never had time to go to Paris—but it is only showing *me* an old figure in a foreign dress, which does not become it like its native costume. But, perhaps, our dramatic entertainment is not a play adapted from the French Drama. Perhaps it is something English —a burlesque. Delightful, I have no doubt, to a fast young farmer from the country, or to a convivial lawyer's clerk who has never read anything but a newspaper in his life. But is it satisfactory to *me?* It is, if I want to go and see the Drama satirized. But I go to enjoy a new play —and I am rewarded by seeing all my favorite ideas and characters in some old play ridiculed. This, like the adapted drama, is the sort of entertainment I do *not* want.

I read at home many original stories, by many original authors, that delight me. I go to the

theater, and naturally want original stories by
original authors which will also delight me there.
Do I get what I ask for? Yes, if I want to see
an old play over again. But if I want a new
play? Why, *then* I must have the French adaptation, or the burlesque. The publisher can understand that there are people among his customers
who possess cultivated tastes, and can cater for
them accordingly, when they ask for something
new. The manager, in the same case, recognizes
no difference between me and my servant. My
footman goes to see the play-actors, and cares
very little what they perform in. If my taste is
not his taste, we may part at the theater door—
he goes in, and I go home. It may be said,
Why is my footman's taste not to be provided
for? By way of answering that question, I will
ask another: Why is my footman not to have the
chance of improving his taste, and making it as
good as mine?

The case between the two countries seems to
stand thus, then: In France, the most eminent
imaginative writers work, as a matter of course,
for the stage, as well as for the library table. In
England, the most eminent imaginative writers
work for the library table alone. What is the
reason of this? To what do you attribute the present shameful dearth of stage literature? To the
dearth of good actors? or, if not to that, to what
other cause?

Of one thing I am certain, that there is no
want of a large and a ready audience for original
English plays possessing genuine dramatic merit,

and appealing, as forcibly as our best novels do, to the tastes, the interests, and tne sympathies of our own time. You, who have had some experience of society, know as well as I do that there is in this country a very large class of persons whose minds are stiffened by no Puritanical scruples, whose circumstances in the world are easy, whose time is at their own disposal, who are the very people to make a good audience and a paying audience at a theater, and who yet hardly ever darken theatrical doors more than two or three times in a year. You know this; and you know also that the systematic neglect of the theater in these people has been forced on them, in the first instance, by the shock inflicted on their good sense by nine-tenths of the so-called new entertainments which are offered to them. I am not speaking now of gorgeous scenic revivals of old plays—for which I have a great respect, because they offer to sensible people the only decent substitute for genuine dramatic novelty to be met with at the present time. I am referring to the "new entertainments" which are, in the vast majority of cases, second-hand entertainments to every man in the theater who is familiar with the French writers—or insufferably coarse entertainments to every man who has elevated his taste by making himself acquainted with the best modern literature of his own land. Let my servant, let my small tradesman, let the fast young farmers and lawyers' clerks, be all catered for! But surely, if they have their theater, I and my large class ought to have our theater too! The fast young farmer has his dramatists, just as he has his novelists in the penny journals. We, on our side, have got our great novelists (whose works the fast young farmer does *not* read)—why, I ask again, are we not to have our great dramatists as well?

With high esteem, yours, my dear sir,

A. READER.

LETTER THE SECOND. FROM MR. AUTHOR TO MR. READER.

MY DEAR SIR—I thoroughly understand your complaint, and I think I can answer your question. My reply will probably a little astonish you—for mean to speak the plain truth boldly. The public ought to know the real state of the case, as regards the present position of the English stage toward English Literature, for the public alone can work the needful reform.

You ask, if I attribute the present dearth of stage literature to the dearth of good actors? I reply to that in the negative. When the good literature comes, the good actors will come also, where they are wanted. In many branches of the theatrical art they are not wanted. We have as good living actors among us now as ever trod the stage. And we should have more if dramatic literature called for more. It is literature that makes the actor—not the actor who makes literature. I could name men to you, now on the stage, whose advance in their profession they owe entirely to the rare opportunities which the occasional appearance of a genuinely good play has afforded to them of stepping out—men whose sense of the picturesque and the natural in their art lay dormant, until the pen of the writer woke it into action. Show me a school of dramatists, and I will show you a school of actors soon afterward—as surely as the effect follows the cause.

You have spoken of France. I will now speak of France also; for the literary comparison with our neighbors is as applicable to the main point of my letter as it was to the main point of yours.

Suppose me to be a French novelist. If I am a successful man, my work has a certain market value at the publisher's. So far my case is the same if I am an English novelist; but there the analogy stops. In France the manager of the theater can compete with the publisher for the purchase of any new idea that I have to sell. In France the market value of my new play is as high, or higher, than the market value of my new novel. Remember, I am not now writing of French theaters which have assistance from the Government, but of French theaters which depend, as our theaters do, entirely on the public. Any one of those theaters will give me as much, I repeat, for the toil of my brains on their behalf, as the publisher will give for the toil of my brains on his. Now, so far is this from being the case in England, that it is a fact perfectly well known to every literary man in the country that, while the remuneration for every other species of literature has enormously increased in the last hundred years, the remuneration for dramatic writing has steadily decreased to such a minimum of pecuniary recognition as to make it impossible for a man who lives by the successful use of his pen, as a writer of books, to alter the nature of his literary practice, and live, or nearly live, in comfortable circumstances, by the use of his pen, as a writer of plays. It is time that this fact was generally known, to justify successful living authors for their apparent neglect of one of the highest branches of their art. I tell you, in plain terms, that I could only write a play for the English stage—a successful play, mind—by consenting to what would be, in my case, and in the cases of all my successful brethren, a serious pecuniary sacrifice.

Let me make the meanness of the remuneration for stage writing in our day, as compared with what that remuneration was in past times, clear to your mind by one or two examples. Rather more than a hundred years ago, Doctor Johnson wrote a very bad play called "Irene," which proved a total failure on representation, and which tottered, rather than "ran," for just nine nights to wretched houses. Excluding his literary copyright of a hundred pounds, the Doctor's dramatic profit on a play that was a failure —remember that!—amounted to one hundred and ninety-five pounds, being just forty-five pounds *more* than the remuneration now paid, to my certain knowledge, for many a play within the last five years which has had a successful run of sixty, and, in some cases, even of a hundred nights!

I can imagine your amazement at reading

this; but I can also assure you that any higher rate of remuneration is exceptional. Let me, however, give the managers the benefit of the exception. Sometimes two hundred pounds have been paid, within the last five years, for a play; and, on one or two rare occasions, three hundred. If Shakespeare came to life again, and took "Macbeth" to an English theater, in this year, eighteen hundred and sixty-three, that is the highest market remuneration he could get for it. You are to understand that this miserable decline in the money reward held out to dramatic literature is peculiar to our own day. Without going back again so long as a century—without going back further than the time of George Colman, the younger—I may remind you that the comedy of "John Bull" brought the author twelve hundred pounds. Since then, six or seven hundred pounds have been paid for a new play; and, later yet, five hundred pounds. We have now dropped to three hundred pounds as the exception, and to one hundred and fifty as the rule. I am speaking, remember, of plays in not less than three acts, which are, or are supposed to be, original—of plays which run from sixty to a hundred nights, and which put their bread (buttered thickly on both sides) into the mouths of actors and managers. As to the remuneration for ordinary translations from the French, I would rather not mention what that is. And, indeed, there is no need I should do so. We are talking of the stage in its present relation to English literature. Suppose I write for it, as some of my friends suggest I should; and suppose I could produce one thoroughly original play, with a story of my own sole invention, with characters of my own sole creation, every year. The utmost annual income the English stage would, at present prices, pay me, after exhausting my brains in its service, would be three hundred pounds!

I use the expression "exhausting my brains" advisedly. For a man who produces a new work every year, which has any real value and completeness as a work of literary art, does, let him be who he may, for a time, exhaust his brain by the process, and leave it sorely in need of an after-period of absolute repose. Three hundred a year, therefore, is the utmost that a fertile original author can expect to get by the English stage, at present market-rates of remuneration.

Such is now the position of the dramatic writer —a special man, with a special faculty. What is now the position of the dramatic performer, when he happens to be a special man, with a special faculty also? Is his income three hundred a year? Is his manager's income three hundred a year? The popular actors of the time when Colman got his twelve hundred pounds would be struck dumb with amazement if they saw what salaries their successors are getting now. If stage remuneration has decreased sordidly in our time for authorship, it has increased splendidly for actorship. When a manager tells me now that his theater cannot afford to pay me as much for my idea in the form of a play as the

publisher can afford to pay me for it in the form
of a novel—he really means that he and his actors take a great deal more now from the nightly
receipts of the theaters than they ever thought of
taking in the time of "John Bull." When the
actor's profits from the theater are largely increased, somebody else's profits from the same
theater must be decreased. That somebody else
is the dramatic author. There you have the real
secret of the mean rate at which the English
stage now estimates the assistance of English
literature.

There are persons whose interest it may be to
deny this, and who will deny it. It is not a
question of assertion or denial, but a question
of figures. How much per week did a popular
actor get in Colman's time? How much per
week does a popular actor get now? The biographies of dead players will answer the first question. And the managers' books, for the past ten
or fifteen years, will answer the second. I must
not give offense by comparisons between living
and dead men—I must not enter into details, because they would lead me too near to the private
affairs of other people. But I tell you again,
that the remuneration for acting has immensely
increased, and the remuneration for dramatic
writing has immensely decreased, in our time;
and I am not afraid of having that assertion
contradicted by proofs.

It is useless to attempt a defense of the present
system by telling me that a different plan of re-
munerating the dramatic author was adopted in

former times, and that a different plan is also practiced on the French stage. I am not discussing which plan is best or which plan is worst. I am only dealing with the plain fact, that the present stage estimate of the author is barbarously low—an estimate which men who had any value for literature, any idea of its importance, any artist-like sympathy with its great difficulties and its great achievements, would be ashamed to make. I prove that fact by reference to the proceedings of a better pastime, and by a plain appeal to the market-value of all kinds of literature, off the stage, at the present time; and I leave the means of effecting a reform to those who are bound in common honor and common justice to make the reform. It is not my business to readjust the commercial machinery of theaters; I don't sit in the treasury, and handle the strings of the money bags. I say that the present system is a base one toward literature, and that the history of the past, and the experience of the present, prove it to be so. All the reasoning in the world which tries to convince us that a wrong is necessary will not succeed in proving that wrong to be right.

Having now established the existence of the abuse, it is easy enough to get on to the consequences that have arisen from it. At the present low rate of remuneration, a man of ability wastes his powers if he writes for the stage—unless he is prepared to put himself out of the category of authors by turning manager and actor, and taking a theater for himself. There are

men still in existence, who occasionally write for
the stage, for the love and honor of their art.
Once, perhaps, in two or three years, one of
these devoted men will try single-handed to dissipate the dense dramatic fog that hangs over
the theater and the audience. For the brief allotted space of time, the one toiling hand lets in a
little light, unthanked by the actors, unaided by
the critics, unnoticed by the audience. The time
expires—the fog gathers back—the toiling hand
disappears. Sometimes it returns once more
bravely to the hard, hopeless work; and out of
all the hundreds whom it has tried to enlighten,
there shall not be one who is grateful enough to
know it again.

These exceptional men—too few, too scattered,
too personally unimportant in the republic of letters, to have any strong or lasting influence—are
not the professed dramatists of our times. These
are not the writers who make so much as a
clerk's income out of the stage. The few men
of practical ability who now write for the English theater are men of the world, who know
that they are throwing away their talents if
they take the trouble to invent for an average
remuneration of one hundred and fifty pounds.
The well-paid Frenchman supplies them with a
story and characters ready-made. The original
adaptation is rattled off in a week; and the dramatic author beats the clerk after all, by getting
so much more money for so much less manual
exercise in the shape of writing. Below this
clever tactician, who foils the theater with its

own weapons, come the rank and file of hack writers, who work still more cheaply, and give still less (I am rejoiced to say) for the money. The stage results of this sort of authorship, as you have already implied, virtually drive the intelligent classes out of the theater. Half a century since, the prosperity of the manager's treasury would have suffered in consequence. But the increase of wealth and population, and the railway connection between London and the country, more than supply in quantity what audiences have lost in quality. Not only does the manager lose nothing in the way of profit—he absolutely gains by getting a vast nightly majority into his theater whose ignorant insensibility nothing can shock. Let him cast what garbage he pleases before them, the unquestioning mouths of his audience open, and snap at it. I am sorry and ashamed to write in this way of any assemblage of my own countrymen; but a large experience of theaters forces me to confess that I am writing the truth. If you want to find out who the people are who know nothing whatever, even by hearsay, of the progress of the literature of their own time—who have caught no chance vestige of any one of the ideas which are floating about before their very eyes—who are, to all social intents and purposes, as far behind the age they live in as any people out of a lunatic asylum can be—go to a theater, and be very careful, in doing so, to pick out the most popular performance of the day. The actors themselves, when they are men of any intelligence, are thoroughly aware of the utter incapacity of the tribunal which is supposed to judge them. Not very long ago, an actor, standing deservedly in the front rank of his profession, happened to play even more admirably than usual in a certain new part. Meeting him soon afterward, I offered him my mite of praise in all sincerity. "Yes," was his reply; "I know that I act my very best in that part, for I hardly get a hand of applause in it through the whole evening." Such is the condition to which the dearth of good literature has now reduced the audiences of English theaters—even in the estimation of the men who act before them.

And what is to remedy this? Nothing can remedy it but a change for the better in the audiences.

I have good hope that this change is slowly, very slowly, beginning. "When things are at the worst they are sure to mend." I really think that, in dramatic matters, they have been at the worst; and I have therefore some belief that the next turn of Fortune's wheel may be in our favor. In certain theaters, I fancy I notice already symptoms of a slight additional sprinkling of intelligence among the audiences. If I am right, if this sprinkling increases, if the few people who have brains in their heads will express themselves boldly, if those who are fit to lead the opinion of their neighbors will resolutely make the attempt to lead it, instead of indolently wrapping themselves up in their own contempt— then there may be a creditable dramatic future

yet in store for the countrymen of Shakespeare.
Perhaps we may yet live to see the day when
managers will be forced to seek out the writers
who are really setting their mark on the literature of the age—when "starvation prices" shall
have given place to a fair remuneration—and
when the prompter shall have his share with the
publisher in the best work that can be done for
him by the best writers of the time.

Meanwhile, there is a large audience of intelligent people, with plenty of money in their pockets, waiting for a theater to go to. Supposing
that such an amazing moral portent should ever
appear in the English firmament as a theatrical
speculator who can actually claim some slight
acquaintance with contemporary literature; and
supposing that unparalleled man to be smitten
with a sudden desire to ascertain what the circulation actually is of serial publications and successful novels which address the educated classes;
I think I may safely predict the consequences
that would follow, as soon as our ideal manager
had received his information and recovered from
his astonishment. London would be startled,
one fine morning, by finding a new theater
opened. Names that are now well known on
title-pages only would then appear on play-bills
also; and tens of thousands of readers, who now
pass the theater door with indifference, would be
turned into tens of thousands of play-goers also.
What a cry of astonishment would be heard
thereupon in the remotest fastness of old theatrical London! "Merciful Heaven! There is

a large public, after all, for well-paid original plays, as well as for well-paid original books. And a man has turned up, at last, of our own managerial order, who has absolutely found it out!''

With true regard, yours, my dear sir,

A. N. AUTHOR.

TO THINK, OR BE THOUGHT FOR.

IF anything I can say here on the subject of
the Painter's Art will encourage intelligent people of any rank to turn a deaf ear to all that
critics, connoisseurs, lecturers, and compilers of
guide-books can tell them; to trust entirely to
their own common sense when they are looking
at pictures; and to express their opinions boldly,
without the slightest reference to any precedents
whatever—I shall have exactly achieved the object with which I now apply myself to the writing of this paper.

Let me first ask, in regard to pictures in general, what it is that prevents the public from
judging for themselves, and why the influence of
Art in England is still limited to select circles—
still unfelt, as the phrase is, by all but the cultivated classes? Why do people want to look at
their guide-books before they can make up their
minds about an old picture? Why do they ask
connoisseurs and professional friends for a
marked catalogue before they venture inside
the walls of the exhibition rooms in Trafalgar
Square? Why, when they are, for the most part,
always ready to tell each other unreservedly
what books they like, or what musical compositions are favorites with them, do they hesitate

the moment pictures turn up as a topic of conversation, and intrench themselves doubtfully behind such cautious phrases as, "I don't pretend to understand the subject," "I believe such and such a picture is much admired," "I am no judge," and so on?

No judge! Does a really good picture want you to be a judge? Does it want you to have anything but eyes in your head, and the undisturbed possession of your senses? Is there any other branch of intellectual art which has such a direct appeal, by the very nature of it, to every sane human being as the art of painting? There it is, able to represent through a medium which offers itself to you palpably, in the shape of so many visible feet of canvas, actual human facts, and distinct aspects of nature, which poetry can only describe, and which music can but obscurely hint at. The art which can do this—and which has done it over and over again both in past and present times—is surely of all arts that one which least requires a course of critical training before it can be approached on familiar terms. Whenever I see an intelligent man, which I often do, standing before a really eloquent and true picture, and asking his marked catalogue, or his newspaper, or his guide-book, whether he may safely admire it or not—I think of a man standing winking both eyes in the full glare of a cloudless August noon, and inquiring deferentially of an astronomical friend whether he is really justified in saying that the sun shines!

But we have not yet fairly got at the main obstacle which hinders the public from judging of pictures for themselves, and which, by a natural consequence, limits the influence of art on the nation generally. For my own part, I have long thought, and shall always continue to believe, that this same obstacle is nothing more nor less than the Conceit of Criticism, which has got obstructively between Art and the people—which has kept them asunder, and will keep them asunder, until it is fairly pulled out of the way, and set aside at once and forever in its proper background place.

This is a bold thing to say; but I think I can advance some proofs that my assertion is not altogether so wild as it may appear at first sight. By the Conceit of Criticism I desire to express, in one word, the conventional laws and formulas, the authoritative rules and regulations which individual men set up to guide the tastes and influence the opinions of their fellow-creatures. When Criticism does not speak in too arbitrary a language, and when the laws it makes are ratified by the consent and approbation of intelligent people in general, I have as much respect for it as any one. But when Criticism sits altogether apart, speaks opinions that find no answering echo in the general heart, and measures the greatness of intellectual work by anything rather than by its power of appealing to all capacities for admiration and enjoyment, from the very highest to the very humblest—then, as it seems to me, criticism becomes the expression of individual conceit, and forfeits all claim to consideration and respect. From that moment, it is obstructive—for it has set itself up fatally between the art of painting and the honest and general appreciation of that art by the people.

Let me try to make this still clearer by an example. A great deal of obstructive criticism undoubtedly continues to hang as closely as it can about poetry and music. But there are, nevertheless, statable instances, in relation to these two arts, of the voice of the critic and the voice of the people being on the same side. The tragedy of "Hamlet," for example, is critically considered to be the masterpiece of dramatic poetry; and the tragedy of "Hamlet" is also, according to the testimony of every sort of manager, the play, of all others, which can be invariably depended on to fill a theater with the greatest certainty, act it when and how you will. Again, in music, the "Don Giovanni" of Mozart, which is the admiration even of the direst pedant producible from the ranks of musical connoisseurs, is also the irresistible popular attraction which is always sure to fill the pit and gallery at the opera. Here, at any rate, are two instances in which two great achievements of the past in poetry and music are alike viewed with admiration by the man who appreciates by instinct and the man who appreciates by rule.

If we apply the same test to the achievements of the past in painting, where shall we find a similar instance of genuine concurrence between the few who are appointed to teach and the many who are expected to learn?

I put myself in the position of a man of fair capacity and average education, who labors under the fatal delusion that he will be helped to a sincere appreciation of the works of the Old Masters by asking critics and connoisseurs to form his opinions for him. I am sent to Italy as a matter of course. A general chorus of learned authorities tells me that Michael Angelo and Raphael are the two greatest painters that ever lived; and that the two recognized masterpieces of the highest high art are the "Last Judgment," in the Sistine Chapel, and the "Transfiguration," in the Vatican picture-gallery. It is not only Lanzi and Vasari, and hosts of later sages running smoothly along the same critical grooves, who give me this information. Even the greatest of English portrait-painters, Sir Joshua Reynolds, sings steadily with the critical chorus, note for note. When experience has made me wiser, I am able to detect clearly enough, in the main principles which Reynolds has adopted in his Lectures on Art, the reason of his notorious want of success whenever he tried to rise above portraits to the regions of historical painting. But at the period of my innocence, I am simply puzzled and amazed, when I come to such a passage as the following in Sir Joshua's famous Fifth Lecture, where he sums up the comparative merits of Michael Angelo and Raphael:

"If we put these great artists in a line of comparison with each other" (lectures Sir Joshua), "Raphael had more taste and fancy, Michael

Angelo more genius and imagination. The one excelled in beauty, the other in energy. Michael Angelo had more of the poetical inspiration; his ideas are vast and sublime; his people are a superior order of beings; there is nothing about them, nothing in the air of their actions or their attitudes, or the style and cast of their limbs or features, that reminds us of their belonging to our own species."

Here I get plainly enough at what Sir Joshua considers to be the crowning excellence of high art. It is one great proof of the poetry and sublimity of Michael Angelo's pictures that the people represented in them never remind us of our own species; which seems equivalent to saying that the representation of a man made in the image of Michael Angelo is a grander sight than the representation of a man made in the image of God. I am a little staggered by these principles of criticism; but as all the learned authorities that I can get at seem to have adopted them, I do my best to follow the example of my teachers, and set off reverently for Rome to see the two works of art which my critical masters tell me are the sublimest pictures that the world has yet beheld.

I go first to the Sistine Chapel; and, on a great blue-colored wall at one end of it, I see painted a confusion of naked, knotty-bodied figures, sprawling up or tumbling down below a single figure, posted aloft in the middle, and apparently threatening the rest with his hand. If I ask Lanzi,

or Vasari, or Sir Joshua Reynolds, or the gentleman who has compiled "Murray's Hand-book for
Central Italy," or any other competent authorities, what this grotesquely startling piece of
painter's work can possibly be, I am answered
that it is actually intended to represent the un-
imaginably awful spectacle of the Last Judgment! And I am further informed that, estimated by the critical tests applied to it by these
competent authorities, the picture is pronounced
to be a masterpiece of grandeur and sublimity.
I resolve to look a little closer at this celebrated
work, and to try if I can get at any fair estimate
of it by employing such plain, uncritical tests as
will do for me and for everybody.

Here is a fresco which aspires to represent the
most impressive of all Christian subjects; it is
painted on the wall of a Christian church, by a
man belonging to a Christian community—what
evidences of religious feeling has it to show me?
I look at the lower part of the composition first,
and see—a combination of the orthodox nursery
notion of the devil, with the heathen idea of the
conveyance to the infernal regions, in the shape
of a horned and tailed ferryman giving condemned souls a cast across a river! Pretty well,
I think, to begin with.

Let me try and discover next what evidences
of extraordinary intellectual ability the picture
presents. I look up toward the top now, by way
of a change, and I find Michael Angelo's conception of the entrance of a martyr into the kingdom
of Heaven, displayed before me in the shape of

a flayed man, presenting his own skin, as a sort
of credential, to the hideous figure with the threatening hand—which I will not, even in writing,
identify with the name of Our Saviour. Elsewhere I see nothing but unnatural distortion and
hopeless confusion; fighting figures, tearing figures, tumbling figures, kicking figures; and, to
crown all, a caricatured portrait, with a pair of
ass's ears, of a certain Messer Biagio, of Sienna,
who had the sense and courage, when the "Last
Judgment" was first shown on completion, to
protest against every figure in it being painted
stark naked!

I see such things as these, and many more
equally preposterous, which it is not worth while
to mention. All other people with eyes in their
heads see them too. They are actual matters of
fact, not debatable matters of taste. But I am
not—on that account—justified, nor is any other
uncritical person justified, in saying a word
against the picture. It may palpably outrage
all the religious proprieties of the subject; but,
then, it is full of "fine foreshortening," and
therefore we uncritical people must hold our
tongues. It may violate just as plainly all the
intellectual proprieties, counting from the flayed
man with his skin in his hand, at the top, to
Messer Biagio, of Sienna, with his ass's ears, at
the bottom; but, then, it exhibits "masterly ana-
tomical detail," and therefore we uncritical spectators must hold our tongues. It may strike us
forcibly that, if people are to be painted at all,
as in this picture, rising out of their graves in

their own bodies as they lived, it is surely important (to say nothing of giving them the benefit
of the shrouds in which they were buried) to represent them as having the usual general proportions of human beings. But Sir Joshua Reynolds interposes critically, and tells us the figures
on the wall and ceiling of the Sistine Chapel are
sublime, because they don't remind us of our own
species. Why should they not remind us of our
own species? Because they are prophets, sibyls,
and such like, cries the chorus of critics indignantly. And what then? If I had been on intimate terms with Jeremiah, or if I had been the
ancient king to whom the sibyl brought the mysterious books, would not my friend in the one
case, and the messenger in the other, have appeared before me bearing the ordinary proportions and exhibiting the usual appearance of my
own species? Does not sacred history inform
me that the prophet was a man, and does not
profane history describe the sibyl as an old woman? Is old age never venerable and striking
in real life? But I am uttering heresies. I am
mutinously summoning reason and common sense
to help me in estimating an old master. This
will never do; I had better follow the example
of all the travelers I see about me, by turning
away in despair, and leaving the "Last Judgment" to the critics and connoisseurs.

Having thus discovered that one masterpiece
of high art does not address itself to me, and
to the large majority whom I represent, let me
go next to the picture gallery, and see how the

second masterpiece (the "Transfiguration," by
Raphael) can vindicate its magnificent reputation among critics and connoisseurs. This picture I approach under the advantage of knowing,
beforehand, that I must make allowances for
minor defects in it, which are recognized by the
learned authorities themselves. 1 am, indeed,
prepared to be disappointed at the outset, because
I have been prepared to make allowances:

First, for defects of color, which spoil the general effect of the picture on the spectator; all the
lights being lividly tinged with green, and all
the shadows being grimly hardened with black.
This mischief is said to have been worked by the
tricks of French cleaners and restorers, who have
so fatally tampered with the whole surface that
Raphael's original coloring must be given up as
lost. Rather a considerable loss, this, to begin
with; but not Raphael's fault. Therefore, let
it by no means depreciate the picture in my estimation.

Secondly, 1 have to make allowances for the
introduction of two Roman Catholic saints (St.
Julian and St. Lawrence), represented by the
painter as being actually present at the Transfiguration, in order to please Cardinal De Medici,
for whom the picture was painted. This *is* Raphael's fault. This sets him forth in the rather
anomalous character of a great painter with no
respect for his art. 1 have some doubts about
him, after that—doubts which my critical friends
might possibly share if Raphael were only a
modern painter.

Thirdly, I have to make allowances for the
scene of the Transfiguration on the high mountain, and the scene of the inability of the disciples
to cure the boy possessed with a devil, being represented, without the slightest division, one at
the top and the other at the bottom of the same
canvas—both events thus appearing to be connected by happening in the same place, within
view of each other, when we know very well that
they were only connected by happening at the
same time.   Also, when I see some of the disciples painted in the act of pointing up to the
Transfiguration, the mountain itself being the
background against which they stand, I am to
remember (though the whole of the rest of the
picture is most absolutely and unflinchingly literal
in treatment) that here Raphael has suddenly
broken out into allegory, and desires to indicate
by the pointing hands of the disciples that it is
the duty of the afflicted to look to Heaven for relief in their calamities.   Having made all these
rather important allowances, I may now look
impartially at the upper half of this famous composition.

I find myself soon looking away again.   It
may be that three figures clothed in gracefully
fluttering drapery, and dancing at symmetrically
exact distances from each other in the air, represent such an unearthly spectacle as the Transfiguration to the satisfaction of great judges of
art.   I can also imagine that some few select
persons may be able to look at the top of the high
mountain, as represented in the picture, without

feeling their gravity in the smallest degree endangered by seeing that the ugly knob of ground on which the disciples are lying prostrate is barely big enough to hold them, and most certainly would not hold them if they all moved briskly on it together. These things are matters of taste on which I have the misfortune to differ with the connoisseurs. Not feeling bold enough to venture on defending myself against the masters who are teaching me to appreciate high art, I can only look away from the upper part of the picture, and try if I can derive any useful or pleasant impressions from the lower half of the composition, in which no supernatural event is depicted, and which it is, therefore, perfectly justifiable to judge by referring it to the standard of dramatic truth, or, in one word, of Nature.

As for this portion of the picture, I can hardly believe my eyes when I first look at it. Excepting the convulsed face of the boy, and a certain hard eagerness in the look of the man who is holding him, all the other faces display a stony inexpressiveness, which, when I think of the great name of Raphael in connection with what I see, fairly amazes me. I look down incredulously at my guide-book. Yes! there is indeed the critical authority of Lanzi quoted for my benefit. Lanzi tells me in plain terms that I behold represented in the picture before me "the most pathetic story Raphael ever conceived," and refers, in proof of it, to the "compassion evinced by the apostles." I look attentively at them all, and behold an assembly of hard-featured, bearded men, standing,

sitting, and gesticulating, in conventional acade-
mic attitudes; their faces not expressing naturally,
not even affecting to express artificially, compassion for the suffering boy, humility at their own
incapability to relieve him, or any other human
emotion likely to be suggested by the situation in
which they are placed. I find it still more dis-
maying to look next at the figure of a brawny
woman, with her back to the spectator, entreating the help of the apostles theatrically on one
knee, with her insensible classical profile turned
in one direction, and both her muscular arms
stretched out in the other; it is still more dismay-
ing to look at such a figure as this, and then to
be gravely told by Lanzi that I am contemplat-
ing "the affliction of a beautiful and interesting
female." I observe, on entering the room in
which the "Transfiguration" is placed, as I have
previously observed on entering the Sistine Chapel,
groups of spectators before the picture consulting
their guide-books—looking attentively at the work
of high art which they are ordered to admire—
trying hard to admire it—then, with dismay in
their faces, looking round at each other, shutting
up their books, and retreating from high art in
despair. I observe these groups for a little while,
and I end in following their example. We members of the general public may admire "Hamlet"
and "Don Giovanni" honestly, along with the
critics, but the two sublimest pictures (according
to the learned authorities) which the world has
yet beheld, appeal to none of us; and we leave
them, altogether discouraged on the subject of

Art for the future.   From that time forth we look
at pictures with a fatal self-distrust.   Some of us
recklessly take our opinions from others; some
of us cautiously keep our opinions to ourselves;
and some of us indolently abstain from having
anything to do with an opinion at all.

Is this exaggerated?   Have I misrepresented
facts in the example I have quoted of obstructive
criticism on art, and of its discouraging effects
on the public mind?   Let the doubting reader,
by all means, judge for himself.   Let him refer
to any recognized authority he pleases, and he
will find that the two pictures of which I have
been writing are critically and officially considered, to this day, as the two master-works of the
highest school of painting.   Having ascertained
that, let him next, if possible, procure a sight of
some print or small copy from any part of either
picture (there is a copy of the whole of the "Transfiguration" in the Gallery at the Crystal Palace),
and practically test the truth of what I have said.
Or, in the event of his not choosing to take that
trouble, let him ask any unprofessional and uncritical friend who has seen the pictures themselves—and the more intelligent and unprejudiced
that friend, the better for my purpose—what the
effect on him was of the "Last Judgment," or
the "Transfiguration."   If I can only be assured
of the sincerity of the witness, I shall not be afraid
of the result of the examination.

Other readers who have visited the Sistine
Chapel and the Vatican Gallery can testify for
themselves (but few of them will—I know them!)

whether I have misrepresented their impressions or not. To that part of my audience I have nothing to say, except that I beg them not to believe that I am a heretic in relation to all works by all old masters, because I have spoken out about the "Last Judgment" and the "Transfiguration." I am not blind, I hope, to the merits of any picture, provided it will bear honest investigation on uncritical principles. I have seen such exceptional works by ones and twos, amid many hundreds of utterly worthless canvases with undeservedly famous names attached to them, in Italy and elsewhere. My *valet de place* has not pointed them out to me; my guide-book, which criticises according to authority, has not recommended me to look at them, except in very rare cases indeed. I discovered them for myself, and others may discover them as readily as I did, if they will only take their minds out of leading-strings when they enter a gallery, and challenge a picture boldly to do its duty by explaining its own merits to them without the assistance of an interpreter. Having given that simple receipt for the finding out and enjoying of good pictures, I need give no more. It is no part of my object to attempt to impose my own tastes and preferences on others. I want—if I may be allowed to repeat my motives once more in the plainest terms—to do all I can to shake the influence of authority in matters of Art, because I see that authority standing drearily and persistently aloof from all popular sympathy; because I see it keeping pictures and the people apart; because

I find it setting up as masterpieces two of the worst of many palpably bad and barbarous works of past times; and, lastly, because I find it purchasing pictures for the National Gallery of England, for which, in nine cases out of ten, the nation has no concern or care, which have no merits but technical merits, and which have not the last and lowest recommendation of winning general approval even among the critics and connoisseurs themselves.

And what remedy against this? I say at the end, as I said at the beginning, the remedy is to judge for ourselves, and to express our opinions, privately and publicly, on every possible occasion, without hesitation, without compromise, without reference to any precedents whatever. Public opinion has had its victories in other matters, and may yet have its victory in matters of art. We, the people, have a gallery that is called ours; let us do our best to have it filled for the future with pictures (no matter when or by whom painted) that we can get some honest enjoyment and benefit from. Let us, in Parliament and out of it, before dinner and after dinner, in the presence of authorities just as coolly as out of the presence of authorities, say plainly, once for all, that the sort of high art which is professedly bought *for us*, and which does actually address itself to nobody but painters, critics and connoisseurs, is not high art at all, but the lowest of the low: because it is the narrowest as to its sphere of action, and the most scantily furnished as to its means of doing good. We shall shock the connoisseurs (especially the elderly ones) by taking this course; we shall get indignantly reprimanded by the critics, and flatly contradicted by the lecturers: but we shall also, sooner or later, get a collection of pictures bought for us that we, mere mankind, can appreciate and understand. It may be a revolutionary sentiment, but I think that the carrying out of this reform (as well as of a few others) is a part of the national business which the people of England have got to do for themselves, and in which no existing authorities will assist them. There is a great deal of social litter accumulating about us. Suppose, when we start the business of setting things to rights, that we try the new broom gently at first by sweeping away a little high art, and having the temerity to form our own opinions.

SOCIAL GRIEVANCES.—IV.

SAVE ME FROM MY FRIENDS.

A FEW days ago, I was walking in a street at the western part of London, and I encountered a mendicant individual of an almost extinct species. Some years since, the oratorical beggar, who addressed himself to the public on each side of the way, in a neat speech spoken from the middle of the road, was almost as constant and regular in his appearances as the postman himself. Of late, however, this well-known figure—this cadger Cicero of modern days—has all but disappeared; the easy public ear having probably grown rather deaf, in course of time, to the persuasive power of orators with only two subjects to illustrate—their moral virtues and their physical destitution.

With these thoughts in my mind, I stopped to look at the rare and wretched object for charity whom I had met by chance, and to listen to the address which he was delivering for the benefit of the street population and the street passengers on both sides of the pavement. He was a tall, sturdy, self-satisfied, healthy-looking vagabond, with a face which would have been almost handsome if it had not been disfigured by the expression which Nature sets, like a brand, on the countenance of a common impostor. As for his style of oratory, I will not do him the injustice of merely describing it. Here is a specimen, faithfully reported for the public, from the original speech:

"Good Christian people, will you be so obliging as to leave off your various occupations for a few minutes only, and listen to the harrowing statement of a father of a family, who is reduced to acknowledge his misfortunes in the public streets? Work, honest work, is all I ask for; and I cannot get it. Why?—I ask, most respectfully, why? Good Christian people, I think it is because I have no friends. Alas! indeed I have no friends. My wife and seven babes are, I am shocked to tell you, without food. Yes, without food. Oh yes, without food. Because we have no friends; I assure you I am right in saying, because we have no friends. Why am I and my wife and my seven babes starving in a land of plenty? Why have I no share in the wholesome necessaries of life, which I see, with my hungry eyes, in butchers' and bakers' shops on each side of me? Can anybody give me a reason for this? 1 think, Good Christian people, nobody can. Must I perish in a land of plenty because I have no work and because 1 have no friends? I cannot perish in a land of plenty. No, 1 cannot perish in a land of plenty. Oh no, I cannot perish in a land of plenty. Bear with my importunity, if you please, and listen to my harrowing statement. 1 am the father of a starving family, and I have got no friends."

With this neat return to the introductory passage of his speech, the mendicant individual paused; collected the pecuniary tokens of public approval; and walked forward, with a funereal slowness of step, to deliver a second edition of his address in another part of the street.

While I had been looking at this man, I had also been insensibly led to compare myself, as I stood on the pavement, with my oratorical vagrant, as he stood in the roadway. In some important respects, I found, to my own astonishment, that the result of the comparison was not by any means flattering on my side. I might certainly assume, without paying myself any extraordinary compliment, that I was the honester man of the two; also that I was better educated, and a little better clad. But here my superiority ceased. The beggar was far in advance of me in all the outward and visible signs of inward mental comfort which combine to form the appearance of a healthily-constituted man. After perplexing myself for some time in the attempt to discover the reason for the enviably prosperous and contented aspect of this vagabond—which appeared palpably to any sharp observer, through his assumed expression of suffering and despair —I came to the singular conclusion that the secret of his personal advantages over me lay in the very circumstance on which he chiefly relied for awakening the sympathies of the charitable public—the circumstance of his having no friends.

"No friends!" I repeated to myself, as I

walked away. "Happily situated vagrant! there is the true cause of your superiority over me—you have no friends! But can the marvelous assertion be true? Can this enviable man really go home and touch up his speech for tomorrow, with the certainty of not being interrupted? I am going home to finish an article, without knowing whether I shall have a clear five minutes to myself all the time I am at work. Can he take his money back to his drawer in broad daylight, and meet nobody by the way who will say to him, 'Remember our old friendship, and lend me a trifle?' I have money waiting for me at my publisher's, and I dare not go and fetch it, except under cover of the night. Is that spoiled child of fortune, from whom I have just separated myself, really and truly never asked to parties and obliged to go to them? He has a button on his coat—I am positively certain I saw it—and is there no human finger and thumb to lay hold of it, and no human tongue to worry him the while? He does not live in the times of the pillory, and he has his ears—the lucky wretch. Have those organs actually enjoyed the indescribable blessedness of freedom from the intrusion of 'well-meant advice'? Can he write—and has he got no letters to answer? Can he read—and has he no dear friend's book to get through, whether he likes it or not? No wonder that he looks prosperous and healthy, though he lives in a dingy slum, and that I look peevish and pale, though I reside on gravel, in an airy neighborhood. Good heavens! does he

dare to speak of his misfortunes, when he has no
calls to make? Irrational Sybarite! what does
he want next, I wonder?"

These are crabbed sentiments. But, perhaps,
as it is the fashion, nowadays, to take an invete-
rately genial view of society in general, my present outbreak of misanthropy may be pardoned,
in consideration of its involving a certain accidental originality of expression in relation to social subjects. It is a dreadful thing to say; but
it is the sad truth that I have never yet been able
to appreciate the advantage of having a large
circle of acquaintances, and that I could positively dispense with a great many of my dearest
friends.

There is my Boisterous Friend, for instance—
an excellent creature, who has been intimate with
me from childhood, and who loves me as his
brother. I always know when he calls, though
my study is at the top of the house. I hear him
in the passage the moment the door is opened—
he is so hearty; and, like other hearty people, he
has such a loud voice. I have told my servant
to say that I am engaged, which means simply
that I am hard at work. "Dear old boy!" I
hear my Boisterous Friend exclaim, with a
genial roar, "writing away just as usual—eh,
Susan? Lord bless you! he knows me—he
knows I don't want to interrupt him. Upstairs, of course? I know my way. Just for
a minute, Susan—just for a minute." The

voice stops, and heavily-shod feet (all boister-ous men wear thick boots) ascend the stairs, two at a time. My door is burst open, as if with a battering-ram (no boisterous man ever knocks), and my friend rushes in like a mad bull. "Ha, ha, ha! I've caught you," says the associate of my childhood. "Don't stop for me, dear old boy; I'm not going to interrupt you (bless my soul, what a lot of writing!)—and you are all right, eh? That's all I wanted to know. By George, it's quite refreshing to see you here forming the public mind! No! I won't sit down; I won't stop another instant. So glad to have seen you, dear fellow—good-by." By this time his affectionate voice has made the room ring again; he has squeezed my hand, in his brotherly way, till my fingers are too sore to hold the pen; and he has put to flight, for the rest of the day, every idea that I had when I sat down to work. And yet (as he would tell me himself) he has not been in the room more than a minute—though he might well have stopped for hours without doing any additional harm. Could I really dispense with him? I don't deny that he has known me from the time when I was in short frocks, and that he loves me like a brother. Nevertheless, I could dispense—yes, I could dis-pense—oh, yes, I could dispense—with my Bois-terous Friend.

Again, there is my Domestic Friend, whose time for calling on me is late in the afternoon, when I have wrought through my day's task; and when a quiet restorative half-hour by myself, over the fire, is precious to me beyond all power of expression. There is my Domestic Friend, who comes to me at such times, and who has no subject of conversation but the maladies of his wife and children. No efforts that I can make to change the subject can get me out of the range of the family sick-room. If I start the weather, I lead to a harrowing narrative of its effect on Mrs. Ricketts, or the Master and Misses Ricketts. If I try politics or literature, my friend apologizes for knowing nothing about any recent events in which ministers or writers are concerned, by telling me how his time has been taken up by illness at home. If I attempt to protect myself by asking him to meet a large party, where the conversation must surely be on general topics, he brings his wife with him (though he told me, when I invited her, that she was unable to stir from her bed), and publicly asks her how she feels at certain intervals; wafting that affectionate question across the table as easily as if he was handing the salt-cellar or passing the bottle. I have given up defending myself against him of late, in sheer despair. I am resigned to my fate. Though not a family man, I know (through the vast array of facts in connection with the subject with which my friend has favored me) as much about the maladies of young mothers and their children as the doctor himself. Does any other unmedical man know when half a pint of raw brandy may be poured down the throat of a delicate and sensitive woman, without producing the slightest effect on

her, except of the restorative kind? I know
when it may be done—when it must be done—
when, I give you my sacred word of honor, the
exhibition of alcohol in large quantities may be
the saving of one precious life—ay, sir, and perhaps of two! Possibly it may yet prove a useful
addition to my stores of information to know
what I know now on such interesting subjects as
these. It may be so; but, good Christian people, it is not the less true that I could also dispense with my Domestic Friend.

My Country Friends—I must not forget them
—and least of all, my hospitable hostess, Lady
Jinkinson, who is in certain respects the type and
symbol of my whole circle of rural acquaintance.

Lady Jinkinson is the widow of a gallant general officer. She has a charming place in the
country. She has also sons who are splendid
fellows, and daughters who are charming girls.
She has a cultivated taste for literature—so have
the charming girls—so have not the splendid fellows. She thinks a little attention to literary
men is very becoming in persons of distinction;
and she is good enough to ask me to come and
stay at her country house, where a room shall be
specially reserved for me, and where I can write
my "fine things" in perfect quiet, away from
London noises and London interruptions. I go
to the country house with my work in my portmanteau—work which must be done by a certain
time. I find a charming little room made ready
for me, opening into my bedroom, and looking
out on the lovely garden terrace, and the noble

trees in the park beyond. I come down to breakfast in the morning; and after the second cup of tea I get up to return to my writing-room. A chorus of family remonstrances rises instantly. Oh, surely I am not going to begin writing on the very first day. Look at the sun, listen to the birds, feel the sweet air. A drive in the country, after the London smoke, is absolutely necessary—a drive to Shockley Bottom, and a picnic luncheon (so nice!), and back by Grimshawe's Folly (such a view from the top!), and a call on the way home, at the Abbey, that lovely old house, where the dear Squire has had my last book read aloud to him (only think of that! the very last thing in the world that I could possibly have expected!) by darling Emily and Matilda, who are both dying to know me. Possessed by a (printer's) devil, I gruffly break through this string of temptations to be idle, and resolutely make my escape.

"Lunch at half-past one," says **Lady Jinkin-son**, as I retire.

"Pray don't wait for me," I answer.

"Lunch at half-past one," persists **Lady Jinkinson**, as if she thought I had not heard her.

"And cigars in the billiard-room," adds one of the splendid fellows.

"And in the greenhouse, too," continues one of the charming girls, "where your horrid smoking is really of some use."

I shut the door desperately. The last words I hear are from Lady Jinkinson. **"Lunch at half-past one."**

I get into my writing-room, and take the following inventory of the contents:

Table of rare inlaid woods, on which a drop of ink would be downright ruin; silver inkstand of enormous size, holding about a thimbleful of ink; clarified pens in scented papier-mache box; blotting-book lined with crimson watered-silk, full of violet and rose-colored note-paper with the Jinkinson crest stamped in silver at the top of each leaf; penwiper, of glossy new cloth, all ablaze with beads; tortoise-shell paper-knife; also paper-weight, exhibiting a view of the Colosseum in rare mosaic; also light-green taper, in ebony candlestick; wax in scented box; matches in scented box; pencil-tray made of fine gold, with a torquoise eruption breaking out all over it: upon the whole, about two hundred pounds' worth of valuable property, as working materials for me to write with.

I remove every portable article carefully from the inlaid table, look about me for the most worthless thing I can discover to throw over it, in case of ink-splashes; find nothing worthless in the room, except my own summer paletot; take that, accordingly, and make a cloth of it, pull out my battered old writing-case, with my provision of cheap paper, and my inky steel pen in my twopenny holder.

With these materials before me on my paletot (price one guinea), I endeavor to persuade myself, by carefully abstaining from looking about the room, that I am immersed in my customary squalor, and upheld by my natural untidiness.

After a little while, I succeed in the effort, and begin to work.

Birds. The poets are all fond of birds. Can they write, I wonder, when their favorites are singing in chorus close outside their window? I, who only produce prose, find birds a nuisance. Cows also. Has that one particular cow who bellows so very regularly a bereavement to mourn? I think we shall have veal for dinner to-day; I do think we shall have nice veal and stuffing. But this is not the train of thought I ought to be engaged in. Let me be deaf to these pastoral noises (including the sharpening of the gardener's scythe on the lawn), and get on with my work.

Tum-dum-tiddy-hidy-dum — tom-tom-tiddy-hiddy-tom — ti-too-tidy-hidy-ti — ti-ti-ti-tum. Yes, yes, that famous tenor bit in the "Trovatore," played with prodigious fire on the piano in the room below, by one of the charming girls. I like the "Trovatore" (not being, fortunately for myself, a musical critic). Let me lean back in my chair on this balmy morning—writing being now clearly out of the question—and float away placidly on the stream of melody. Brava! Brava! Bravissima! She is going through the whole opera, now in one part of it, and now in another. No, she stops, after only an hour's practice. A voice calls to her—I hear her ringing laugh in answer; no more piano—silence. Work, work, you must be done! Oh, my ideas, my only stock in trade, mercifully come back to me—or, like the famous Roman, I have lost a day.

Let me see; where was I when the "Trovatore" began? At the following passage apparently, for the sentence is left unfinished:

"The further we enter into this interesting subject, the more light—" What had I got to say about light when the "Trovatore" began? Was it, "flows in upon us"? No; nothing so commonplace as that. I had surely a good long metaphor, and a fine round close to the sentence. "The more light"—shines? beams? bursts? dawns? floods? bathes? quivers? Oh, me! what was the precious next word I had in my head when the "Trovatore" took possession of my poor crazy brains? It is useless to search for it. Strike out "the more light," and try something else.

"The further we enter into this interesting subject, the more prodigally we find scattered before us the gems of truth which—so seldom ride over to see us now."

"So seldom ride over to see us now?" Mercy on me, what am I about? Ending my unfortunate sentence by mechanically taking down a few polite words spoken by the melodious voice of one of the charming girls on the garden terrace under my window. What do I hear in a man's voice? "Regret being so long an absentee, but my schools and my poor—" Oh, a young clerical visitor; I know him by his way of talking. All young clergymen speak alike—who teaches them, I wonder? Let me peep out of window.

I am right. It *is* a young clergyman—no

whiskers, apostolic hair, sickly smile, long frock-coat, a wisp of muslin round his neck, and a canonical black waistcoat with no gap in it for the display of profane linen. The charming girl is respectfully devouring him with her eyes. Are they going to have their morning chat under my window? Evidently they are. This is pleasant. Every word of their small, fluent, ceaseless, sentimental gabble comes into my room. If I ask them to get out of hearing, I am rude. If I go to the window, and announce my presence by a cough, I confuse the charming girl. No help for it but to lay the pen down again and wait. This is a change for the worse, with a vengeance. The "Trovatore" was something pleasant to listen to; but the reverend gentleman's opinions on the terrace flowers which he has come to admire, on the last volume of modern poetry which he has borrowed from the charming girl, on the merits of the church system in the Ages of Faith, and on the difficulties he has had to contend with in his Infant-school, are, upon the whole, rather wearisome to listen to. And this is the house that I entered, in the full belief that it would offer me the luxury of perfect quiet to work in! And downstairs sits Lady Jinkinson, firmly believing that she has given me such an opportunity of distinguishing myself with my pen as I have never before enjoyed in all my life! Patience, patience.

Half an hour; three-quarters of an hour. Do I hear him taking his leave? Yes, at last. Pen again; paper again. Where was I?

"The further we enter into this interesting subject, the more prodigally do we find scattered before us the gems of truth, which—"

What was I going to say the gems of truth did, when the young clergyman and the charming girl began their sentimental interview on the terrace? Gone—utterly gone. Strike out the gems of truth, and try another way.

"The further we enter into this interesting subject, the more its vast capabilities—"

A knock at the door.

"Yes."

"Her ladyship wishes me to say, sir, that luncheon is ready."

"Very well."

"The further we enter into this interesting subject, the more clearly its vast capabilities display themselves to our view. The mind, indeed, can hardly be pronounced competent—"

A knock at the door.

"Yes."

"Her ladyship wishes me to remind you, sir, that luncheon is ready."

"Pray beg Lady Jinkinson not to wait for me."

"The mind, indeed, can hardly be pronounced competent to survey the extended field of observation—"

A knock at the door.

"Yes."

"I beg your pardon, sir, but her ladyship desires me to say that a friar's omelet has just come

up, which she very much wishes you to taste.
And she is afraid it will get cold, unless you will
be so good as to come downstairs at once."

"Say I will come directly."

"The mind, indeed, can hardly be pronounced
competent to survey the extended field of observation, which"—which?—which?—Gone again!
What else could I expect? A nice chance literature has in this house against luncheon.

I descend to the dining-room, and am politely
told that I look as if I had just achieved a wonderful morning's work. "I dare say you have
not written in such perfect quiet as this for
months past?" says Lady Jinkinson, helping
me to the friar's omelet. I begin with that
dainty; where I end is more than my recollection enables me to say. Everybody feeds me,
under the impression that I am exhausted with
writing. All the splendid fellows will drink
wine with me, "to set me going again." Nobody believes my rueful assertion that I have
done nothing, which they ascribe to excessive
modesty. When we rise from table (a process
which is performed with extreme difficulty,
speaking for myself), I am told that the carriage will be ready in an hour. Lady Jinkinson will not hear of any objections. "No!
No!" she says. "I have not asked you here
to overwork yourself. I really can't allow
that."

I get back to my room with an extraordinary
tightness in my waistcoat, and with slight symp-

toms of a determination of sherry to the head. Under these circumstances, returning to work immediately is not to be thought of. Returning to bed is by far the wiser proceeding. I lie down to arrange my ideas. Having none to arrange, I yield to nature, and go to sleep.

When I wake, my head is clear again. I see my way now to the end of that bit about "the extended field of observation," and make for my table in high spirits. Just as I sit down comes another knock at the door. The carriage is ready. The carriage! I had forgotten all about it. There is no way of escape, however. Hours must give way to me when I am at home; I must give way to hours when I am at Lady Jinkinson's. My papers are soon shuffled together in my case, and I am once more united with the hospitable party downstairs. "More bright ideas?" cry the ladies, interrogatively, as I take my place in the carriage. "Not the dimmest vestige of one," I answer. Lady Jinkinson shakes her parasol reproachfully at me. "My dear friend, you were always absurdly modest when speaking of yourself; and, do you know, I think it grows on you."

We get back in time to dress for dinner. After dinner there is the social evening and more "Trovatore." After that, cigars with the splendid fellows in the billiard-room. I look over my day's work, with the calmness of despair, when I get to bed at last. It amounts to four sentences and a half, every line of which is perfectly worthless as a literary composition.

The next morning I rise before the rest of the family are up, leave a note of apology on my table, and take the early train for London. This is very ungrateful behavior to people who have treated me with extreme kindness. But here, again, I must confess the hard truth. The demands of my business in life are imperative; and, sad to say, they absolutely oblige me to dispense with Lady Jinkinson.

I have now been confessing my misanthropical sentiments at some length, but I have not by any means done yet with the number of my dear friends whom I could dispense with. To say nothing of my friend who borrows money of me (an obvious nuisance), there is my self-satisfied friend, who can talk of nothing but himself, and his successes in life; there is my inattentive friend, who is perpetually asking me irrelevant questions, and who has no power of listening to my answers; there is my accidental friend, whom I always meet when I go out; there is my hospitable friend, who is continually telling me that he wants so much to ask me to dinner, and who never does really ask me by any chance. All these intimate associates of mine are persons of fundamentally irreproachable characters, and of well-defined positions in the world; and yet so unhappily is my nature constituted, that I am not exaggerating when I acknowledge that 1 could positively dispense with every one of them. To proceed a little further, now that I have begun to unburden my mind—

A double knock at the street door stops **my** pen suddenly. I make no complaint, for I have been, to my own amazement, filling these pages for the last three hours, in my parlor after dinner, without interruption. A well known voice in the passage smites my ear, inquiring for me on very particular business, and asking the servant to take in the name. The servant appears at my door, and I make up my mind to send these leaves to the printer, unfinished as they are. No necessity, Susan, to mention the name; I have recognized the voice. This is my friend who does not at all like the state of my health. He comes, I know beforehand, with the address of a new doctor, cr the recipe of a new remedy; and he will stay for hours, persuading me that I am in a bad way. No escaping from him, as I know by experience. Well, well, I have made my confession, and eased my mind. Let my friend who doesn't like the state of my health end the list, for the present, of the dear friends whom I could dispense with. Show him in, Susan—show **him in.**

CASES WORTH LOOKING AT.—III

THE CALDRON OF OIL.

ABOUT one French league distant from the city of Toulouse there is a village called Croix-Daurade. In the military history of England, this place is associated with a famous charge of the Eighteenth Hussars, which united two separated columns of the British army on the day before the Duke of Wellington fought the battle of Toulouse. In the criminal history of France, the village is memorable as the scene of a daring crime, which was discovered and punished under circumstances sufficiently remarkable to merit preservation in the form of a plain narrative.

I. THE PERSONS OF THE DRAMA.

In the year seventeen hundred, the resident priest of the village of Croix-Daurade was Monsieur Pierre-Celestin Chaubard. He was a man of no extraordinary energy or capacity, simple in his habits, and sociable in his disposition. His character was irreproachable; he was strictly conscientious in the performance of his duties; and he was universally respected and beloved by all his parishioners.

Among the members of his flock there was a family named Siadoux. The head of the household, Saturnin Siadoux, had been long established in business at Croix-Daurade as an oil manufacturer. At the period of the events now to be narrated, he had attained the age of sixty, and was a widower. His family consisted of five children—three young men, who helped him in the business, and two daughters. His nearest living relative was his sister, the widow Mirailhe.

The widow resided principally at Toulouse. Her time in that city was mainly occupied in winding up the business affairs of her deceased husband, which had remained unsettled for a considerable period after his death, through delays in realizing certain sums of money owing to his representative. The widow had been left very well provided for—she was still a comely, attractive woman—and more than one substantial citizen of Toulouse had shown himself anxious to persuade her into marrying for the second time. But the widow Mirailhe lived on terms of great intimacy and affection with her brother Siadoux and his family; she was sincerely attached to them, and sincerely unwilling, at her age, to deprive her nephews and nieces, by a second marriage, of the inheritance, or even of a portion of the inheritance, which would otherwise fall to them on her death. Animated by these motives, she closed her doors resolutely on all suitors who attempted to pay their court to her, with the one exception of a master-butcher of Toulouse, whose name was Cantegrel.

This man was a neighbor of the widow's, and had made himself useful by assisting her in the business complications which still hung about the realization of her late husband's estate. The preference which she showed for the master-butcher was thus far of the purely negative kind. She gave him no absolute encouragement; she would not for a moment admit that there was the slightest prospect of her ever marrying him; but, at the same time, she continued to receive his visits, and she showed no disposition to restrict the neighborly intercourse between them. for the future, within purely formal bounds. Under these circumstances, Saturnin Siadoux began to be alarmed, and to think it time to bestir himself. He had no personal acquaintance with Cantegrel, who never visited the village; and Monsieur Chaubard (to whom he might otherwise have applied for advice) was not in a position to give an opinion; the priest and the master-butcher did not even know each other by sight. In this difficulty, Siadoux bethought himself of inquiring privately at Toulouse, in the hope of discovering some scandalous passages in Cantegrel's early life which might fatally degrade him in the estimation of the widow Mirailhe. The investigation, as usual in such cases, produced rumors and reports in plenty, the greater part of which dated back to a period of the butcher's life when he had resided in the ancient town of Narbonne. One of these rumors, especially, was of so serious a nature that Siadoux determined to test the truth or falsehood of it personally by traveling to Narbonne. He kept his intention a secret not only from his sister and his daughters, but also from his sons; they were young men, not overpatient in their tempers, and he doubted their discretion. Thus, nobody knew his real purpose but himself when he left home.

His safe arrival at Narbonne was notified in a letter to his family. The letter entered into no particulars relating to his secret errand: it merely informed his children of the day when they might expect him back, and of certain social arrangements which he wished to be made to welcome him on his return. He proposed, on his way home, to stay two days at Castelnaudry, for the purpose of paying a visit to an old friend who was settled there. According to this plan, his return to Croix-Daurade would be deferred until Tuesday, the twenty-sixth of April, when his family might expect to see him about sunset, in good time for supper. He further desired that a little party of friends might be invited to the meal, to celebrate the twenty-sixth of April (which was a feast-day in the village), as well as to celebrate his return. The guests whom he wished to be invited were, first, his sister; secondly, Monsieur Chaubard, whose pleasant disposition made him a welcome guest at all the village festivals; thirdly and fourthly, two neighbors, business men like himself, with whom he lived on terms of the friendliest intimacy. That was the party; and the family of Siadoux took especial pains, as the time approached, to provide a supper worthy of the guests, who had all shown

the heartiest readiness in accepting their invitations.

This was the domestic position, these were the
family prospects, on the morning of the twenty-
sixth of April—a memorable day, for years afterward, in the village of Croix-Daurade.

II. THE EVENTS OF THE DAY.

Besides the curacy of the village church, good
Monsieur Chaubard held some ecclesiastical pre-
ferment in the cathedral church of St. Stephen at
Toulouse.   Early in the forenoon of the twenty-
sixth, certain matters connected with this prefer-
ment took him from his village curacy to the city
—a distance which has been already described as
not greater than one French league, or between
two and three English miles.

After transacting his business, Monsieur Chaubard parted with his clerical brethren, who left
him by himself in the sacristy (or vestry) of the
church.   Before he had quitted the room, in his
turn, the beadle entered it, and inquired for the
Abbe de Mariotte, one of the officiating priests
attached to the cathedral.

"The Abbe has just gone out," replied Monsieur Chaubard.   "Who wants him?"

"A respectable-looking man," said the beadle.
"I thought he seemed to be in some distress of
mind when he spoke to me."

"Did he mention his business with the Abbe?"

"Yes, sir; he expressed himself as anxious to
make his confession immediately."

"In that case," said Monsieur Chaubard, "I

may be of use to him in the Abbe's absence, for
I have authority to act here as confessor. Let
us go into the church and see if this person feels
disposed to accept my services."

When they went into the church, they found
the man walking backward and forward in a
restless, disordered manner. His looks were so
strikingly suggestive of some serious mental per-
turbation, that Monsieur Chaubard found it no
easy matter to preserve his composure when he
first addressed himself to the stranger.

"I am sorry," he began, "that the Abbe de
Mariotte is not here to offer you his services—"

"I want to make my confession," said the
man, looking about him vacantly, as if the
priest's words had not attracted his attention.

"You can do so at once, if you please," said
Monsieur Chaubard. "I am attached to this
church, and I possess the necessary authority to
receive confessions in it. Perhaps, however, you
are personally acquainted with the Abbe de Mariotte? Perhaps you would prefer waiting—"

"No!" said the man, roughly. "I would as
soon, or sooner, confess to a stranger."

"In that case," replied Monsieur Chaubard,
"be so good as to follow me."

He led the way to the confessional. The beadle, whose curiosity was excited, waited a little,
and looked after them. In a few minutes he
saw the curtains, which were sometimes used to
conceal the face of the officiating priest, suddenly
drawn. The penitent knelt with his back turned
to the church. There was literally nothing to

see; but the beadle waited, nevertheless, **in ex-**
pectation of the end.

After a long lapse of time the curtain was
withdrawn, and priest and penitent left the
confessional.

The change which the interval had worked in
Monsieur Chaubard was so extraordinary that
the beadle's attention was altogether withdrawn,
in the interest of observing it, from the man who
had made the confession. He did not remark by
which door the stranger left the church—his eyes
were fixed on Monsieur Chaubard. The priest's
naturally ruddy face was as white as if he had
just risen from a long sickness; he looked straight
before him, with a stare of terror, and he left the
church as hurriedly as if he had been a man
escaping from prison; left it without a parting
word, or a farewell look, although he was noted
for his courtesy to his inferiors on all ordinary
occasions.

"Good Monsieur Chaubard has heard more
than he bargained for," said the beadle, wandering back to the empty confessional with an interest which he had never felt in it till that moment.

The day wore on as quitely as usual in the village of Croix-Daurade. At the appointed time
the supper-table was laid for the guests in the
house of Saturnin Siadoux. The widow Mirailhe
and the two neighbors arrived a little before sunset. Monsieur Chaubard, who was usually punc-
tual, did not make his appearance with them; and
when the daughters of Saturnin Siadoux looked

out from the upper windows, they saw no signs on the highroad of their father's return.

Sunset came, and still neither Siadoux nor the priest appeared. The little party sat waiting rou d the table, and waited in vain. Before long a message was sent up from the kitchen, representing that the supper must be eaten forthwith, or be spoiled; and the company began to debate the two alternatives—of waiting, or not waiting, any longer.

"It is my belief," said the widow Mirailhe, "that my brother is not coming home to-night. When Monsieur Chaubard joins us, we had better sit down to supper."

"Can any accident have happened to my father?" asked one of the two daughters, anxiously.

"God forbid!" said the widow.

"God forbid!" repeated the two neighbors, looking expectantly at the empty supper-table.

"It has been a wretched day for traveling," said Louis, the eldest son.

"It rained in torrents all yesterday," added Thomas, the second son.

"And your father's rheumatism makes him averse to traveling in wet weather," suggested the widow, thoughtfully.

"Very true!" said the first of the two neighbors, shaking his head piteously at his passive knife and fork.

Another message came up from the kitchen, and peremptorily forbade the company to wait any longer.

"But where is Monsieur Chaubard?" said the widow. "Has he been taking a journey too? Why is *he* absent? Has anybody seen him to-day?"

"I have seen him to-day," said the youngest son, who had not spoken yet. This young man's name was Jean; he was little given to talking, but he had proved himself, on various domestic occasions, to be the quickest and most observant member of the family.

"Where did you see him?" asked the widow.

"I met him this morning, on his way in to Toulouse."

"He has not fallen ill, I hope? Did he look out of sorts when you met him?"

"He was in excellent health and spirits," said Jean. "I never saw him look better—"

"And *I* never saw him look worse," said the second of the neighbors, striking into the conversation with the aggressive fretfulness of a hungry man.

"What! this morning?" cried Jean, in astonishment.

"No; this afternoon," said the neighbor. "I saw him going into our church here. He was as white as our plates will be—when they come up. And what is almost as extraordinary, he passed without taking the slightest notice of me."

Jean relapsed into his customary silence. It was getting dark; the clouds had gathered while the company had been talking; and, at the first pause in the conversation, the rain, falling again in torrents, made itself drearily audible

"Dear, dear me!" said the widow. "If it was not raining so hard, we might send somebody to inquire after good Monsieur Chaubard."

"I'll go and inquire," said Thomas Siadoux. "It's not five minutes' walk. Have up the supper; I'll take a cloak with me; and if our excellent Monsieur Chaubard is out of his bed, I'll bring him back, to answer for himself."

With those words he left the room. The supper was put on the table forthwith. The hungry neighbor disputed with nobody from that moment, and the melancholy neighbor recovered his spirits.

On reaching the priest's house, Thomas Siadoux found him sitting alone in his study. He started to his feet, with every appearance of the most violent alarm, when the young man entered the room.

"I beg your pardon, sir," said Thomas; "I am afraid I have startled you."

"What do you want?" asked Monsieur Chaubard, in a singularly abrupt, bewildered manner.

"Have you forgotten, sir, that this is the night of our supper?" remonstrated Thomas. "My father has not come back, and we can only suppose—"

At those words the priest dropped into his chair again, and trembled from head to foot. Amazed to the last degree by this extraordinary reception of his remonstrance, Thomas Siadoux remembered, at the same time, that he had engaged to bring Monsieur Chaubard back with him; and

he determined to finish his civil speech as if noth-
ing had happened.

"We are all of opinion," he resumed, "that
the weather has kept my father on the road.   But
that is no reason, sir, why the supper should be
wasted, or why you should not make one of
us, as you promised.   Here is a good warm
cloak—"

"I can't come," said the priest.   "I'm ill; I'm
in bad spirits; l'm not fit to go out."   He sighed
bitterly, and hid his face in his hands.

"Don't say that, sir," persisted Thomas.   "If
you are out of spirits, let us try to cheer you.
And you, in your turn, will enliven us.   They
are all waiting for you at home.   Don't refuse,
sir," pleaded the young man, "or we shall think
we have offended you in some way.   You have
always been a good friend to our family—"

Monsieur Chaubard again rose from his chair,
with a second change of manner, as extraordinary and as perplexing as the first.   His eyes
moistened as if the tears were rising in them; he
took the hand of Thomas Siadoux, and pressed
it long and warmly in his own.   There was a
curious mixed expression of pity and fear in the
look which he now fixed on the young man.

"Of all the days in the year," he said, very
earnestly, "don't doubt my friendship to-day.
Ill as I am, I will make one of the supper party,
for your sake—"

"And for my father's sake?" added Thomas,
persuasively.

"Let us go to the supper," said the priest.

Thomas Siadoux wrapped the cloak round him, and they left the house.

Every one at the table noticed the change in Monsieur Chaubard. He accounted for it by declaring, confusedly, that he was suffering from nervous illness; and then added that he would do his best, notwithstanding, to promote the social enjoyment of the evening. His talk was fragmentary, and his cheerfulness was sadly forced; but he contrived, with these drawbacks, to take his part in the conversation—except in the case when it happened to turn on the absent master of the house. Whenever the name of Saturnin Siadoux was mentioned—either by the neighbors, who politely regretted that he was not present, or by the family, who naturally talked about the resting-place which he might have chosen for the night—Monsieur Chaubard either relapsed into blank silence, or abruptly changed the topic. Under these circumstances, the company, by whom he was respected and beloved, made the necessary allowances for his state of health; the only person among them who showed no desire to cheer the priest's spirits, and to humor him in his temporary fretfulness, being the silent younger son of Saturnin Siadoux.

Both Louis and Thomas noticed that, from the moment when Monsieur Chaubard's manner first betrayed his singular unwillingness to touch on the subject of their father's absence, Jean fixed his eyes on the priest with an expression of suspicious attention, and never looked away from him for the rest of the evening. The young

man's absolute silence at table did not surprise
his brothers, for they were accustomed to his
taciturn habits. But the sullen distrust betrayed
in his close observation of the honored guest and
friend of the family surprised and angered them.
The priest himself seemed once or twice to be
aware of the scrutiny to which he was subjected,
and to feel uneasy and offended, as he naturally
might. He abstained, however, from openly
noticing Jean's strange behavior; and Louis
and Thomas were bound, therefore, in common
politeness, to abstain from noticing it also.

The inhabitants of Croix-Daurade kept early
hours. Toward eleven o'clock, the company
rose and separated for the night. Except the
two neighbors, nobody had enjoyed the supper,
and even the two neighbors, having eaten their
fill, were as glad to get home as the rest. In the
little confusion of parting, Monsieur Chaubard
completed the astonishment of the guests at the
extraordinary change in him, by slipping away
alone, without waiting to bid anybody good-night.

The widow Mirailhe and her nieces withdrew
to their bedrooms, and left the three brothers by
themselves in the parlor.

"Jean," said Thomas Siadoux, "I have a word
to say to you. You stared at our good Monsieur
Chaubard in a very offensive manner all through
the evening. What did you mean by it?"

"Wait till to-morrow," said Jean, "and perhaps I may tell you."

He lit his candle, and left them. Both the
brothers observed that his hand trembled, and

that his manner—never very winning—was on that night more serious and more unsociable than usual.

III. THE YOUNGER BROTHER.

When post-time came on the morning of the twenty-seventh, no letter arrived from Saturnin Siadoux. On consideration, the family interpreted this circumstance in a favorable light. If the master of the house had not written to them, it followed, surely, that he meant to make writing unnecessary by returning on that day.

As the hours passed, the widow and her nieces looked out, from time to time, for the absent man. Toward noon they observed a little assembly of people approaching the village. Ere long, on a nearer view, they recognized at the head of the assembly the chief magistrate of Toulouse, in his official dress. He was accompanied by his assessor (also in official dress), by an escort of archers, and by certain subordinates attached to the town-hall. These last appeared to be carrying some burden, which was hidden from view by the escort of archers. The procession stopped at the house of Saturnin Siadoux; and the two daughters, hastening to the door to discover what had happened, met the burden which the men were carrying, and saw, stretched on a litter, the dead body of their father.

The corpse had been found that morning on the banks of the river Lers. It was stabbed in eleven places with knife or dagger wounds. None of the valuables about the dead man's person had been touched; his watch and his money were still in his pockets. Whoever had murdered him, had murdered him for vengeance, not for gain.

Some time elapsed before even the male members of the family were sufficiently composed to hear what the officers of justice had to say to them. When this result had been at length achieved, and when the necessary inquiries had been made, no information of any kind was obtained which pointed to the murderer, in the eye of the law. After expressing his sympathy, and promising that every available means should be tried to effect the discovery of the criminal, the chief magistrate gave his orders to his escort, and withdrew.

When night came, the sister and the daughters of the murdered man retired to the upper part of the house, exhausted by the violence of their grief. The three brothers were left once more alone in the parlor, to speak together of the awful calamity which had befallen them. They were of hot Southern blood, and they looked on one another with a Southern thirst for vengeance in their tearless eyes.

The silent younger son was now the first to open his lips.

"You charged me yesterday," he said to his brother Thomas, "with looking strangely at Monsieur Chaubard all the evening; and I answered, that I might tell you *why* I looked at him when to-morrow came. To-morrow has come, and I am ready to tell you."

He waited a little, and lowered his voice to a whisper when he spoke again.

"When Monsieur Chaubard was at our supper-table last night," he said, "I had it in my mind that something had happned to our father, and that the priest knew it."

The two elder brothers looked at him in speech-less astonisment.

"Our father has been brought back to us a murdered man!" Jean went on, still in a whis-per. "I tell you, Louis—and you, Thomas—that the priest knows who murdered him."

Louis and Thomas shrank from their younger brother as if he had spoken blasphemy.

"Listen," said Jean. "No clew has been found to the secret of the murder. The magistrate has promised us to do his best; but I saw in his face that he had little hope. We must make the dis-covery ourselves, or our father's blood will have cried to us for vengeance, and cried in vain. Re-member that, and mark my next words. You heard me say yesterday evening that I had met Monsieur Chaubard on his way to Toulouse, in excellent health and spirits. You heard our old friend and neighbor contradict me at the supper-table, and declare that he had seen the priest, some hours later, go into our church here with the face of a panic-stricken man. You saw, Thomas, how he behaved when you went to fetch him to our house. You saw, Louis, what his looks were like when he came in. The change was noticed by everybody—what was the cause of it? *I* saw the cause in the priest's own face

when our father's name turned up in the talk
round the supper - table. Did Monsieur Chaubard join in that talk? He was the only person
present who never joined in it once. Did he
change it on a sudden whenever it came his way?
It came his way four times; and four times he
changed it — trembling, stammering, turning
whiter and whiter, but still, as true as the
heaven above us, shifting the talk off himself
every time! Are you men? Have you brains
in your heads? Don't you see, as I see, what
this leads to? On my salvation I swear it—the
priest knows the hand that killed our father!"

The faces of the two elder brothers darkened
vindictively, as the conviction of the truth fastened itself on their minds.

"*How* could he know it?" they inquired,
eagerly.

"He must tell us himself," said Jean.

"And if he hesitates—if he refuses to open his
lips?"

"We must open them by main force."

They drew their chairs together after that
last answer, and consulted for some time in
whispers.

When the consultation was over, the brothers
rose and went into the room where the dead body
of their father was laid out. The three kissed
him, in turn, on the forehead—then took hands
together, and looked meaningly in each other's
faces—then separated. Louis and Thomas put
on their hats, and went at once to the priest's
residence; while Jean withdrew by himself to

the great room at the back of the house, which was used for the purposes of the oil factory.

Only one of the workmen was left in the place. He was watching an immense caldron of boiling linseed-oil.

"You can go home," said Jean, patting the man kindly on the shoulder. "There is no hope of a night's rest for me, after the affliction that has befallen us; I will take your place at the caldron. Go home, my good fellow—go home."

The man thanked him, and withdrew. Jean followed, and satisfied himself that the workman had really left the house. He then returned, and sat down by the boiling caldron.

Meanwhile, Louis and Thomas presented themselves at the priest's house. He had not yet retired to bed, and he received them kindly, but with the same extraordinary agitation in his face and manner which had surprised all who saw him on the previous day. The brothers were prepared beforehand with an answer when he inquired what they wanted of him. They replied immediately that the shock of their father's horrible death had so seriously affected their aunt and their elder sister, that it was feared the minds of both might give way, unless spiritual consolation and assistance were afforded to them that night. The unhappy priest — always faithful and self-sacrificing where the duties of his ministry were in question—at once rose to accompany the young men back to the house. He even put on his surplice, and took the crucifix with him, to impress his words of comfort all the more solemnly on the afflicted women whom he was called on to succor.

Thus innocent of all suspicion of the conspiracy to which he had fallen a victim, he was taken into the room where Jean sat waiting by the caldron of oil, and the door was locked behind him.

Before he could speak, Thomas Siadoux openly avowed the truth.

"It is we three who want you," he said; "not our aunt, and not our sister. If you answer our questions truly, you have nothing to fear. If you refuse—" He stopped, and looked toward Jean and the boiling caldron.

Never, at the best of times, a resolute man; deprived, since the day before, of such resources of energy as he possessed, by the mental suffering which he had undergone in secret, the unfortunate priest trembled from head to foot as the three brothers closed round him. Louis took the crucifix from him, and held it; Thomas forced him to place his right hand on it; Jean stood in front of him and put the questions.

"Our father has been brought home a murdered man," he said. "Do you know who killed him?"

The priest hesitated, and the two elder brothers moved him nearer to the caldron.

"Answer us, on peril of your life," said Jean. "Say, with your hand on the blessed crucifix, do you know the man who killed our father?"

"I do know him."

"When did you make the discovery?"

"Yesterday."

"Where?"

"At Toulouse."

"Name the murderer."

At those words the priest closed his hand fast on the crucifix, and rallied his sinking courage.

"Never!" he said, firmly. "The knowledge I possess was obtained in the confessional. The secrets of the confessional are sacred. If I betray them, I commit sacrilege. I will die first!"

"Think!" said Jean. "If you keep silence, you screen the murderer. If you keep silence, you are the murderer's accomplice. We have sworn over our father's dead body to avenge him; if you refuse to speak, we will avenge him on *you*. I charge you again, name the man who killed him."

"I will die first," the priest reiterated, as firmly as before.

"Die, then!" said Jean. "Die in that caldron of boiling oil."

"Give him time," cried Louis and Thomas, earnestly pleading together.

"We will give him time," said the younger brother. "There is the clock yonder, against the wall. We will count five minutes by it. In those five minutes, let him make his peace with God, or make up his mind to speak."

They waited, watching the clock. In that dreadful interval, the priest dropped on his knees and hid his face. The time passed in dead silence.

"Speak! for your own sake, for our sakes, speak!" said Thomas Siadoux, as the minute-hand reached the point at which the five minutes expired.

The priest looked up; his voice died away on his lips; the mortal agony broke out on his face in great drops of sweat; his head sank forward on his breast.

"Lift him!" cried Jean, seizing the priest on one side. "Lift him, and throw him in!"

The two elder brothers advanced a step, and hesitated.

"Lift him, on your oath over our father's body!"

The two brothers seized him on the other side. As they lifted him to a level with the caldron, the horror of the death that threatened him burst from the lips of the miserable man in a scream of terror. The brothers held him firm at the caldron's edge. "Name the man!" they said for the last time.

The priest's teeth chattered—he was speechless. But he made a sign with his head—a sign in the affirmative. They placed him in a chair, and waited patiently until he was able to speak.

His first words were words of entreaty. He begged Thomas Siadoux to give him back the crucifix. When it was placed in his possession, he kissed it, and said, faintly: "I ask pardon of God for the sin that I am about to commit." He paused, and then looked up at the younger brother, who still stood in front of him. "I am ready," he said. "Question me, and I will answer."

Jean repeated the questions which he had put when the priest was first brought into the room.

"You know the murderer of our father?"

"I know him."

"Since when?"

"Since he made his confession to me yesterday in the Cathedral of Toulouse."

"Name him."

"His name is Cantegrel."

"The man who wanted to marry our aunt?"

"The same."

"What brought him to the confessional?"

"His own remorse."

"What were the motives for his crime?"

"There were reports against his character, and he discovered that your father had gone privately to Narbonne to make sure that they were true."

"Did our father make sure of their truth?"

"He did."

"Would those discoveries have separated our aunt from Cantegrel if our father had lived to tell her of them?"

"They would. If your father had lived, he would have told your aunt that Cantegrel was married already; that he had deserted his wife at Narbonne; that she was living there with another man, under another name; and that she had herself confessed it in your father's presence."

"Where was the murder committed?"

"Between Villefranche and this village. Cantegrel had followed your father to Narbonne, and had followed him back again to Villefranche. As far as that place, he traveled in company with others, both going and returning. Beyond Villefranche, he was left alone at the ford over the river. There Cantegrel drew the knife to kill him before he reached home and told his news to your aunt."

"How was the murder committed?"

"It was committed while your father was watering his pony by the bank of the stream. Cantegrel stole on him from behind, and struck him as he was stooping over the saddle-bow."

"This is the truth, on your oath?"

"On my oath, it is the truth."

"You may leave us."

The priest rose from his chair without assistance. From the time when the terror of death had forced him to reveal the murderer's name a great change had passed over him. He had given his answers with the immovable calmness of a man on whose mind all human interests had lost their hold. He now left the room, strangely absorbed in himself; moving with the mechanical regularity of a sleep-walker; lost to all perception of things and persons about him. At the door he stopped—woke, as it seemed, from the trance that possessed him — and looked at the three brothers with a steady, changeless sorrow, which they had never seen in him before, which they never afterward forgot.

"I forgive you," he said, quietly and solemnly. "Pray for me when my time comes."

With those last words, he left them.

IV. THE END.

The night was far advanced; but the three brothers determined to set forth instantly for Toulouse, and to place their information in the magistrate's hands before the morning dawned.

Thus far no suspicion had occurred to them of the terrible consequences which were to follow their night-interview with the priest. They were absolutely ignorant of the punishment to which a man in holy orders exposed himself, if he revealed the secrets of the confessional. No infliction of that punishment had been known in their neighborhood; for at that time, as at this, the rarest of all priestly offenses was a violation of the sacred trust confided to the confessor by the Roman Church. Conscious that they had forced the priest into the commission of a clerical offense, the brothers sincerely believed that the loss of his curacy would be the heaviest penalty which the law could exact from him. They entered Toulouse that night, discussing the atonement which they might offer to Monsieur Chaubard, and the means which they might best employ to make his future easy to him.

The first disclosure of the consequences which would certainly follow the outrage they had committed, was revealed to them when they made their deposition before the officer of justice. The magistrate listened to their narrative with horror vividly expressed in his face and manner.

"Better you had never been born," he said,

"than have avenged your father's death as you three have avenged it. Your own act has doomed the guilty and the innocent to suffer alike."

Those words proved prophetic of the truth. The end came quickly, as the priest had foreseen it, when he spoke his parting words.

The arrest of Cantegrel was accomplished without difficulty the next morning. In the absence of any other evidence on which to justify this proceeding, the private disclosure to the authorities of the secret which the priest had violated became inevitable. The Parliament of Languedoc was, under these circumstances, the tribunal appealed to; and the decision of that assembly immediately ordered the priest and the three brothers to be placed in confinement, as well as the murderer Cantegrel. Evidence was then immediately sought for, which might convict this last criminal without any reference to the revelation that had been forced from the priest—and evidence enough was found to satisfy judges whose minds already possessed the foregone certainty of the prisoner's guilt. He was put on his trial, was convicted of the murder, and was condemned to be broken on the wheel. The sentence was rigidly executed, with as little delay as the law would permit.

The cases of Monsieur Chaubard, and of the three sons of Siadoux, next occupied the judges. The three brothers were found guilty of having forced the secret of a confession from a man in holy orders, and were sentenced to death by hanging. A far more terrible expiation of his offense awaited the unfortunate priest. He was condemned to have his limbs broken on the wheel, and to be afterward, while still living, bound to the stake and destroyed by fire.

Barbarous as the punishments of that period were, accustomed as the population was to hear of their infliction, and even to witness it, the sentences pronounced in these two cases dismayed the public mind; and the authorities were surprised by receiving petitions for mercy from Toulouse, and from all the surrounding neighborhood. But the priest's doom had been sealed. All that could be obtained, by the intercession of persons of the highest distinction, was, that the executioner should grant him the mercy of death before his body was committed to the flames. With this one modification, the sentence was executed, as the sentence had been pronounced, on the curate of Croix-Daurade.

The punishment of the three sons of Siadoux remained to be inflicted. But the people, roused by the death of the ill-fated priest, rose against this third execution with a resolution before which the local government gave way. The cause of the young men was taken up by the hot-blooded populace, as the cause of all fathers and all sons; their filial piety was exalted to the skies; their youth was pleaded in their behalf; their ignorance of the terrible responsibility which they had confronted in forcing the secret from the priest was loudly alleged in their favor. More than this, the authorities were actually warned that the appearance of the prisoners on the scaffold would be the signal for an organized revolt and rescue. Under this serious pressure, the execution was deferred, and the prisoners were kept in confinement until the popular ferment had subsided.

The delay not only saved their lives, it gave them back their liberty as well. The infection of the popular sympathy had penetrated through the prison doors. All three brothers were handsome, well-grown young men. The gentlest of the three in disposition—Thomas Siadoux—aroused the interest and won the affection of the head-jailer's daughter. Her father was prevailed on at her intercession to relax a little in his customary vigilance; and the rest was accomplished by the girl herself. One morning the population of Toulouse heard, with every testimony of the most extravagant rejoicing, that the three brothers had escaped, accompanied by the jailer's daughter. As a necessary legal formality, they were pursued, but no extraordinary efforts were used to overtake them; and they succeeded, accordingly, in crossing the nearest frontier.

Twenty days later, orders were received from the capital to execute their sentence in effigy. They were then permitted to return to France, on condition that they never again appeared in their native place, or in any other part of the province of Languedoc. With this reservation they were left free to live where they pleased, and to repent the fatal act which had avenged them on the murderer of their father at the cost of the priest's life.

Beyond this point the official documents do not enable us to follow their career. All that is now known has been now told of the village tragedy at Croix-Daurade.

BOLD WORDS BY A BACHELOR.

THE postman's knocks at my door have been
latterly more frequent than usual; and out of the
increased number of letters left for me, it has
happened that an unusually large proportion have
contained wedding-cards.   Just as there seem to
be certain days when all the beautiful women in
London take to going out together, certain days
when all the people we know appear to be con-
spiring to meet us at every turn in one afternoon's walk—so there seem to be times and seasons when all our friends are inexplicably bent
on getting married together. Capricious in everything, the law of chances is especially whimsical,
according to my experience, in its influence over
the solemnization of matrimony. Six months
ago, there was no need for me to leave a single
complimentary card anywhere, for weeks and
weeks together. Just at the present time, I find
myself in danger of wearing out my card-case
by incessant use.   My friends are marrying recklessly in all sorts of opposite directions, and are
making the bells a greater nuisance than usual
in every parish of London.

These curious circumstances have set me
thinking on the subject of marriage, and have

recalled to my mind certain reflections in connection with that important change in life, which I first made when I was not quite such an incurably settled old bachelor as I am at the present moment.

It occurred to me, at that past time, and it occurs to me still, that while great stress is laid in ordinary books and ordinary talk on the personal interest which a man has himself, and on the family interest which his near relations have also, in his marrying an affectionate and sensible woman, sufficient importance has not been attached to the interest of another sort, which the tried and worthy friends of his bachelor days ought to feel, and, for the most part, do feel, in his getting a good wife. It really and truly depends upon her, in more cases than I should like to enumerate, whether her husband's friendships are to be continued, after his marriage, in all their integrity, or are only to be maintained as a mere social form. It is hardly necessary for me to repeat—but I will do so, in order to avoid the slightest chance of misconstruction—that I am here speaking only of the worthiest, the truest, the longest-tried friends of a man's bachelor days. Toward these every sensible married woman feels, as I believe, that she owes a duty for her husband's sake. But, unfortunately, there are such female phenomena in the world as fond wives and devoted mothers, who are anything rather than sensible women the moment they are required to step out of the sphere of their conjugal and maternal instincts. Women of this sort have an unreasonable jealousy of their husbands in small things; and on the misuse of their influence to serve the interests of that jealousy, lies but too often the responsibility of severing such friendships as no man can hope to form for the second time in the course of his life. By the severing of friendships, I do not mean the breaking off of all intercourse, but the fatal changing of the terms on which a man lives with his friend—the casting of the first slight shadow which alters the look of the whole prospect. It is astonishing by what a multitude of slight threads the firm continuity of brotherly regard is maintained. Many a woman has snapped asunder all the finer ligaments which once connected her husband and his friend; and has thought it enough if she left the two still attached by the coarser ties which are at the common disposal of all the world. Many a woman —delicate, affectionate, and kind within her own narrow limits—has committed that heavy social offense, and has never felt afterward a single pang of pity or remorse.

These bold words will be unpopular enough, I am afraid, with certain readers; but I am an old bachelor, and I must have license to speak the unwelcome truth. I respect and admire a good husband and father, but I cannot shake off the equally sincere reverence that I feel for a good friend; and I must be allowed to tell some married ladies—what Society ought to tell them a little oftener—that there are other affections in this world which are noble and honorable besides those of conjugal and parental origin. It may be an assertion of a very shocking and unexpected kind, but I must nevertheless be excused for saying that some of the best wives and mothers in the land have given the heartache to some of the best friends. While they have been behaving like patterns of conjugal propriety, they have been estranging men who would once have gone to the world's end to serve each other. I, as a single man, can say nothing of the dreadful wrench—not the less dreadful because it is inevitable—when a father and mother lose a daughter, in order that a lover may gain a wife. But I can speak feelingly of the shock of losing a dear friend, in order that a bride may gain a devoted husband. Nothing shall ever persuade me (possibly because I am not married) that there is not a flaw of some sort in the love for a wife which is made complete, in some people's eyes, by forced contributions from the love which belongs to a friend. I know that a man and woman who make a happy marriage have gained the summit of earthly felicity; but do they never reach that enviable eminence without having trampled underfoot something venerable, or something tender, by the way?

Bear with me, indignant wives, if I recall the long-past time when one of the handsomest women I ever saw took my dearest friend away from me, and destroyed, in one short day, the whole pleasant edifice that we two had been building up together since we were boys at school.

I shall never be as fond of any human being again as I was of that one friend; and, until the beautiful woman came between us, I believe there was nothing in this world that he would not have sacrificed and have done for me. Even while he was courting, I kept my hold on him. Against opposition on the part of his bride and her family, he stipulated that I should be his best man on the wedding-day. The beautiful woman grudged me my one small corner in his heart, even at that time; but he was true to me —he persisted—and I was the first to shake hands with him when he was a married man. I had no suspicion then that I was to lose him from that moment. I only discovered the truth when I went to pay my first visit to the bride and bridegroom at their abode in the country. I found a beautiful house, exquisitely kept from top to bottom; I found a hearty welcome; I found a good dinner and an airy bedroom; I found a pattern husband and a pattern wife; the one thing I did not find was my old friend. Something stood up in his clothes, shook hands with me, pressed wine on me, called me by my Christian name, and inquired what I was doing in my profession. It was certainly something that had a trick of looking like my former comrade and brother; something that nobody in my situation could have complained of with the smallest reason; something with all the brightness of the old metal about it, but without the sterling old ring; something, in short, which made me instinctively take my chamber-candlestick early on the first night of my arrival, and say good-night while the beautiful woman and pattern wife was present to keep her eye on me.

Can I ever forget the language of that eye on that occasion!—the volumes it spoke in one glance of cruel triumph! "No more sacred secrets between you two," it said, brightly. "When you trust him now, you must trust me. You may sacrifice yourself for your love of him over and over again still, but he shall make no sacrifices now for you, until he has first found out how they affect my convenience and my pleasure. Your place in his heart now is where I choose it to be. I have stormed the citadel, and I will bring children by-and-by to keep the ramparts; and you, the faithful old soldier of former years —you have got your discharge, and may sit and sun yourself as well as you can at the outer gates. You have been his truest friend, but he has another now, and need trouble you no longer, except in the capacity of witness of his happiness. This, you will observe, is in the order of nature, and in the recognized fitness of things; and he hopes you will see it—and so do I. And he trusts you will sleep well under his (and my) new roof—and so do I. And he wishes you good-night—and so do I!"

Many, many years have passed since I first learned these hard truths; but I can never forget the pang that it cost me to get them by heart at a moment's notice. My old friend lives still —that is to say, I have an intimate acquaintance who asks me to all his dinners, and who made me godfather to one of his children; but the brother of my love, who died to me on the day when I paid him the marriage visit, has never come back to life since that time. On the altar at which we two once sacrificed, the ashes lie cold. A model husband and father has risen from them, and that result is, I suppose, the only one that any third person has a right to expect. It may be so; but, to this day, I cannot help thinking that the beautiful woman would have done better if she could have made a fond husband, without at the same time marring a good friend.

Readers will, I am afraid, not be wanting who will be inclined to tell me that the lady to whom I have been referring only asserted the fair privilege that was hers by right of marriage, and that my sense of injury springs from the touchy selfishness of an old bachelor. Without attempting to defend myself, I may at least be allowed to inquire into the lady's motive for using her privilege—or, in plainer terms, for altering the relations in which my friend and I had stood toward one another since boyhood.

Her idea I presume to have been that, if I preserved my old footing with her husband, I should be taking away some part of his affection that belonged to her. According to my idea of it, she was taking away something which had belonged to me, and which no effort on her part could afterward convert to her own use. It is hard to make some women understand that a husband's heart—let him be ever so devoted and affection-

ate—has vacant places in it which they can never
hope to fill. It is a house in which they and
their children, naturally and properly, occupy all
the largest apartments and supply all the pretti-
est furniture; but there are spare rooms which
they cannot enter, which are reserved all through
the lease of life for inevitable guests of some sort
from the world outside. It is better to let in the
old friend than some of the substituted visitors,
who are sure, sooner or later, to enter ˌwhere
there are rooms ready for them, by means of
pass-keys obtained without the permission of the
permanent tenants. Am I wrong in making
such assertions as these? I should be willing
enough to think it probable—being only a bachelor—if my views were based on mere theory.
But my opinions, such as they are, have been
formed with the help of proofs and facts. I have
met with bright examples of wives who have
strengthened their husbands' friendships as they
never could have been strengthened except under
the influence of a woman's care, employed in the
truest, the tenderest, the most delicate way. I
have seen men rescued from the bad habits of
half a lifetime by the luck of keeping faithful
friends who were the husbands of sensible wives.
It is a very trite and true re mark that the deadli
est enmities between men have been occasioned
by women. It is not less certain—though it is a
far less widely-accepted truth—that some (I wish
I could say many) of the strongest friendships
have been knit most closely by women's helping
hands.

The real fact seems to be, that the general idea of the scope and purpose of the Institution of Marriage is a miserably narrow one. The same senseless prejudice which leads some people, when driven to extremes, to the practical confession (though it may not be made in plain words), that they would rather see murder committed under their own eyes than approve of any project for obtaining a law of divorce which shall be equal in its operation on husbands and wives of all ranks who cannot live together, is answerable also for the mischievous error in principle of narrowing the practice of the social virtues, in married people, to themselves and their children. A man loves his wife—which is, in other words, loving himself—and loves his offspring, which is equivalent to saying that he has the natural instincts of humanity; and, when he has gone thus far, he has asserted himself as a model of all the virtues of life, in the estimation of some people. In my estimation, he has only begun with the best virtues, and has others yet to practice before he can approach to the standard of a socially complete man. Can there be a lower idea of Marriage than the idea which makes it, in fact, an institution for the development of selfishness on a large and respectable scale? If I am not justified in using the word selfishness, tell me what character a good husband presents (viewed plainly as a man) when he goes out into the world, leaving all his sympathies in his wife's boudoir, and all his affections upstairs in the nursery, and giving to his friends such shreds and patches of formal recognition, in place of true love and regard, as consist in asking them to an occasional dinner-party, and granting them the privilege of presenting his children with silver mugs? He is a model of a husband, the ladies will say. I dare not contradict them; but I should like to know whether he is also a model of a friend?

No. Bachelor as I am, I have a higher idea of Marriage than this. The social advantages which it is fitted to produce ought to extend beyond one man and one woman, to the circle of society amid which they move. The light of its beauty must not be shut up within the four walls which inclose the parents and the family, but must flow out into the world, and shine upon the childless and the solitary, because it has warmth enough and to spare, and because it may make them, even in their way, happy too. I began these few lines by asking sympathy and attention for the interest which a man's true friends have, when he marries, in his choosing a wife who will let them be friends still, who will even help them to mingling in closer brotherhood, if help they need. I lay down the pen, suggesting to some ladies—affectionately suggesting, if they will let me use the word, after some of the bold things I have said—that it is in their power to deprive the bachelor of the sole claim he has left to social recognition and pre-eminence, by making married men what many of them are, and what more might be—the best and truest friends that are to be found in the world.

SOCIAL GRIEVANCES.—IV.

MRS. BULLWINKLE.

LADIES and gentlemen. Give me five minutes' sympathy and attention. I have something serious to say to you.

I am a married man, with an income which is too miserably limited to be worth mentioning.

About a month since, my wife advanced me one step nearer to the Court for the Relief of Insolvent Debtors, by presenting me with another child. On five previous occasions her name had appeared in the List of British Mothers which adorns the daily Supplement of the *Times* newspaper. At each of these trying periods (1 speak entirely of myself when I use the word "trying") she was attended by the same monthly nurse. On this last, and sixth, occasion we were not so fortunate as to secure the services of our regular functionary. She was already engaged; and a new nurse, with excellent recommendations, was therefore employed in her stead. When I first heard of her, and was told that her name was Mrs. Bullwinkle, I laughed. It was then the beginning of the month. It is now the end of it, and I write down that once comical name with a settled gravity which nothing can disturb.

We all know Mrs. Gamp. My late monthly nurse is the exact antipodes of her. Mrs. Bullwinkle is tall and dignified; her complexion is fair; her Grecian nose is innocent of all convivial coloring; her figure is not more than agreeably plump; her manners are icily composed; her dress is quiet and neat; her age cannot be more than five-and-thirty; her style of conversation, when she talks, is flowing and grammatical—upon the whole, she appears to be a woman who is much too lady-like for her station in life. When I first met Mrs. Bullwinkle on the stairs, I felt inclined to apologize for my wife's presumption in engaging her services. Though I checked this absurd impulse, I could not resist answering the new nurse's magnificent courtesy by expressing a polite hope that she would find her situation everything that she could wish, under my roof.

"I am not accustomed to exact much, sir," said Mrs. Bullwinkle. "The cook seems, I am rejoiced to say, to be an intelligent and attentive person. I have been giving her some little hints on the subject of my meals. I have ventured to tell her that I eat little and often; and I think she thoroughly understands me."

I am ashamed to say I was not so sharp as the cook. I did not thoroughly understand Mrs. Bullwinkle until it became my duty, through my wife's inability to manage our domestic business, to settle the weekly bills. I then became sensible of an alarming increase in our household expenditure. If I had given two dinner-parties in the course of the week, the bills could not have been more exorbitant: the butcher, the baker, and the grocer could not have taken me at a heavier pecuniary disadvantage. My heart sank as I thought of my miserable income. I locked up piteously from the bills to the cook for an explanation.

The cook looked back at me compassionately, shook her head, and said:

"Mrs. Bullwinkle."

I reckoned up additional joints, additional chops, additional steaks, fillets, kidneys, gravy beef. I told off a terrible supplement to the usual family consumption of bread, flour, tea, sugar, and alcoholic liquids. I appealed to the cook again; and again the cook shook her head, and said:

"Mrs. Bullwinkle."

My miserable income obliges me to look after sixpences as other men look after five-pound notes. Ruin sat immovable on the pile of weekly bills, and stared me sternly in the face. I went up into my wife's room. The new nurse was not there. The unhappy partner of my pecuniary embarrassments was reading a novel. My innocent infant was smiling in his sleep. I had taken the bills with me. Ruin followed them upstairs, and sat spectral on one side of the bed, while I sat on the other.

"Don't be alarmed, love," I said, "if you hear the police in the house. Mrs. Bullwinkle has a large family, and feeds them all out of our provisions. A search shall be instituted, and slumbering Justice shall be aroused. Look at these joints, these chops, these steaks, these fillets, these kidneys, these gravy beefs!"

My wife shook her head, exactly as the cook had shaken hers; and answered, precisely as the cook had answered:

"Mrs. Bullwinkle."

"But where does she hide it all?" I exclaimed. My wife shut her eyes and shuddered.

"John!" she said, "I have privately consulted the doctor; and the doctor says Mrs. Bullwinkle is a cow."

"If the doctor had to pay these bills," I retorted, savagely, "he would not be quite so free with his jokes."

"He is in earnest, dear. He explained to me, what I never knew before, that a cow is an animal with many stomachs—"

"What!" I cried out, in amazement; "do you mean to tell me that all these joints, these chops, these steaks, these fillets, these kidneys, these gravy beefs—these loaves, these muffins, these mixed biscuits—these teas, these sugars, these brandies, gins, sherries, and beers have disappeared in one week down Mrs. Bullwinkle's throat?"

"All, John," said my wife, sinking back on the pillow with a groan.

It was impossible to look at the bills and believe it. I questioned and cross-questioned my wife, and still elicited nothing but the one be-

wildering answer: "All, John." Determined—
for I am a man of a logical and judicial mind
—to have this extraordinary and alarming case
properly investigated, I took out my pocketbook
and pencil, and asked my wife if she felt strong
enough to make a few private entries for my
satisfaction.   Finding that she willingly accepted
the responsibility, I directed her to take down,
from her own personal investigation, a statement of Mrs. Bullwinkle's meals, and of the
time at which she partook of each of them, for
twenty-four hours, beginning with one morning
and ending with another. After making this
arrangement, I descended to the parlor, and
took the necessary business measures for using
the cook as a check upon her mistress. Having
carefully instructed her to enter on the kitchen
slate everything that was sent up to Mrs. Bullwinkle for twenty-four hours, I felt that my machinery for investigating the truth was now complete.   If the statement of the mistress, in bed on
the second floor, agreed with the statement of the
cook, in the distant sphere of the kitchen, there
could be no doubt that I had obtained reliable
information on the mysterious subject of Mrs.
Bullwinkle's meals.

In due time the two reports were sent in, and
I had an opportunity of understanding at last
what "eating little and often" really meant, in
the case of my wife's monthly nurse. Except
in one particular, to be hereafter adverted to,
both statements agreed exactly. Here is the list,
accompanied by a correct time-table, of Mrs. Bull-

winkle's meals, beginning with the morning of Monday and ending with the morning of Tuesday. I certify, on my honor as a British husband and housekeeper, that the copy is correctly taken from my wife's entries in my pocketbook, checked impartially by the cook's slate:*

A.M.

7. Breakfast. — Tea, Toast, Half - quartern Loaf, Butter, Eggs, Bacon.

9.30. First Morning Snack. — A glass of pale Sherry, and a plate of Mixed Biscuits.

11. Second Morning Snack.—A basin of Beef-tea, and a tumbler of Brandy-and-water.

P.M.

12.45. Dinner.—A Roast Loin of Mutton and Mashed Potatoes. With Dinner, Ale, spiced and warmed. After Dinner, a tumbler of Hot Gin-and-water.

P.M.

3. Afternoon Snack.—A glass of pale Sherry, and a plate of Mixed Biscuits.

4.30. Tea and Muffins.

7. Evening Snack.—Stewed Cheese, Toast, and a tumbler of Brandy-and-water.

9. Supper.—Nice juicy Steak, and two glasses of Beer. Second Course. — Stewed Cheese, and a tumbler of Gin-and-water.

---

* This time-table is no invention of mine. It is accurately copied from an "original document" sent to me by the victim of a monthly nurse.

ADDITIONAL PARTICULARS. (Not vouched
for by the cook's slate.)—During the
night of Monday Mrs. Bullwinkle partook, at intervals, of Caudle. At 4.30
A.M., on the morning of Tuesday, my
wife was awakened by hearing the
nurse walking up and down the room,
and sighing bitterly. The following
conversation then took place between
them:

My Wife. Are you ill?

Mrs. Bullwinkle. No. Hungry.

———

I can certify that the above list correctly, and
even moderately, represents Mrs. Bullwinkle's
daily bill of fare for one month. I can assert,
from my own observation, that every dish, at
every hour of the day, which went up to her full,
invariably came down from her empty. Mrs.
Bullwinkle was not a wasteful eater. She could
fully appreciate, in roast meat, for example, the
great value of "lean"; but she was not, on that
account, insensible to the humbler merits of fat,
skin, and "outside." All—emphatically, all—
was fish that came to her net; and the net itself,
as I can personally testify, was never once over-
weighted and never out of order. I have watched,
in the case of this perfectly unparalleled human
cormorant, for symptoms of apoplexy, or at least
of visible repletion, with a dreadful and absorb-
ing interest; and have on no occasion been re-

warded by making the smallest discovery. Mrs. Bullwinkle was never, while in my service, even so much as partially intoxicated. Her face was never flushed; her articulation was never thickened; her brain was never confused; her movements were never uncertain. After the breakfast, the two morning snacks, and the dinner—all occurring within the space of six hours—she could move about the room with unimpeded freedom of action; could keep my wife and the baby in a state of the strictest discipline; could courtesy magnificently when the unoffending master, whom she was eating out of house and home, entered the room, preserving her color, her equilibrium, and her stay-laces, when she sank down and when she swelled up again, without the vestige of an apparent effort. During the month of her devastating residence under my roof, she had two hundred and forty-eight meals, including the snacks; and she went out of the house no larger and no redder than she came in. After the statement of one such fact as that, further comment is superfluous.

I leave this case in the hands of the medical and the married public. I present it, as a problem, to physiological science. I offer it, as a warning, to British husbands with limited incomes. While I write these lines, while I give my married countrymen this friendly caution, my wife is weeping over the tradesmen's bills; my children are on half-allowance of food; my cook is worked off her legs; my purse is empty. Young husbands, and persons about to marry, commit to memory the description here given of my late monthly nurse! Avoid a tall and dignified woman, with a flowing style of conversation and impressively lady - like manners! Beware, my struggling friends, my fellow-toilers along the heavily-taxed highways of domestic happiness —beware of Mrs. Bullwinkle!

END OF VOLUME TWENTY.

DATE DUE

#47-0108 Peel Off Pressure Sensitive